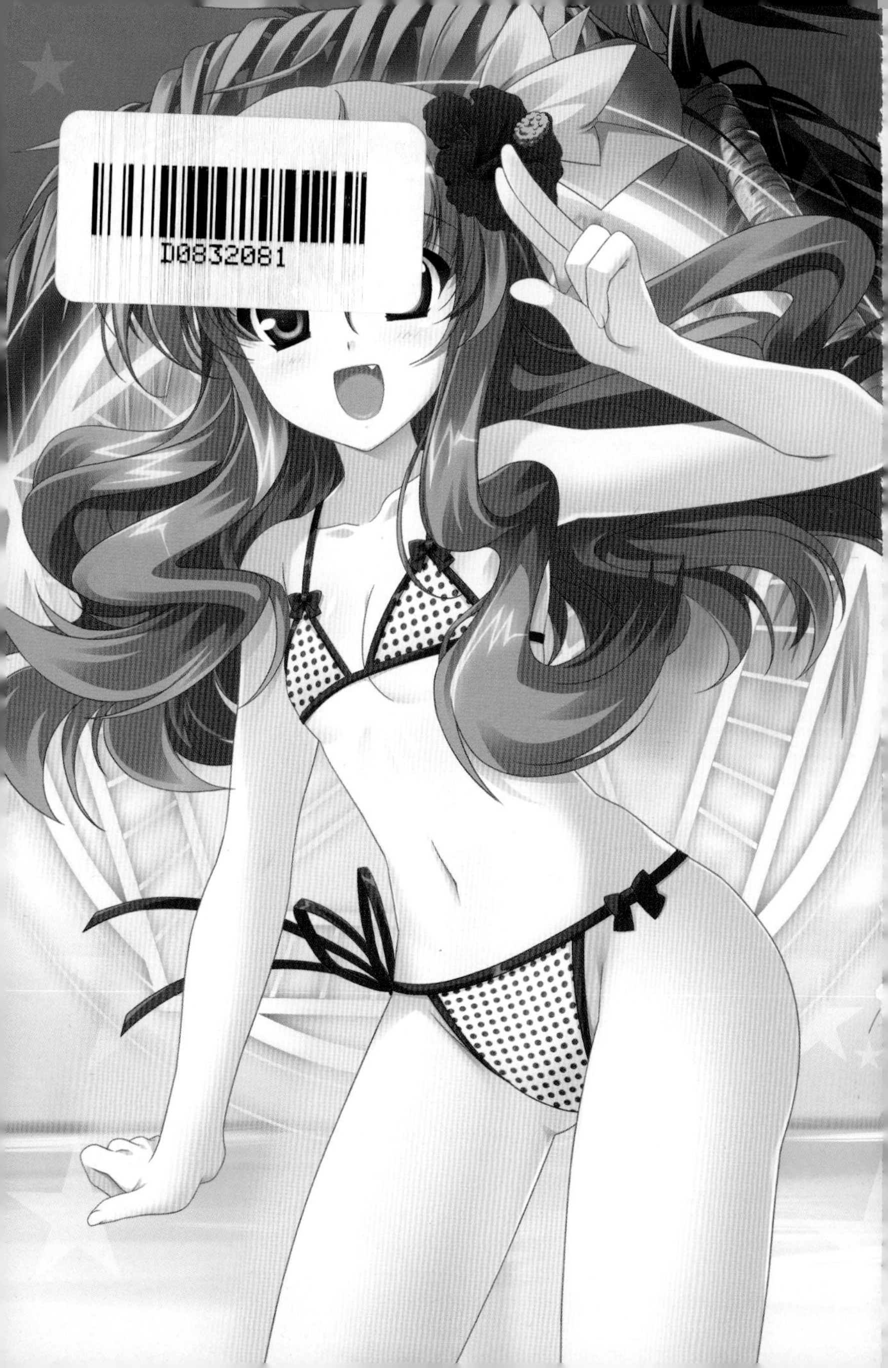

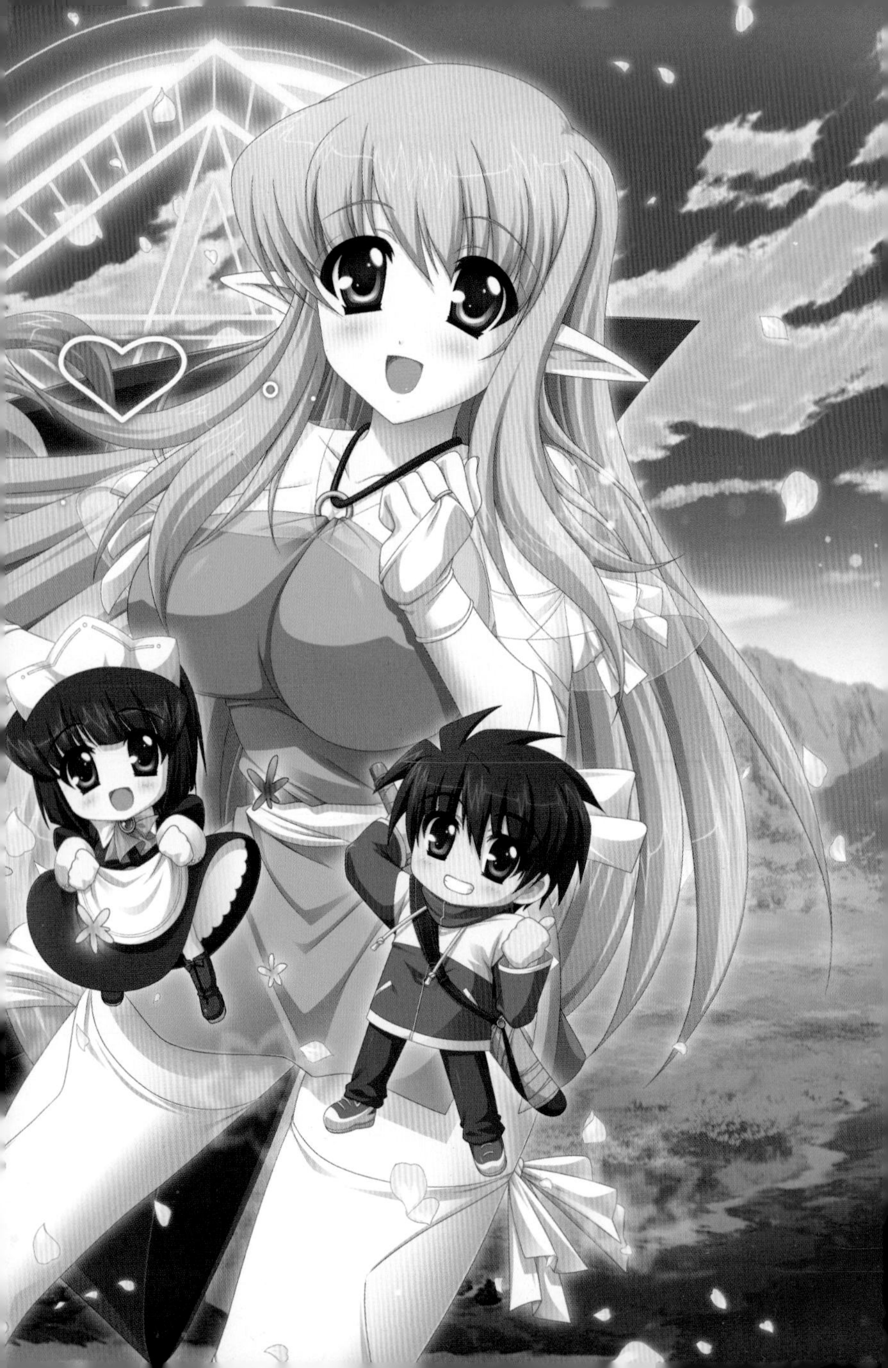

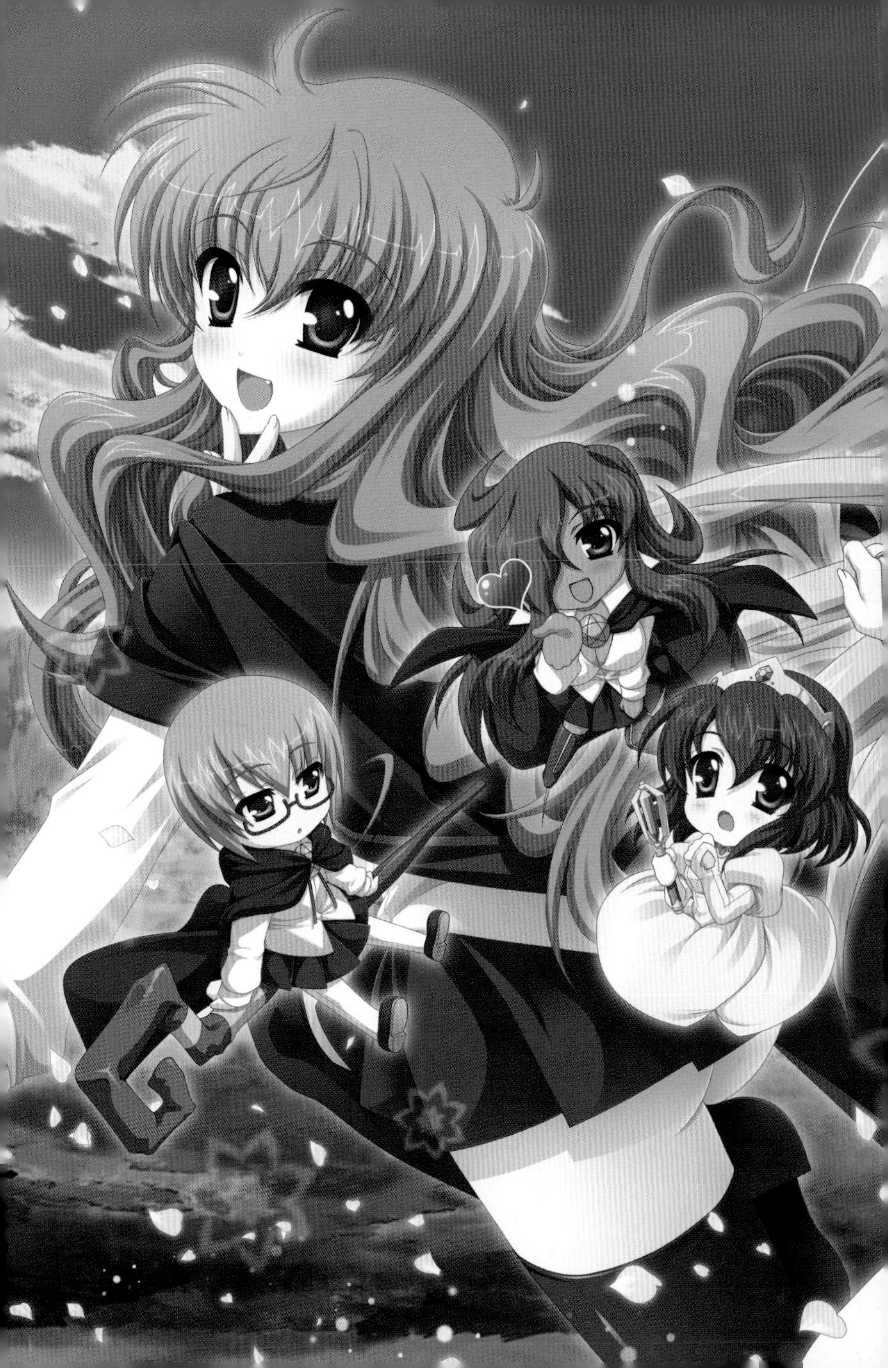

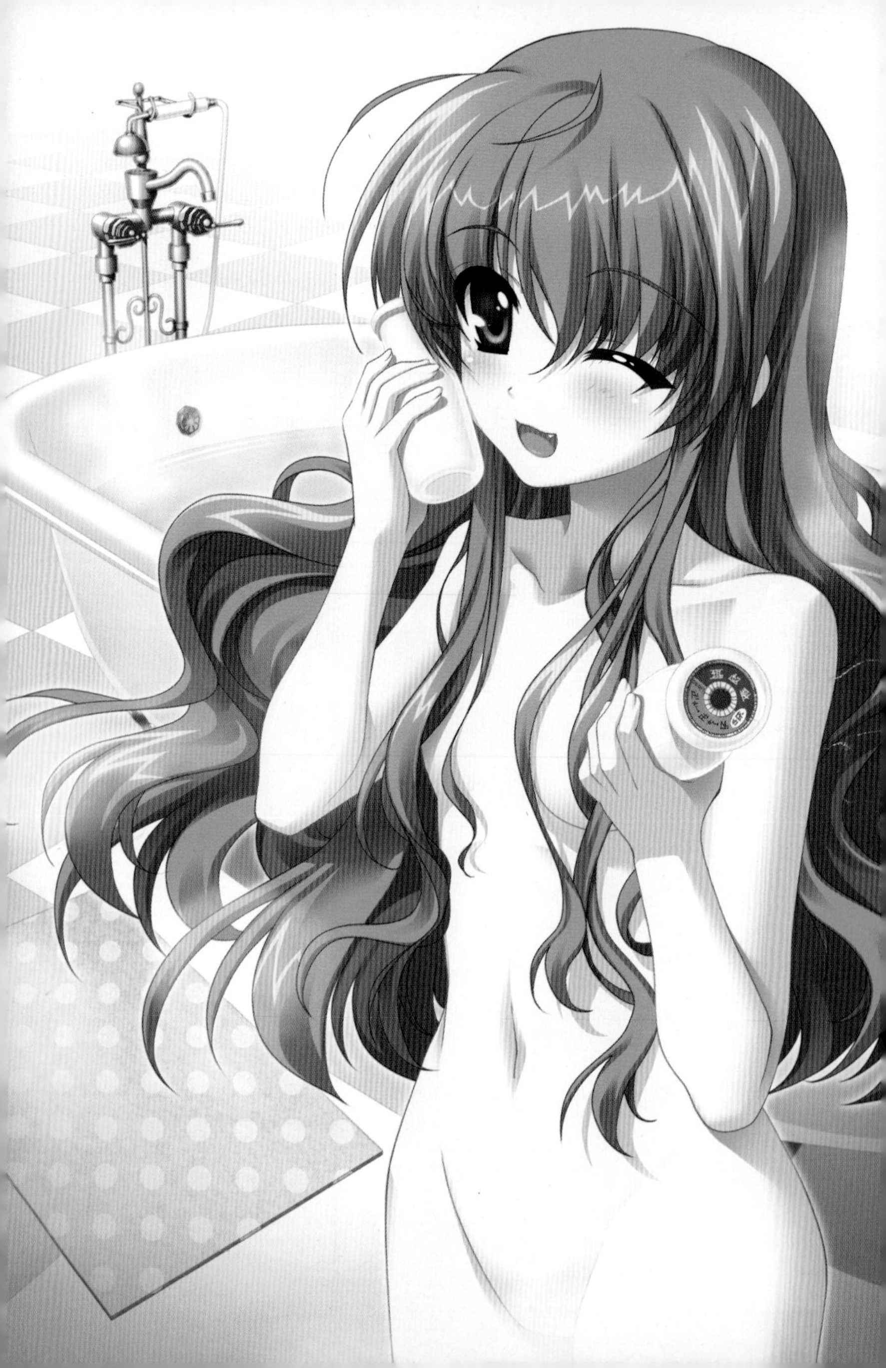

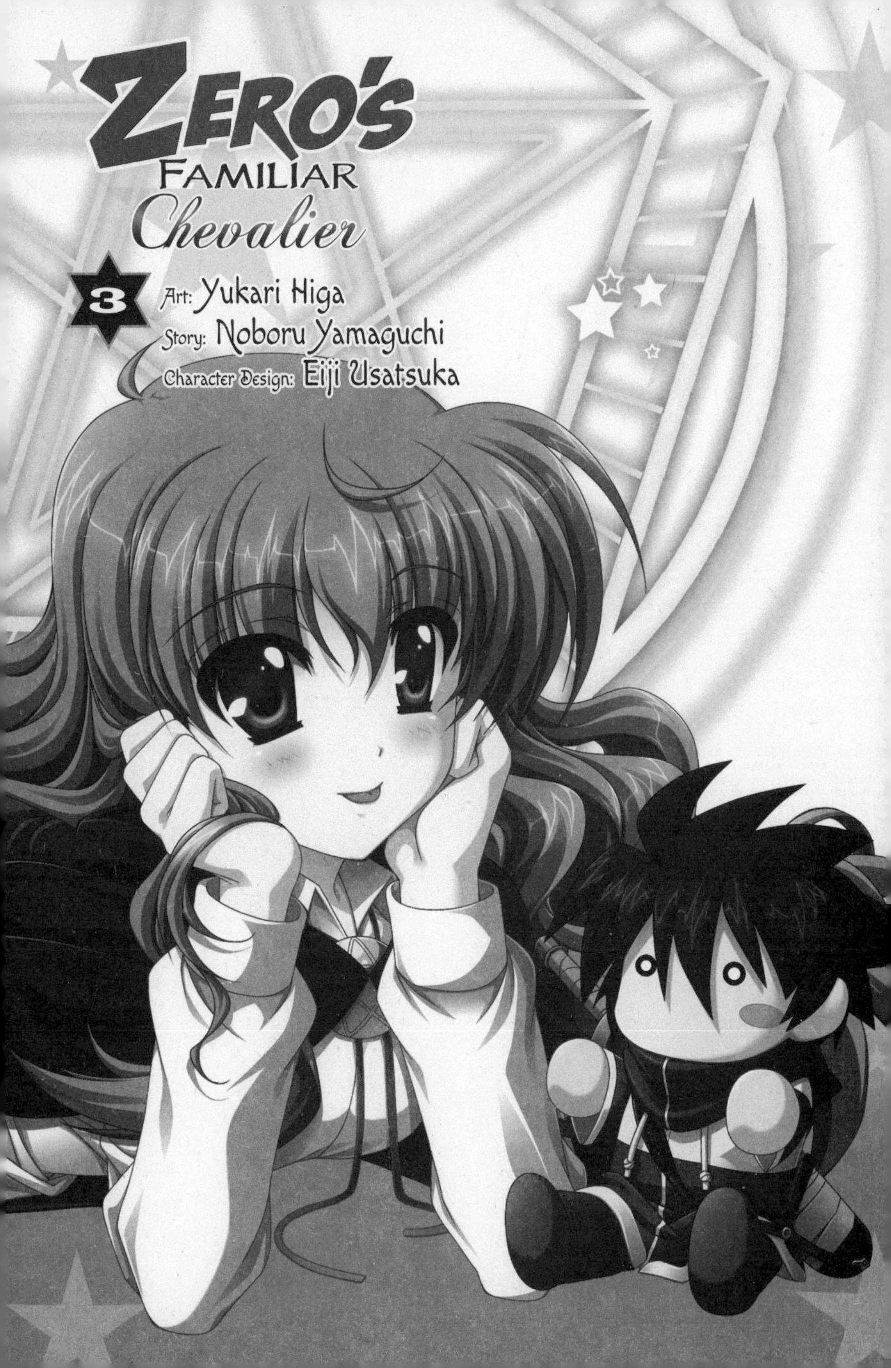
ZERO'S
FAMILIAR
Chevalier
3
Art: Yukari Higa
Story: Noboru Yamaguchi
Character Design: Eiji Usatsuka

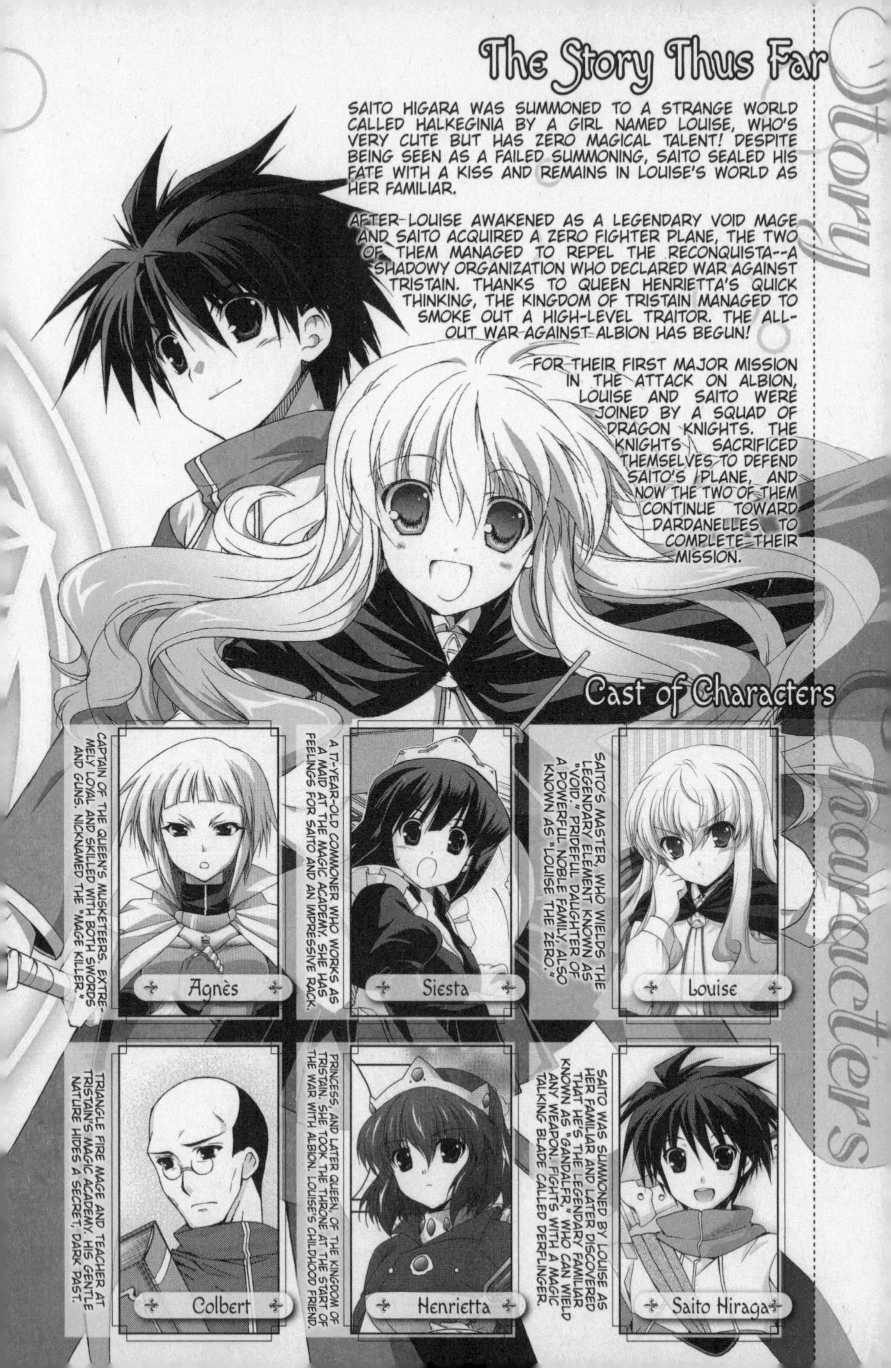

The Story Thus Far

SAITO HIGARA WAS SUMMONED TO A STRANGE WORLD CALLED HALKEGINIA BY A GIRL NAMED LOUISE, WHO'S VERY CUTE BUT HAS ZERO MAGICAL TALENT! DESPITE BEING SEEN AS A FAILED SUMMONING, SAITO SEALED HIS FATE WITH A KISS AND REMAINS IN LOUISE'S WORLD AS HER FAMILIAR.

AFTER LOUISE AWAKENED AS A LEGENDARY VOID MAGE AND SAITO ACQUIRED A ZERO FIGHTER PLANE, THE TWO OF THEM MANAGED TO REPEL THE RECONQUISTA--A SHADOWY ORGANIZATION WHO DECLARED WAR AGAINST TRISTAIN. THANKS TO QUEEN HENRIETTA'S QUICK THINKING, THE KINGDOM OF TRISTAIN MANAGED TO SMOKE OUT A HIGH-LEVEL TRAITOR. THE ALL-OUT WAR AGAINST ALBION HAS BEGUN!

FOR THEIR FIRST MAJOR MISSION IN THE ATTACK ON ALBION, LOUISE AND SAITO WERE JOINED BY A SQUAD OF DRAGON KNIGHTS. THE KNIGHTS SACRIFICED THEMSELVES TO DEFEND SAITO'S PLANE, AND NOW THE TWO OF THEM CONTINUE TOWARD DARDANELLES TO COMPLETE THEIR MISSION.

Cast of Characters

Louise

SAITO'S MASTER, WHO WIELDS THE LEGENDARY ELEMENT KNOWN AS "VOID." PRIDEFUL NOBLE DAUGHTER OF A POWERFUL NOBLE FAMILY, ALSO KNOWN AS "LOUISE THE ZERO."

Siesta

A 17-YEAR-OLD COMMONER WHO WORKS AS A MAID AT THE MAGIC ACADEMY. SHE HAS FEELINGS FOR SAITO AND AN IMPRESSIVE RACK.

Agnès

CAPTAIN OF THE QUEEN'S MUSKETEERS. EXTREMELY LOYAL AND SKILLED WITH BOTH SWORDS AND GUNS. NICKNAMED THE "MAGE KILLER."

Saito Hiraga

SAITO WAS SUMMONED BY LOUISE AS HER FAMILIAR AND LATER DISCOVERED THAT HE'S THE LEGENDARY FAMILIAR KNOWN AS "GANDALFR," WHO CAN WIELD ANY WEAPON. FIGHTS WITH A MAGIC TALKING BLADE CALLED DERFLINGER.

Henrietta

PRINCESS, AND LATER QUEEN, OF THE KINGDOM OF TRISTAIN. SHE TOOK THE THRONE AT THE START OF THE WAR WITH ALBION. LOUISE'S CHILDHOOD FRIEND.

Colbert

TRIANGLE FIRE MAGE AND TEACHER AT TRISTAIN'S MAGIC ACADEMY. HIS GENTLE NATURE HIDES A SECRET, DARK PAST.

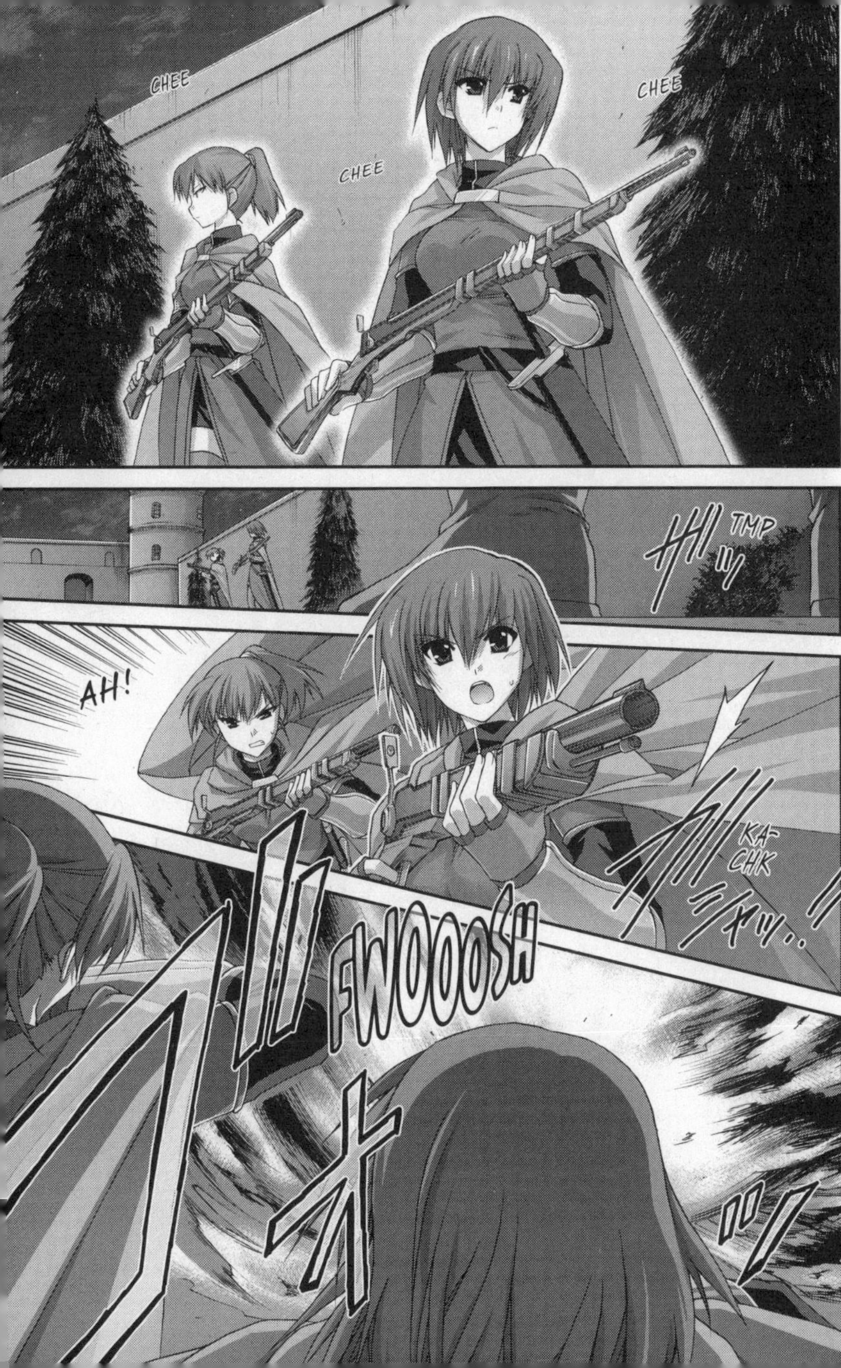
CHEE
CHEE
CHEE
TMP
KA-CHK
シャッ..!!
AH!
FWOOOSH

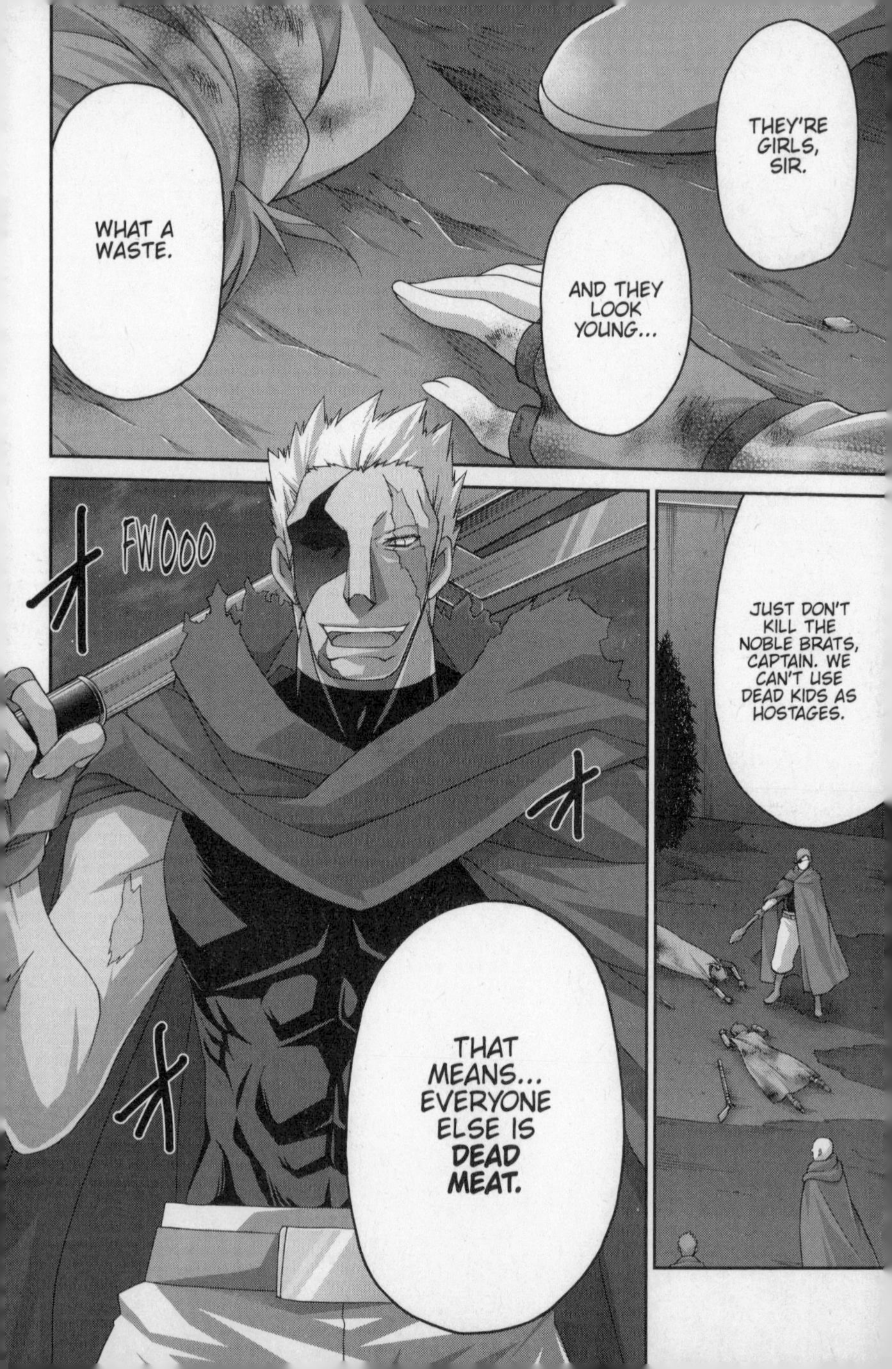
THEY'RE GIRLS, SIR.
AND THEY LOOK YOUNG...
WHAT A WASTE.
JUST DON'T KILL THE NOBLE BRATS, CAPTAIN. WE CAN'T USE DEAD KIDS AS HOSTAGES.
FWOOO
THAT MEANS... EVERYONE ELSE IS **DEAD MEAT.**

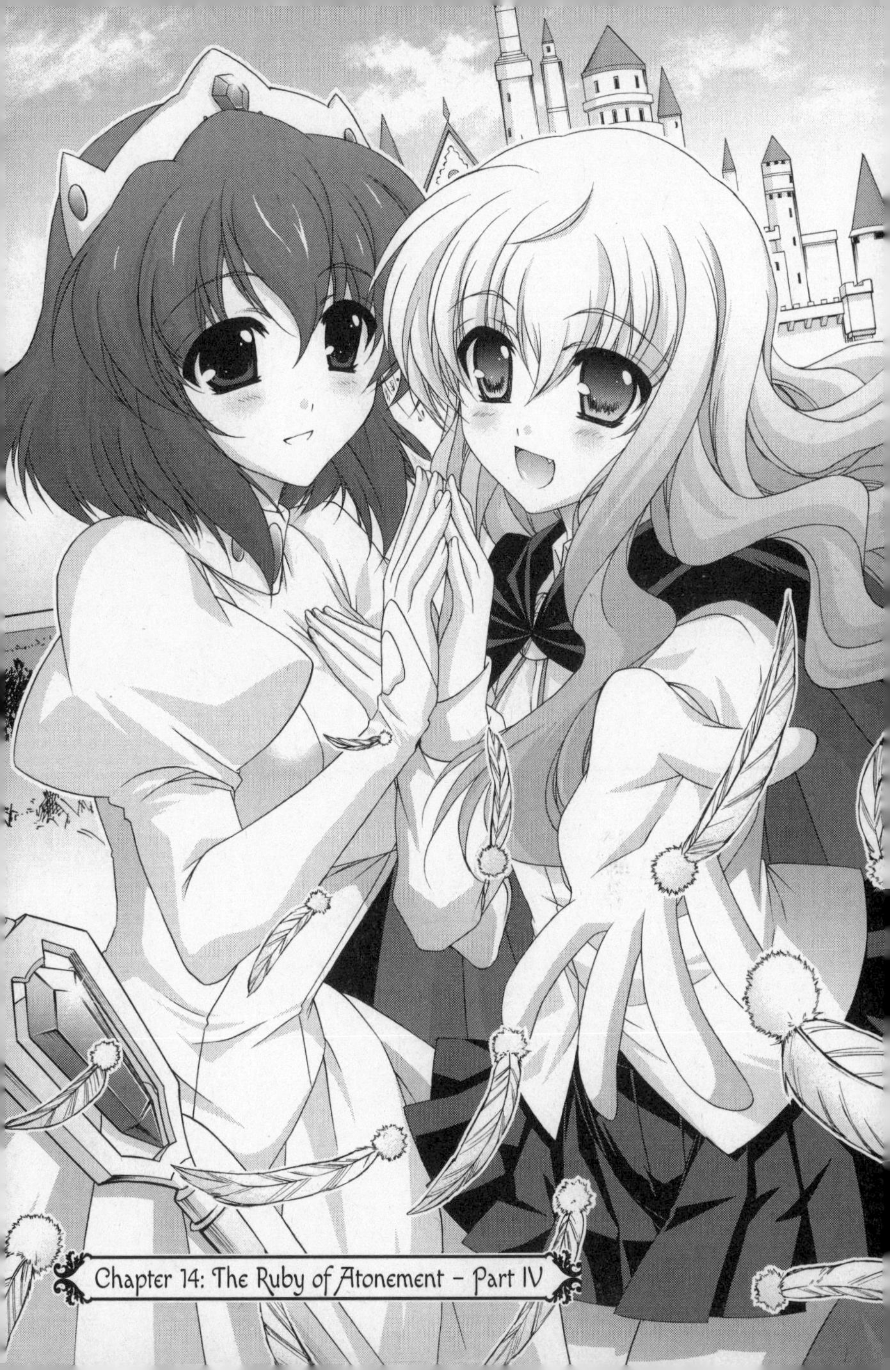

Chapter 14: The Ruby of Atonement – Part IV

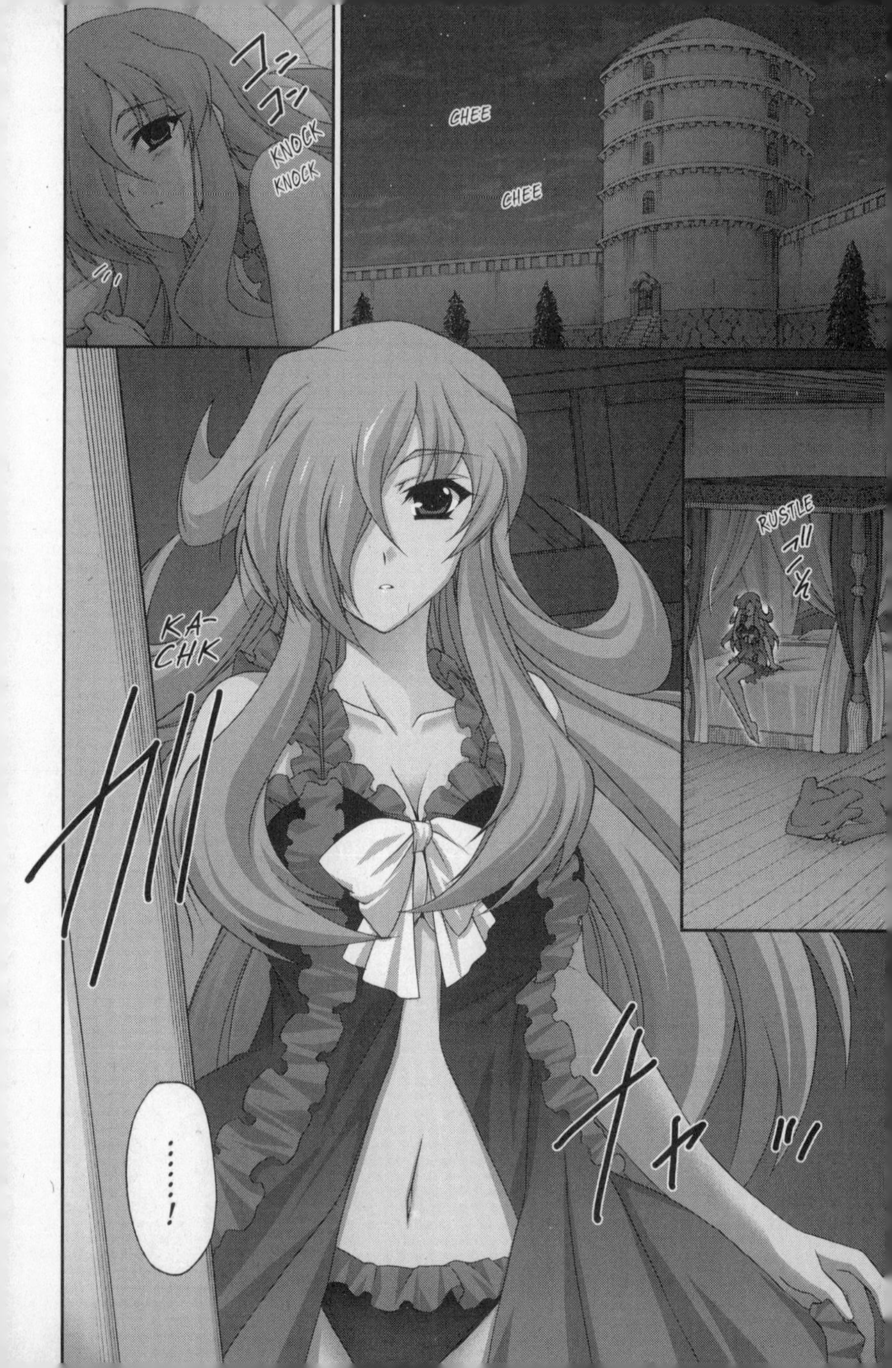
CHEE
CHEE
KNOCK KNOCK
RUSTLE
KA-CHK
......!

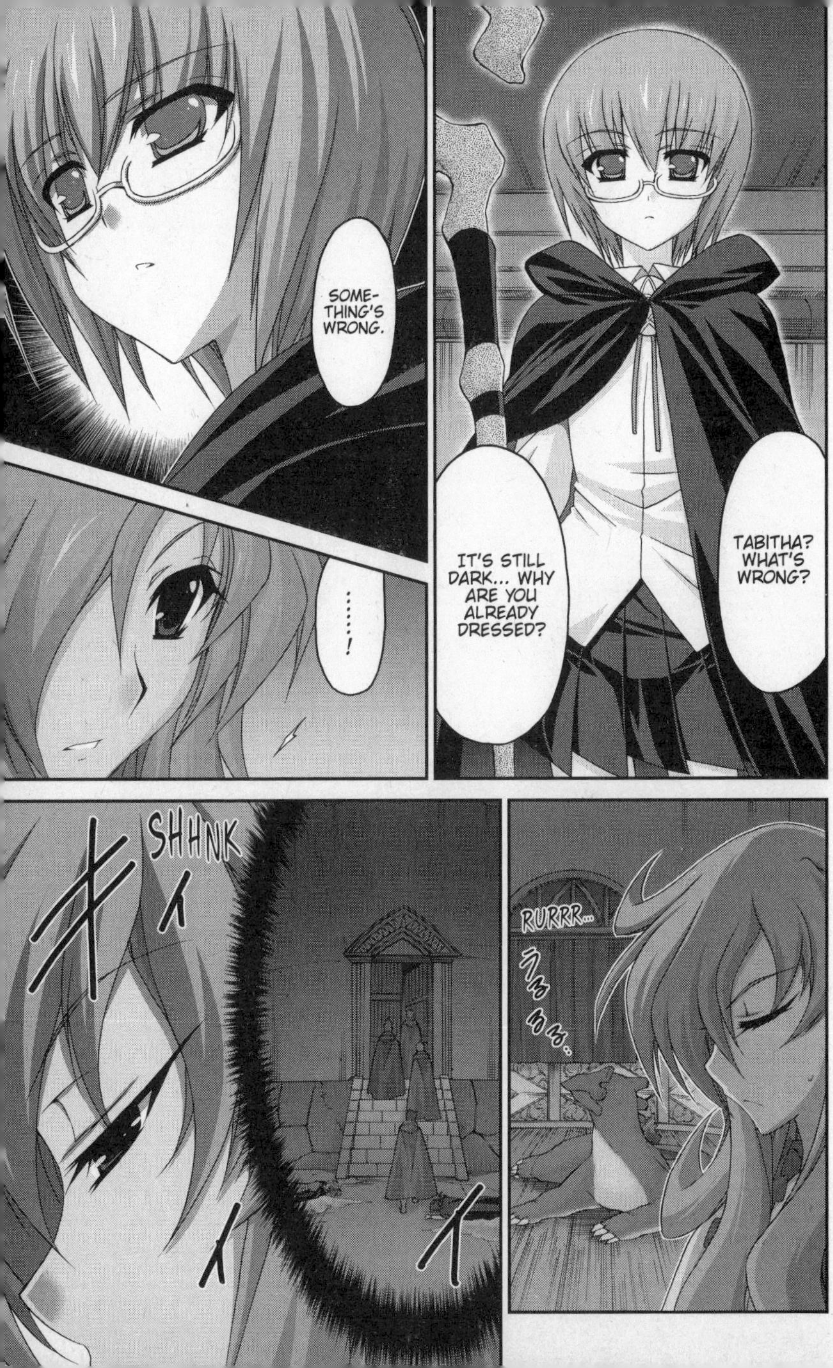
TABITHA? WHAT'S WRONG?
IT'S STILL DARK... WHY ARE YOU ALREADY DRESSED?
SOME-THING'S WRONG.
......!
RURRR...
るるる..
SHHNK
キィ

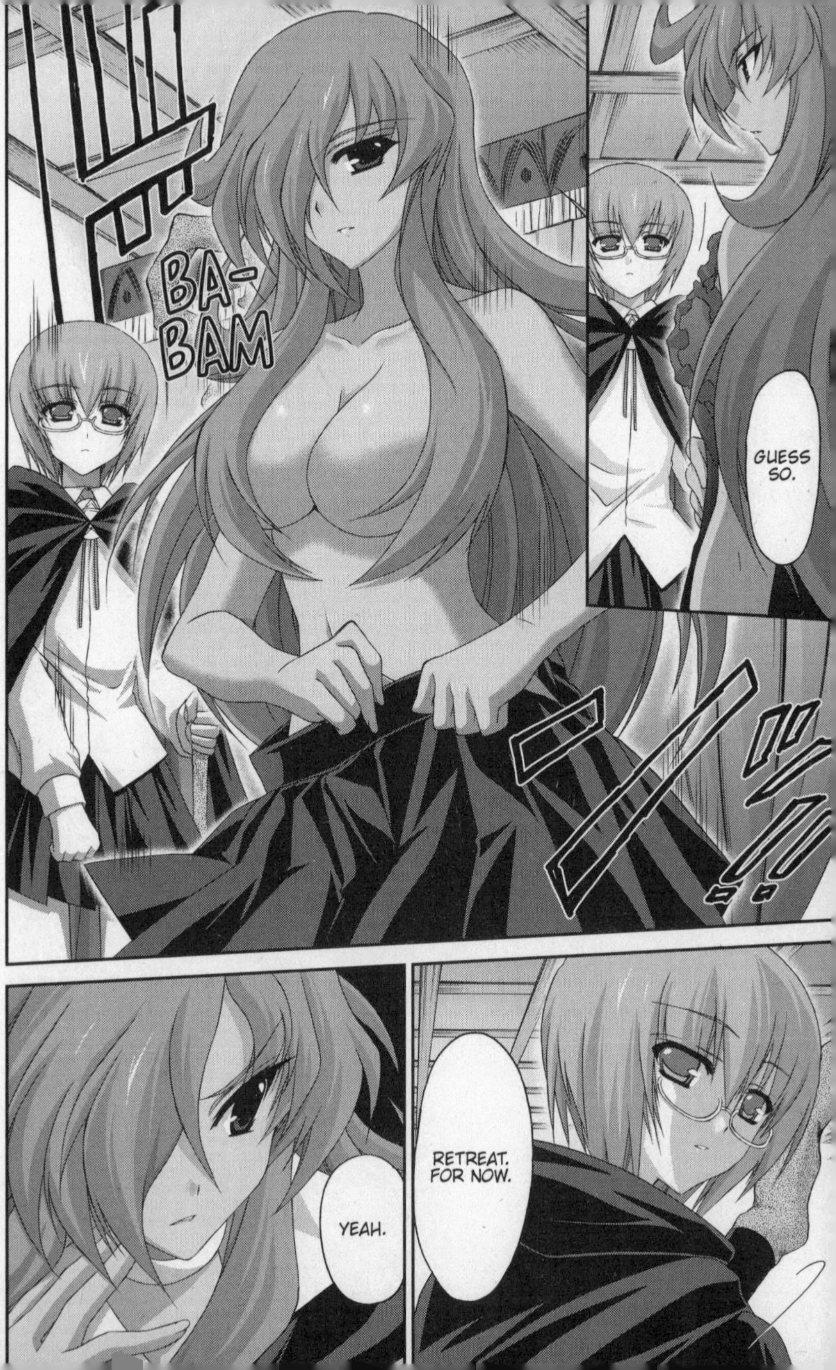
GUESS SO.
BA-BAM
RETREAT. FOR NOW.
YEAH.

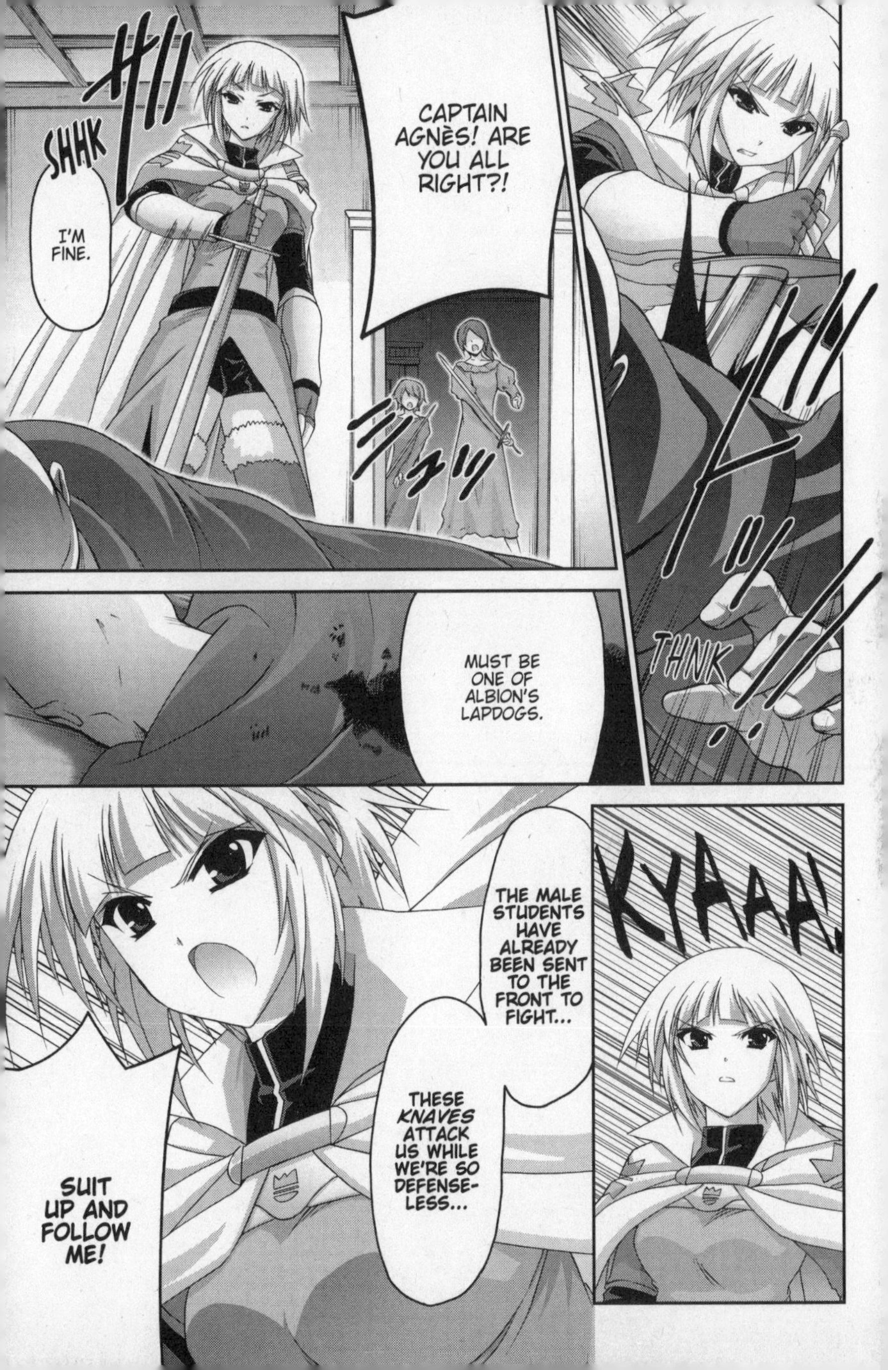
THNK
CAPTAIN AGNÈS! ARE YOU ALL RIGHT?!
SHHK
I'M FINE.
MUST BE ONE OF ALBION'S LAPDOGS.
KYAAA!
THE MALE STUDENTS HAVE ALREADY BEEN SENT TO THE FRONT TO FIGHT...
THESE *KNAVES* ATTACK US WHILE WE'RE SO DEFENSE-LESS...
SUIT UP AND FOLLOW ME!

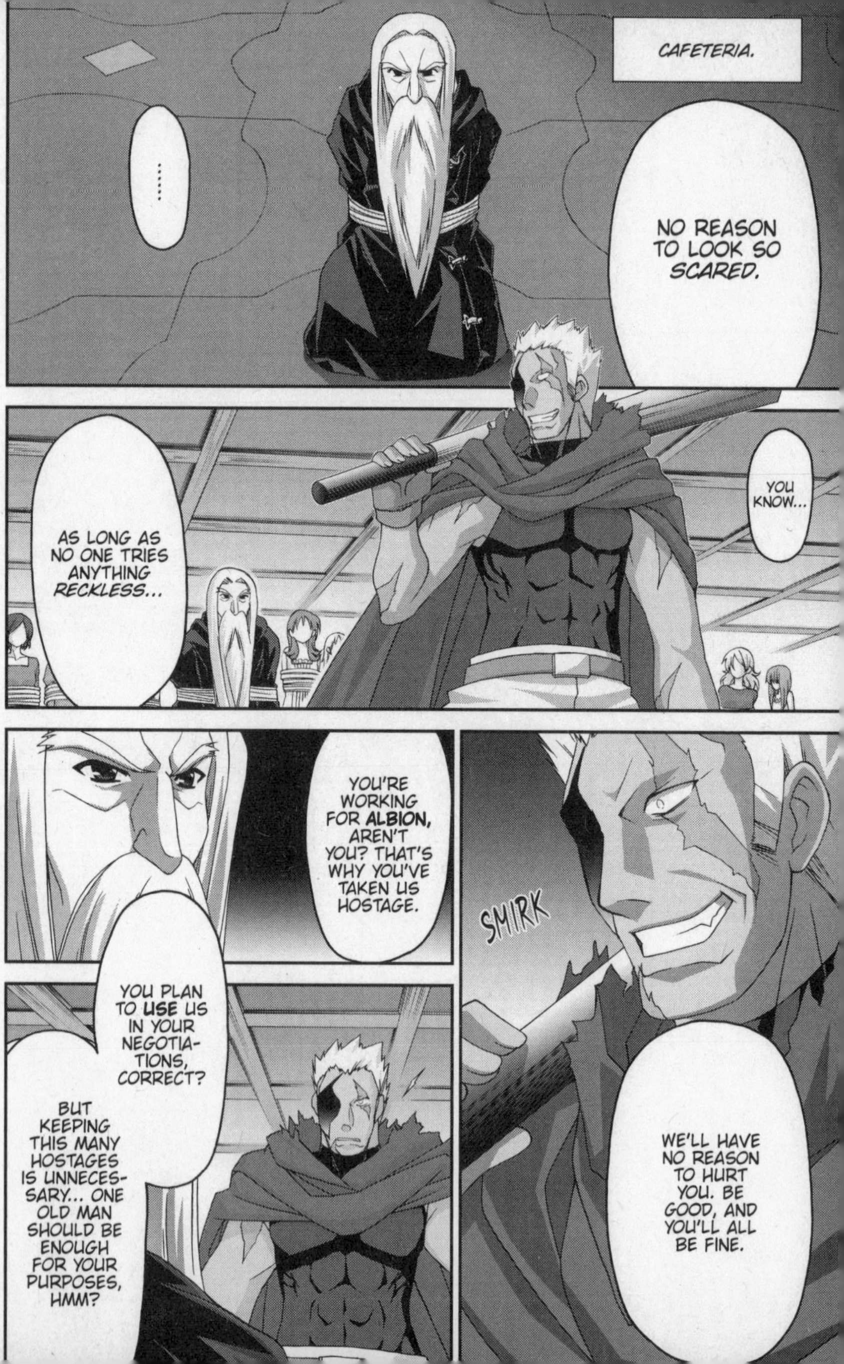
CAFETERIA.
NO REASON TO LOOK SO SCARED.
......
YOU KNOW...
AS LONG AS NO ONE TRIES ANYTHING RECKLESS...
SMIRK
WE'LL HAVE NO REASON TO HURT YOU. BE GOOD, AND YOU'LL ALL BE FINE.
YOU'RE WORKING FOR ALBION, AREN'T YOU? THAT'S WHY YOU'VE TAKEN US HOSTAGE.
YOU PLAN TO USE US IN YOUR NEGOTIATIONS, CORRECT?
BUT KEEPING THIS MANY HOSTAGES IS UNNECESSARY... ONE OLD MAN SHOULD BE ENOUGH FOR YOUR PURPOSES, HMM?

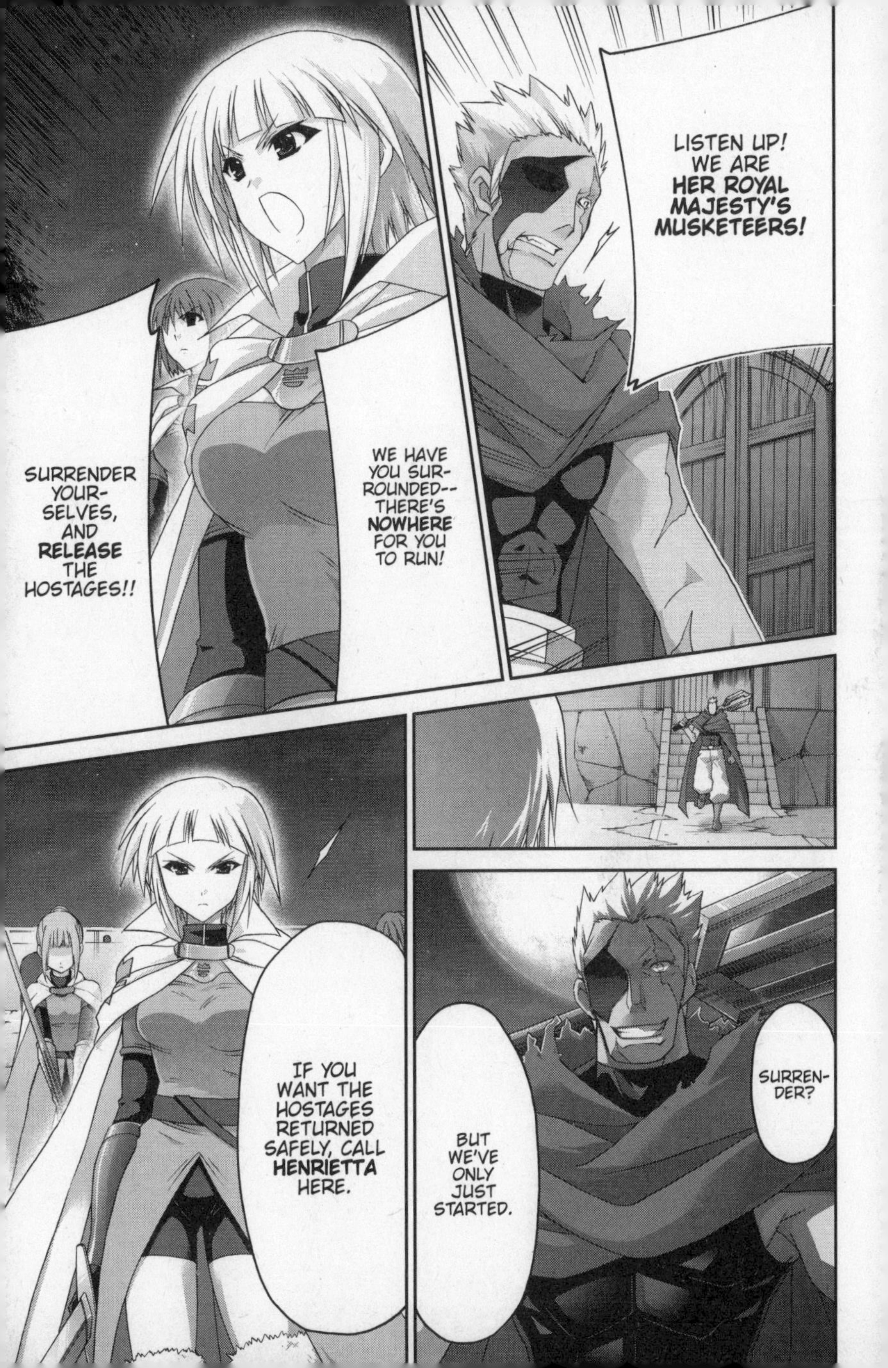
LISTEN UP! WE ARE **HER ROYAL MAJESTY'S MUSKETEERS!**
WE HAVE YOU SURROUNDED-- THERE'S **NOWHERE** FOR YOU TO RUN!
SURRENDER YOURSELVES, AND **RELEASE** THE HOSTAGES!!
SURRENDER?
BUT WE'VE ONLY JUST STARTED.
IF YOU WANT THE HOSTAGES RETURNED SAFELY, CALL **HENRIETTA** HERE.

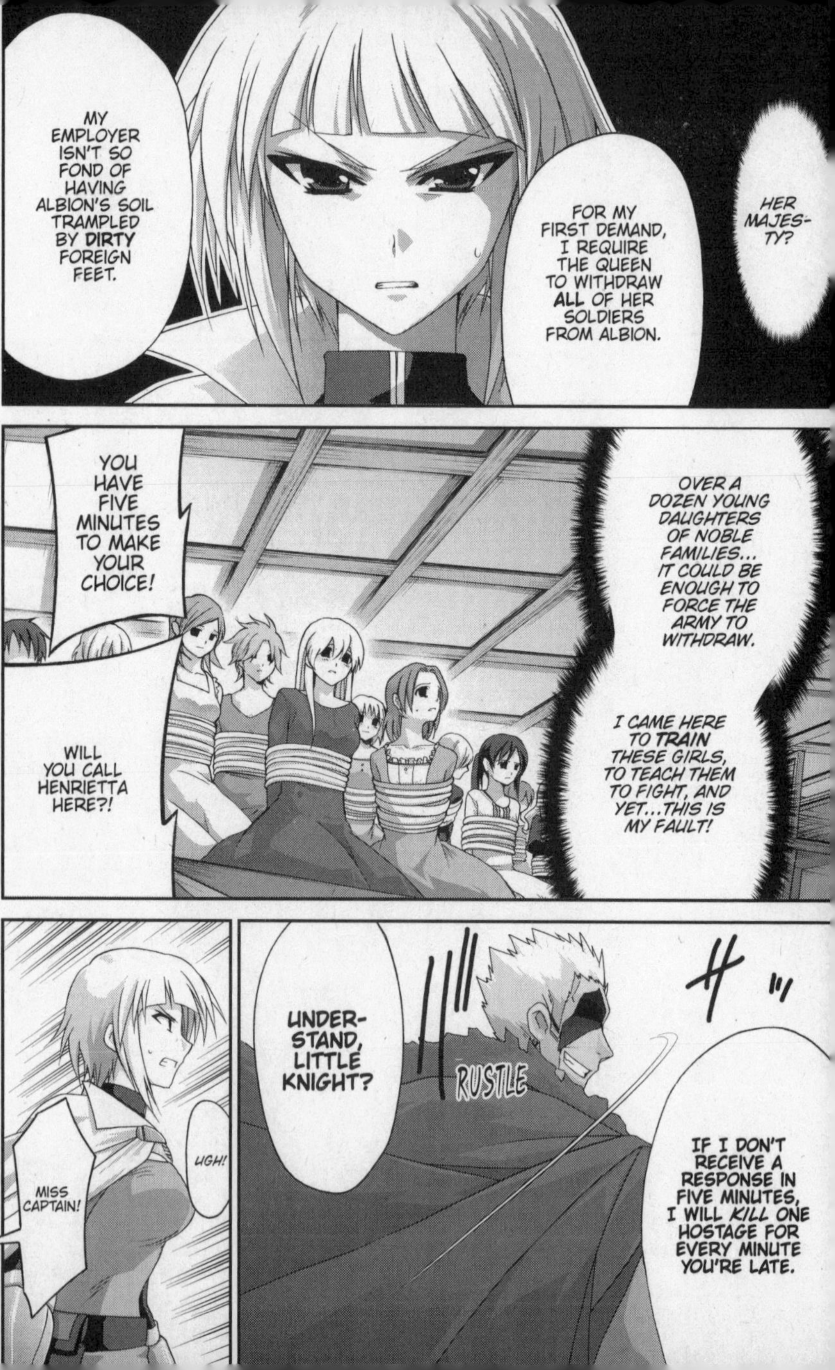
HER MAJESTY?
FOR MY FIRST DEMAND, I REQUIRE THE QUEEN TO WITHDRAW **ALL** OF HER SOLDIERS FROM ALBION.
MY EMPLOYER ISN'T SO FOND OF HAVING ALBION'S SOIL TRAMPLED BY **DIRTY** FOREIGN FEET.
OVER A DOZEN YOUNG DAUGHTERS OF NOBLE FAMILIES... IT COULD BE ENOUGH TO FORCE THE ARMY TO WITHDRAW.
YOU HAVE FIVE MINUTES TO MAKE YOUR CHOICE!
I CAME HERE TO ***TRAIN*** *THESE GIRLS, TO TEACH THEM TO FIGHT, AND YET...THIS IS MY FAULT!*
WILL YOU CALL HENRIETTA HERE?!
IF I DON'T RECEIVE A RESPONSE IN FIVE MINUTES, I WILL *KILL* ONE HOSTAGE FOR EVERY MINUTE YOU'RE LATE.
UNDER-STAND, LITTLE KNIGHT?
RUSTLE
UGH!
MISS CAPTAIN!

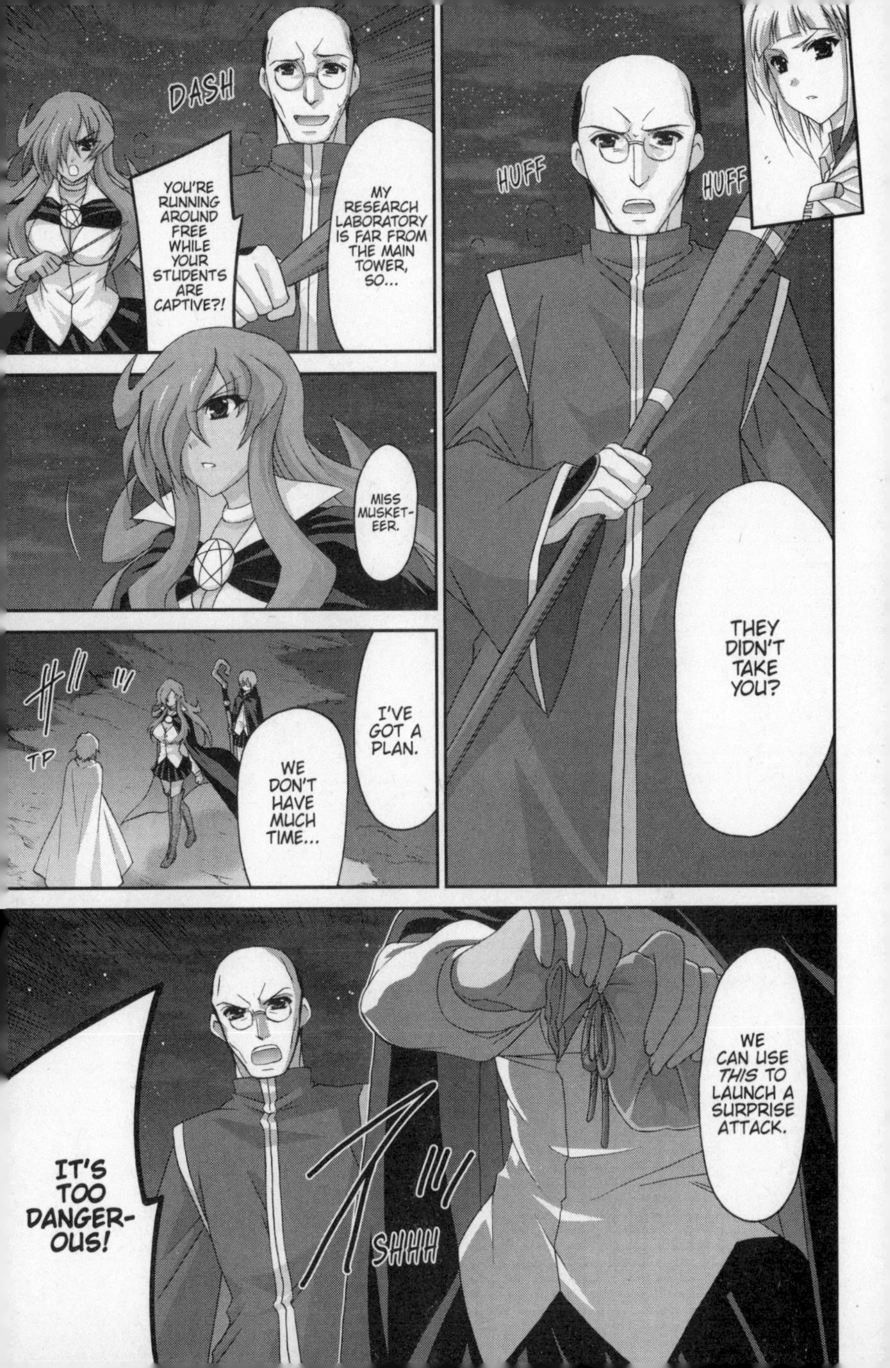

HUFF
HUFF
THEY DIDN'T TAKE YOU?
DASH
MY RESEARCH LABORATORY IS FAR FROM THE MAIN TOWER, SO...
YOU'RE RUNNING AROUND FREE WHILE YOUR STUDENTS ARE CAPTIVE?!
MISS MUSKETEER.
I'VE GOT A PLAN.
WE DON'T HAVE MUCH TIME...
TP
WE CAN USE *THIS* TO LAUNCH A SURPRISE ATTACK.
SHHH
IT'S TOO DANGEROUS!

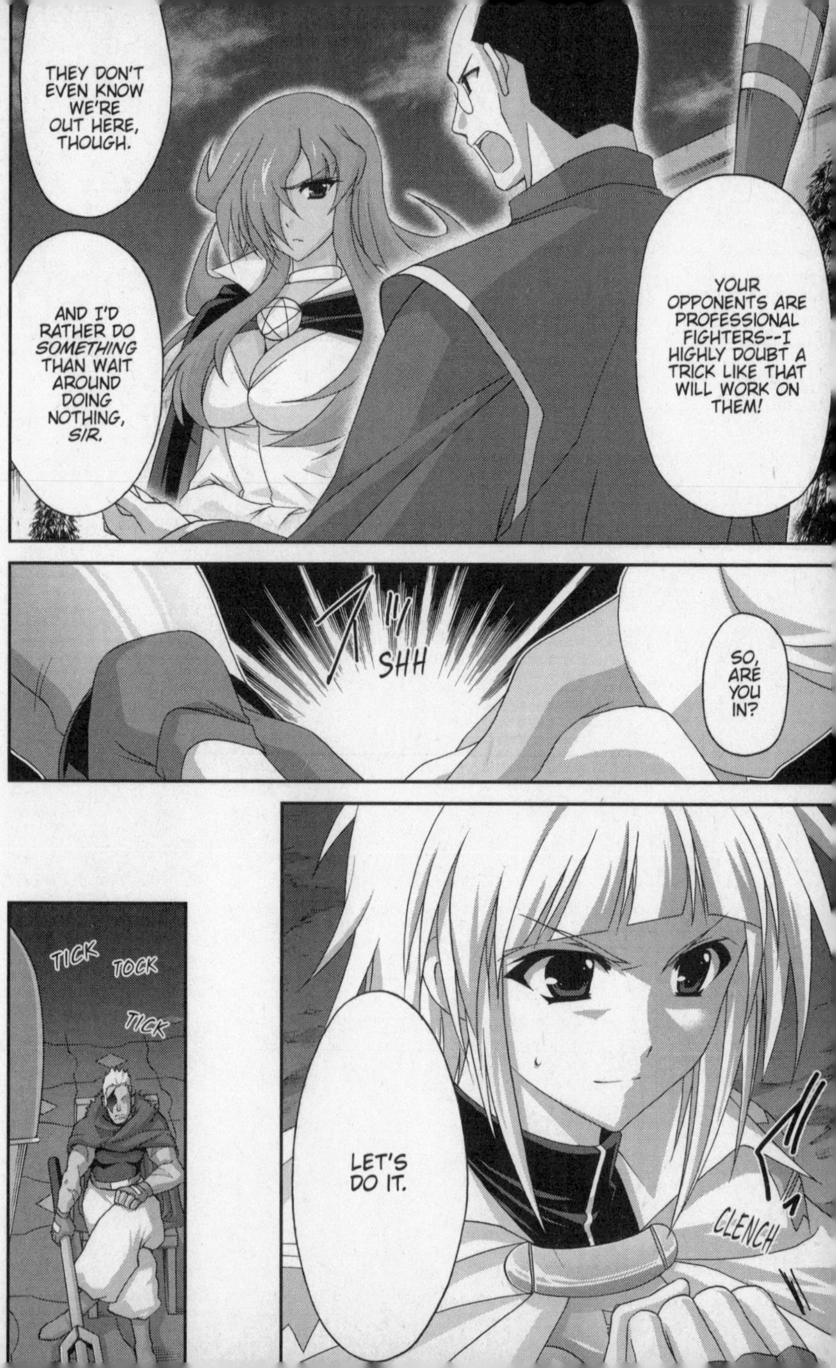
YOUR OPPONENTS ARE PROFESSIONAL FIGHTERS--I HIGHLY DOUBT A TRICK LIKE THAT WILL WORK ON THEM!
THEY DON'T EVEN KNOW WE'RE OUT HERE, THOUGH.
AND I'D RATHER DO *SOMETHING* THAN WAIT AROUND DOING NOTHING, *SIR.*
SO, ARE YOU IN?
SHH
CLENCH
LET'S DO IT.
TICK
TOCK
TICK

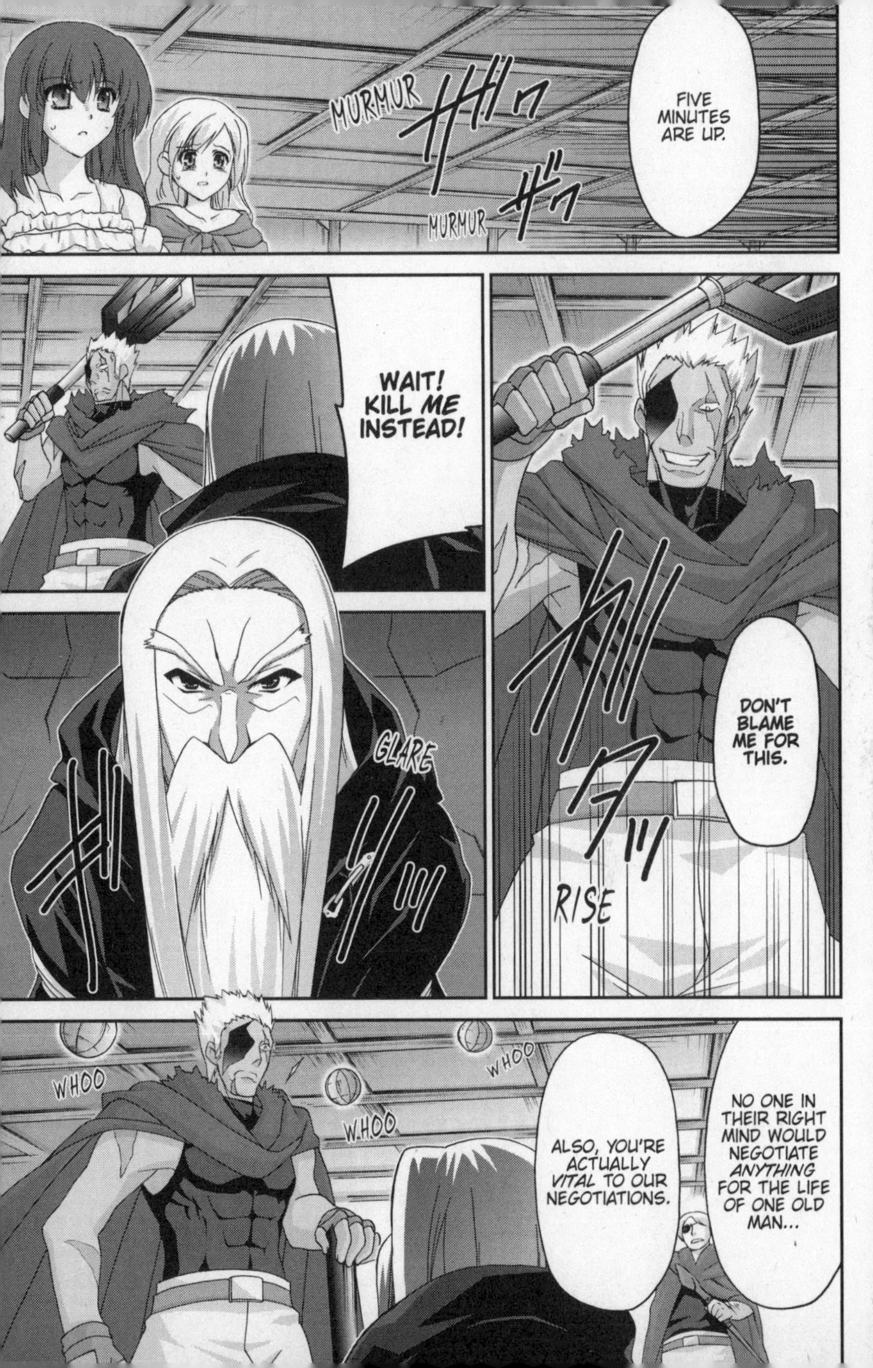
FIVE MINUTES ARE UP.
MURMUR
MURMUR
DON'T BLAME ME FOR THIS.
RISE
WAIT! KILL ME INSTEAD!
GLARE
WHOO
NO ONE IN THEIR RIGHT MIND WOULD NEGOTIATE *ANYTHING* FOR THE LIFE OF ONE OLD MAN...
ALSO, YOU'RE ACTUALLY *VITAL* TO OUR NEGOTIATIONS.
WHOO
WHOO

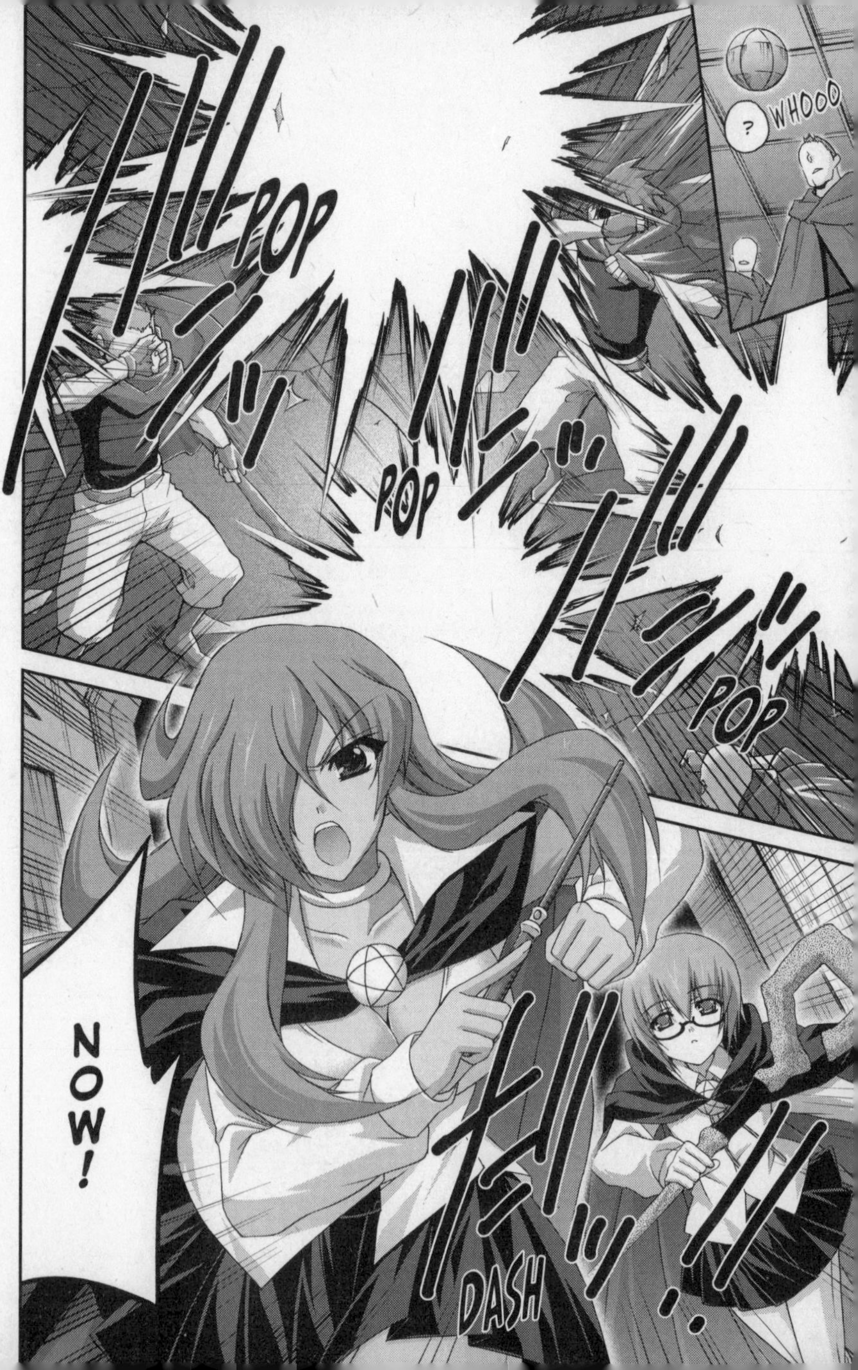
WHOOO
?
POP
POP
POP
NOW!
DASH

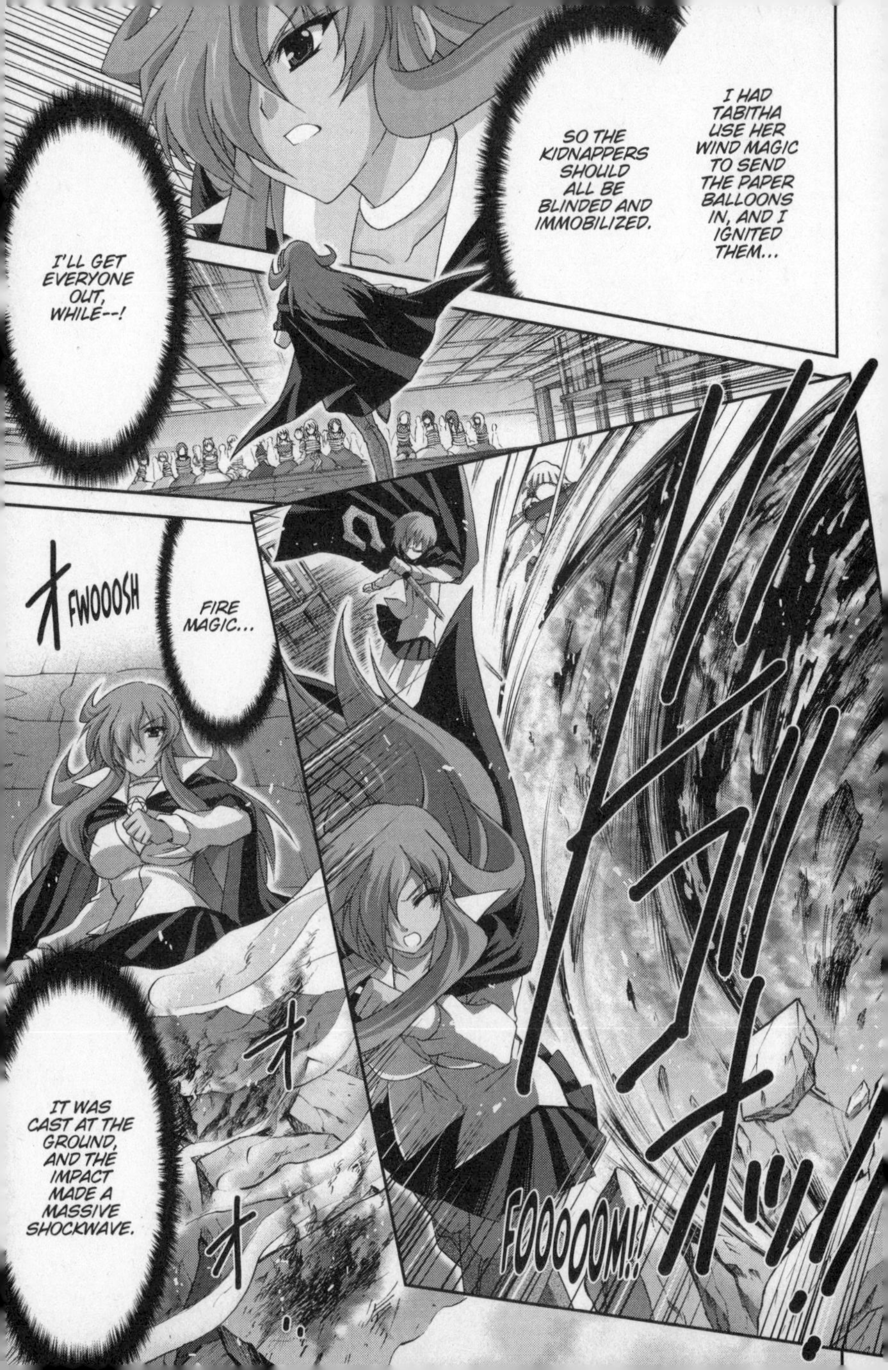
I HAD TABITHA USE HER WIND MAGIC TO SEND THE PAPER BALLOONS IN, AND I IGNITED THEM...
SO THE KIDNAPPERS SHOULD ALL BE BLINDED AND IMMOBILIZED.
I'LL GET EVERYONE OUT, WHILE--!
FOOOOOM!!
FIRE MAGIC...
FWOOOSH
IT WAS CAST AT THE GROUND, AND THE IMPACT MADE A MASSIVE SHOCKWAVE.

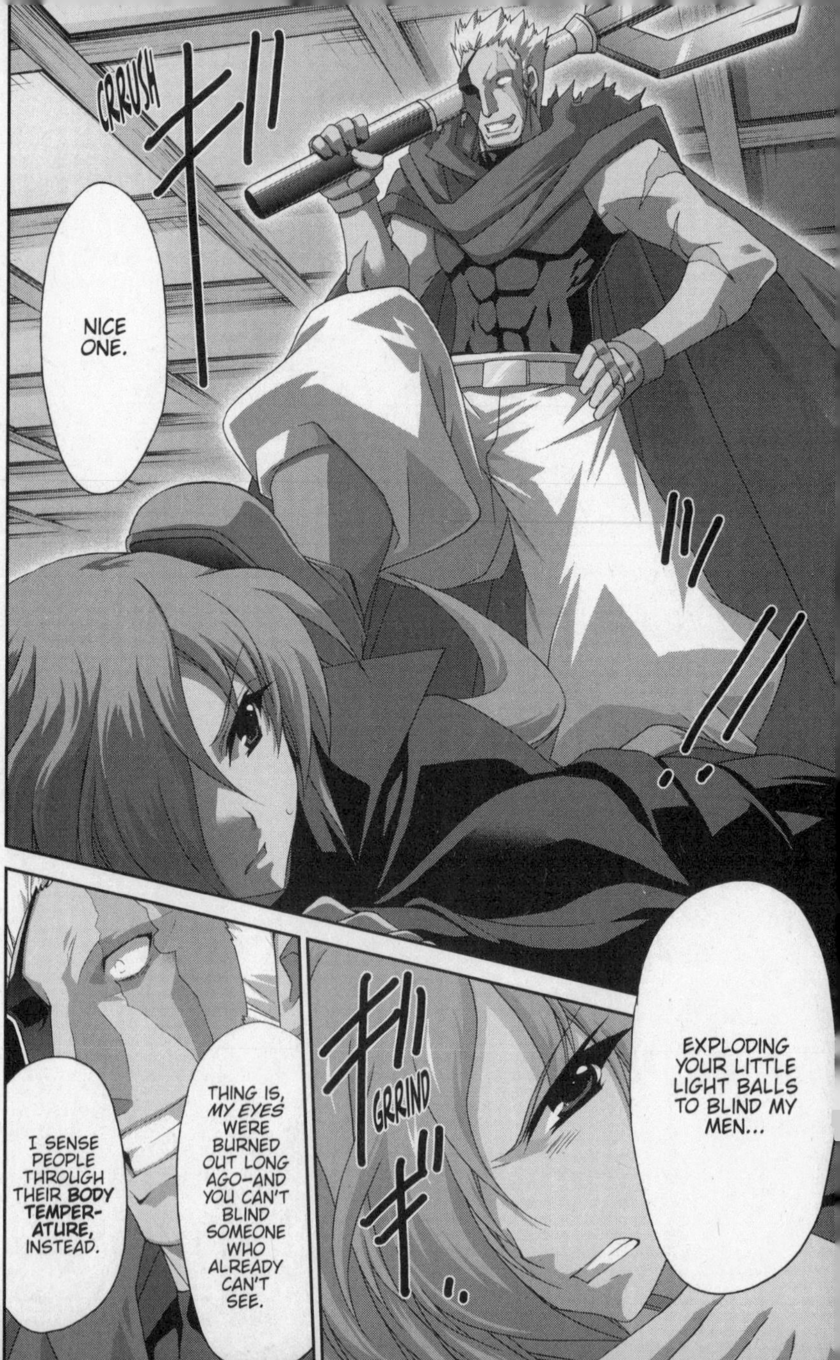
CRRUSH
NICE ONE.
EXPLODING YOUR LITTLE LIGHT BALLS TO BLIND MY MEN...
GRRIND
THING IS, *MY EYES* WERE BURNED OUT LONG AGO—AND YOU CAN'T BLIND SOMEONE WHO ALREADY CAN'T SEE.
I SENSE PEOPLE THROUGH THEIR **BODY TEMPERATURE,** INSTEAD.

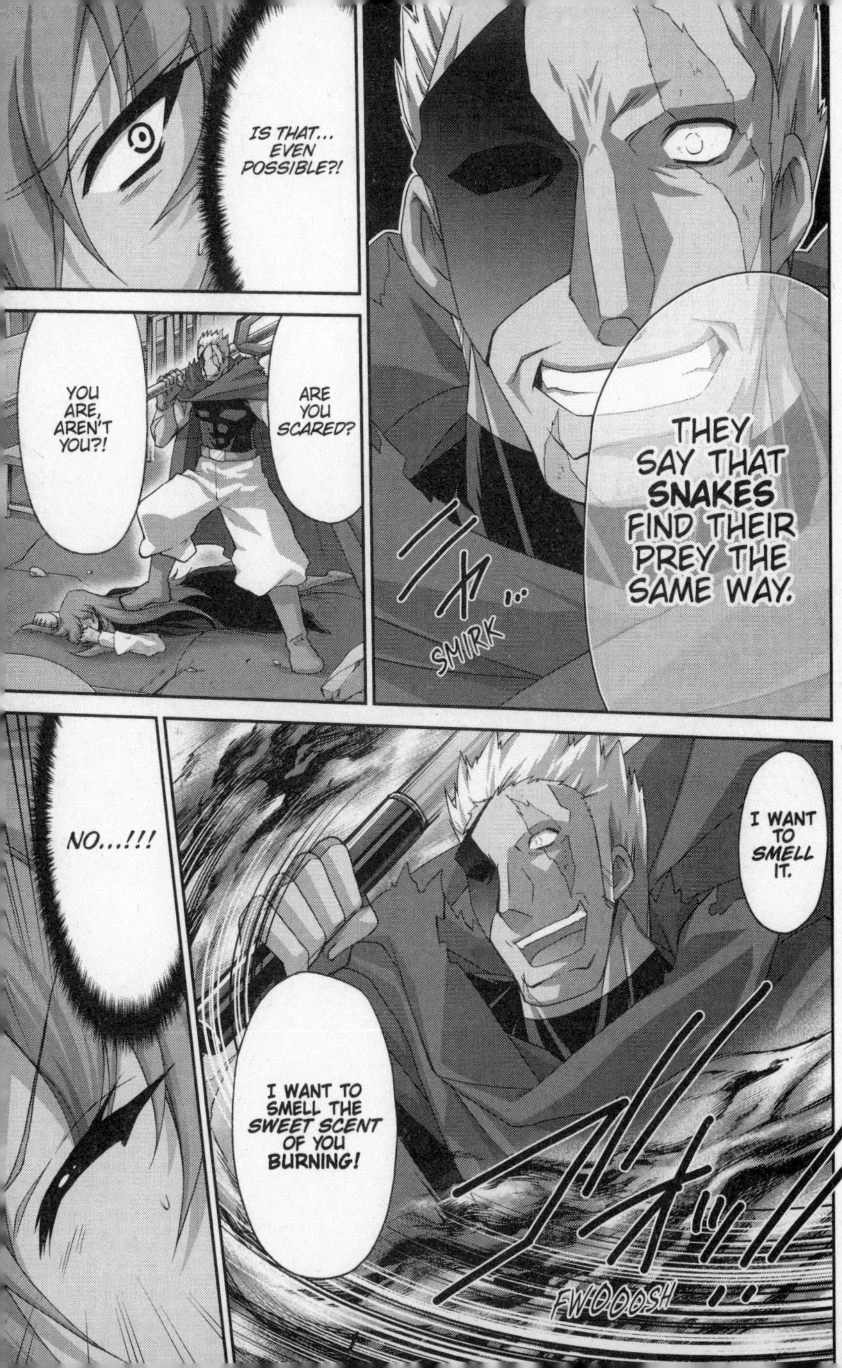
THEY SAY THAT SNAKES FIND THEIR PREY THE SAME WAY.
SMIRK
IS THAT... EVEN POSSIBLE?!
ARE YOU SCARED?
YOU ARE, AREN'T YOU?!
I WANT TO SMELL IT.
I WANT TO SMELL THE SWEET SCENT OF YOU BURNING!
FWOOOSH
NO...!!!

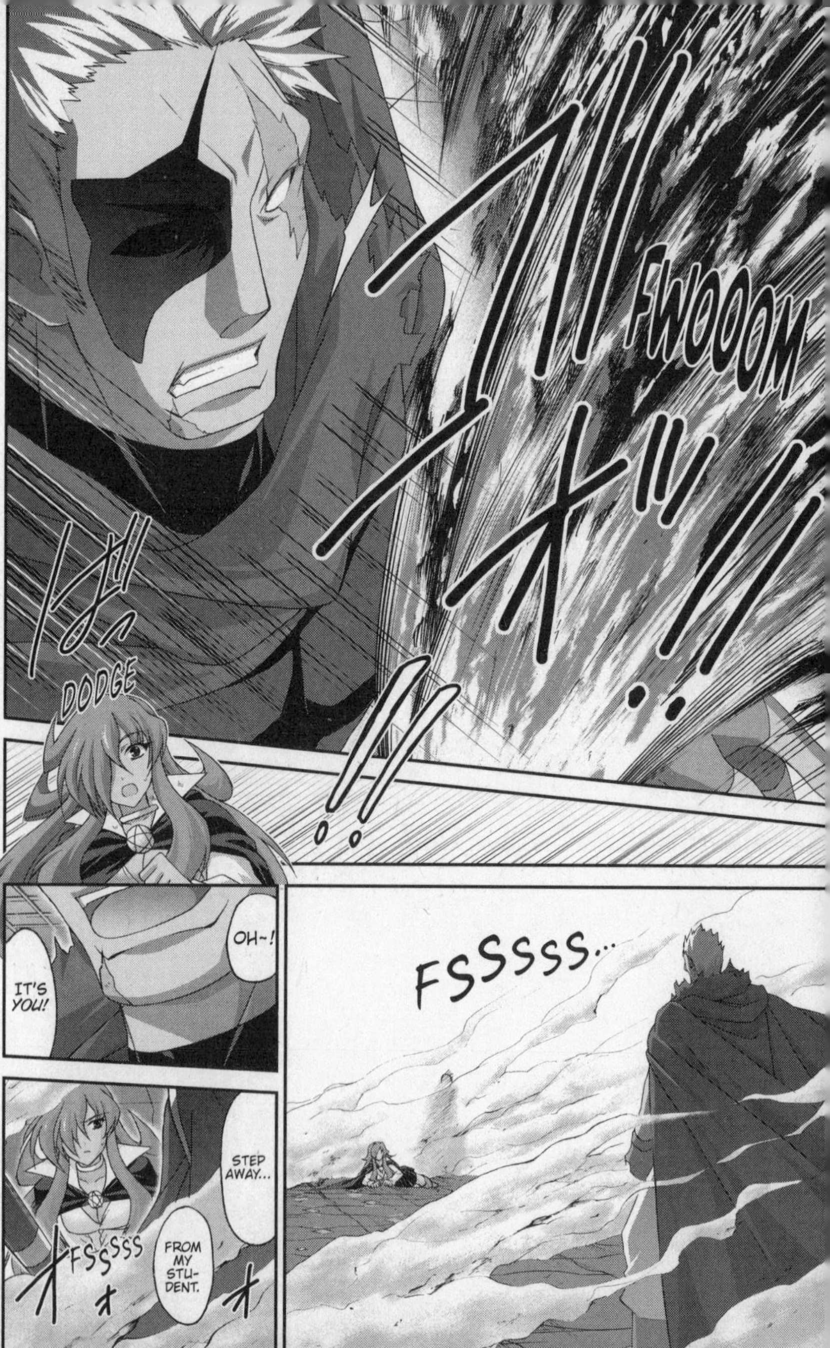
FWOOOM
DODGE
FSSSSS...
OH~!
IT'S YOU!
STEP AWAY...
FROM MY STU-DENT.
FSSSSS

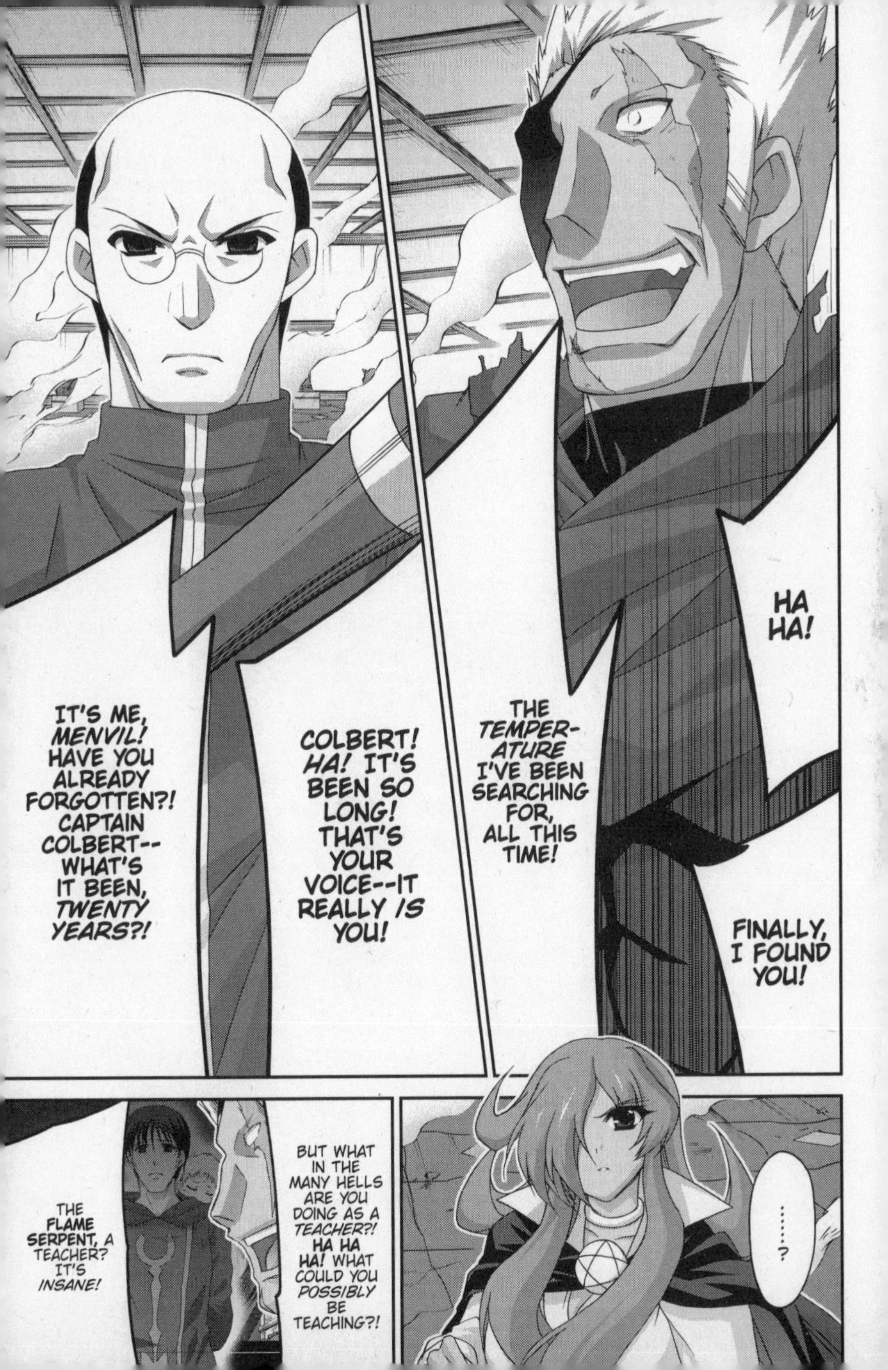

HA HA!
THE TEMPER-ATURE I'VE BEEN SEARCHING FOR, ALL THIS TIME!
FINALLY, I FOUND YOU!
COLBERT! *HA!* IT'S BEEN SO LONG! THAT'S YOUR VOICE--IT REALLY *IS* YOU!
IT'S ME, *MENVIL!* HAVE YOU ALREADY FORGOTTEN?! CAPTAIN COLBERT--WHAT'S IT BEEN, *TWENTY YEARS?!*
......?
BUT WHAT IN THE MANY HELLS ARE YOU DOING AS A *TEACHER?!* HA HA HA! WHAT COULD YOU *POSSIBLY* BE TEACHING?!
THE FLAME SERPENT, A TEACHER? IT'S *INSANE!*

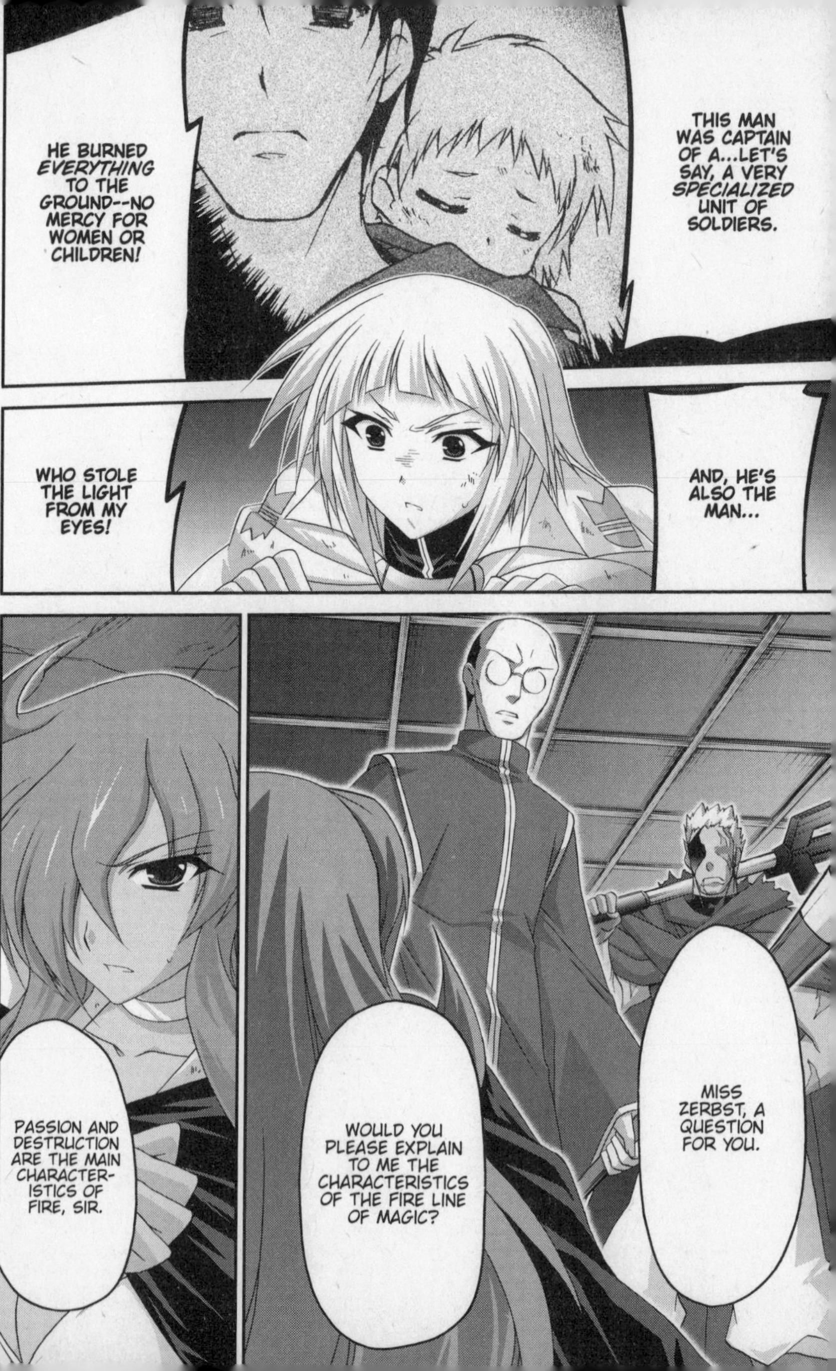
THIS MAN WAS CAPTAIN OF A...LET'S SAY, A VERY *SPECIALIZED* UNIT OF SOLDIERS.
HE BURNED *EVERYTHING* TO THE GROUND--NO MERCY FOR WOMEN OR CHILDREN!
AND, HE'S ALSO THE MAN...
WHO STOLE THE LIGHT FROM MY EYES!
MISS ZERBST, A QUESTION FOR YOU.
WOULD YOU PLEASE EXPLAIN TO ME THE CHARACTERISTICS OF THE FIRE LINE OF MAGIC?
PASSION AND DESTRUCTION ARE THE MAIN CHARACTER-ISTICS OF FIRE, SIR.

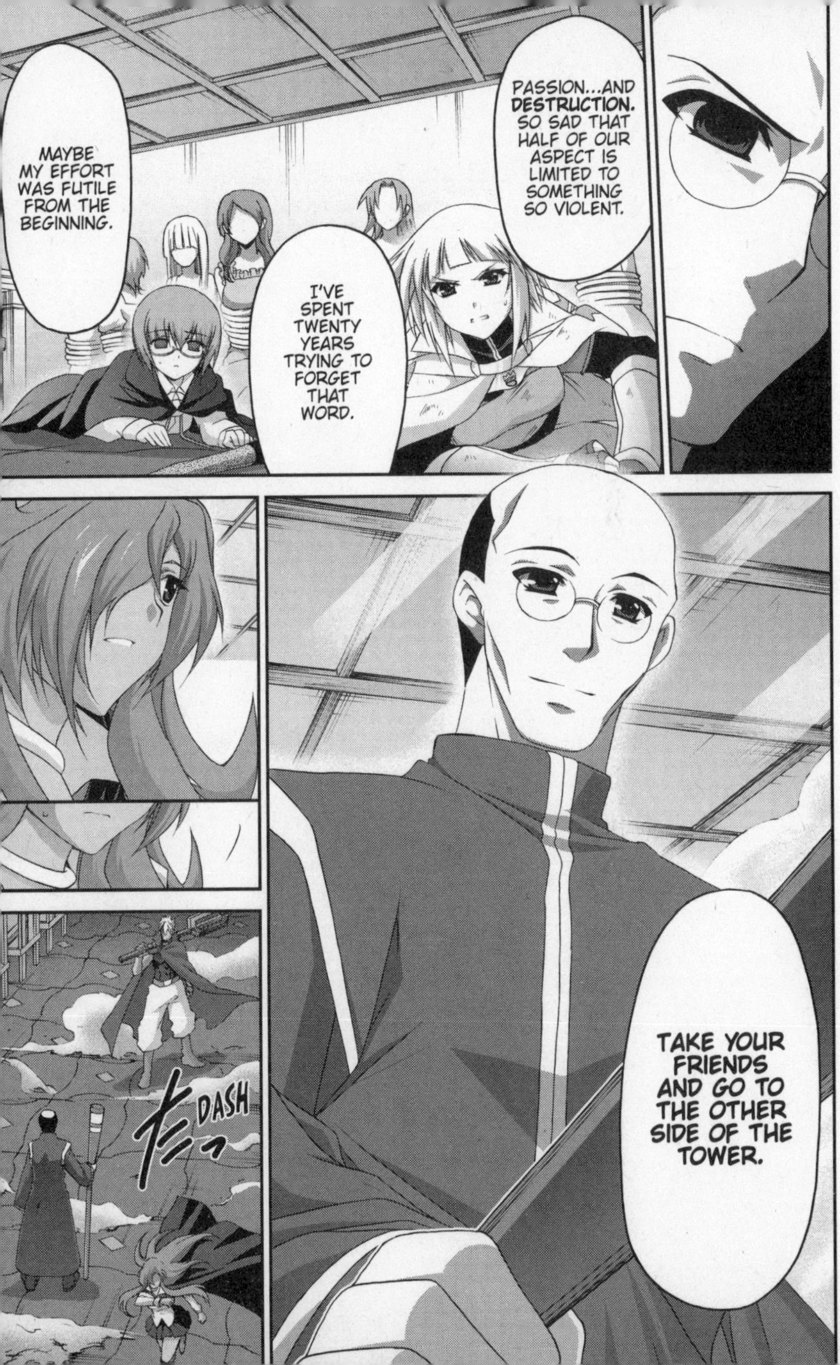
PASSION...AND **DESTRUCTION.** SO SAD THAT HALF OF OUR ASPECT IS LIMITED TO SOMETHING SO VIOLENT.
I'VE SPENT TWENTY YEARS TRYING TO FORGET THAT WORD.
MAYBE MY EFFORT WAS FUTILE FROM THE BEGINNING.
TAKE YOUR FRIENDS AND GO TO THE OTHER SIDE OF THE TOWER.
DASH

Le Familier de Zero Chevalier

ZERO'S
FAMILIAR
Chevalier

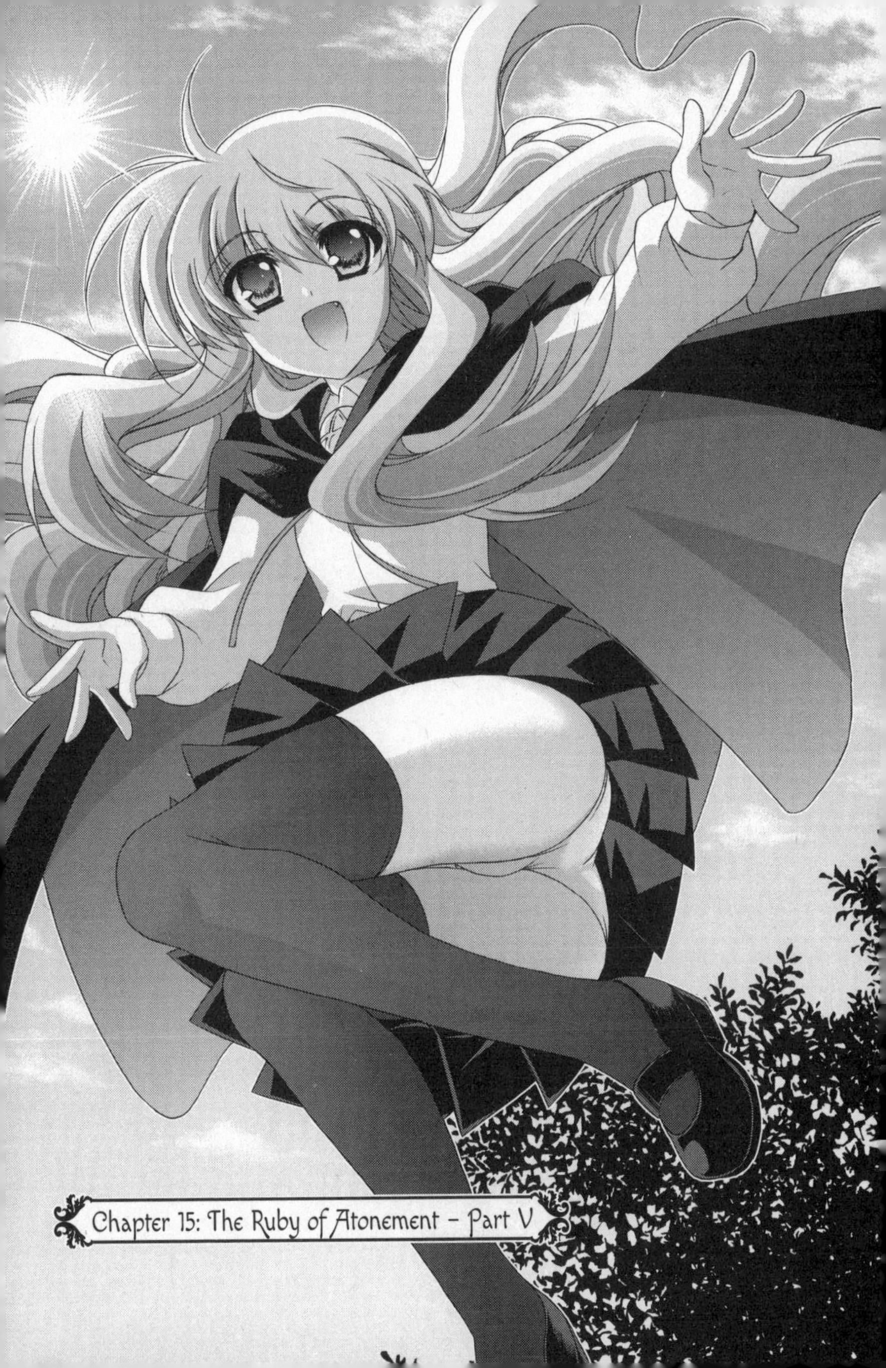

Chapter 15: The Ruby of Atonement - Part V

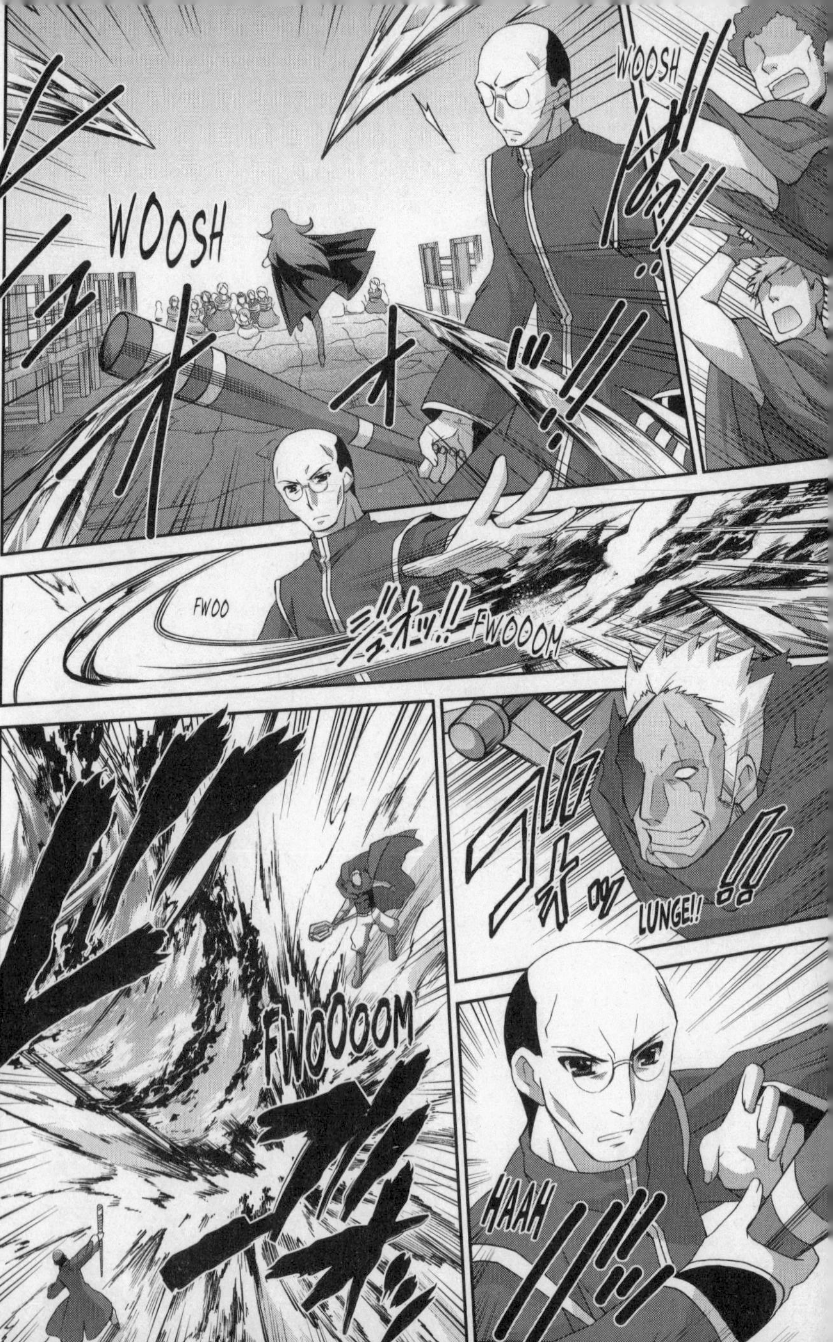
WOOSH
WOOSH
FWOO
ジュオッ!!
FWOOOM
LUNGE!!
HAAH
FWOOOOM

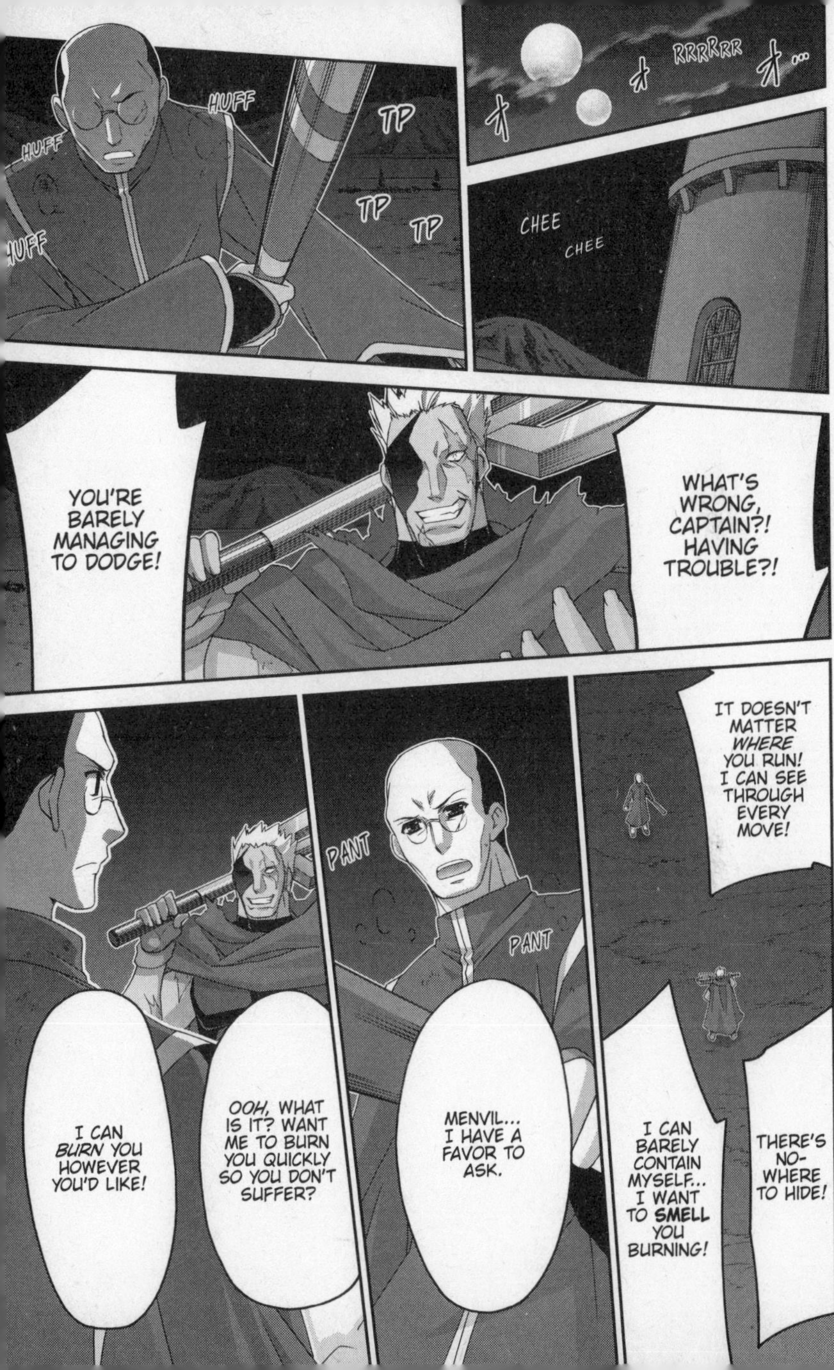

オ
オ
RRRRRR
オ…
CHEE
CHEE
HUFF
HUFF
HUFF
TP
TP
TP
WHAT'S WRONG, CAPTAIN?! HAVING TROUBLE?!
YOU'RE BARELY MANAGING TO DODGE!
IT DOESN'T MATTER *WHERE* YOU RUN! I CAN SEE THROUGH EVERY MOVE!
THERE'S NO-WHERE TO HIDE!
I CAN BARELY CONTAIN MYSELF... I WANT TO **SMELL** YOU BURNING!
PANT
PANT
MENVIL... I HAVE A FAVOR TO ASK.
OOH, WHAT IS IT? WANT ME TO BURN YOU QUICKLY SO YOU DON'T SUFFER?
I CAN *BURN* YOU HOWEVER YOU'D LIKE!

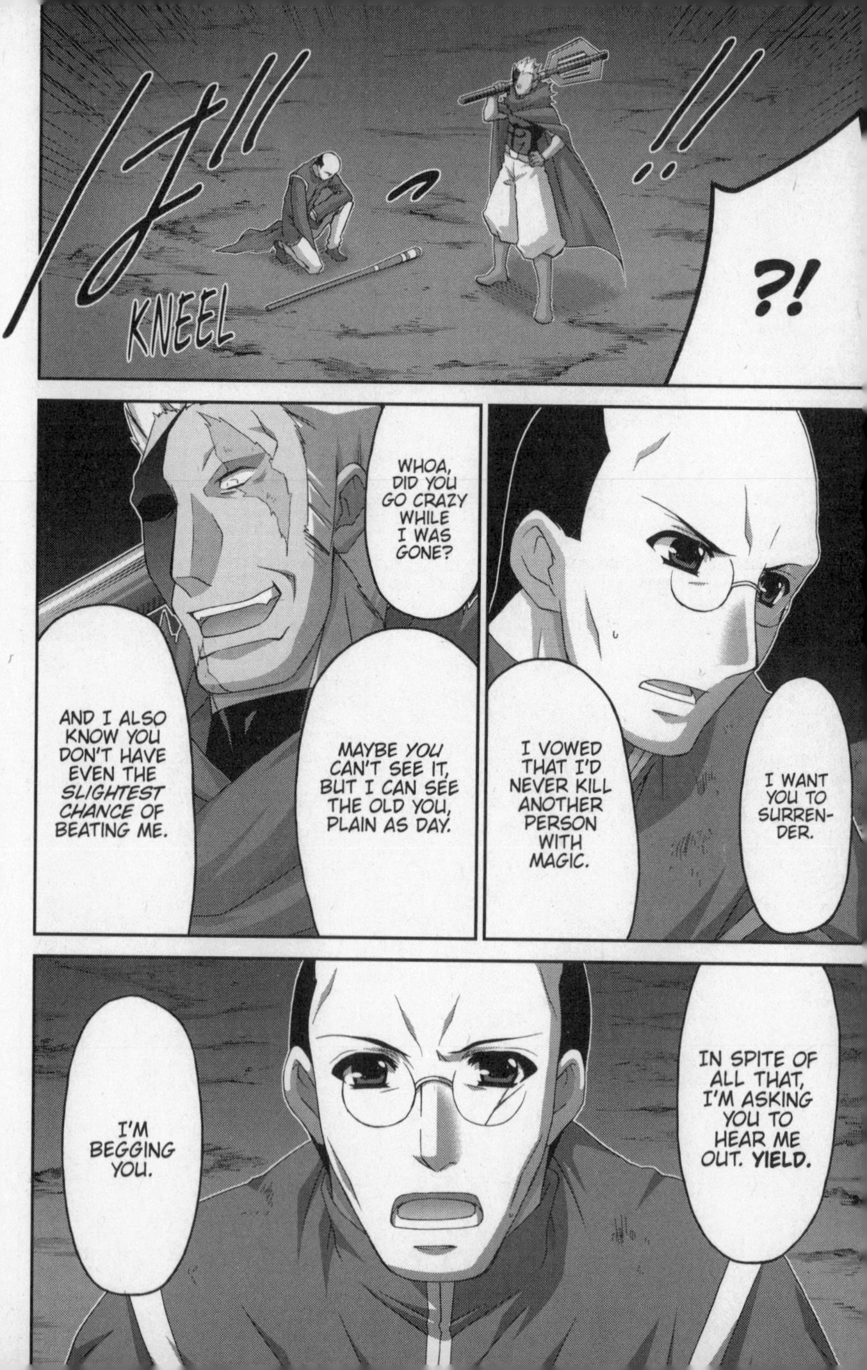
?!
KNEEL
I WANT YOU TO SURRENDER.
I VOWED THAT I'D NEVER KILL ANOTHER PERSON WITH MAGIC.
WHOA, DID YOU GO CRAZY WHILE I WAS GONE?
MAYBE *YOU* CAN'T SEE IT, BUT I CAN SEE THE OLD YOU, PLAIN AS DAY.
AND I ALSO KNOW YOU DON'T HAVE EVEN THE *SLIGHTEST CHANCE* OF BEATING ME.
IN SPITE OF ALL THAT, I'M ASKING YOU TO HEAR ME OUT. **YIELD.**
I'M BEGGING YOU.

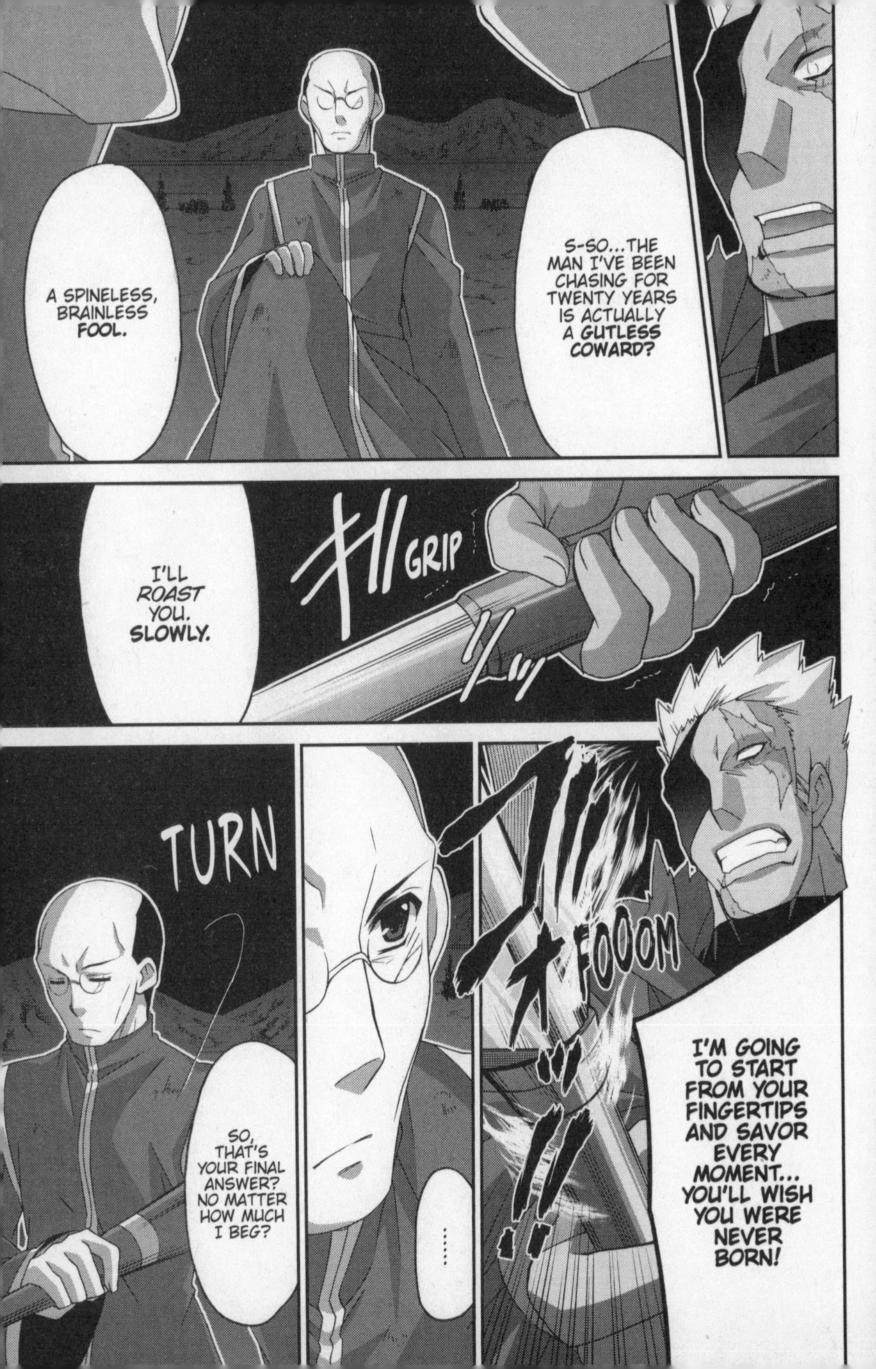
S-SO...THE MAN I'VE BEEN CHASING FOR TWENTY YEARS IS ACTUALLY A GUTLESS COWARD?
A SPINELESS, BRAINLESS FOOL.
GRIP
I'LL ROAST YOU. SLOWLY.
FOOOM
I'M GOING TO START FROM YOUR FINGERTIPS AND SAVOR EVERY MOMENT... YOU'LL WISH YOU WERE NEVER BORN!
......
TURN
SO, THAT'S YOUR FINAL ANSWER? NO MATTER HOW MUCH I BEG?

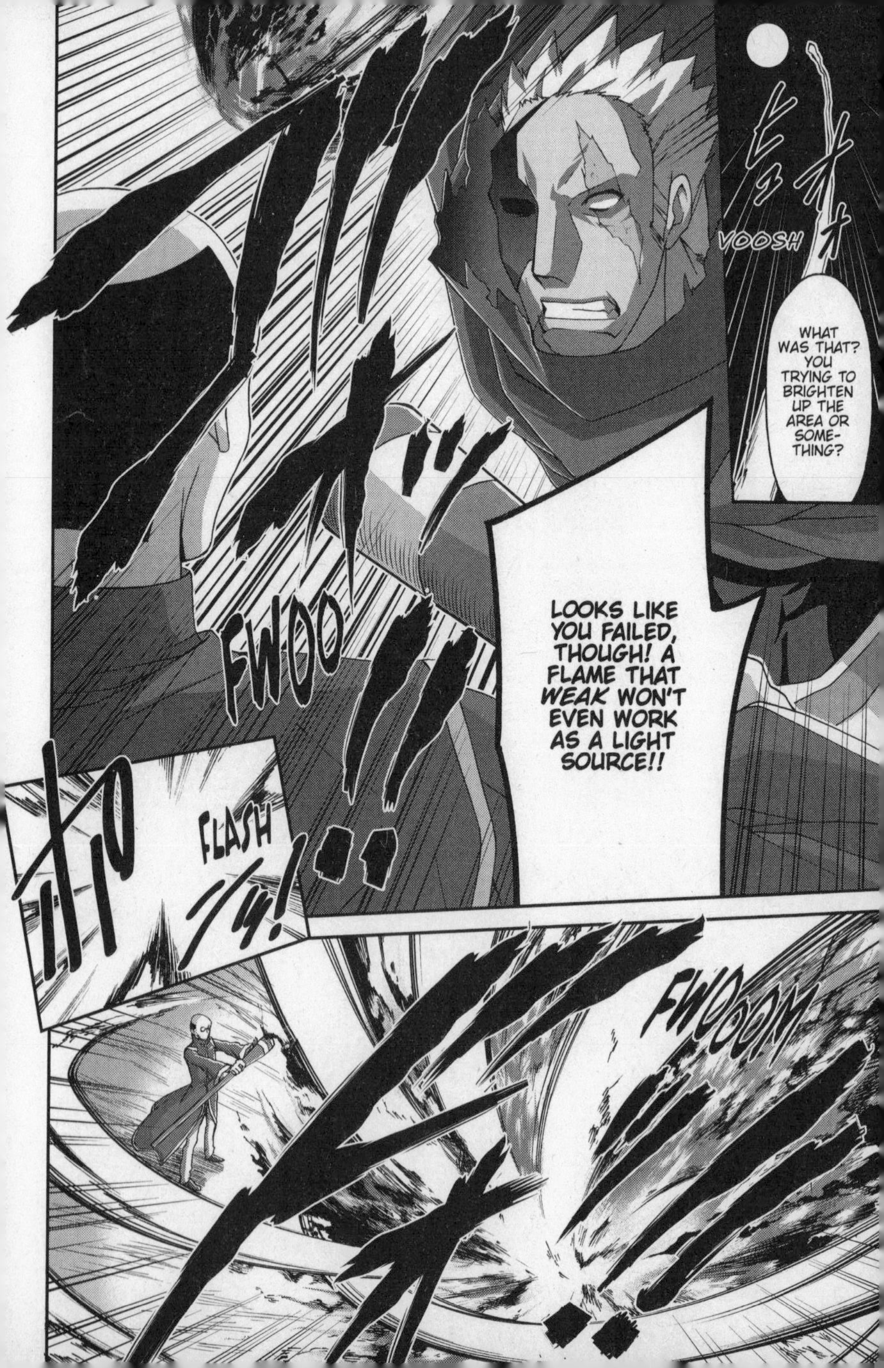
VOOSH
WHAT WAS THAT? YOU TRYING TO BRIGHTEN UP THE AREA OR SOME-THING?
LOOKS LIKE YOU FAILED, THOUGH! A FLAME THAT WEAK WON'T EVEN WORK AS A LIGHT SOURCE!!
FWOO
FLASH
FWOOOM

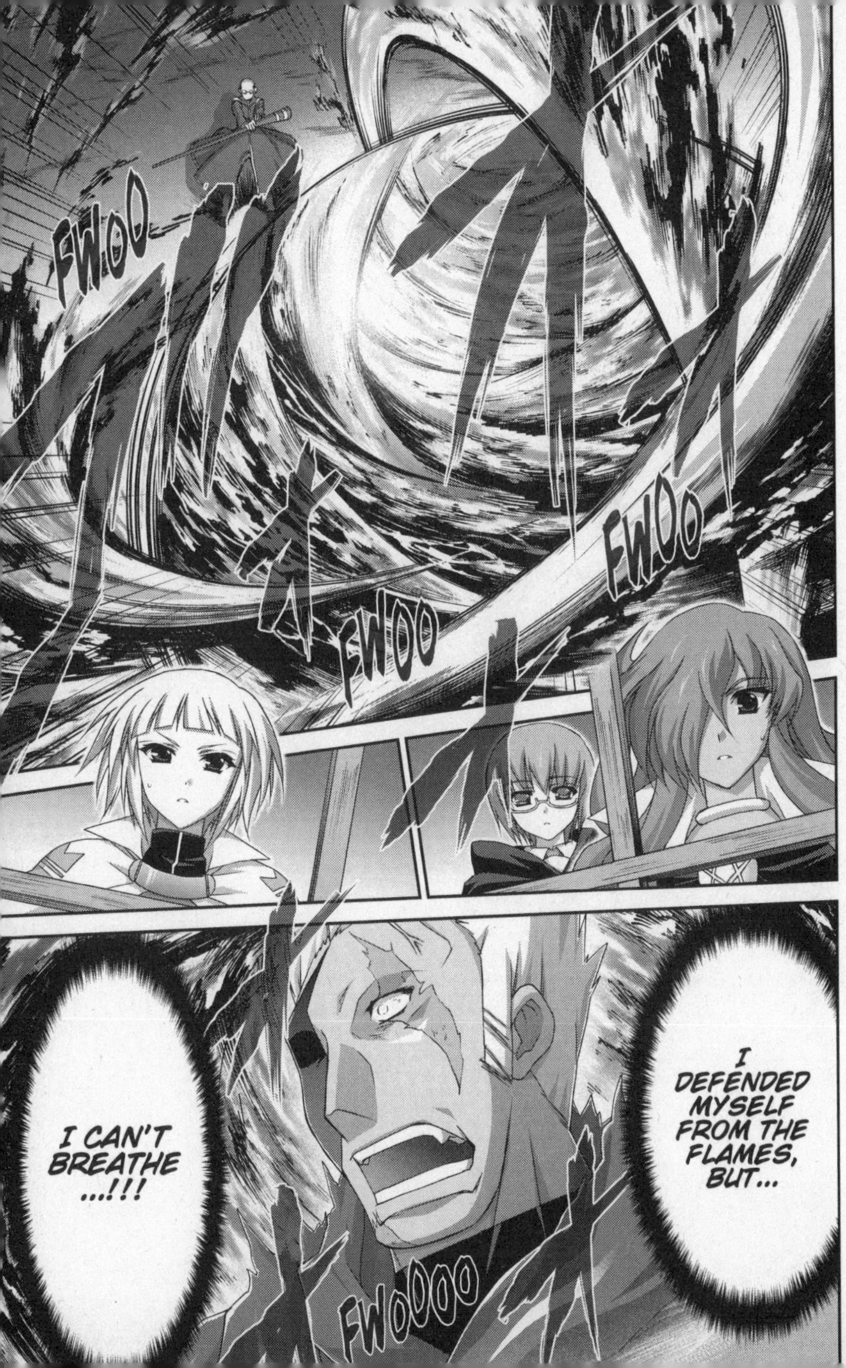
FWOO
FWOO
FWOO
I DEFENDED MYSELF FROM THE FLAMES, BUT...
I CAN'T BREATHE ...!!!
FWOOOO

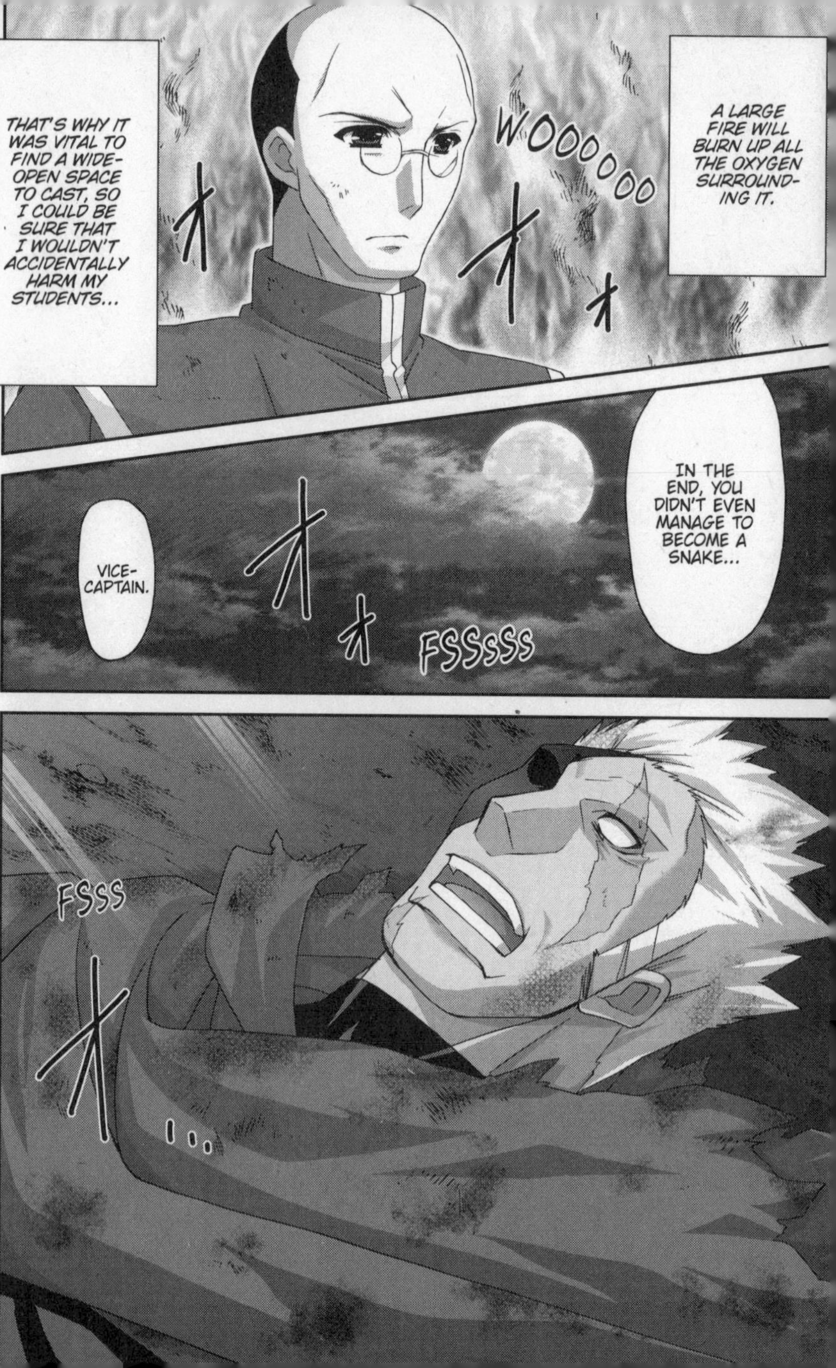
A LARGE FIRE WILL BURN UP ALL THE OXYGEN SURROUNDING IT.
WOOOOOOO
THAT'S WHY IT WAS VITAL TO FIND A WIDE-OPEN SPACE TO CAST, SO I COULD BE SURE THAT I WOULDN'T ACCIDENTALLY HARM MY STUDENTS...
IN THE END, YOU DIDN'T EVEN MANAGE TO BECOME A SNAKE...
FSSSSS
VICE-CAPTAIN.
FSSS
...

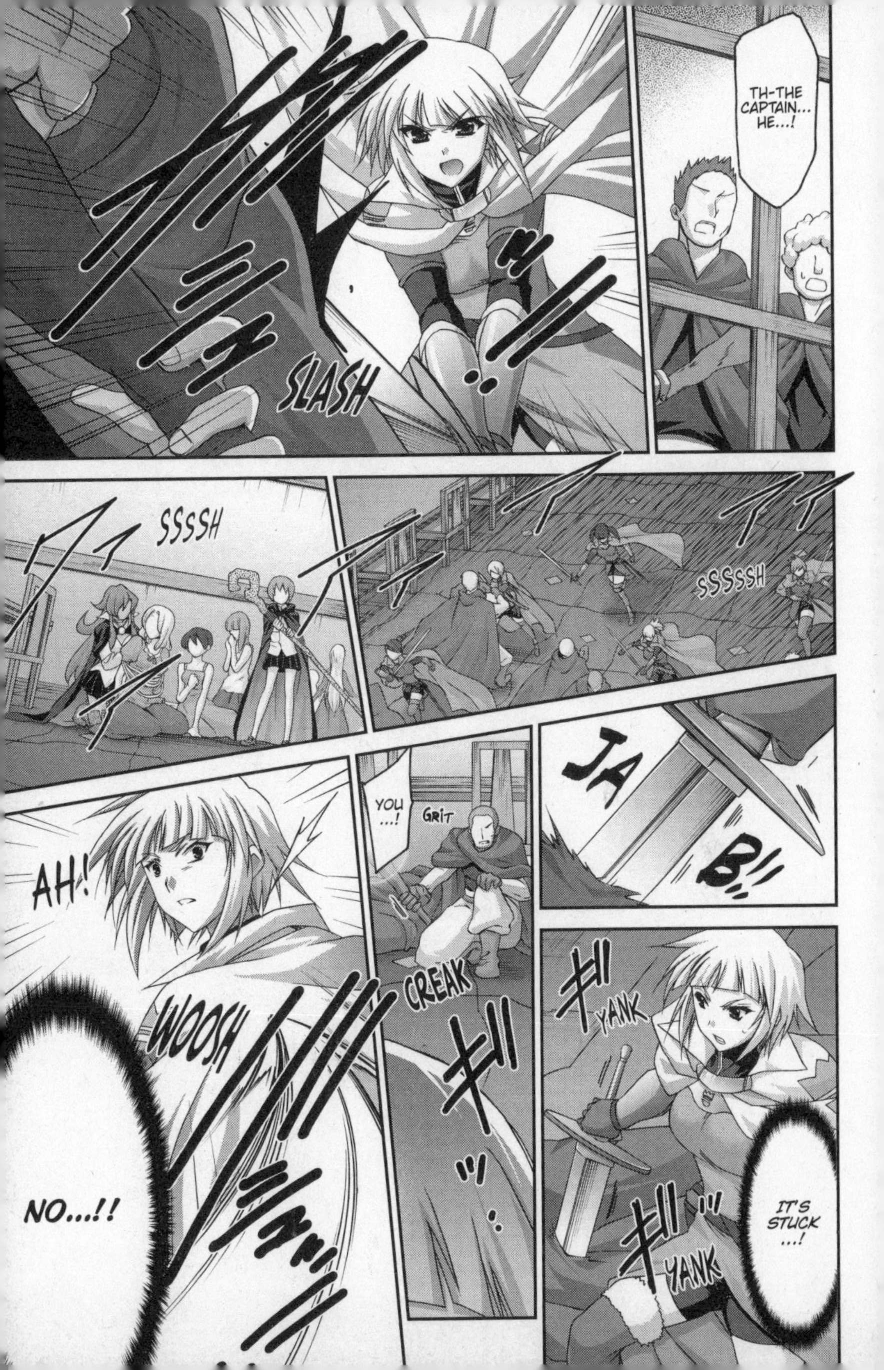
TH-THE CAPTAIN... HE...!
SLASH
SSSSSH
SSSSH
JAB!!
YANK
IT'S STUCK ...!
YANK
YOU ...!
GRIT
CREAK
AH!
WOOSH
NO...!!

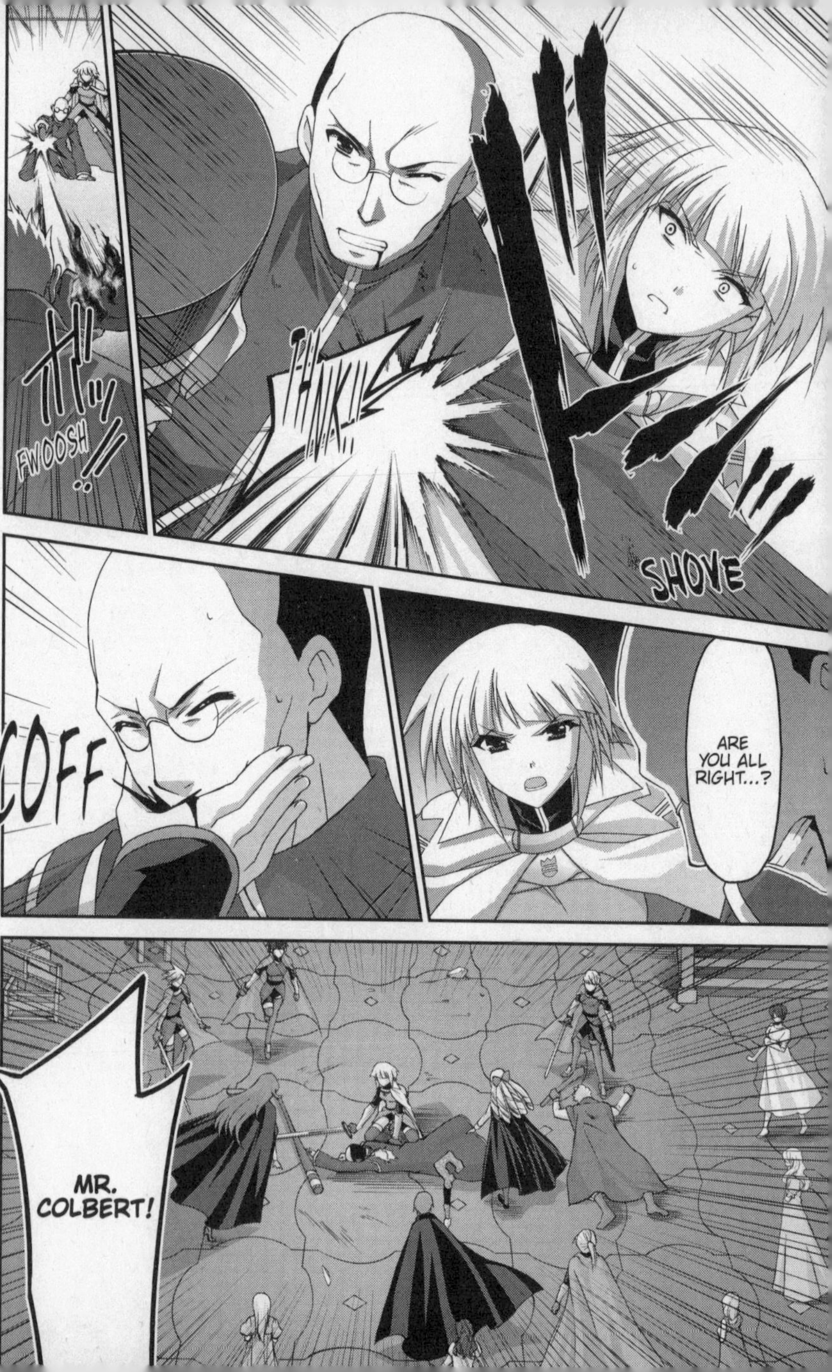
SHOVE
THUNK!!
FWOOSH!!
ARE YOU ALL RIGHT...?
COFF
MR. COLBERT!

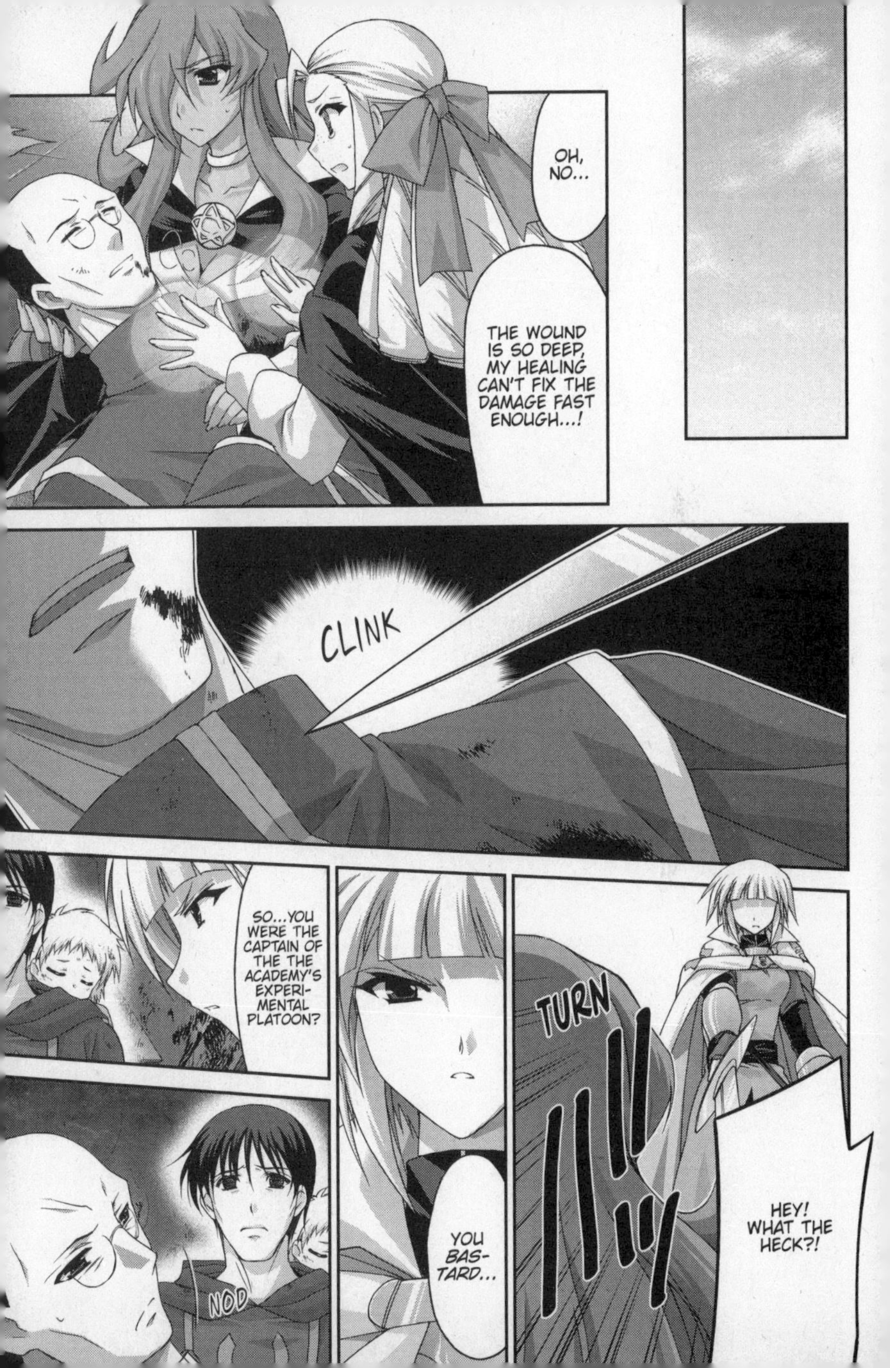
OH, NO...
THE WOUND IS SO DEEP, MY HEALING CAN'T FIX THE DAMAGE FAST ENOUGH...!
CLINK
TURN
HEY! WHAT THE HECK?!
YOU BAS-TARD...
SO...YOU WERE THE CAPTAIN OF THE THE ACADEMY'S EXPERI-MENTAL PLATOON?
NOD

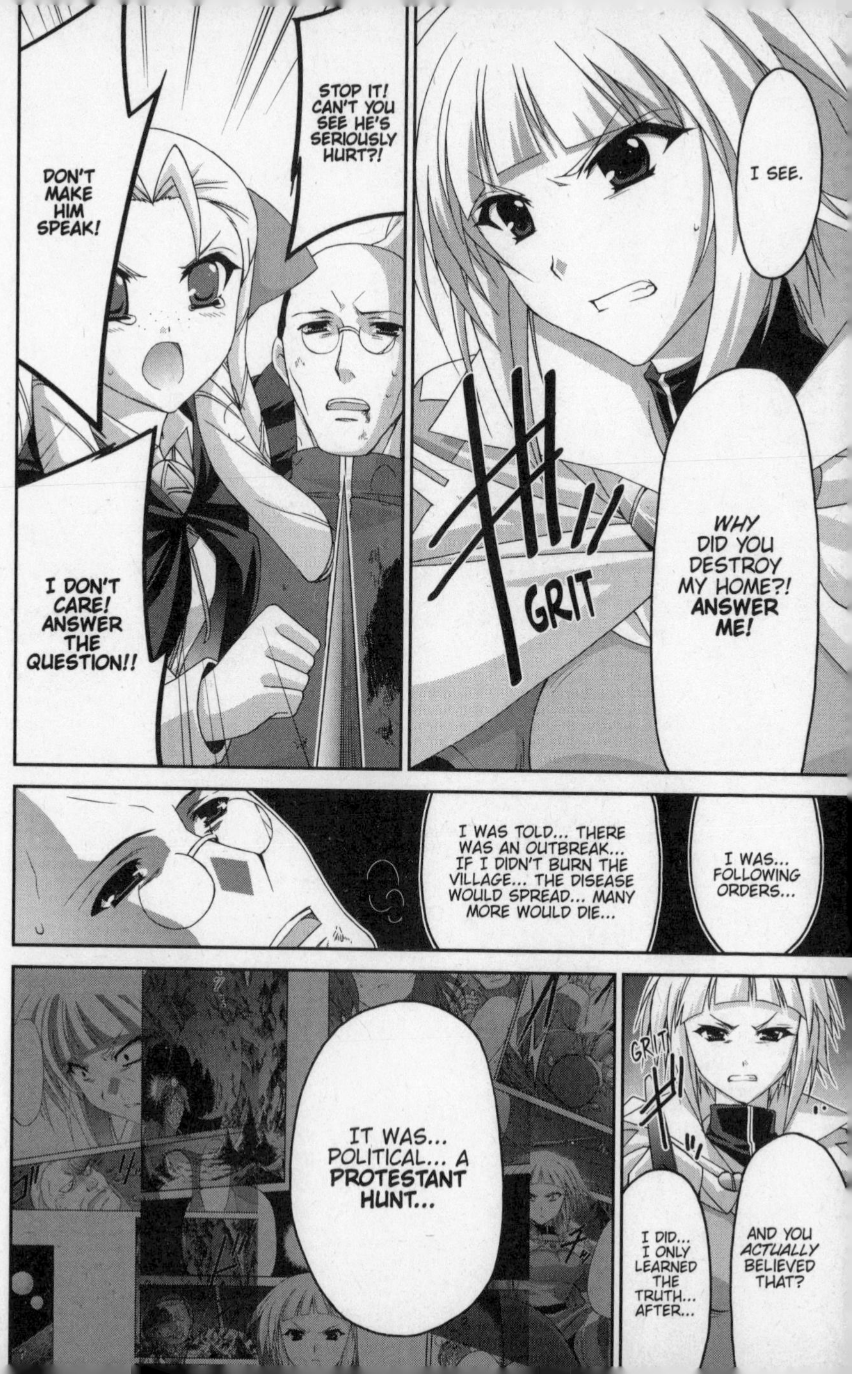
I SEE.
WHY DID YOU DESTROY MY HOME?! ANSWER ME!
GRIT
STOP IT! CAN'T YOU SEE HE'S SERIOUSLY HURT?!
DON'T MAKE HIM SPEAK!
I DON'T CARE! ANSWER THE QUESTION!!
I WAS... FOLLOWING ORDERS...
I WAS TOLD... THERE WAS AN OUTBREAK... IF I DIDN'T BURN THE VILLAGE... THE DISEASE WOULD SPREAD... MANY MORE WOULD DIE...
GRIT
AND YOU ACTUALLY BELIEVED THAT?
I DID... I ONLY LEARNED THE TRUTH... AFTER...
IT WAS... POLITICAL... A PROTESTANT HUNT...

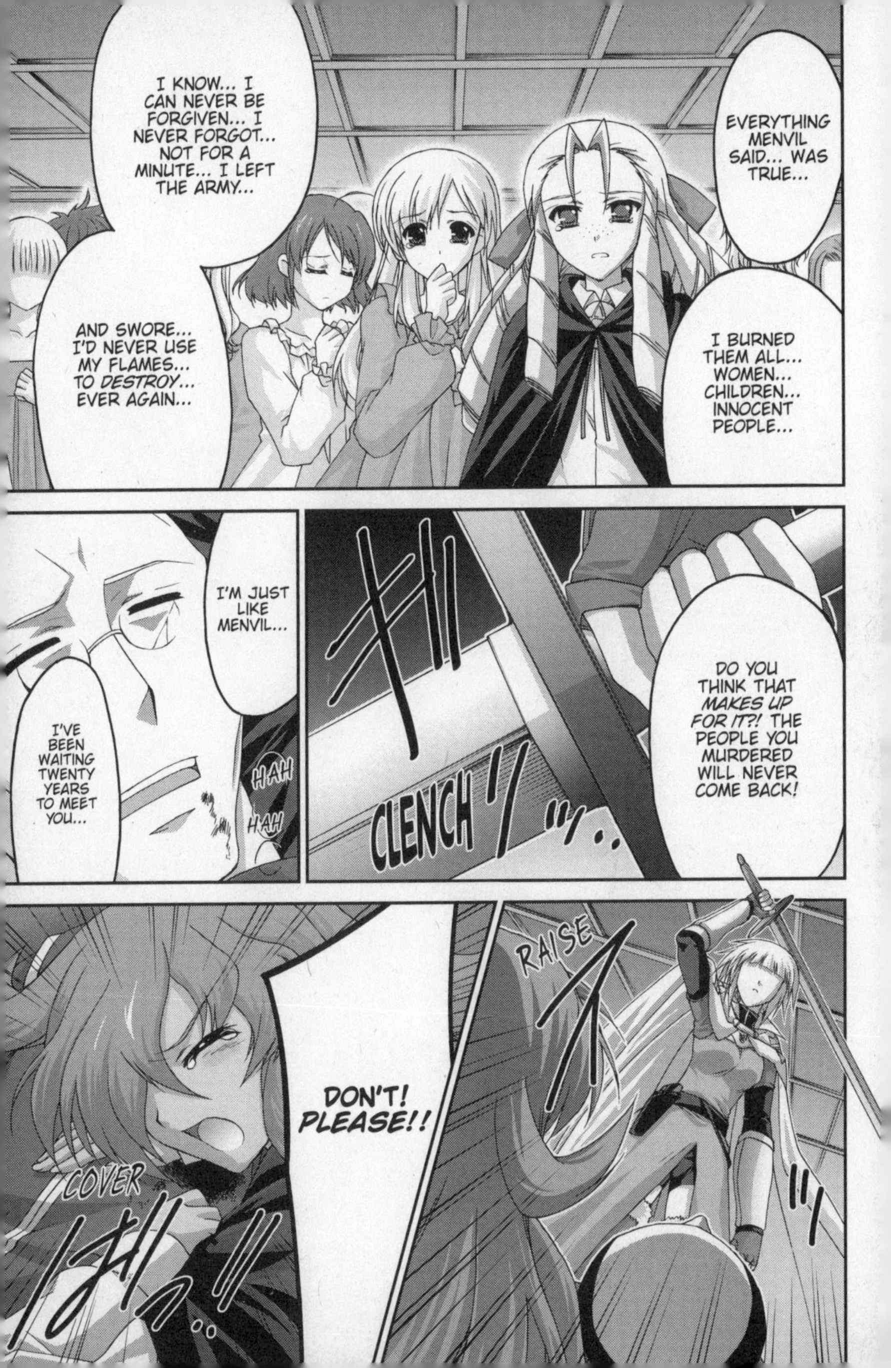
EVERYTHING MENVIL SAID... WAS TRUE...
I BURNED THEM ALL... WOMEN... CHILDREN... INNOCENT PEOPLE...
I KNOW... I CAN NEVER BE FORGIVEN... I NEVER FORGOT... NOT FOR A MINUTE... I LEFT THE ARMY...
AND SWORE... I'D NEVER USE MY FLAMES... TO *DESTROY*... EVER AGAIN...
DO YOU THINK THAT *MAKES UP FOR IT?!* THE PEOPLE YOU MURDERED WILL NEVER COME BACK!
CLENCH
I'M JUST LIKE MENVIL...
HAH
HAH
I'VE BEEN WAITING TWENTY YEARS TO MEET YOU...
RAISE
DON'T! *PLEASE!!*
COVER
ばっ

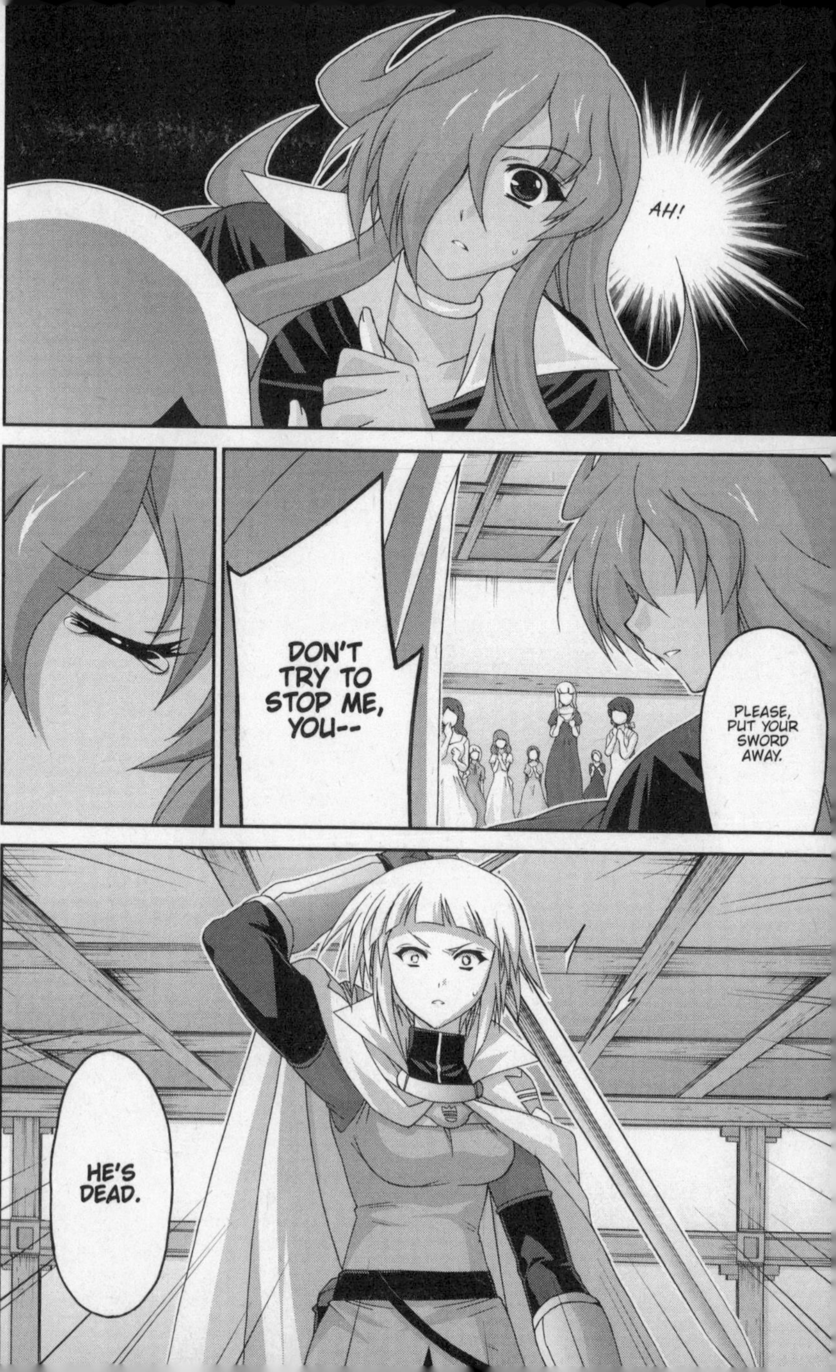
AH!
PLEASE, PUT YOUR SWORD AWAY.
DON'T TRY TO STOP ME, YOU--
HE'S DEAD.

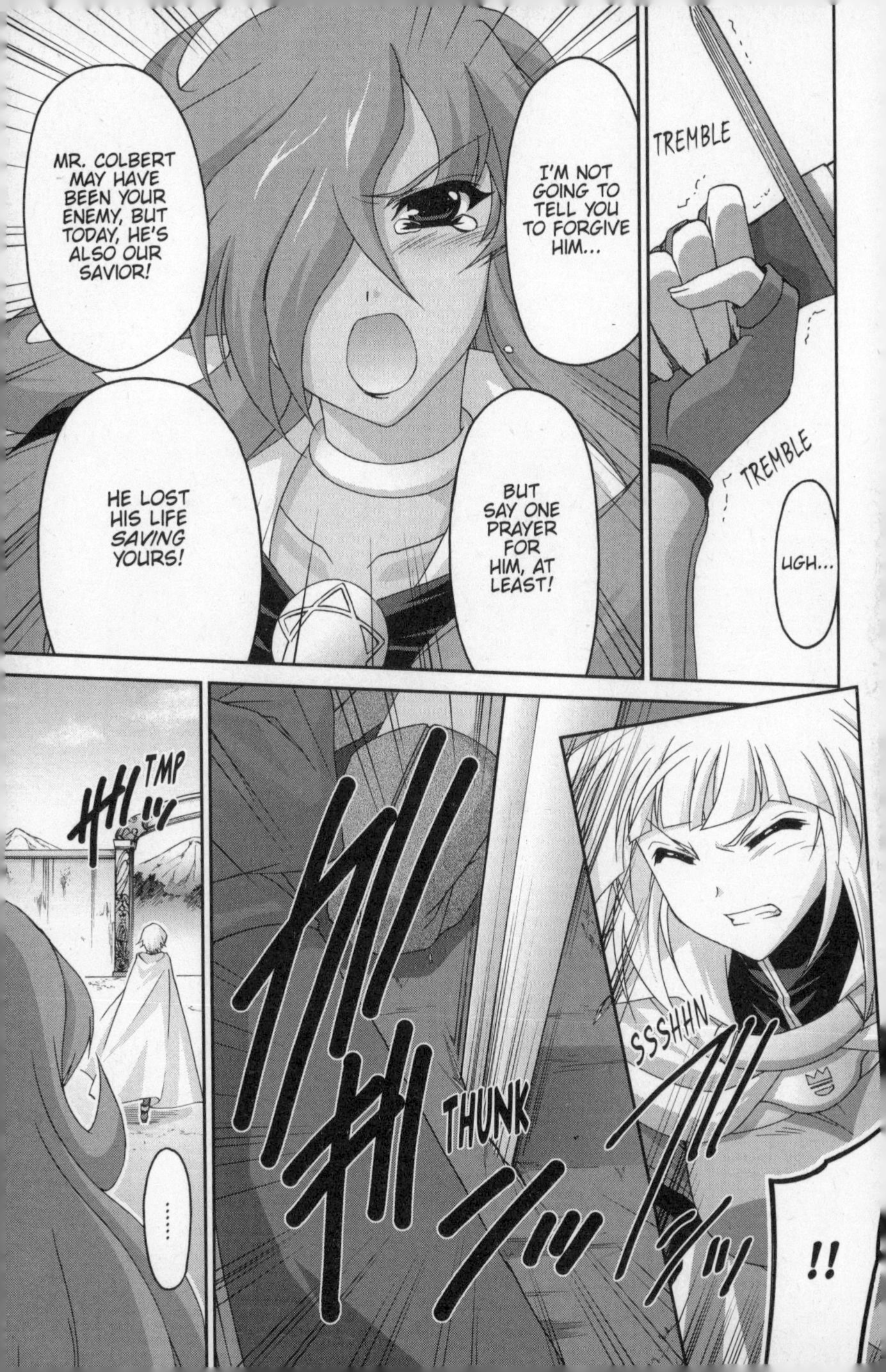
TREMBLE
TREMBLE
UGH...
I'M NOT GOING TO TELL YOU TO FORGIVE HIM...
MR. COLBERT MAY HAVE BEEN YOUR ENEMY, BUT TODAY, HE'S ALSO OUR SAVIOR!
BUT SAY ONE PRAYER FOR HIM, AT LEAST!
HE LOST HIS LIFE *SAVING* YOURS!
SSSHHN
!!
THUNK
TMP
......

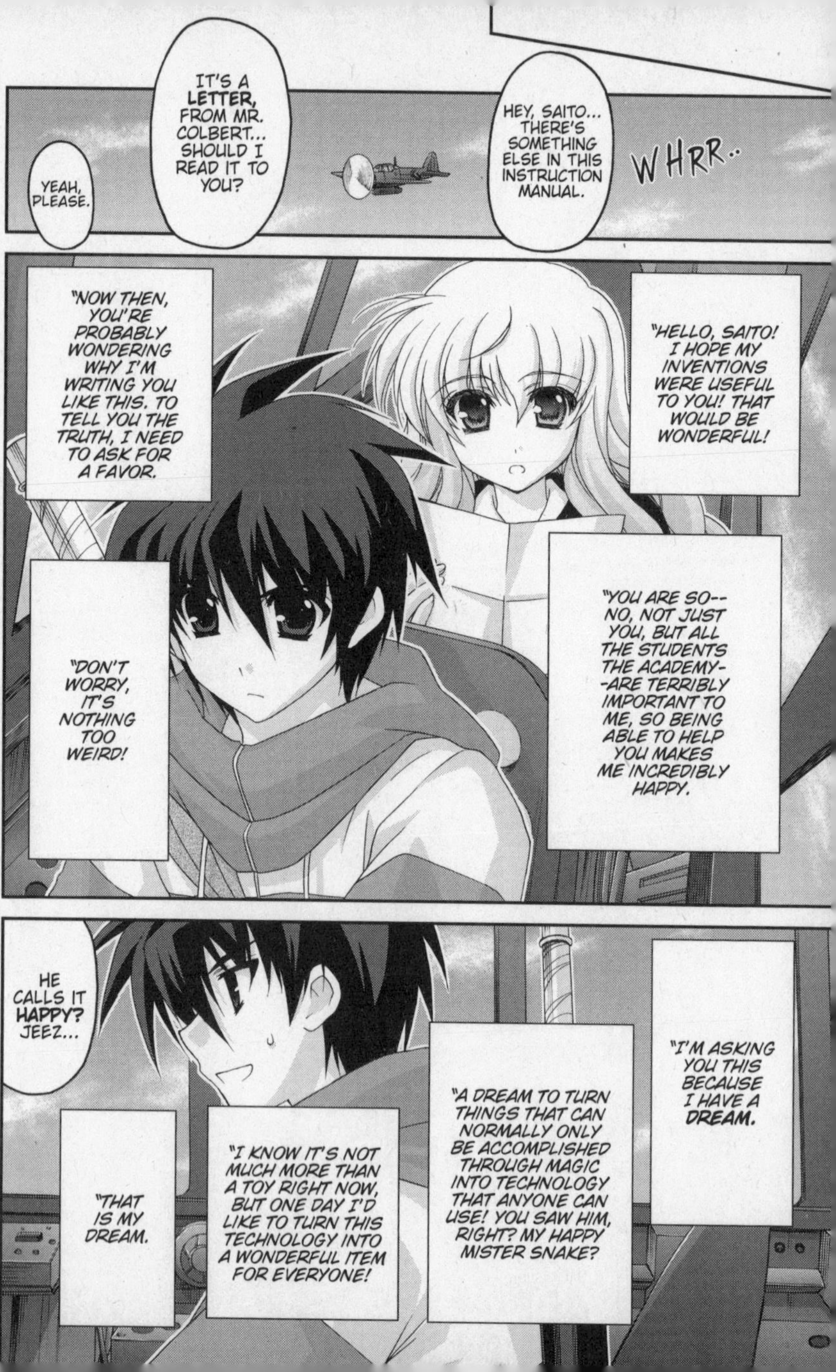
WHRR..
HEY, SAITO... THERE'S SOMETHING ELSE IN THIS INSTRUCTION MANUAL.
IT'S A **LETTER**, FROM MR. COLBERT... SHOULD I READ IT TO YOU?
YEAH, PLEASE.
"HELLO, SAITO! I HOPE MY INVENTIONS WERE USEFUL TO YOU! THAT WOULD BE WONDERFUL!
"YOU ARE SO-- NO, NOT JUST YOU, BUT ALL THE STUDENTS THE ACADEMY--ARE TERRIBLY IMPORTANT TO ME, SO BEING ABLE TO HELP YOU MAKES ME INCREDIBLY HAPPY.
"NOW THEN, YOU'RE PROBABLY WONDERING WHY I'M WRITING YOU LIKE THIS. TO TELL YOU THE TRUTH, I NEED TO ASK FOR A FAVOR.
"DON'T WORRY, IT'S NOTHING TOO WEIRD!
"I'M ASKING YOU THIS BECAUSE I HAVE A **DREAM.**
"A DREAM TO TURN THINGS THAT CAN NORMALLY ONLY BE ACCOMPLISHED THROUGH MAGIC INTO TECHNOLOGY THAT ANYONE CAN USE! YOU SAW HIM, RIGHT? MY HAPPY MISTER SNAKE?
"I KNOW IT'S NOT MUCH MORE THAN A TOY RIGHT NOW, BUT ONE DAY I'D LIKE TO TURN THIS TECHNOLOGY INTO A WONDERFUL ITEM FOR EVERYONE!
"THAT IS MY DREAM.
HE CALLS IT **HAPPY?** JEEZ...

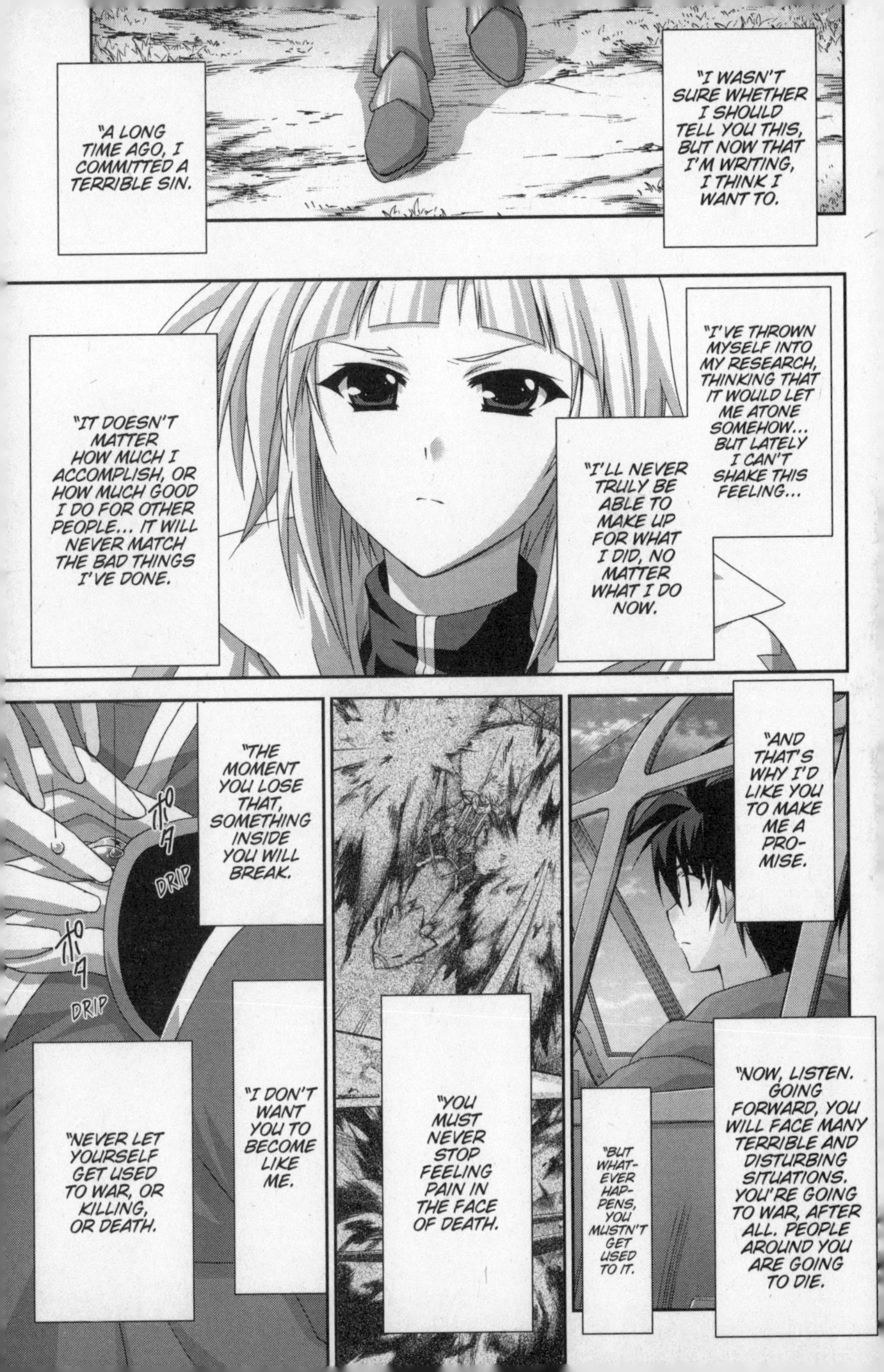
"I WASN'T SURE WHETHER I SHOULD TELL YOU THIS, BUT NOW THAT I'M WRITING, I THINK I WANT TO.
"A LONG TIME AGO, I COMMITTED A TERRIBLE SIN.
"I'VE THROWN MYSELF INTO MY RESEARCH, THINKING THAT IT WOULD LET ME ATONE SOMEHOW... BUT LATELY I CAN'T SHAKE THIS FEELING...
"I'LL NEVER TRULY BE ABLE TO MAKE UP FOR WHAT I DID, NO MATTER WHAT I DO NOW.
"IT DOESN'T MATTER HOW MUCH I ACCOMPLISH, OR HOW MUCH GOOD I DO FOR OTHER PEOPLE... IT WILL NEVER MATCH THE BAD THINGS I'VE DONE.
"AND THAT'S WHY I'D LIKE YOU TO MAKE ME A PRO-MISE.
"NOW, LISTEN. GOING FORWARD, YOU WILL FACE MANY TERRIBLE AND DISTURBING SITUATIONS. YOU'RE GOING TO WAR, AFTER ALL. PEOPLE AROUND YOU ARE GOING TO DIE.
"BUT WHAT-EVER HAP-PENS, YOU MUSTN'T GET USED TO IT.
"YOU MUST NEVER STOP FEELING PAIN IN THE FACE OF DEATH.
ポタ
DRIP
"THE MOMENT YOU LOSE THAT, SOMETHING INSIDE YOU WILL BREAK.
ポタ
DRIP
"I DON'T WANT YOU TO BECOME LIKE ME.
"NEVER LET YOURSELF GET USED TO WAR, OR KILLING, OR DEATH.

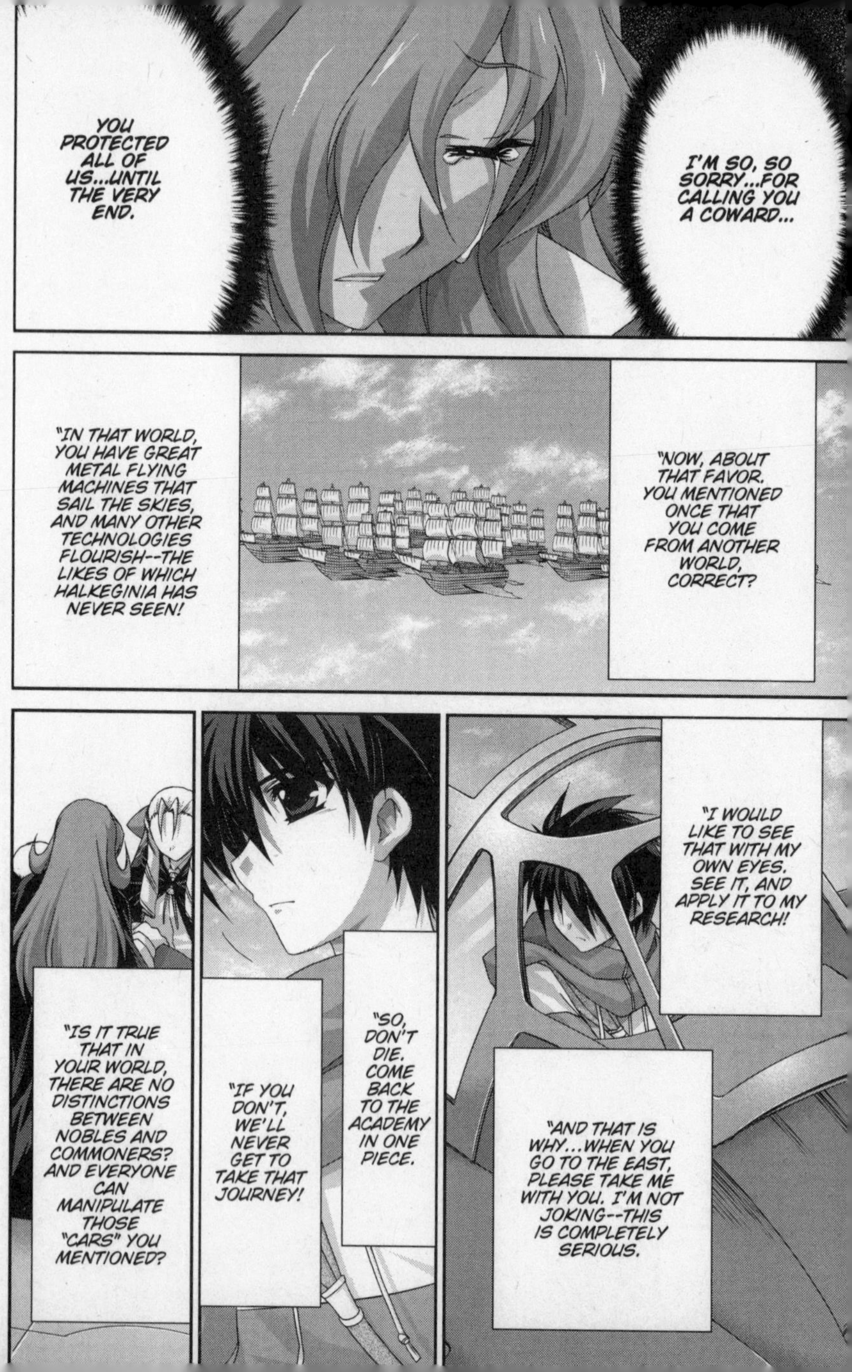
I'M SO, SO SORRY...FOR CALLING YOU A COWARD...
YOU PROTECTED ALL OF US...UNTIL THE VERY END.
"NOW, ABOUT THAT FAVOR. YOU MENTIONED ONCE THAT YOU COME FROM ANOTHER WORLD, CORRECT?
"IN THAT WORLD, YOU HAVE GREAT METAL FLYING MACHINES THAT SAIL THE SKIES, AND MANY OTHER TECHNOLOGIES FLOURISH--THE LIKES OF WHICH HALKEGINIA HAS NEVER SEEN!
"I WOULD LIKE TO SEE THAT WITH MY OWN EYES. SEE IT, AND APPLY IT TO MY RESEARCH!
"AND THAT IS WHY...WHEN YOU GO TO THE EAST, PLEASE TAKE ME WITH YOU. I'M NOT JOKING--THIS IS COMPLETELY SERIOUS.
"SO, DON'T DIE. COME BACK TO THE ACADEMY IN ONE PIECE.
"IF YOU DON'T, WE'LL NEVER GET TO TAKE THAT JOURNEY!
"IS IT TRUE THAT IN YOUR WORLD, THERE ARE NO DISTINCTIONS BETWEEN NOBLES AND COMMONERS? AND EVERYONE CAN MANIPULATE THOSE "CARS" YOU MENTIONED?

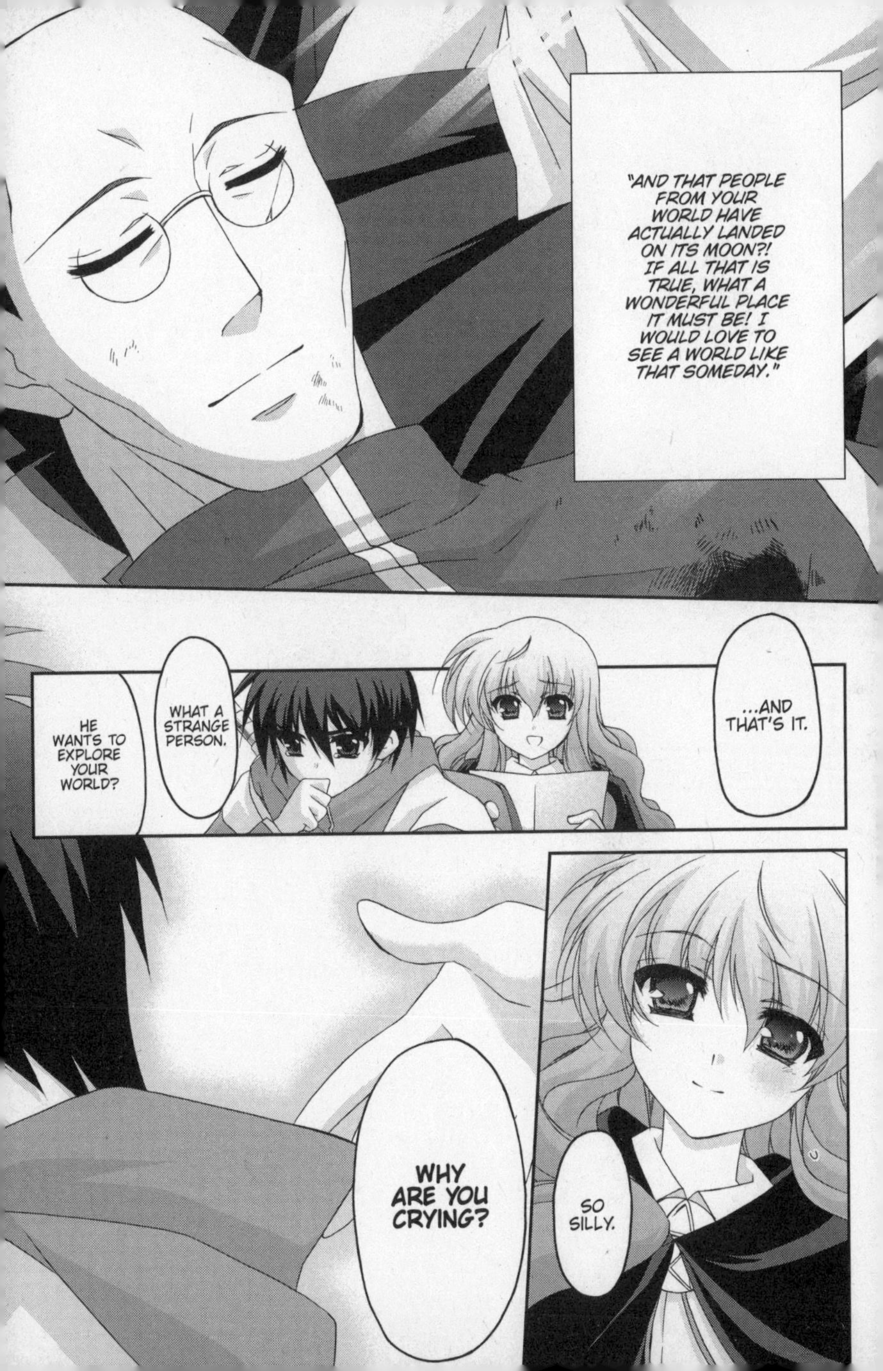
"AND THAT PEOPLE FROM YOUR WORLD HAVE ACTUALLY LANDED ON ITS MOON?! IF ALL THAT IS TRUE, WHAT A WONDERFUL PLACE IT MUST BE! I WOULD LOVE TO SEE A WORLD LIKE THAT SOMEDAY."
...AND THAT'S IT.
WHAT A STRANGE PERSON.
HE WANTS TO EXPLORE YOUR WORLD?
SO SILLY.
WHY ARE YOU CRYING?

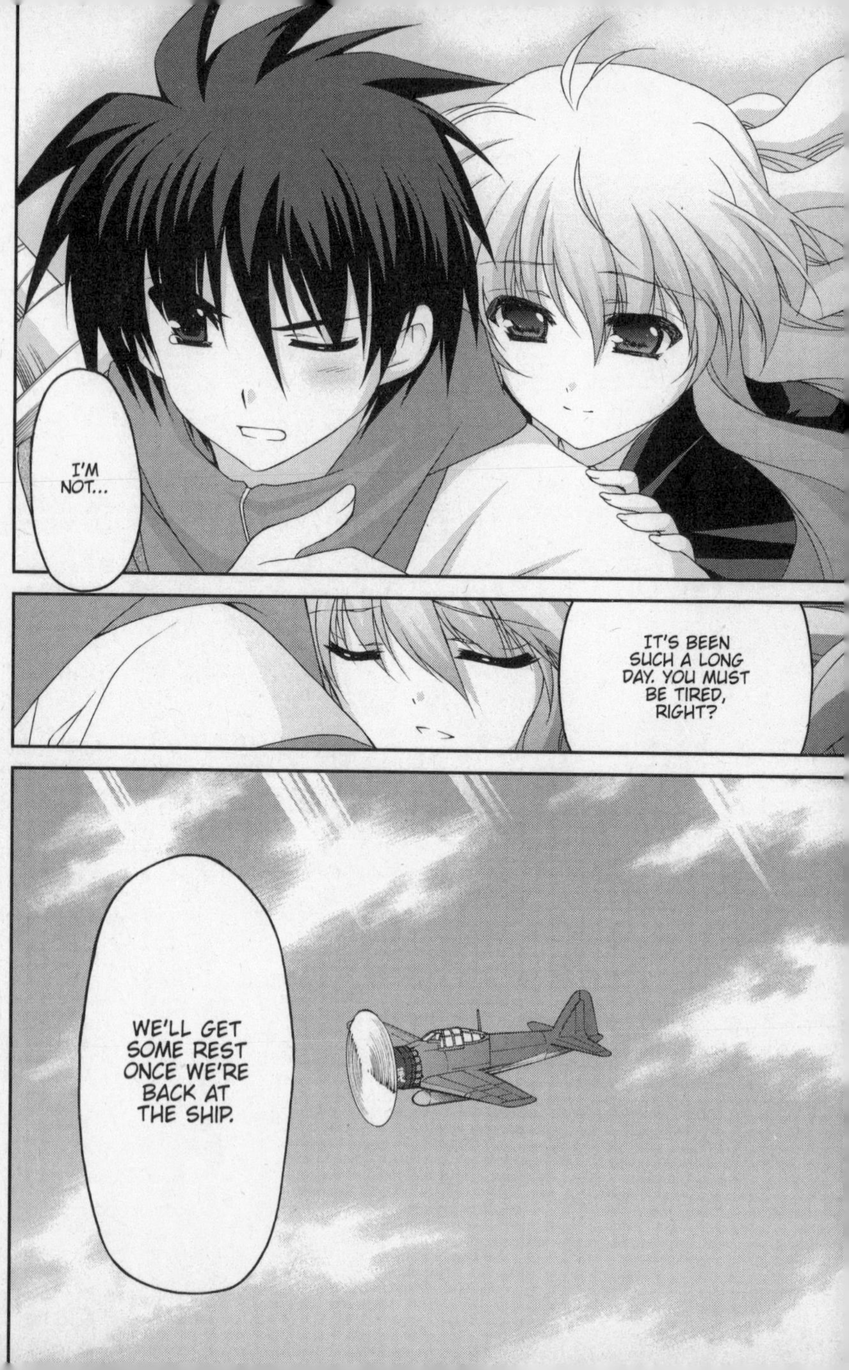
I'M NOT...
IT'S BEEN SUCH A LONG DAY. YOU MUST BE TIRED, RIGHT?
WE'LL GET SOME REST ONCE WE'RE BACK AT THE SHIP.

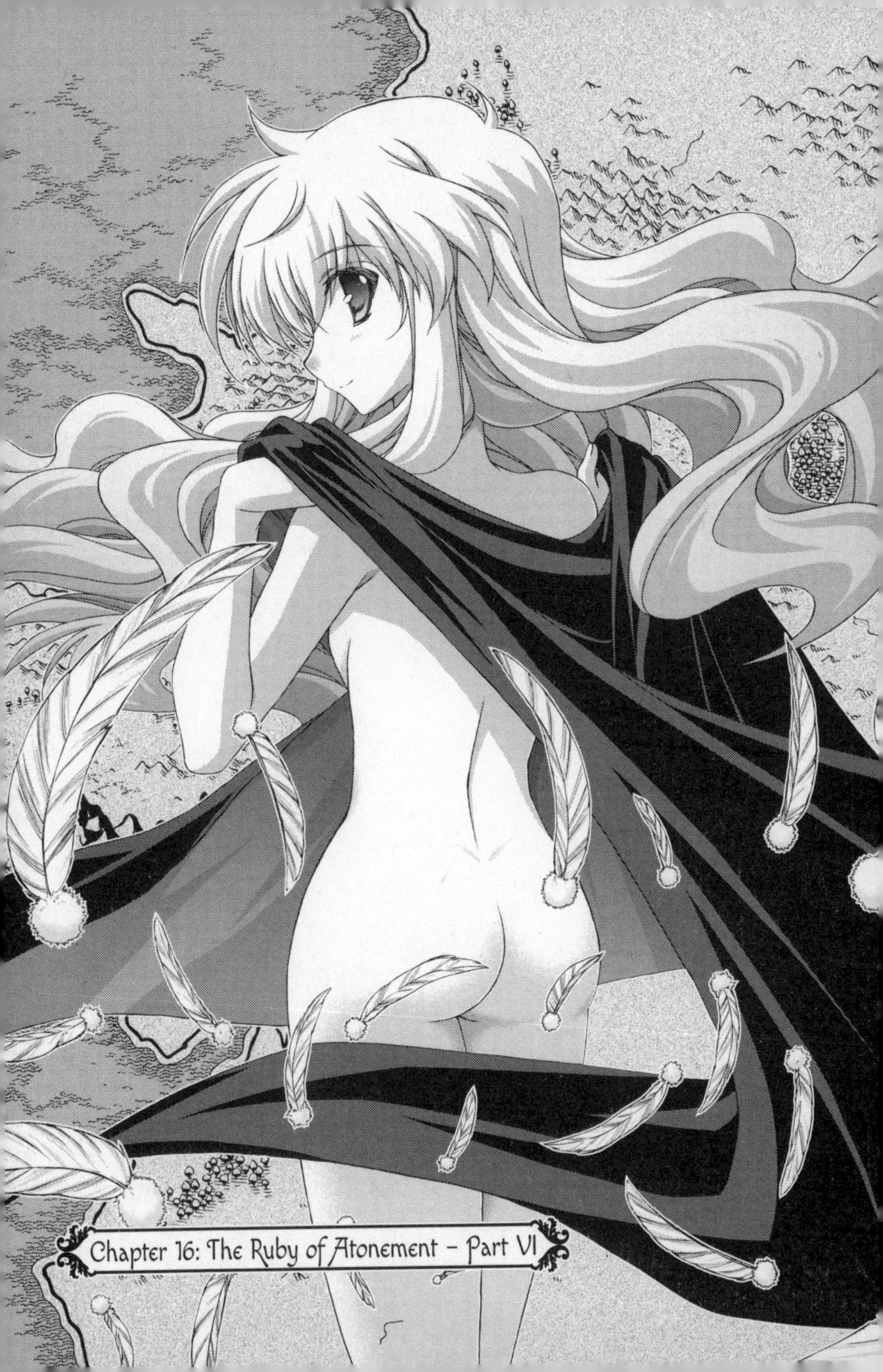
Chapter 16: The Ruby of Atonement - Part VI

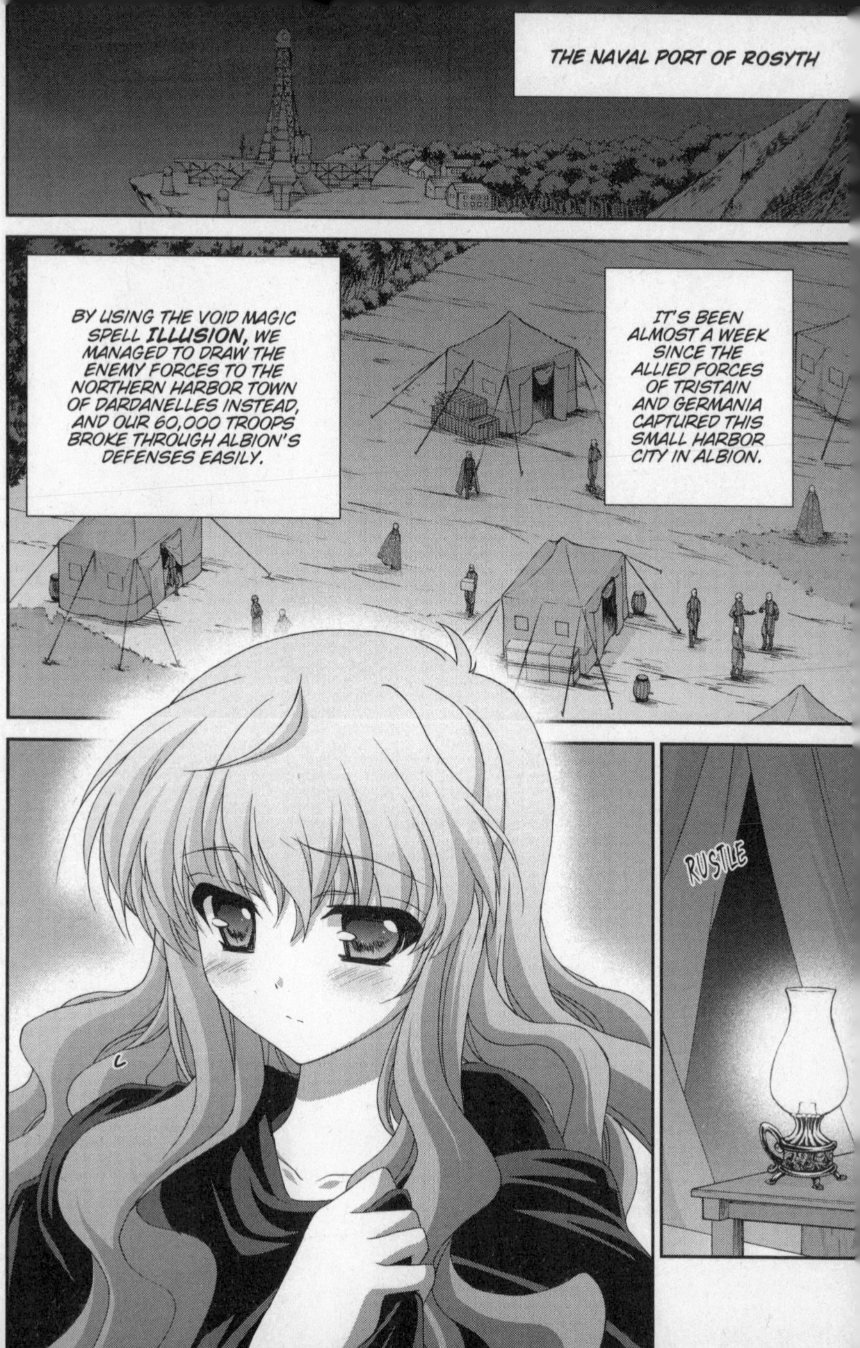
THE NAVAL PORT OF ROSYTH
IT'S BEEN ALMOST A WEEK SINCE THE ALLIED FORCES OF TRISTAIN AND GERMANIA CAPTURED THIS SMALL HARBOR CITY IN ALBION.
BY USING THE VOID MAGIC SPELL **ILLUSION,** WE MANAGED TO DRAW THE ENEMY FORCES TO THE NORTHERN HARBOR TOWN OF DARDANELLES INSTEAD, AND OUR 60,000 TROOPS BROKE THROUGH ALBION'S DEFENSES EASILY.
RUSTLE

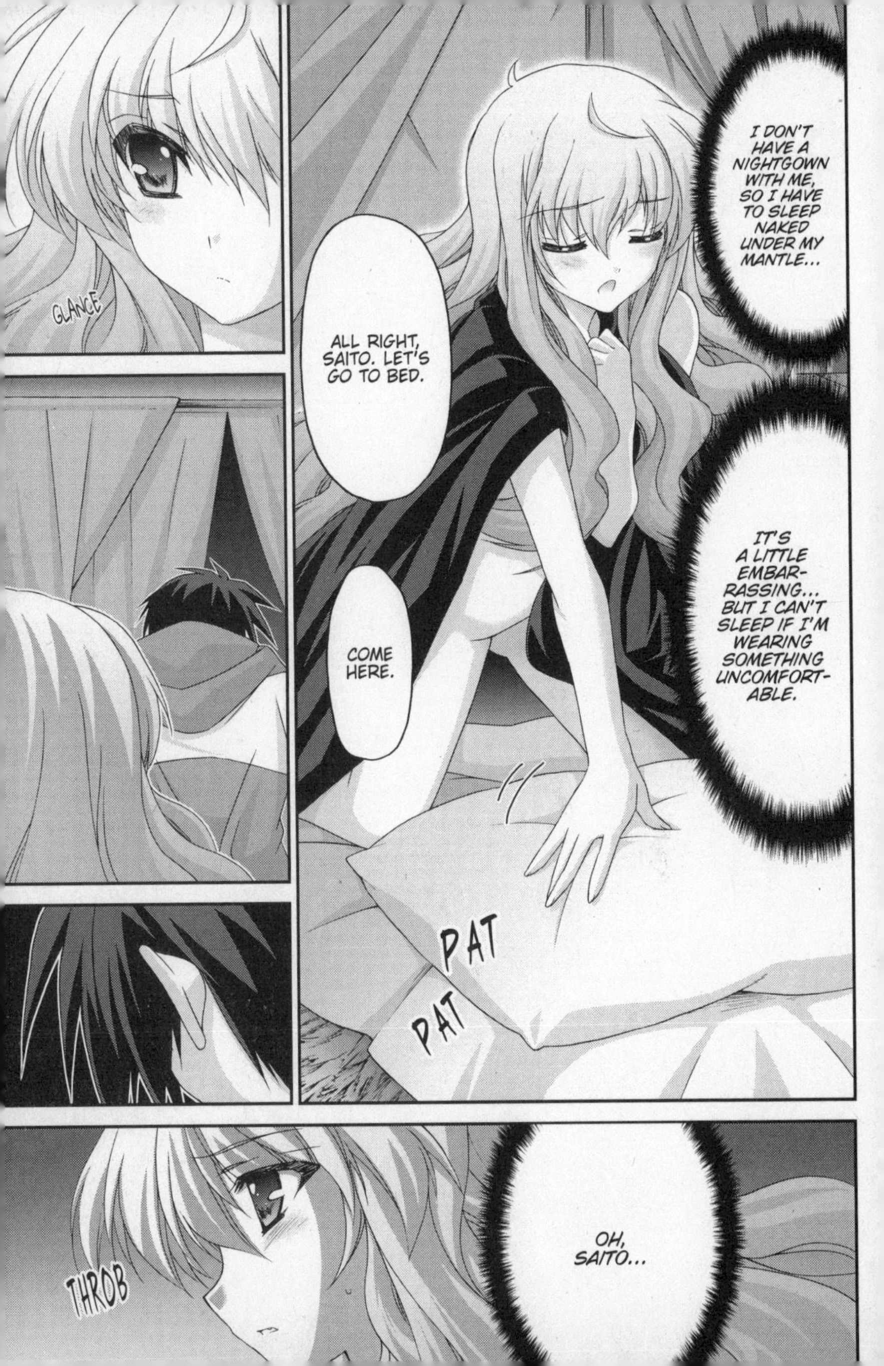
I DON'T HAVE A NIGHTGOWN WITH ME, SO I HAVE TO SLEEP NAKED UNDER MY MANTLE...
ALL RIGHT, SAITO. LET'S GO TO BED.
IT'S A LITTLE EMBAR-RASSING... BUT I CAN'T SLEEP IF I'M WEARING SOMETHING UNCOMFORT-ABLE.
COME HERE.
PAT
PAT
GLANCE
OH, SAITO...
THROB

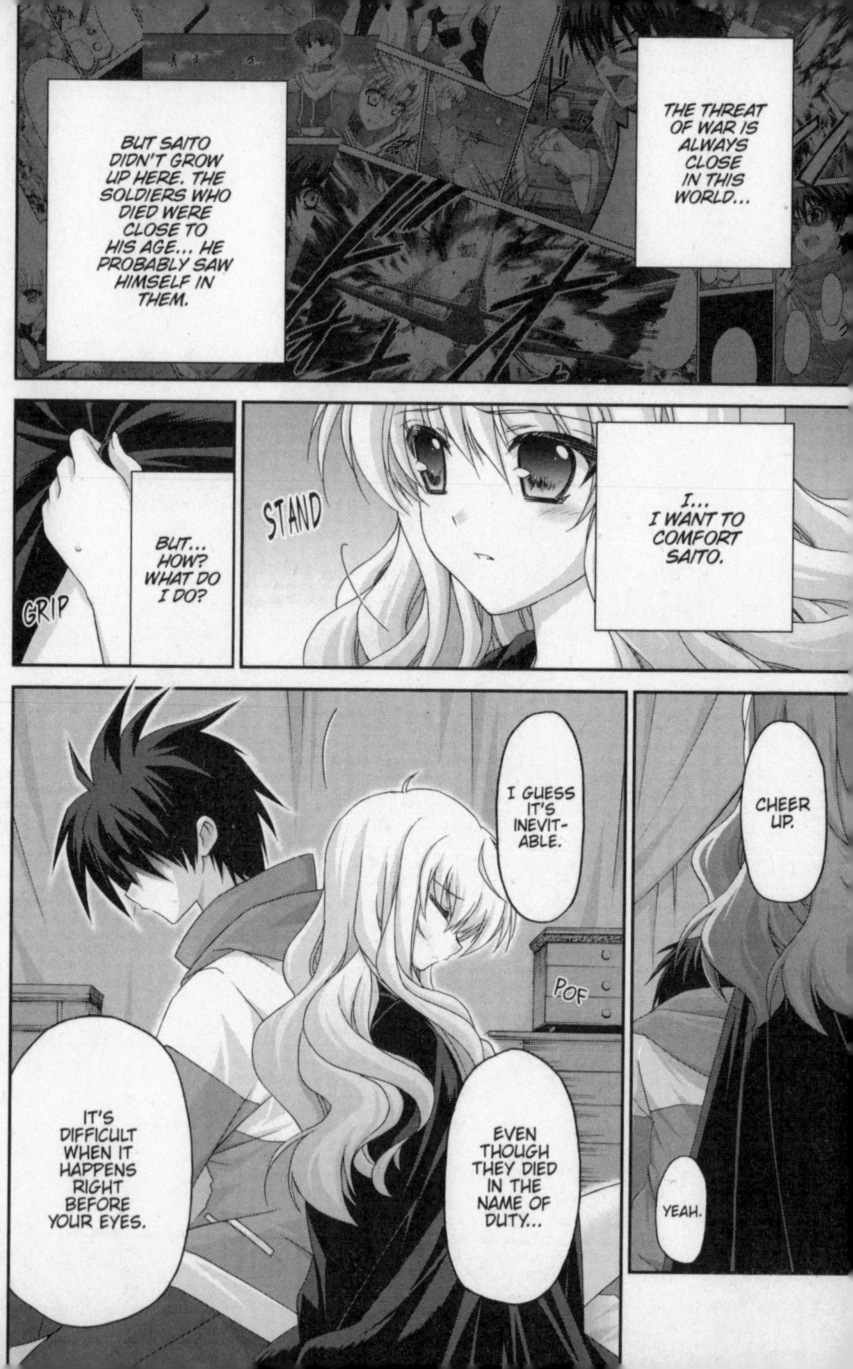
THE THREAT OF WAR IS ALWAYS CLOSE IN THIS WORLD...
BUT SAITO DIDN'T GROW UP HERE. THE SOLDIERS WHO DIED WERE CLOSE TO HIS AGE... HE PROBABLY SAW HIMSELF IN THEM.
I... I WANT TO COMFORT SAITO.
STAND
BUT... HOW? WHAT DO I DO?
GRIP
CHEER UP.
YEAH.
I GUESS IT'S INEVIT-ABLE.
POF
EVEN THOUGH THEY DIED IN THE NAME OF DUTY...
IT'S DIFFICULT WHEN IT HAPPENS RIGHT BEFORE YOUR EYES.

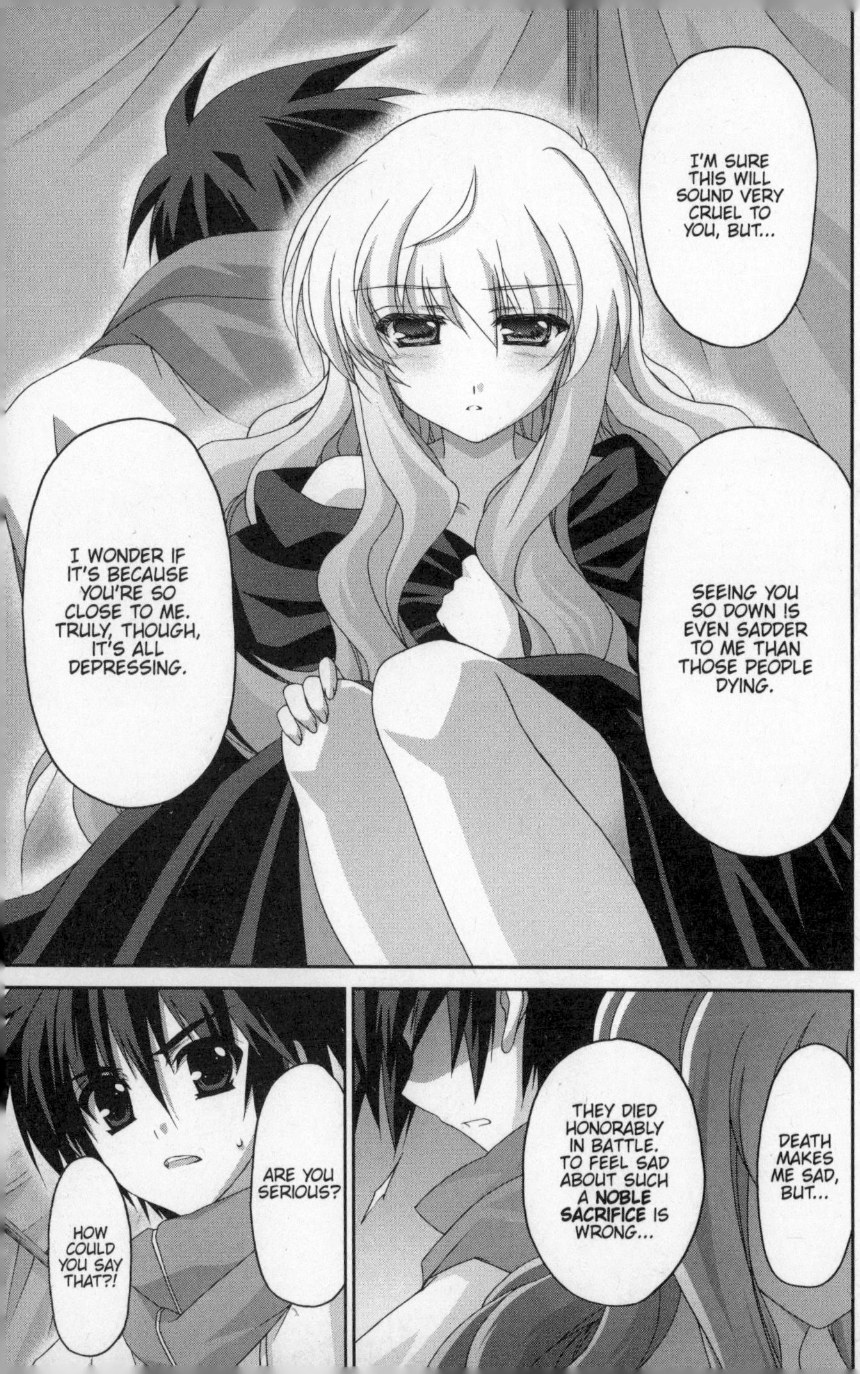
I'M SURE THIS WILL SOUND VERY CRUEL TO YOU, BUT...
SEEING YOU SO DOWN IS EVEN SADDER TO ME THAN THOSE PEOPLE DYING.
I WONDER IF IT'S BECAUSE YOU'RE SO CLOSE TO ME. TRULY, THOUGH, IT'S ALL DEPRESSING.
DEATH MAKES ME SAD, BUT...
THEY DIED HONORABLY IN BATTLE. TO FEEL SAD ABOUT SUCH A **NOBLE SACRIFICE** IS WRONG...
ARE YOU SERIOUS?
HOW COULD YOU SAY THAT?!

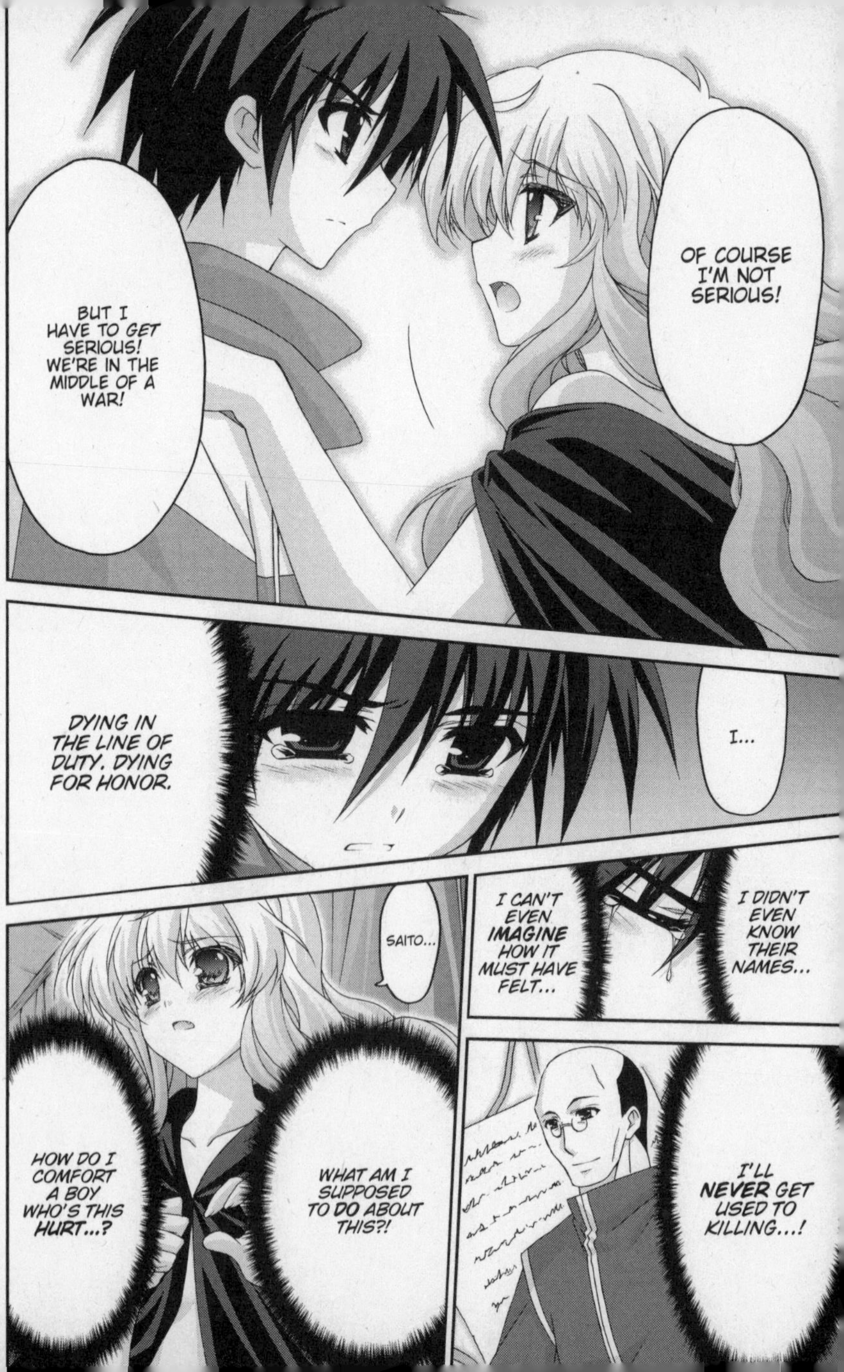
OF COURSE I'M NOT SERIOUS!
BUT I HAVE TO GET SERIOUS! WE'RE IN THE MIDDLE OF A WAR!
I...
DYING IN THE LINE OF DUTY. DYING FOR HONOR.
I DIDN'T EVEN KNOW THEIR NAMES...
I CAN'T EVEN IMAGINE HOW IT MUST HAVE FELT...
I'LL NEVER GET USED TO KILLING...!
SAITO...
WHAT AM I SUPPOSED TO DO ABOUT THIS?!
HOW DO I COMFORT A BOY WHO'S THIS HURT...?

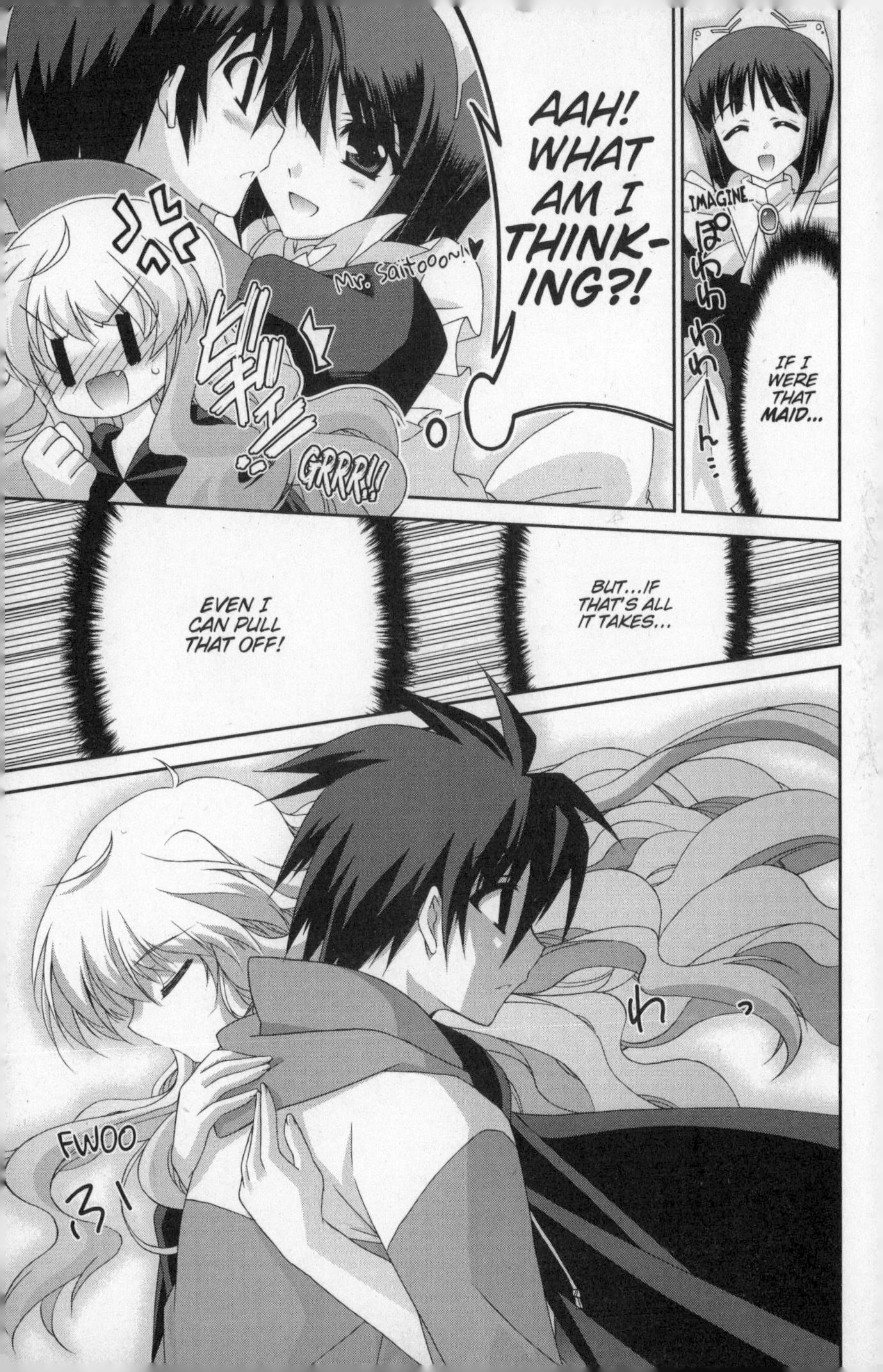
IMAGINE...
IF I WERE THAT MAID...
AAH! WHAT AM I THINKING?!
Mr. Saitooon~!♥
GRRR!!
BUT...IF THAT'S ALL IT TAKES...
EVEN I CAN PULL THAT OFF!
FWOO

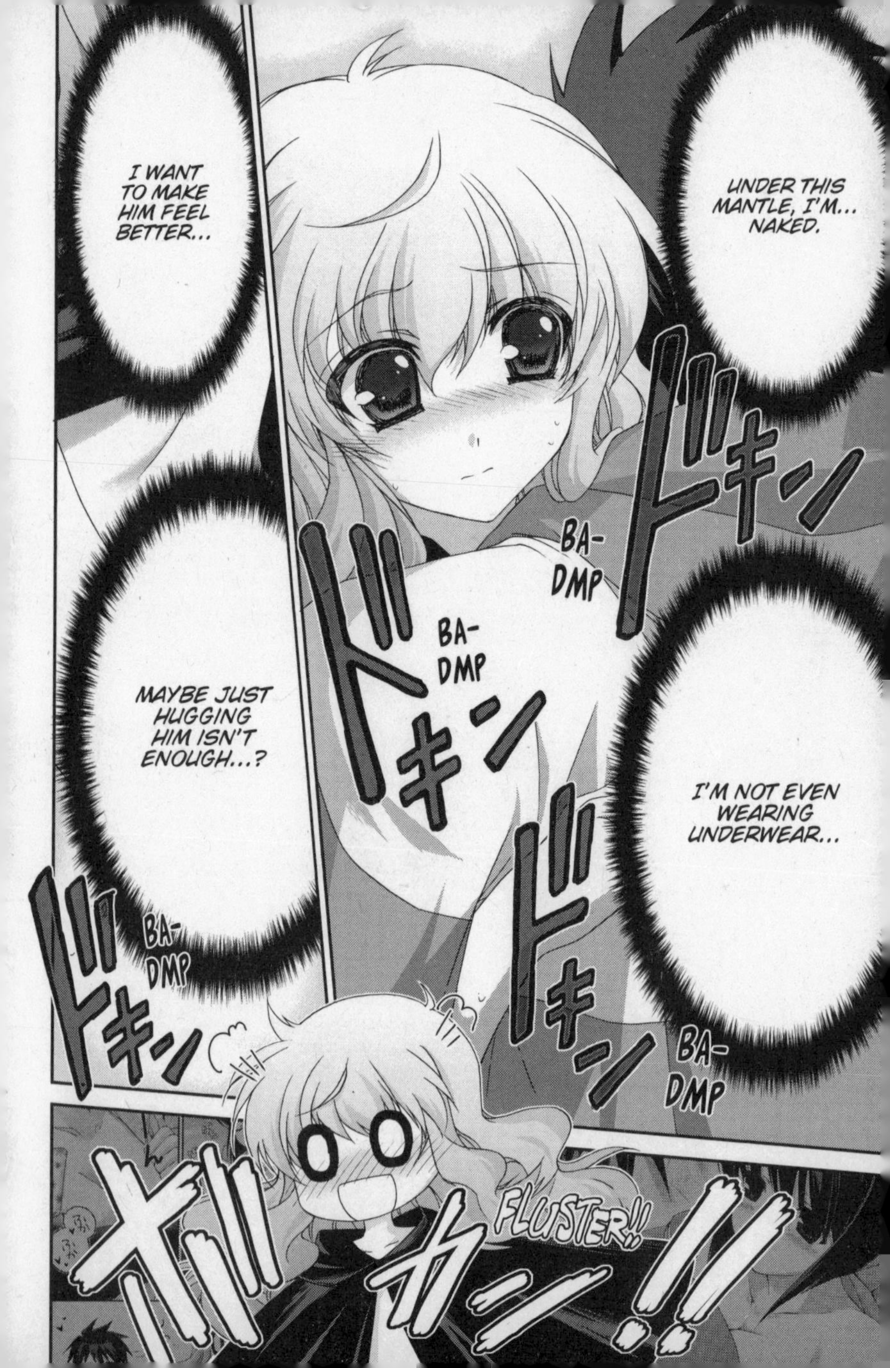
UNDER THIS MANTLE, I'M... NAKED.
BA-DMP
BA-DMP
I'M NOT EVEN WEARING UNDERWEAR...
BA-DMP
I WANT TO MAKE HIM FEEL BETTER...
MAYBE JUST HUGGING HIM ISN'T ENOUGH...?
BA-DMP
FLUSTER!!

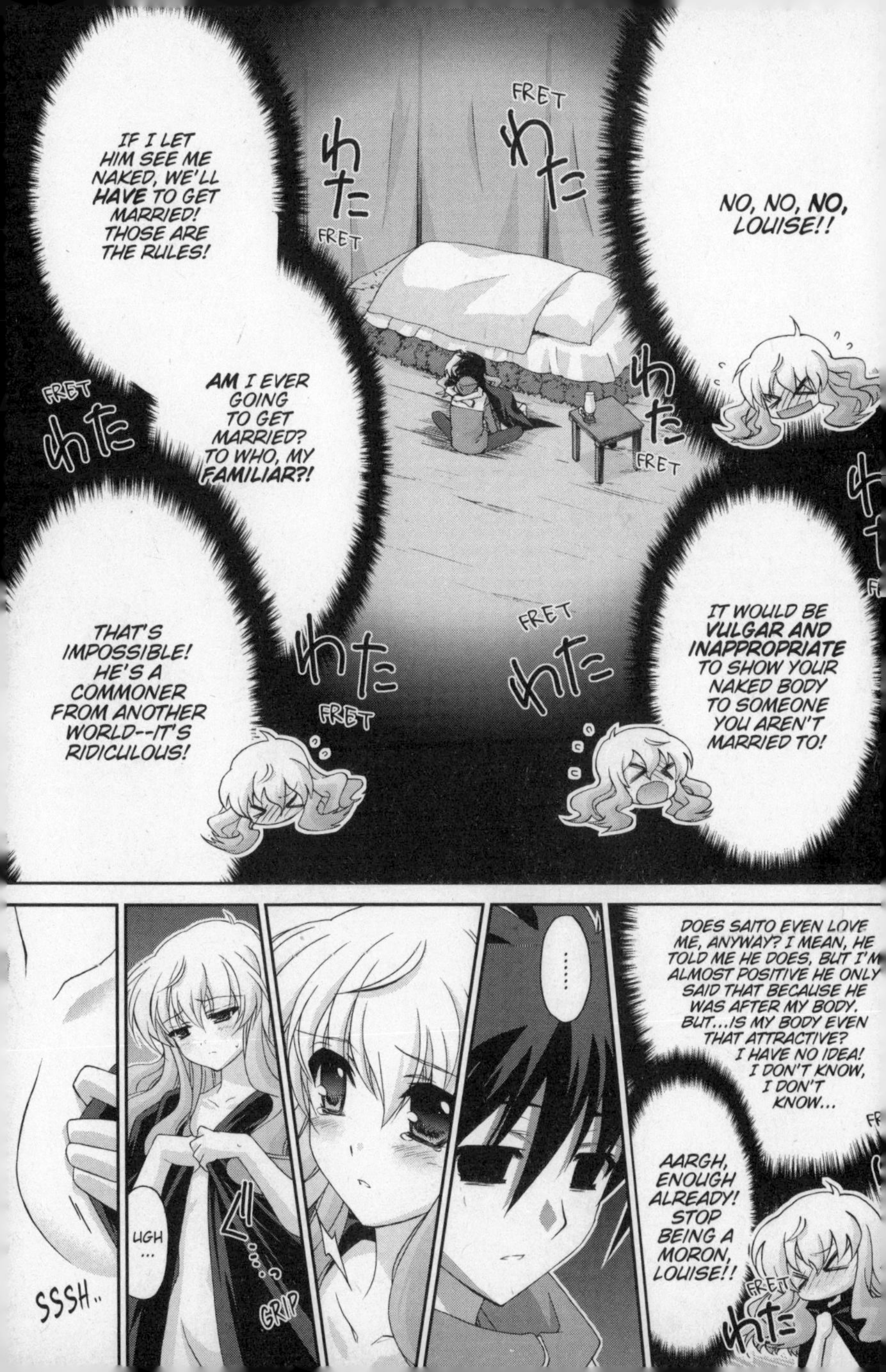
NO, NO, **NO,** LOUISE!!
FRET
わた
わた
FRET
IF I LET HIM SEE ME NAKED, WE'LL **HAVE** TO GET MARRIED! THOSE ARE THE RULES!
わた
FRET
AM I EVER GOING TO GET MARRIED? TO WHO, MY **FAMILIAR**?!
FRET
わた
IT WOULD BE **VULGAR AND INAPPROPRIATE** TO SHOW YOUR NAKED BODY TO SOMEONE YOU AREN'T MARRIED TO!
FRET
わた
わた
FRET
THAT'S IMPOSSIBLE! HE'S A COMMONER FROM ANOTHER WORLD--IT'S RIDICULOUS!
DOES SAITO EVEN LOVE ME, ANYWAY? I MEAN, HE TOLD ME HE DOES, BUT I'M ALMOST POSITIVE HE ONLY SAID THAT BECAUSE HE WAS AFTER MY BODY. BUT...IS MY BODY EVEN THAT ATTRACTIVE? I HAVE NO IDEA! I DON'T KNOW, I DON'T KNOW...
AARGH, ENOUGH ALREADY! STOP BEING A MORON, LOUISE!!
FRET
わた
......
UGH...
GRIP
SSSH..

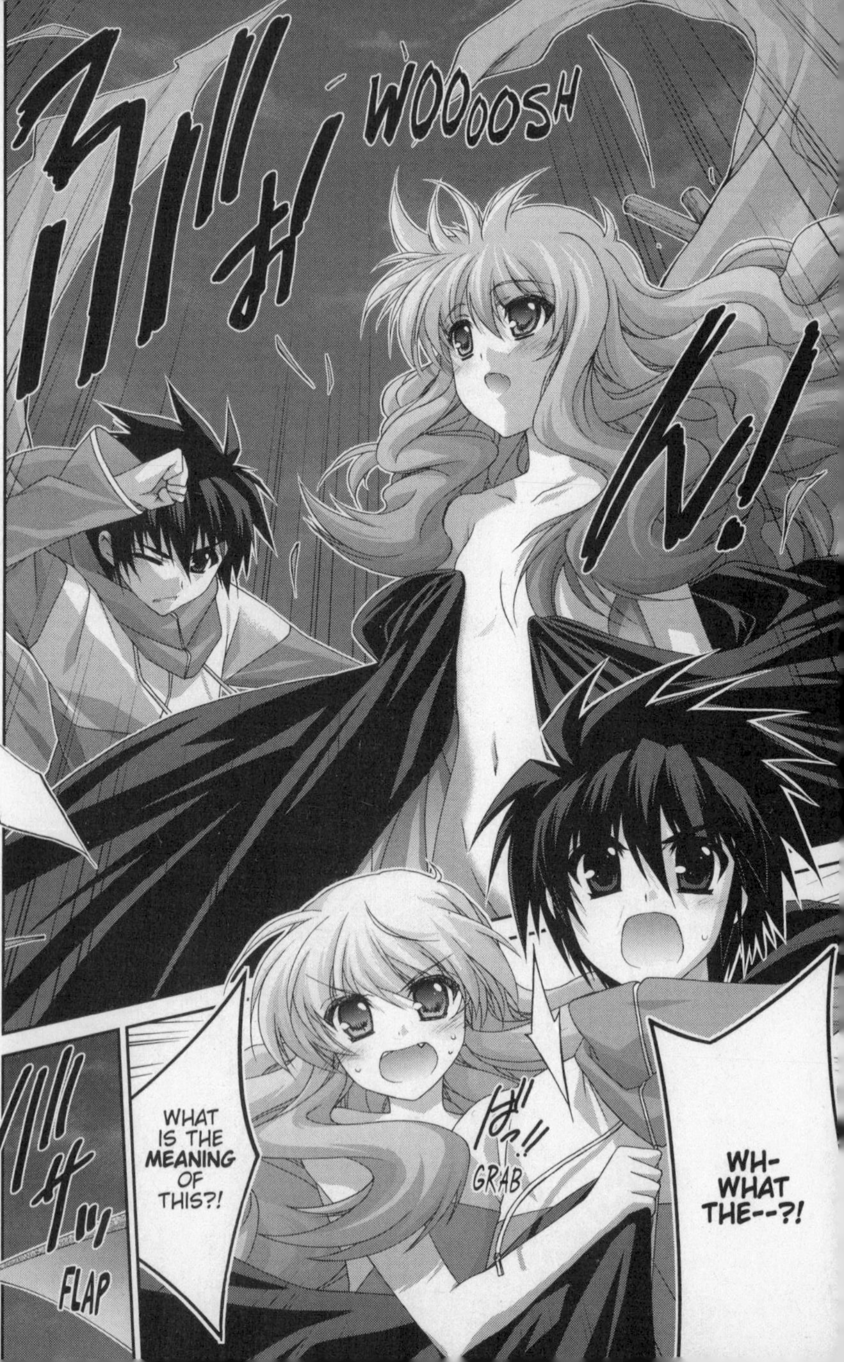
WOOOOSH
WH-WHAT THE--?!
GRAB
WHAT IS THE MEANING OF THIS?!
FLAP

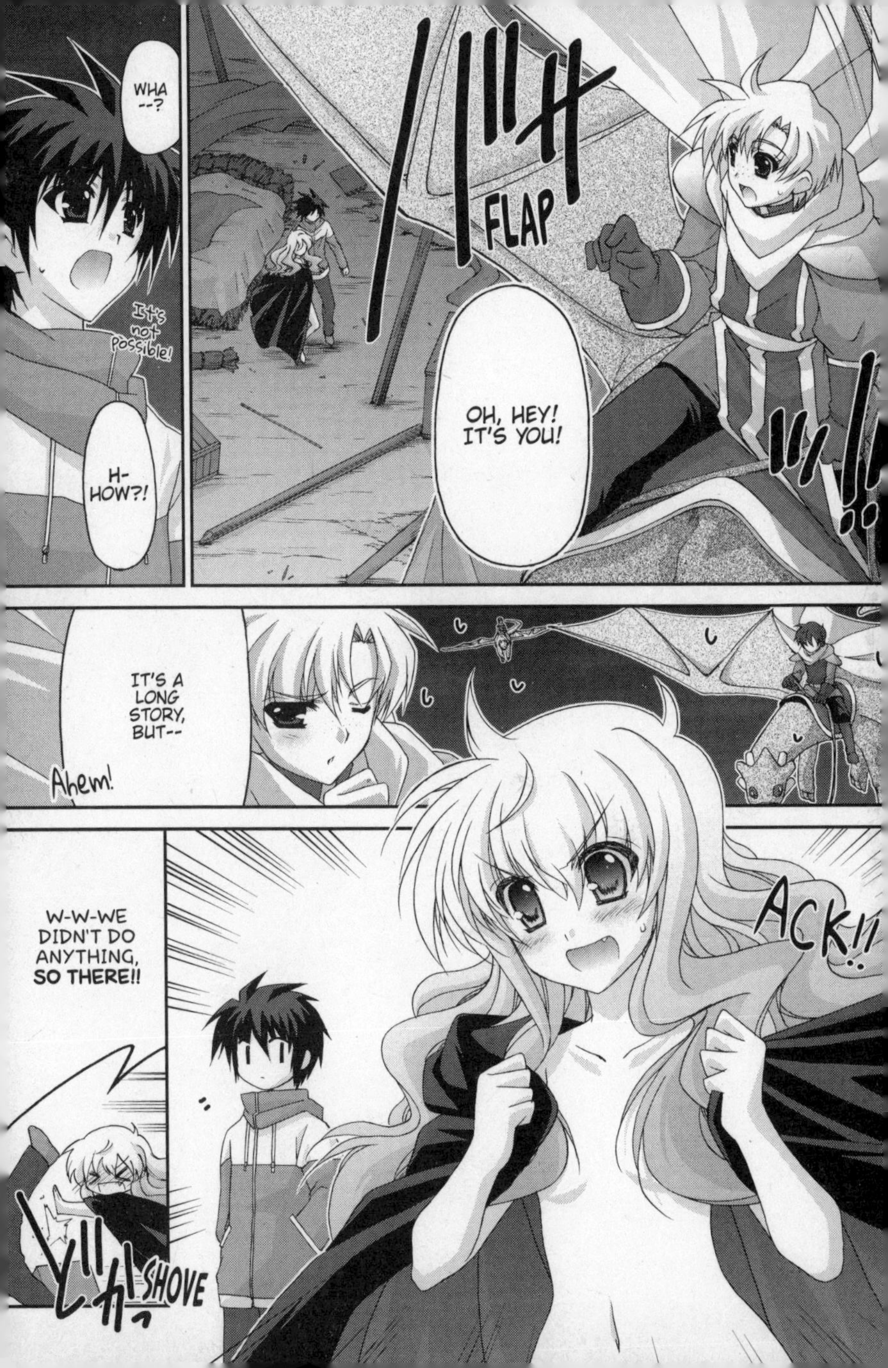
FLAP
OH, HEY! IT'S YOU!
WHA --?
It's not possible!
H- HOW?!
IT'S A LONG STORY, BUT--
Ahem!
ACK!!
W-W-WE DIDN'T DO ANYTHING, SO THERE!!
SHOVE

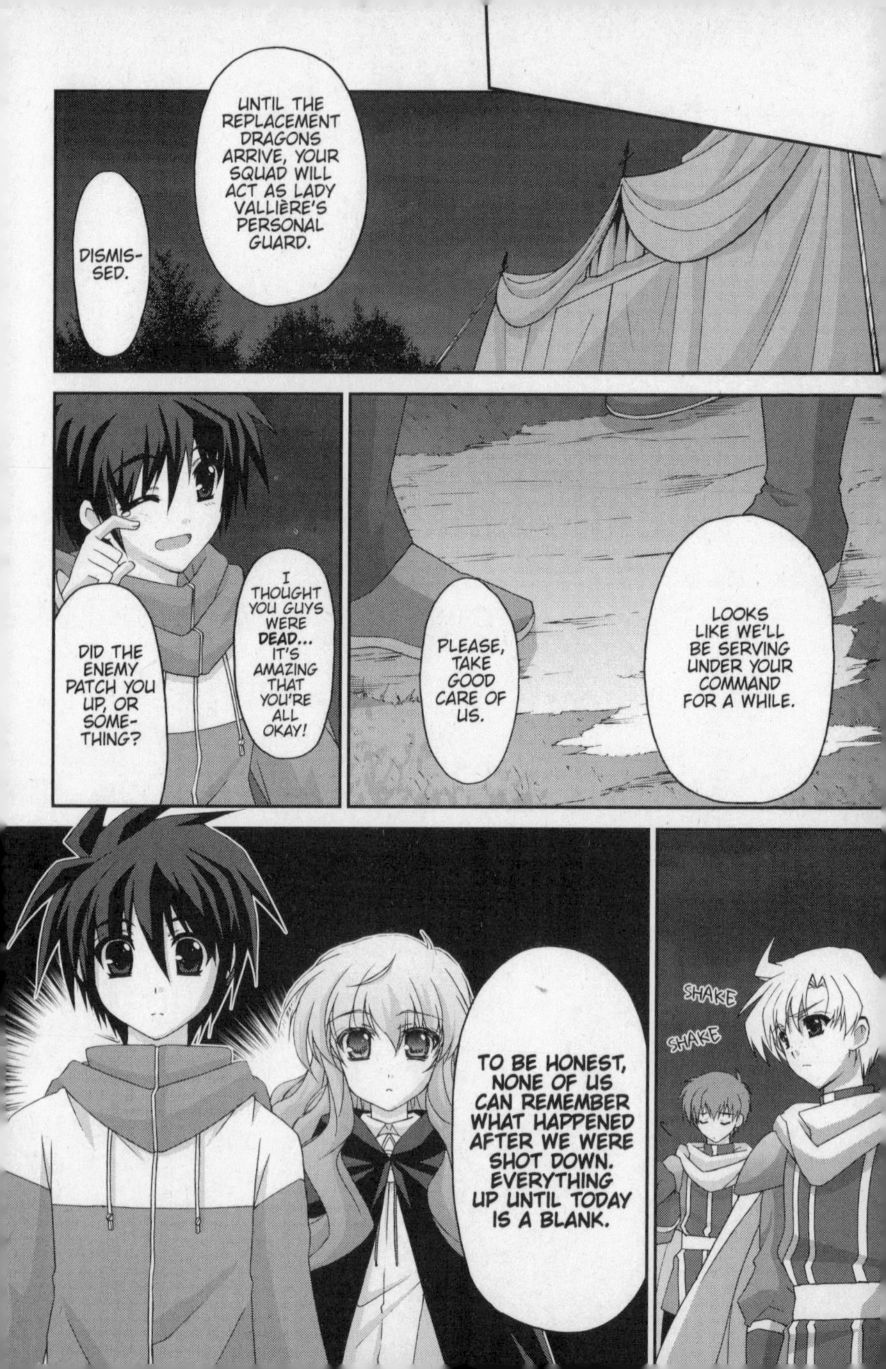
UNTIL THE REPLACEMENT DRAGONS ARRIVE, YOUR SQUAD WILL ACT AS LADY VALLIÈRE'S PERSONAL GUARD.
DISMIS-SED.
LOOKS LIKE WE'LL BE SERVING UNDER YOUR COMMAND FOR A WHILE.
PLEASE, TAKE GOOD CARE OF US.
I THOUGHT YOU GUYS WERE **DEAD**... IT'S AMAZING THAT YOU'RE ALL OKAY!
DID THE ENEMY PATCH YOU UP, OR SOME-THING?
SHAKE
SHAKE
TO BE HONEST, NONE OF US CAN REMEMBER WHAT HAPPENED AFTER WE WERE SHOT DOWN. EVERYTHING UP UNTIL TODAY IS A BLANK.

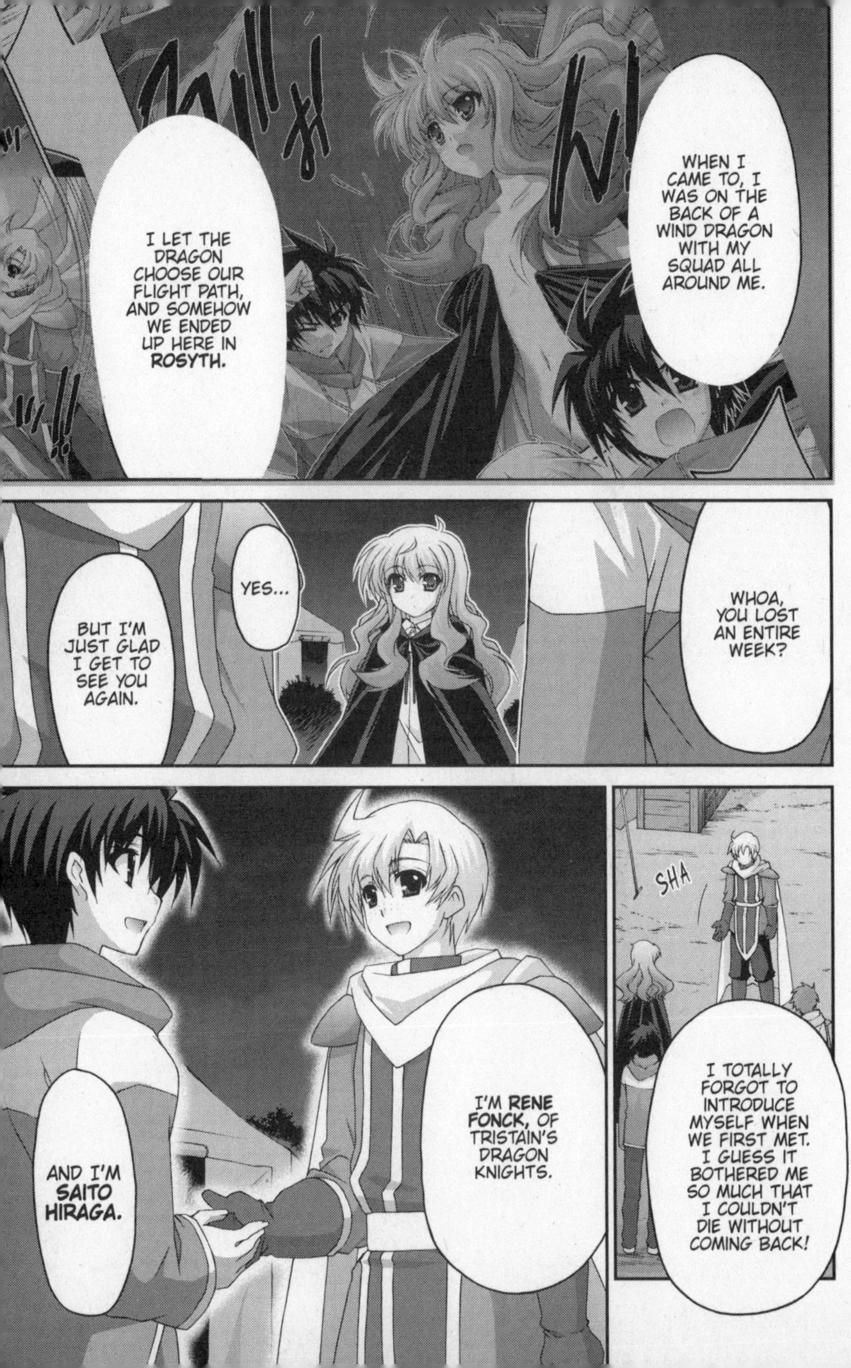
WHEN I CAME TO, I WAS ON THE BACK OF A WIND DRAGON WITH MY SQUAD ALL AROUND ME.
I LET THE DRAGON CHOOSE OUR FLIGHT PATH, AND SOMEHOW WE ENDED UP HERE IN ROSYTH.
WHOA, YOU LOST AN ENTIRE WEEK?
YES...
BUT I'M JUST GLAD I GET TO SEE YOU AGAIN.
SHA
I TOTALLY FORGOT TO INTRODUCE MYSELF WHEN WE FIRST MET. I GUESS IT BOTHERED ME SO MUCH THAT I COULDN'T DIE WITHOUT COMING BACK!
I'M RENE FONCK, OF TRISTAIN'S DRAGON KNIGHTS.
AND I'M SAITO HIRAGA.

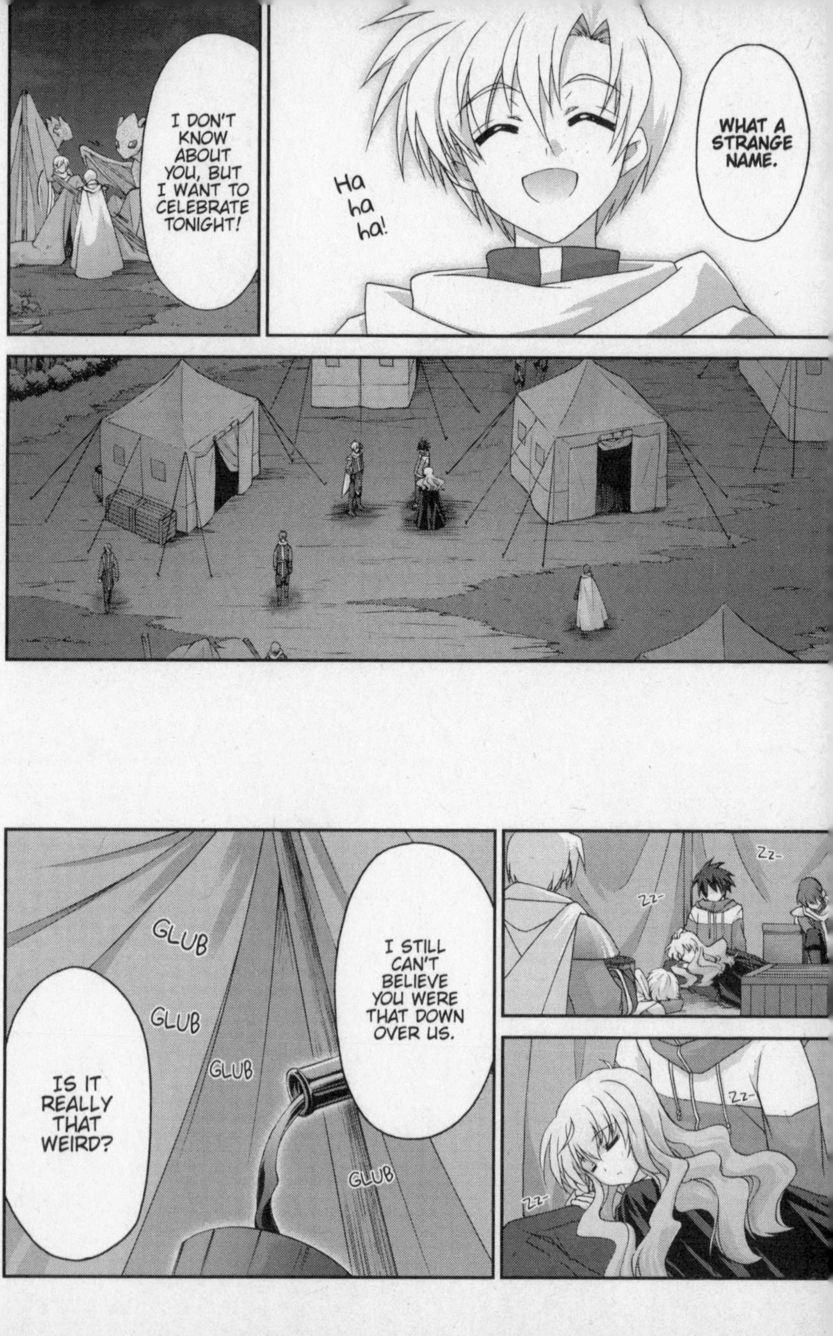
WHAT A STRANGE NAME.
Ha ha ha!
I DON'T KNOW ABOUT YOU, BUT I WANT TO CELEBRATE TONIGHT!
Zz-
Zz-
Zz-
Zz-
I STILL CAN'T BELIEVE YOU WERE THAT DOWN OVER US.
GLUB
GLUB
GLUB
GLUB
IS IT REALLY THAT WEIRD?

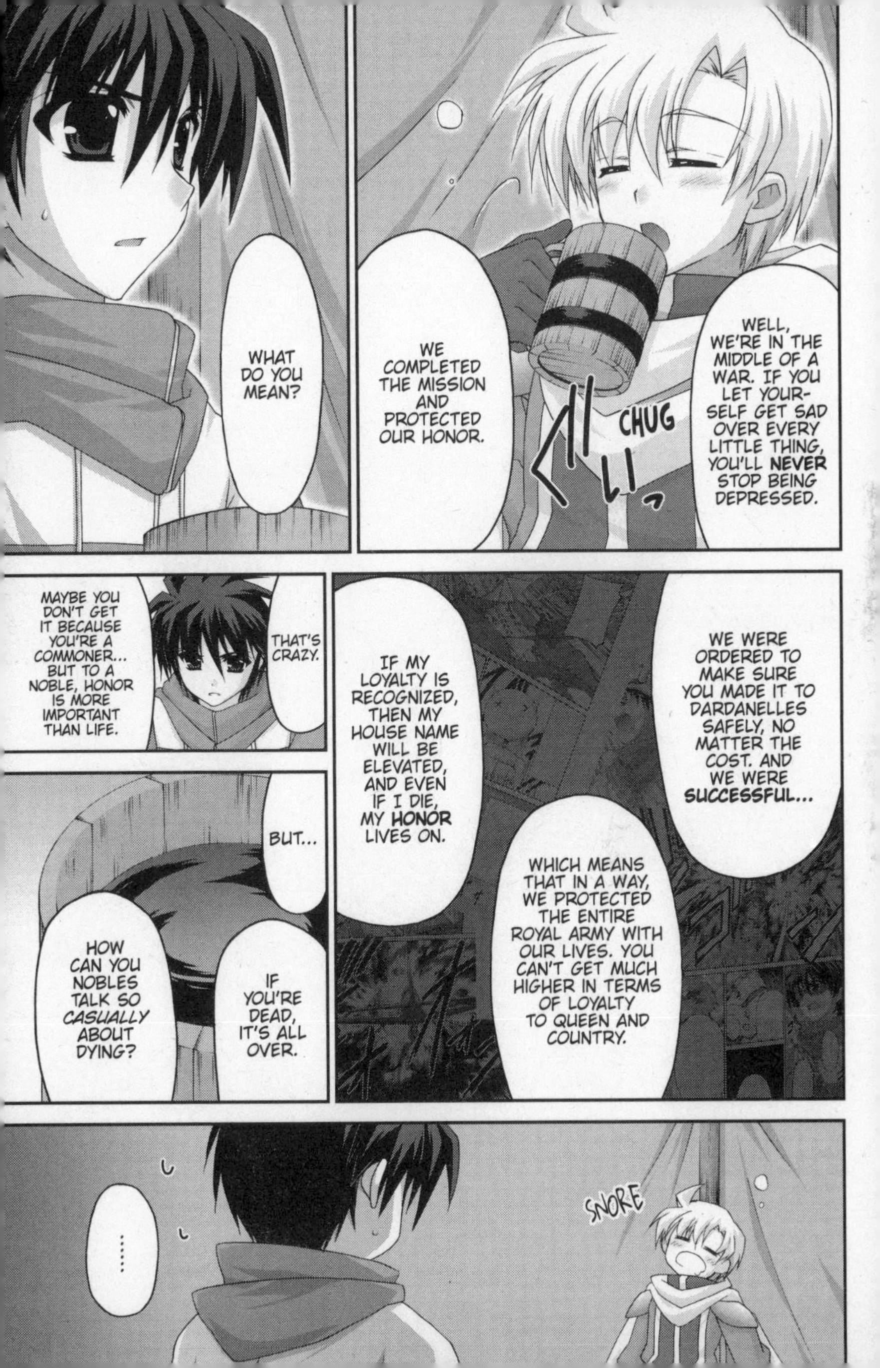
WELL, WE'RE IN THE MIDDLE OF A WAR. IF YOU LET YOURSELF GET SAD OVER EVERY LITTLE THING, YOU'LL **NEVER** STOP BEING DEPRESSED.
CHUG
WE COMPLETED THE MISSION AND PROTECTED OUR HONOR.
WHAT DO YOU MEAN?
WE WERE ORDERED TO MAKE SURE YOU MADE IT TO DARDANELLES SAFELY, NO MATTER THE COST. AND WE WERE **SUCCESSFUL...**
WHICH MEANS THAT IN A WAY, WE PROTECTED THE ENTIRE ROYAL ARMY WITH OUR LIVES. YOU CAN'T GET MUCH HIGHER IN TERMS OF LOYALTY TO QUEEN AND COUNTRY.
IF MY LOYALTY IS RECOGNIZED, THEN MY HOUSE NAME WILL BE ELEVATED, AND EVEN IF I DIE, MY **HONOR** LIVES ON.
THAT'S CRAZY.
MAYBE YOU DON'T GET IT BECAUSE YOU'RE A COMMONER... BUT TO A NOBLE, HONOR IS MORE IMPORTANT THAN LIFE.
BUT...
IF YOU'RE DEAD, IT'S ALL OVER.
HOW CAN YOU NOBLES TALK SO *CASUALLY* ABOUT DYING?
SNORE
......

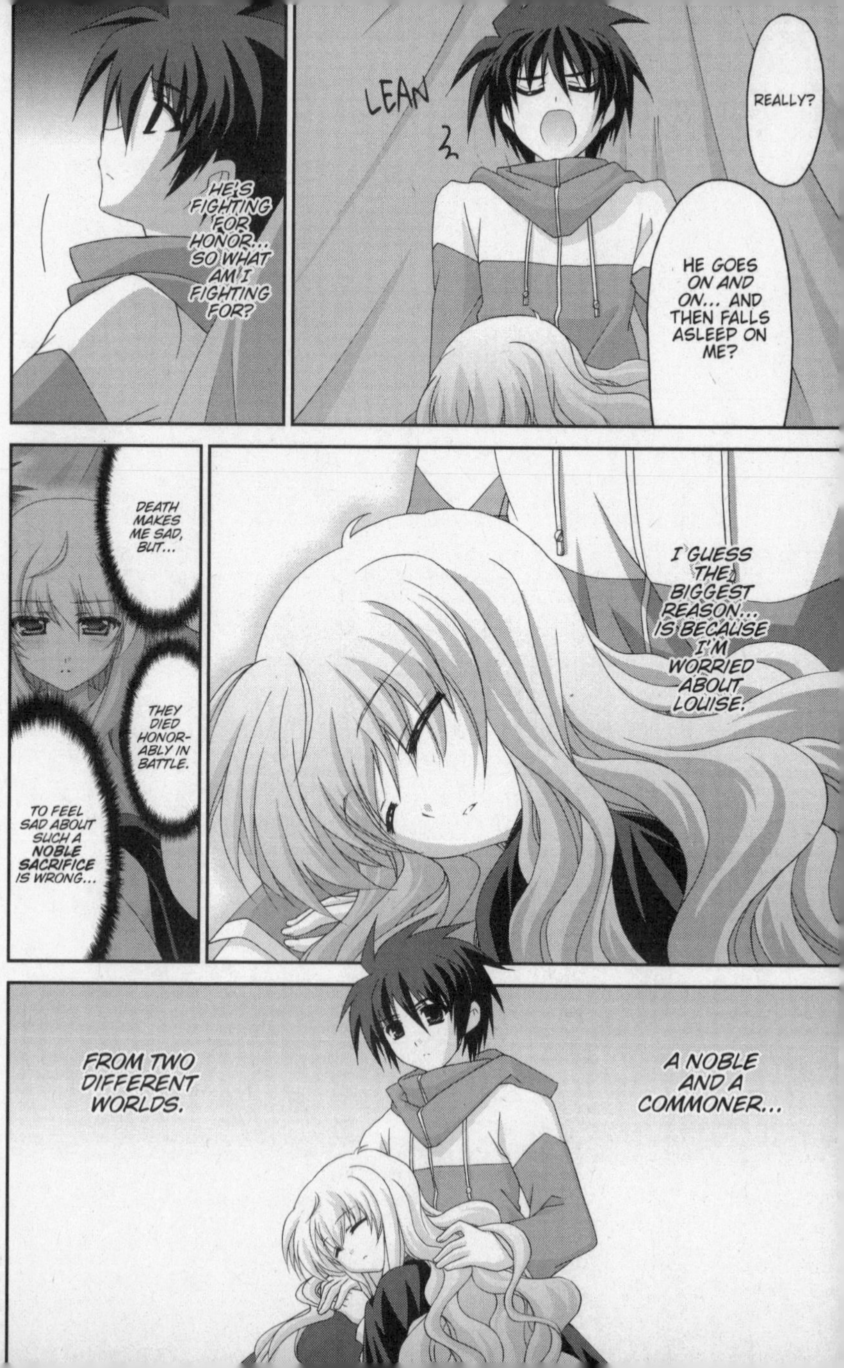
REALLY?
LEAN
HE GOES ON AND ON... AND THEN FALLS ASLEEP ON ME?
HE'S FIGHTING FOR HONOR... SO WHAT AM I FIGHTING FOR?
I GUESS THE BIGGEST REASON... IS BECAUSE I'M WORRIED ABOUT LOUISE.
DEATH MAKES ME SAD, BUT...
THEY DIED HONORABLY IN BATTLE.
TO FEEL SAD ABOUT SUCH A NOBLE SACRIFICE IS WRONG...
A NOBLE AND A COMMONER...
FROM TWO DIFFERENT WORLDS.

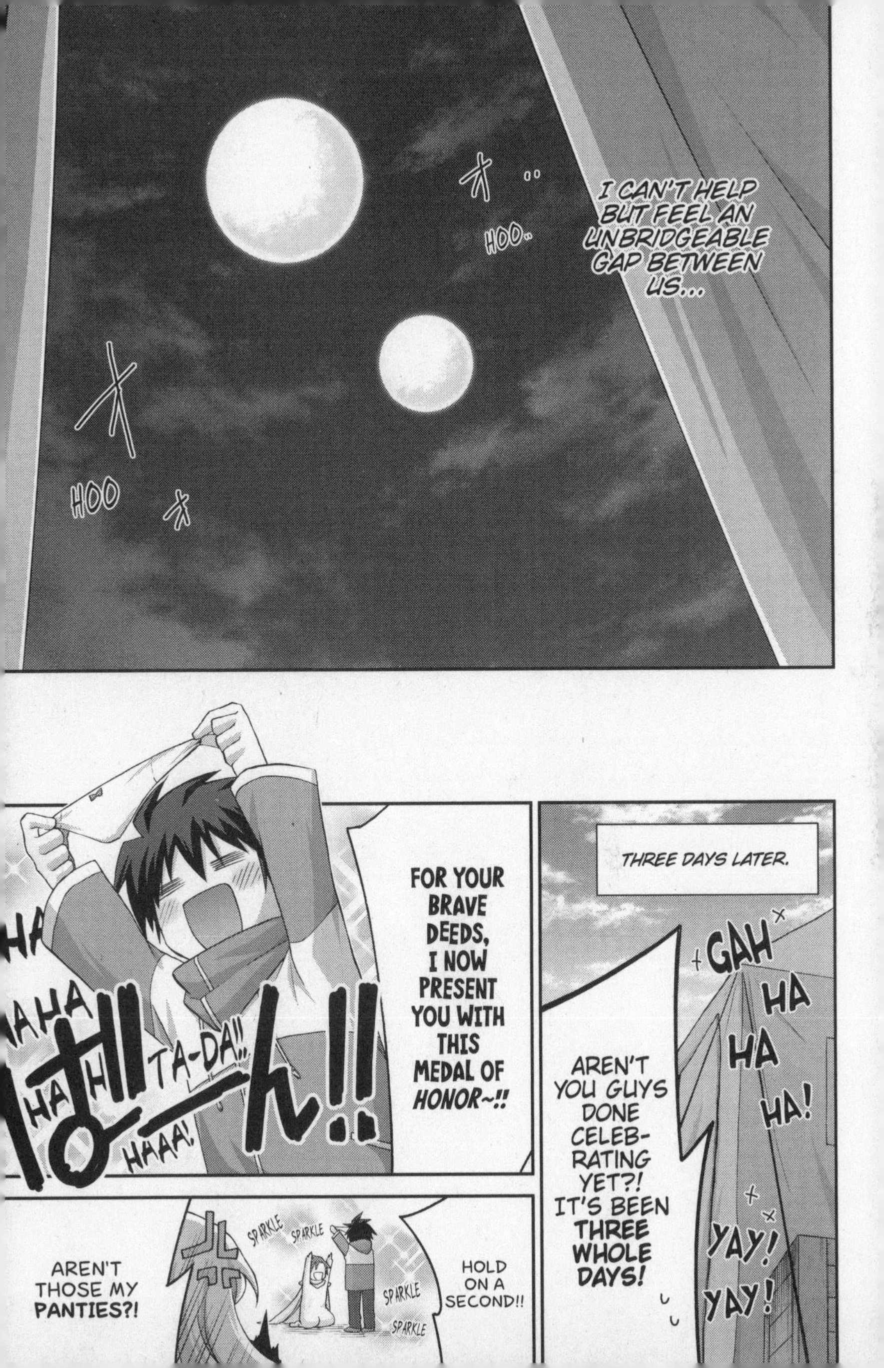
I CAN'T HELP BUT FEEL AN UNBRIDGEABLE GAP BETWEEN US...
HOO..
HOO
THREE DAYS LATER.
GAH HA HA HA!
AREN'T YOU GUYS DONE CELEB-RATING YET?! IT'S BEEN THREE WHOLE DAYS!
YAY! YAY!
FOR YOUR BRAVE DEEDS, I NOW PRESENT YOU WITH THIS MEDAL OF HONOR~!!
TA-DA!!
HAHA HA HA HAAA!
HOLD ON A SECOND!!
SPARKLE SPARKLE
SPARKLE SPARKLE
AREN'T THOSE MY PANTIES?!

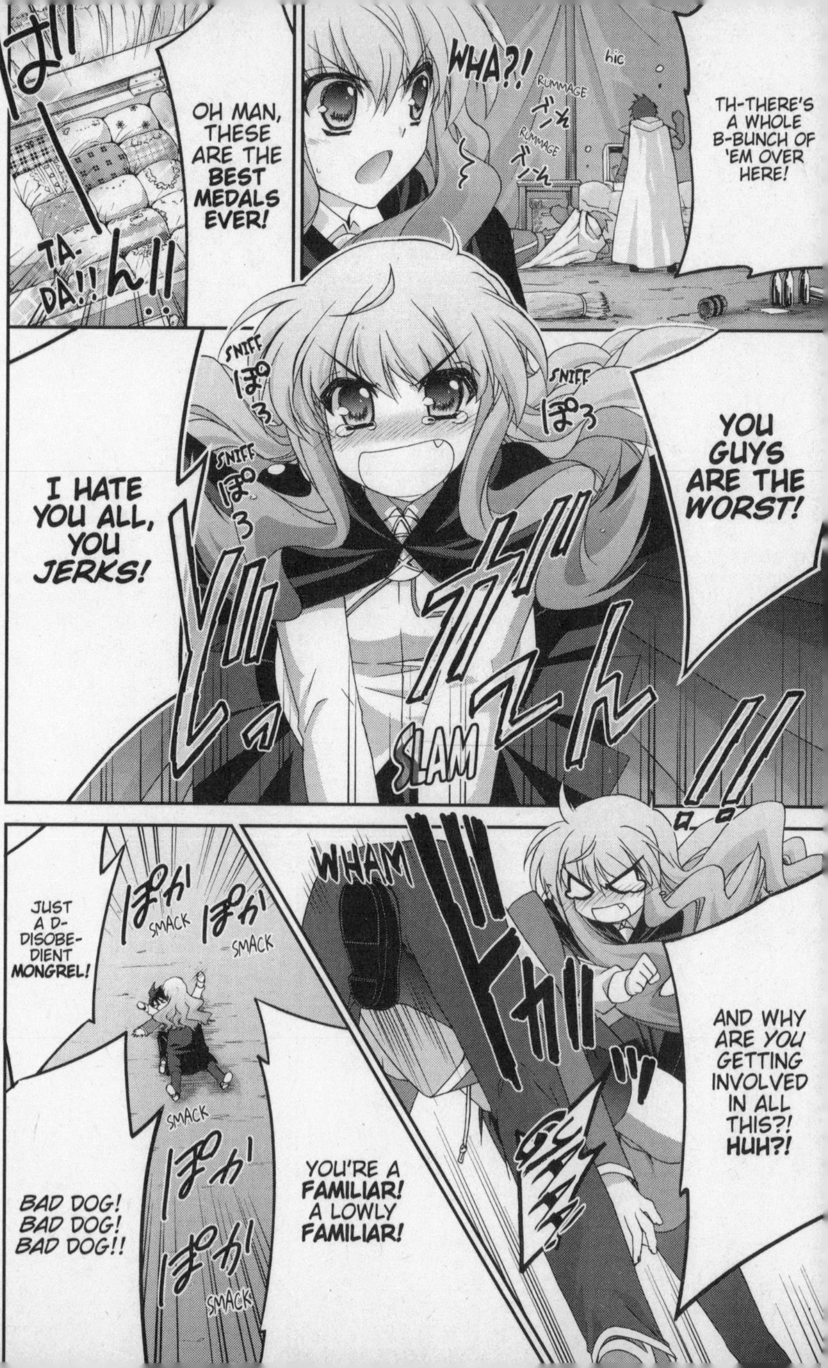
hic
RUMMAGE
RUMMAGE
TH-THERE'S A WHOLE B-BUNCH OF 'EM OVER HERE!
WHA?!
OH MAN, THESE ARE THE BEST MEDALS EVER!
TA-DA!!
YOU GUYS ARE THE WORST!
SNIFF
SNIFF
SNIFF
I HATE YOU ALL, YOU JERKS!
SLAM
AND WHY ARE YOU GETTING INVOLVED IN ALL THIS?! HUH?!
GAH
WHAM
YOU'RE A FAMILIAR! A LOWLY FAMILIAR!
SMACK
SMACK
JUST A D-DISOBEDIENT MONGREL!
SMACK
BAD DOG! BAD DOG! BAD DOG!!
SMACK

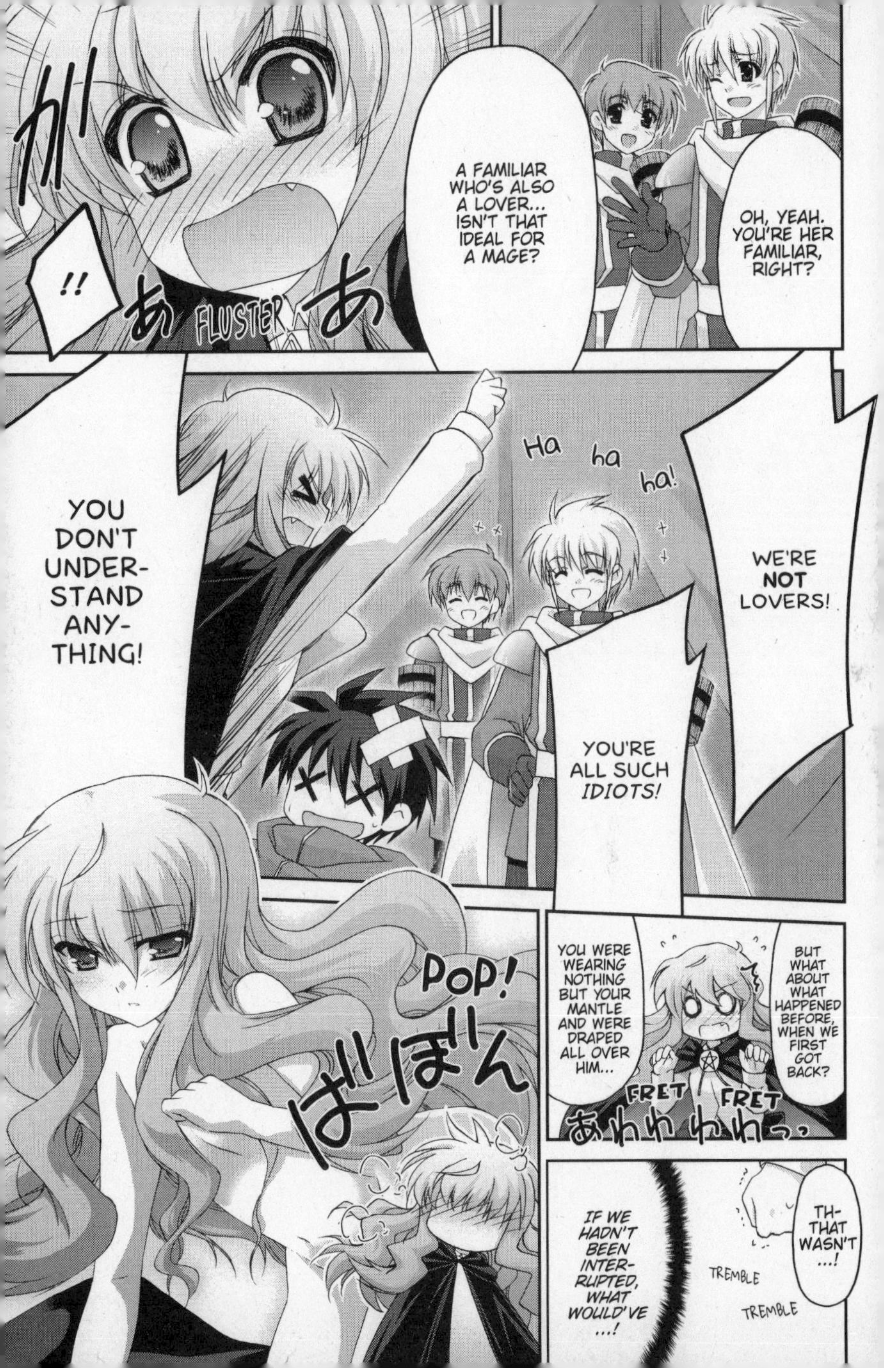
OH, YEAH. YOU'RE HER FAMILIAR, RIGHT?
A FAMILIAR WHO'S ALSO A LOVER... ISN'T THAT IDEAL FOR A MAGE?
!!
FLUSTER
WE'RE NOT LOVERS!
Ha ha ha!
YOU'RE ALL SUCH IDIOTS!
YOU DON'T UNDER-STAND ANY-THING!
BUT WHAT ABOUT WHAT HAPPENED BEFORE, WHEN WE FIRST GOT BACK?
YOU WERE WEARING NOTHING BUT YOUR MANTLE AND WERE DRAPED ALL OVER HIM...
FRET FRET
TH-THAT WASN'T ...!
TREMBLE TREMBLE
IF WE HADN'T BEEN INTER-RUPTED, WHAT WOULD'VE ...!
POP!

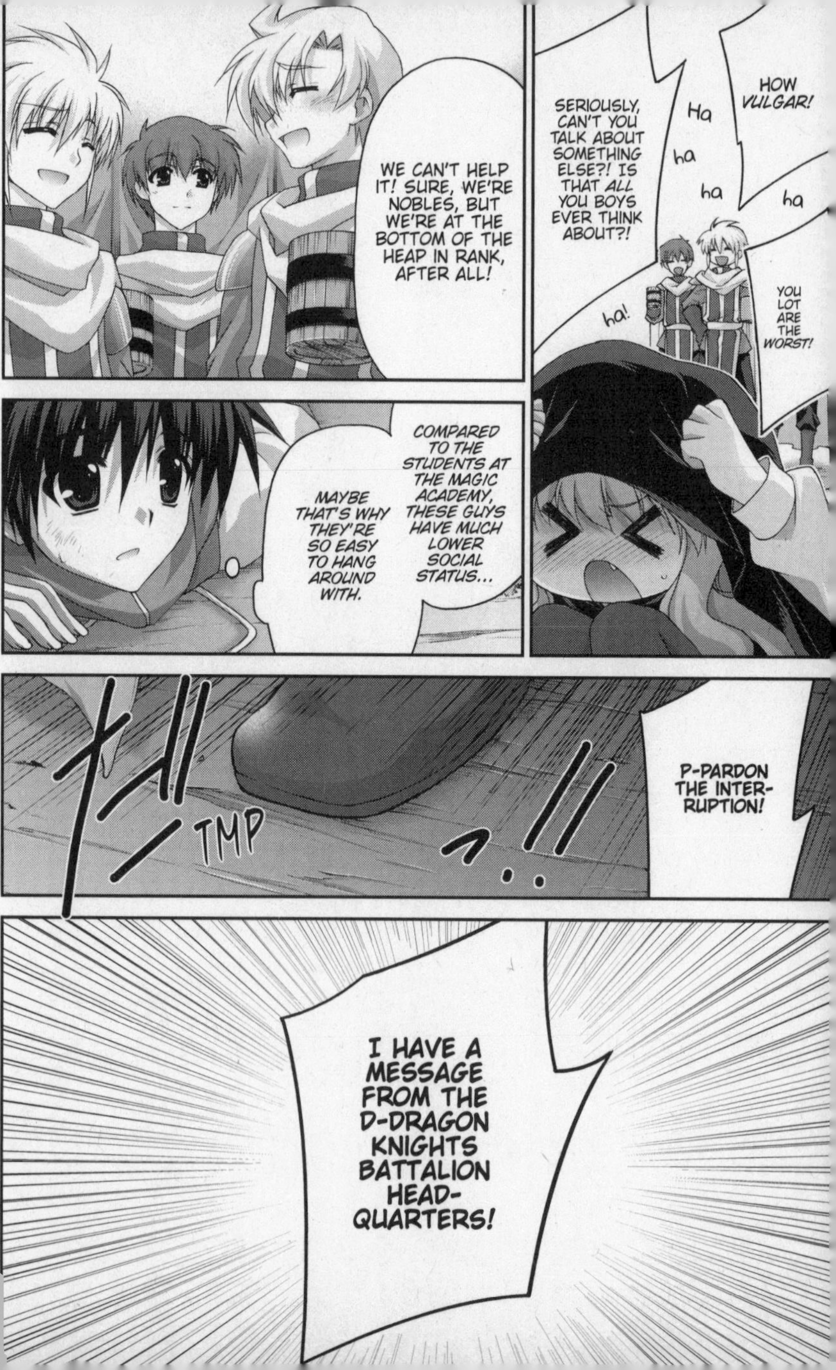
HOW VULGAR!
Ha
ha
ha
ha
SERIOUSLY, CAN'T YOU TALK ABOUT SOMETHING ELSE?! IS THAT ALL YOU BOYS EVER THINK ABOUT?!
YOU LOT ARE THE WORST!
ha!
WE CAN'T HELP IT! SURE, WE'RE NOBLES, BUT WE'RE AT THE BOTTOM OF THE HEAP IN RANK, AFTER ALL!
COMPARED TO THE STUDENTS AT THE MAGIC ACADEMY, THESE GUYS HAVE MUCH LOWER SOCIAL STATUS...
MAYBE THAT'S WHY THEY'RE SO EASY TO HANG AROUND WITH.
P-PARDON THE INTER-RUPTION!
TMP
I HAVE A MESSAGE FROM THE D-DRAGON KNIGHTS BATTALION HEAD-QUARTERS!

Chapter 17: Fairy

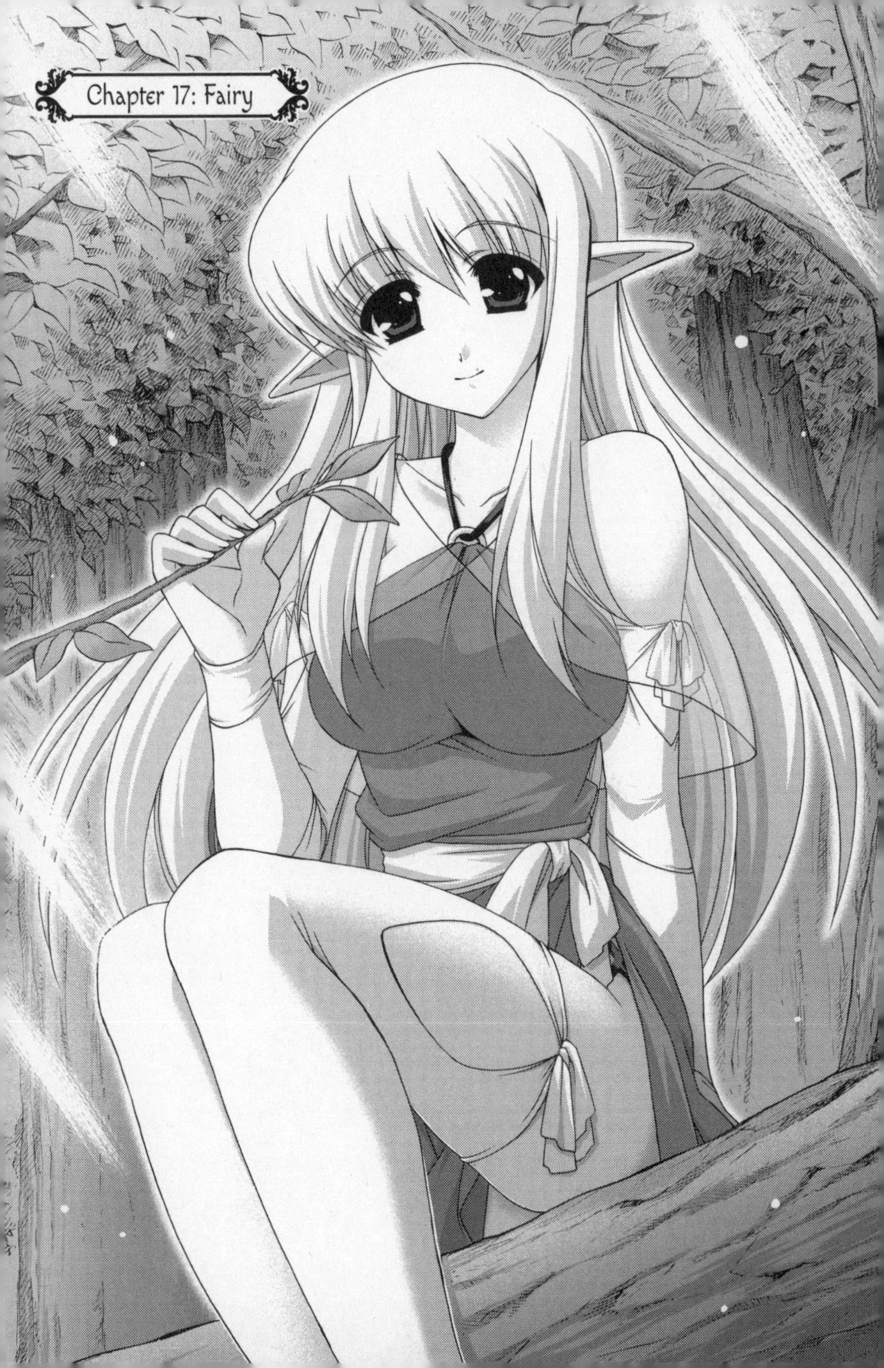

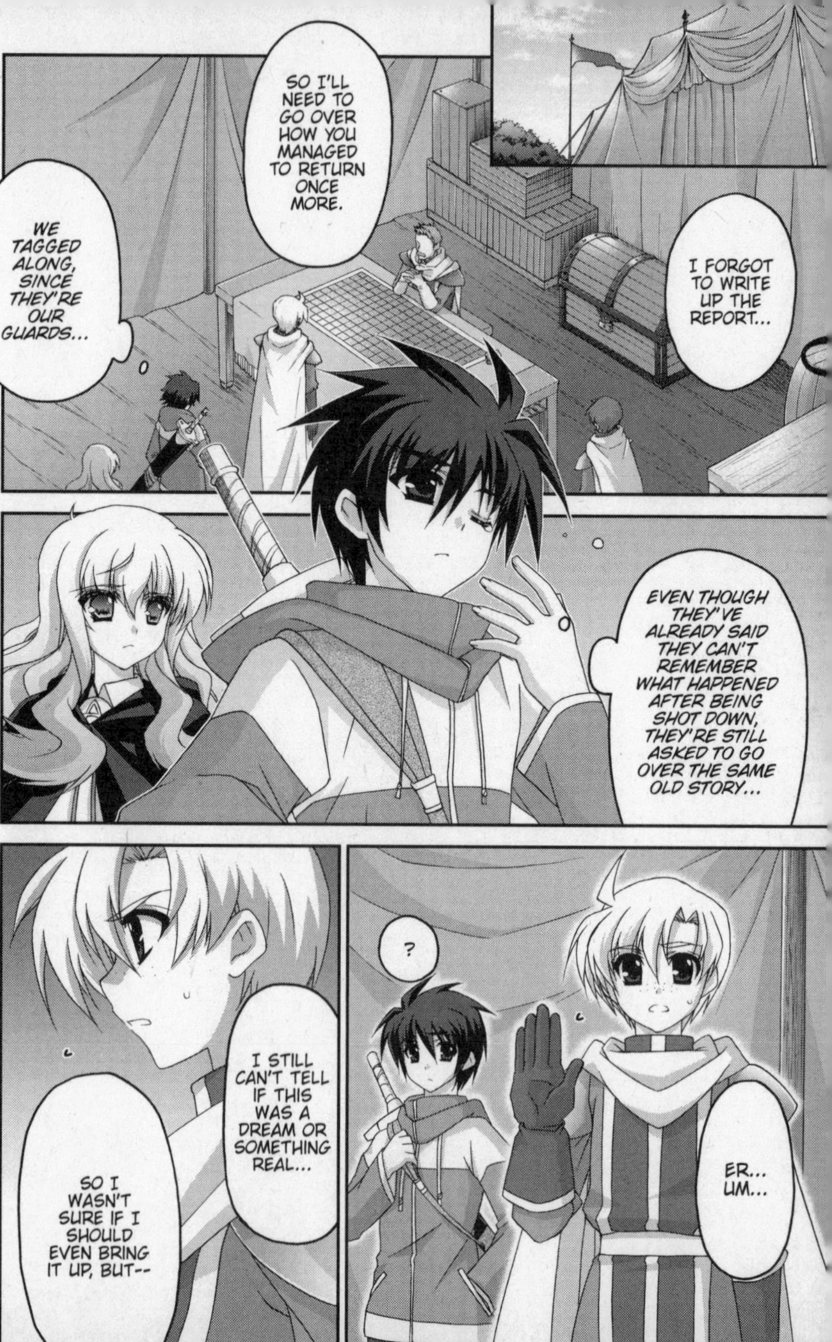
I FORGOT TO WRITE UP THE REPORT...
SO I'LL NEED TO GO OVER HOW YOU MANAGED TO RETURN ONCE MORE.
WE TAGGED ALONG, SINCE THEY'RE OUR GUARDS...
EVEN THOUGH THEY'VE ALREADY SAID THEY CAN'T REMEMBER WHAT HAPPENED AFTER BEING SHOT DOWN, THEY'RE STILL ASKED TO GO OVER THE SAME OLD STORY...
?
ER... UM...
I STILL CAN'T TELL IF THIS WAS A DREAM OR SOMETHING REAL...
SO I WASN'T SURE IF I SHOULD EVEN BRING IT UP, BUT--

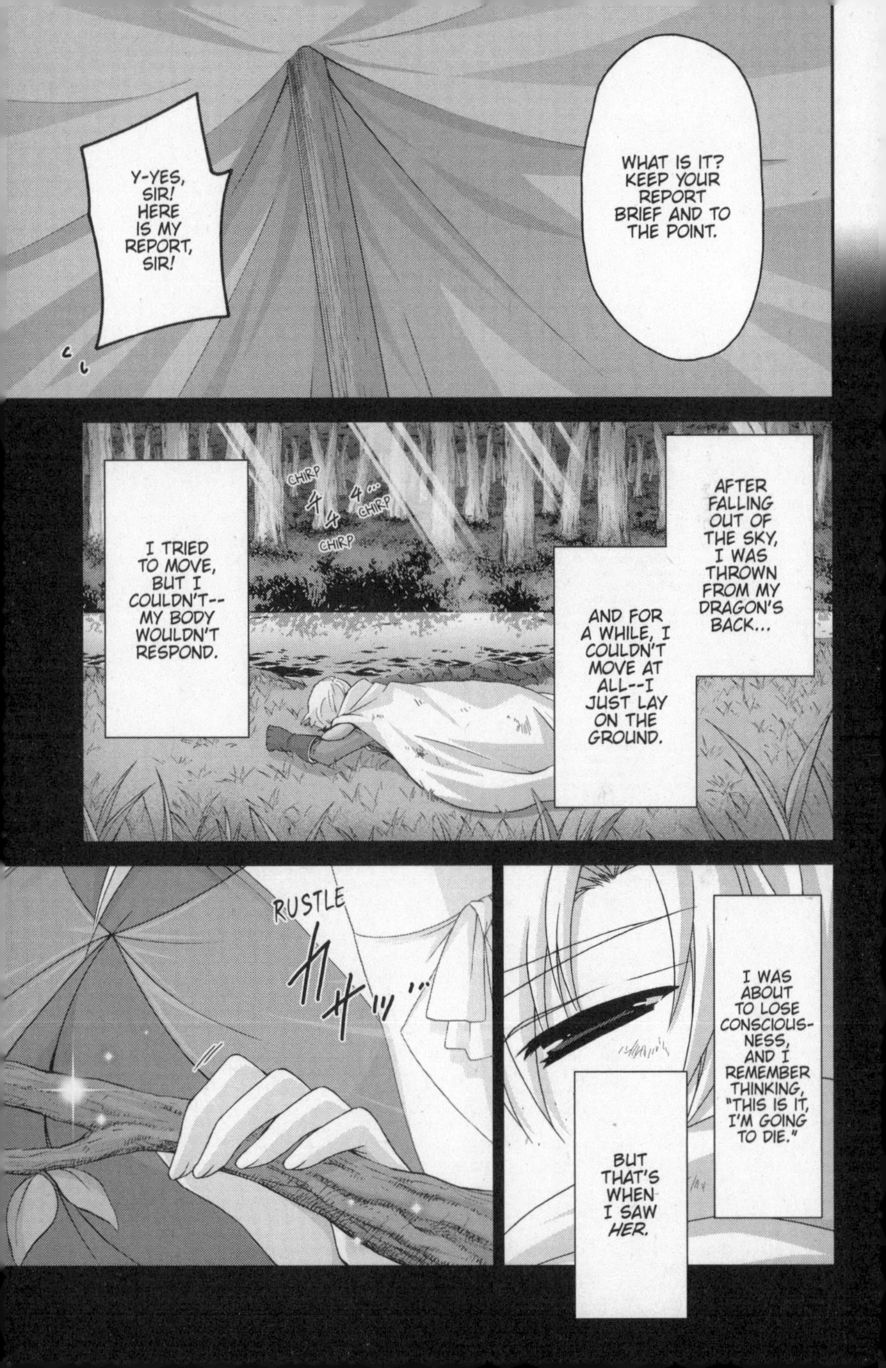
WHAT IS IT? KEEP YOUR REPORT BRIEF AND TO THE POINT.
Y-YES, SIR! HERE IS MY REPORT, SIR!
AFTER FALLING OUT OF THE SKY, I WAS THROWN FROM MY DRAGON'S BACK...
AND FOR A WHILE, I COULDN'T MOVE AT ALL--I JUST LAY ON THE GROUND.
CHIRP
CHIRP
CHIRP
I TRIED TO MOVE, BUT I COULDN'T--MY BODY WOULDN'T RESPOND.
I WAS ABOUT TO LOSE CONSCIOUS-NESS, AND I REMEMBER THINKING, "THIS IS IT, I'M GOING TO DIE."
BUT THAT'S WHEN I SAW *HER*.
RUSTLE
ガサッ…

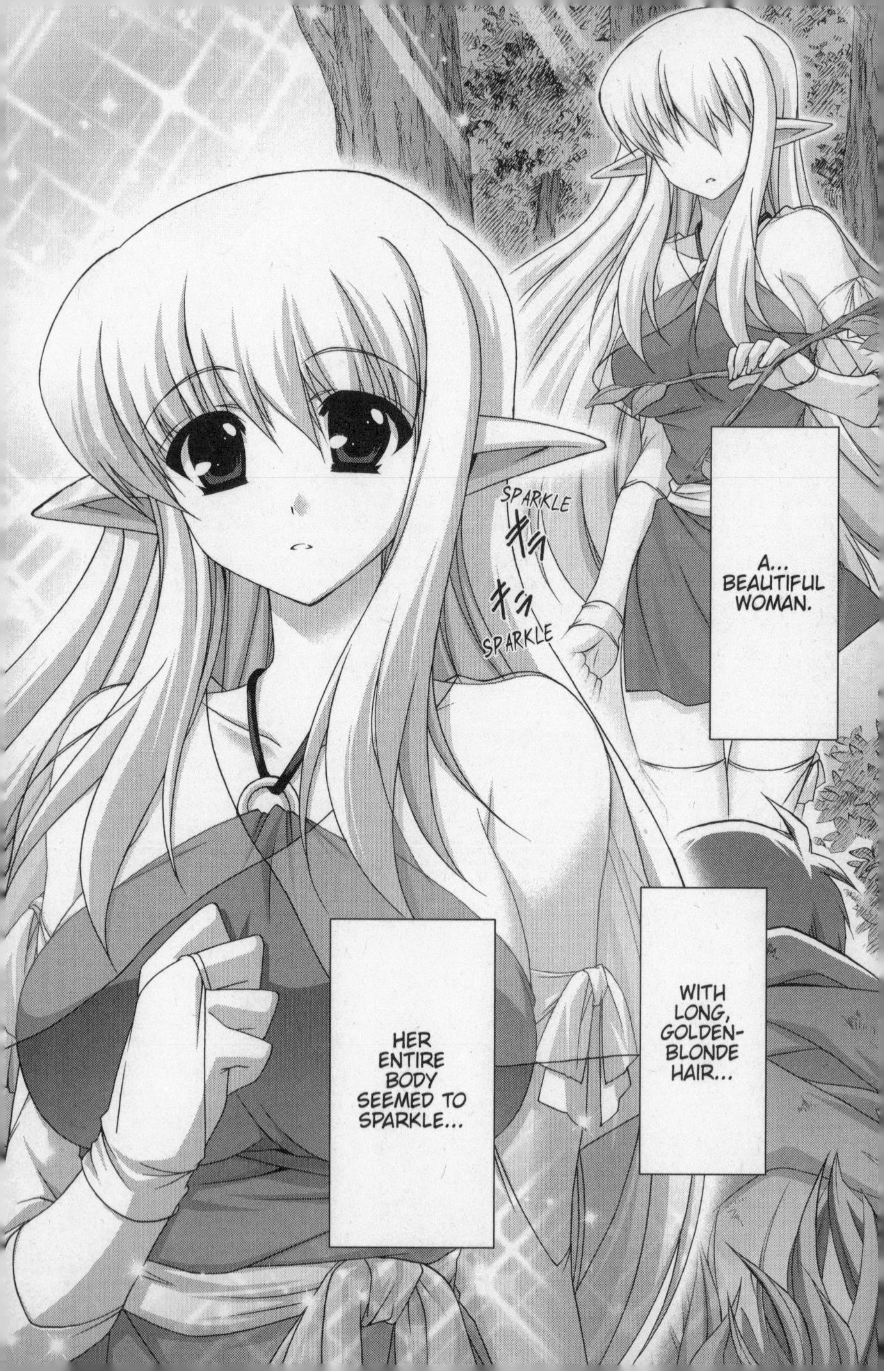
A... BEAUTIFUL WOMAN.
SPARKLE
キラ
キラ
SPARKLE
WITH LONG, GOLDEN-BLONDE HAIR...
HER ENTIRE BODY SEEMED TO SPARKLE...

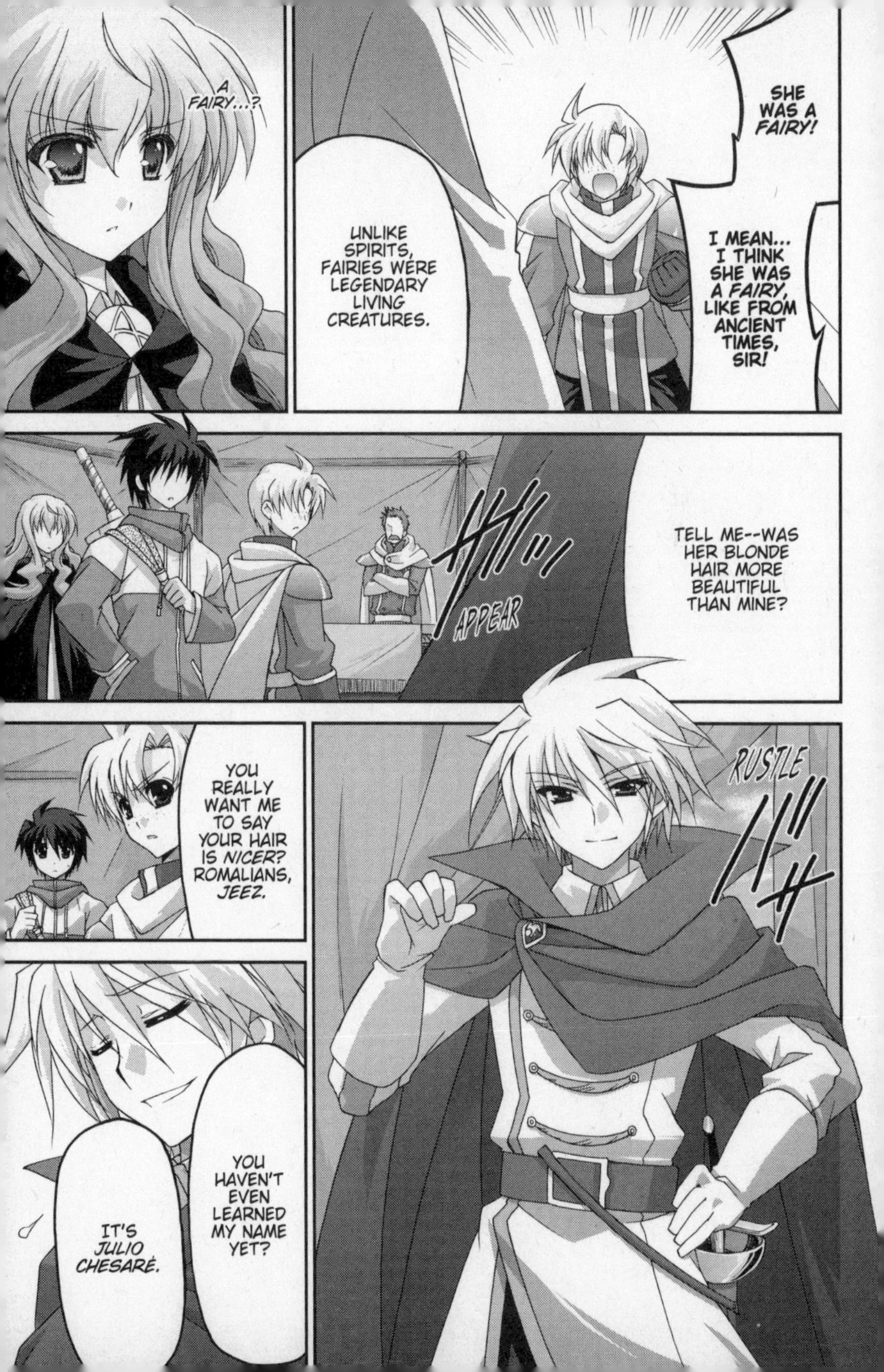
SHE WAS A FAIRY!
I MEAN... I THINK SHE WAS A FAIRY, LIKE FROM ANCIENT TIMES, SIR!
UNLIKE SPIRITS, FAIRIES WERE LEGENDARY LIVING CREATURES.
A FAIRY...?
TELL ME--WAS HER BLONDE HAIR MORE BEAUTIFUL THAN MINE?
APPEAR
RUSTLE
YOU REALLY WANT ME TO SAY YOUR HAIR IS NICER? ROMALIANS, JEEZ.
YOU HAVEN'T EVEN LEARNED MY NAME YET?
IT'S JULIO CHESARÉ.

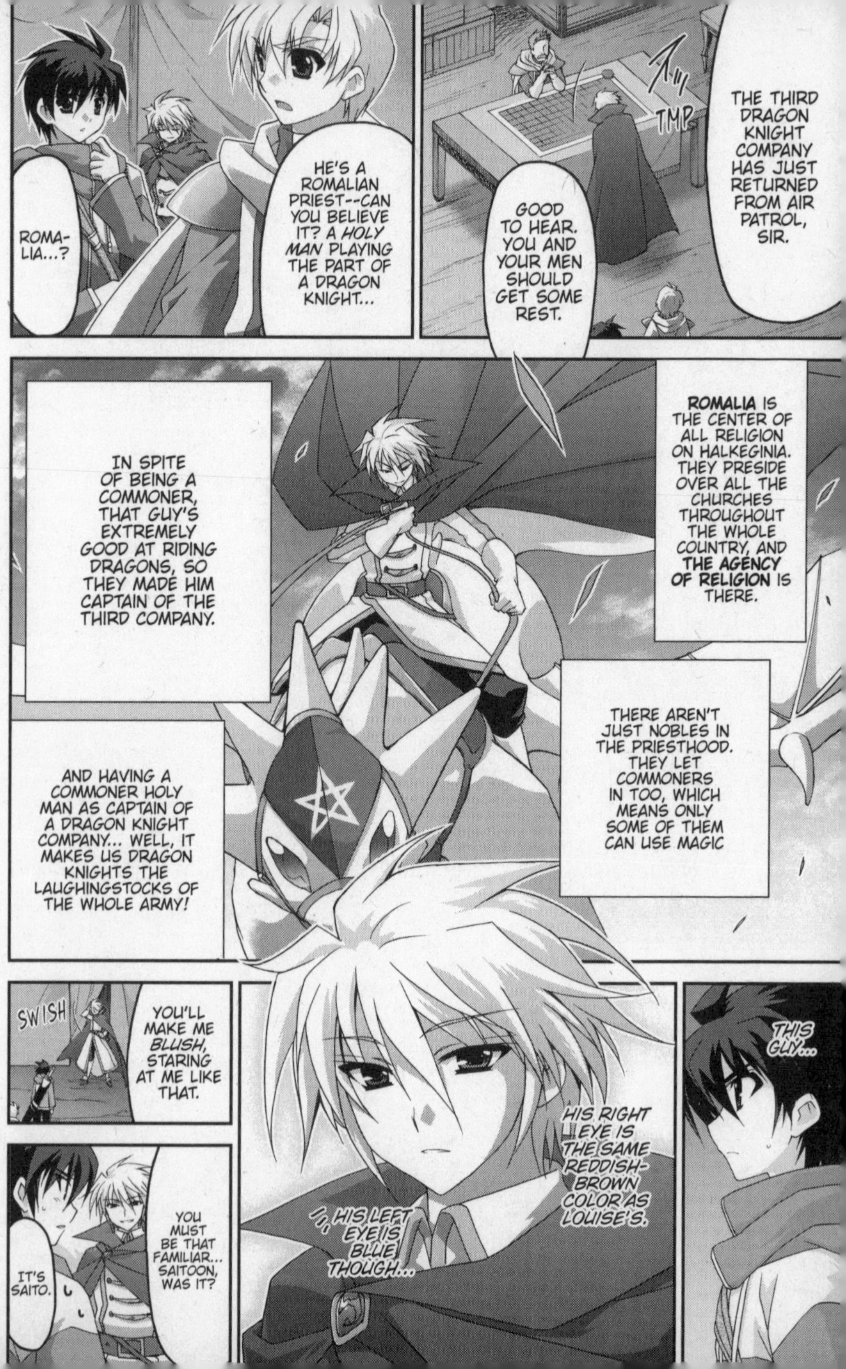
THE THIRD DRAGON KNIGHT COMPANY HAS JUST RETURNED FROM AIR PATROL, SIR.
TMP
GOOD TO HEAR. YOU AND YOUR MEN SHOULD GET SOME REST.
HE'S A ROMALIAN PRIEST--CAN YOU BELIEVE IT? A *HOLY MAN* PLAYING THE PART OF A DRAGON KNIGHT...
ROMA-LIA...?
ROMALIA IS THE CENTER OF ALL RELIGION ON HALKEGINIA. THEY PRESIDE OVER ALL THE CHURCHES THROUGHOUT THE WHOLE COUNTRY, AND **THE AGENCY OF RELIGION** IS THERE.
IN SPITE OF BEING A COMMONER, THAT GUY'S EXTREMELY GOOD AT RIDING DRAGONS, SO THEY MADE HIM CAPTAIN OF THE THIRD COMPANY.
THERE AREN'T JUST NOBLES IN THE PRIESTHOOD. THEY LET COMMONERS IN TOO, WHICH MEANS ONLY SOME OF THEM CAN USE MAGIC
AND HAVING A COMMONER HOLY MAN AS CAPTAIN OF A DRAGON KNIGHT COMPANY... WELL, IT MAKES US DRAGON KNIGHTS THE LAUGHINGSTOCKS OF THE WHOLE ARMY!
THIS GUY...
HIS RIGHT EYE IS THE SAME REDDISH-BROWN COLOR AS LOUISE'S.
HIS LEFT EYE IS BLUE THOUGH...
SWISH
YOU'LL MAKE ME *BLUSH*, STARING AT ME LIKE THAT.
YOU MUST BE THAT FAMILIAR... SAITOON, WAS IT?
IT'S SAITO.

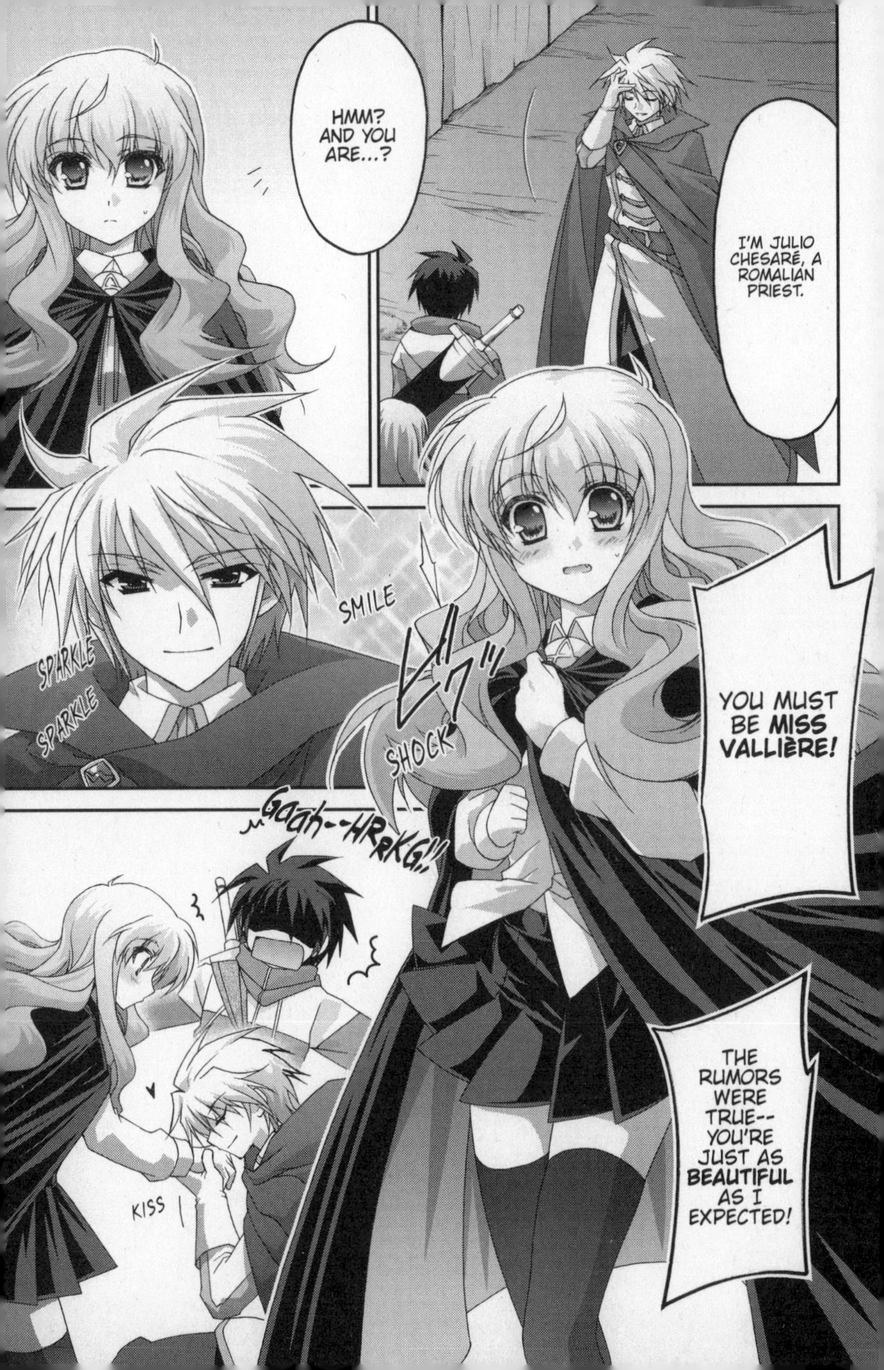
HMM? AND YOU ARE...?
I'M JULIO CHESARÉ, A ROMALIAN PRIEST.
YOU MUST BE **MISS VALLIÈRE!**
SMILE
SHOCK
SPARKLE
SPARKLE
THE RUMORS WERE TRUE-- YOU'RE JUST AS **BEAUTIFUL** AS I EXPECTED!
Gaah--HRRKG!!
KISS

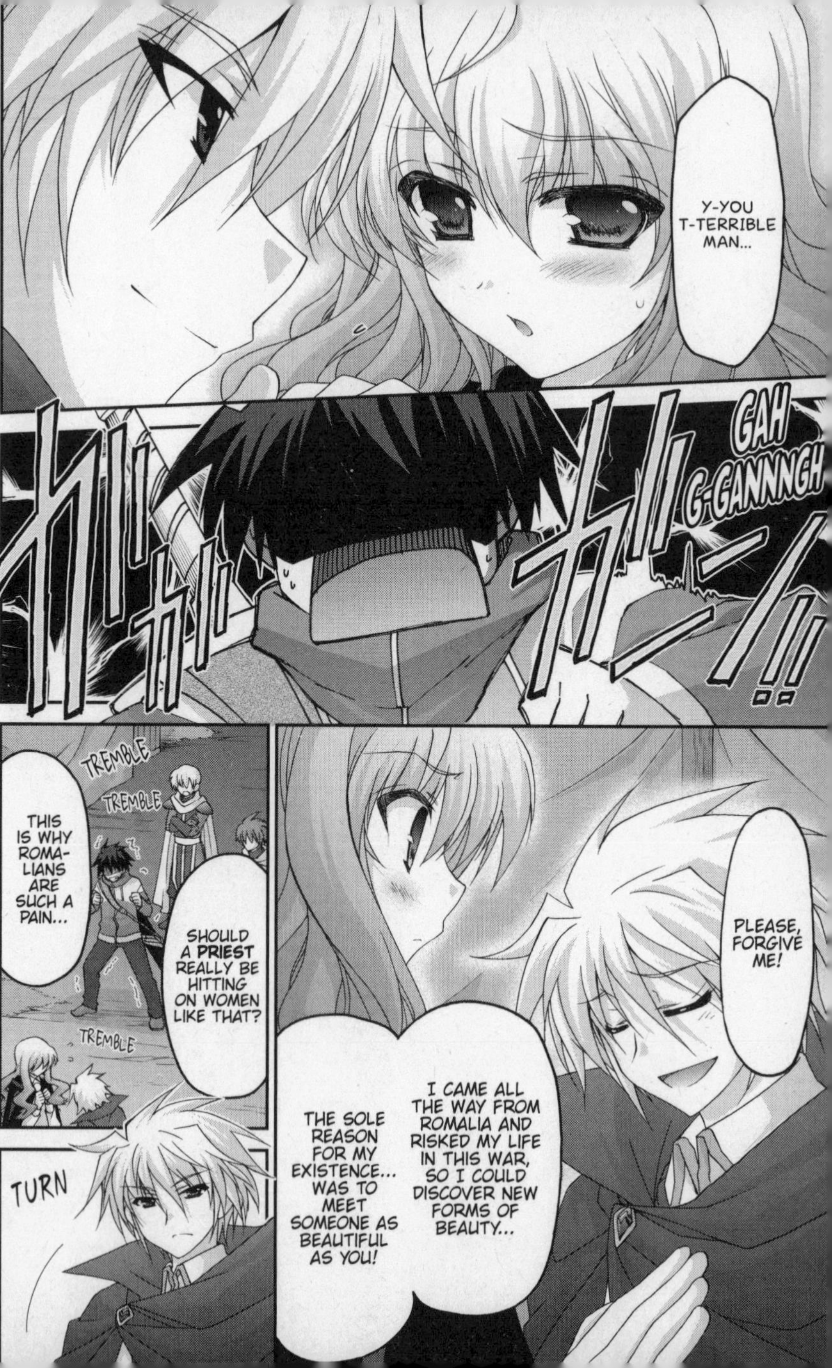
Y-YOU T-TERRIBLE MAN...
GAH G-GANNNGH
PLEASE, FORGIVE ME!
I CAME ALL THE WAY FROM ROMALIA AND RISKED MY LIFE IN THIS WAR, SO I COULD DISCOVER NEW FORMS OF BEAUTY...
THE SOLE REASON FOR MY EXISTENCE... WAS TO MEET SOMEONE AS BEAUTIFUL AS YOU!
TREMBLE
TREMBLE
THIS IS WHY ROMALIANS ARE SUCH A PAIN...
SHOULD A PRIEST REALLY BE HITTING ON WOMEN LIKE THAT?
TREMBLE
TURN

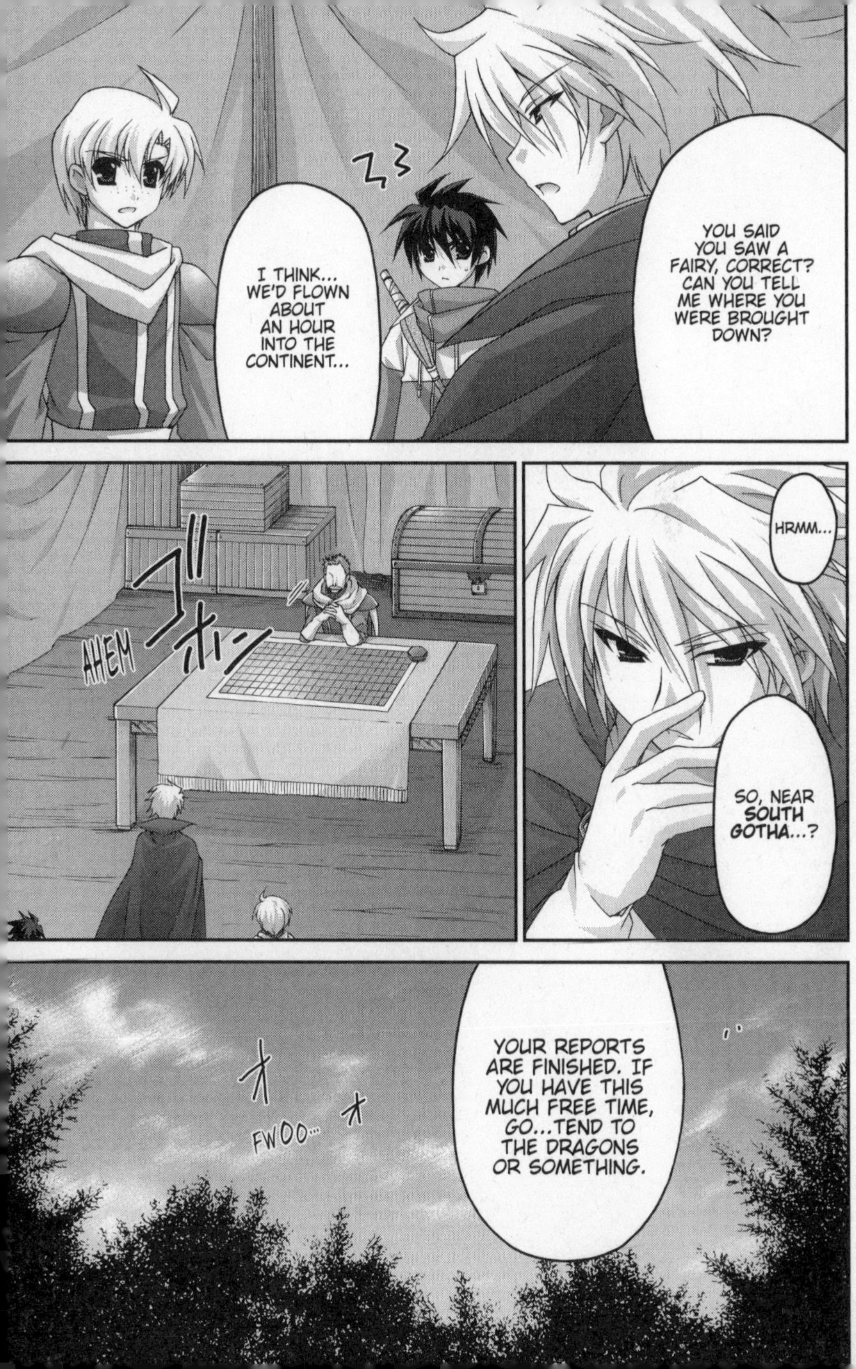
YOU SAID YOU SAW A FAIRY, CORRECT? CAN YOU TELL ME WHERE YOU WERE BROUGHT DOWN?
I THINK... WE'D FLOWN ABOUT AN HOUR INTO THE CONTINENT...
HRMM...
SO, NEAR SOUTH GOTHA...?
AHEM
YOUR REPORTS ARE FINISHED. IF YOU HAVE THIS MUCH FREE TIME, GO...TEND TO THE DRAGONS OR SOMETHING.
FWOO...

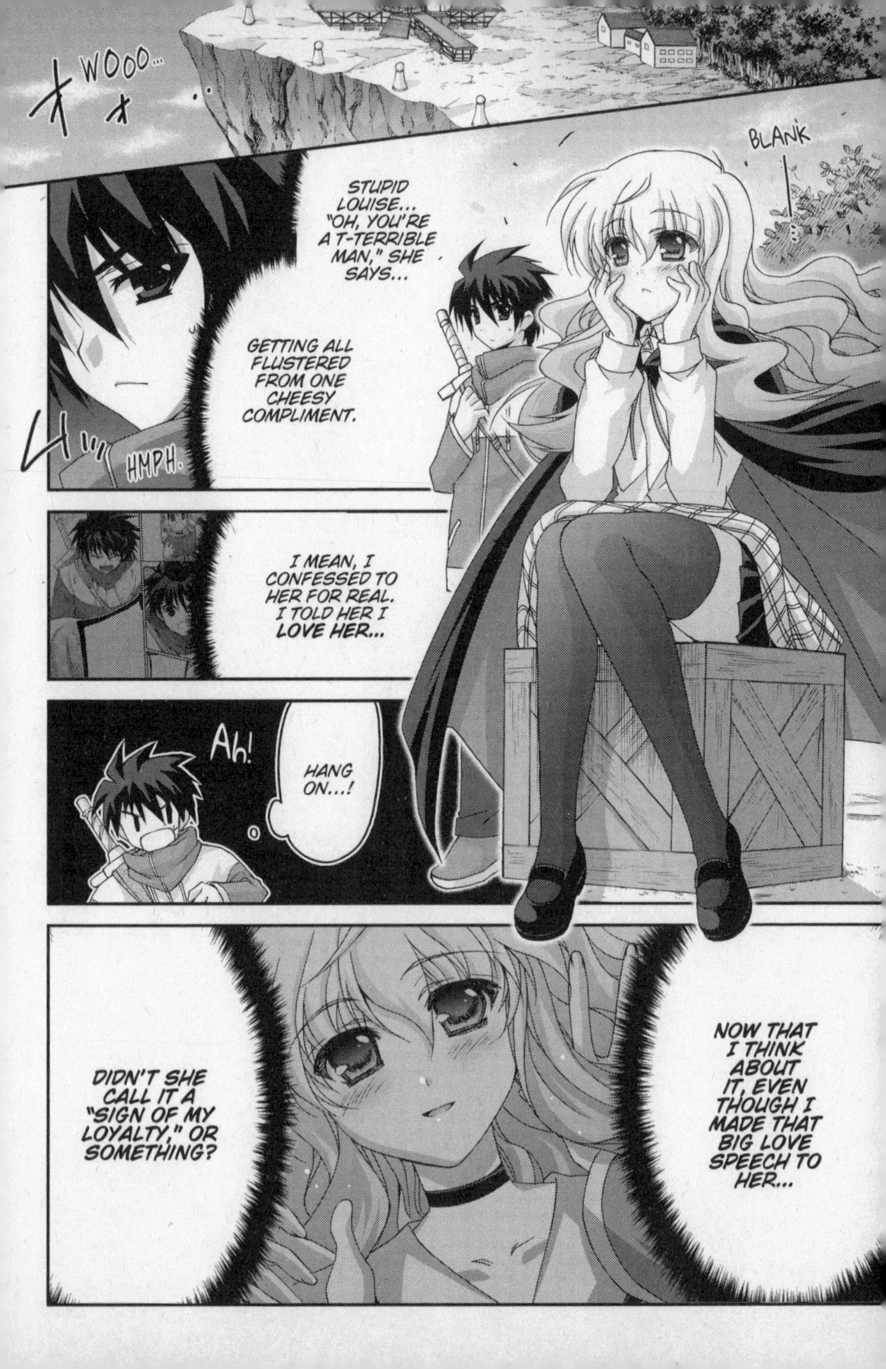

WOOO...
BLANK
STUPID LOUISE... "OH, YOU'RE A T-TERRIBLE MAN," SHE SAYS...
GETTING ALL FLUSTERED FROM ONE CHEESY COMPLIMENT.
HMPH.
I MEAN, I CONFESSED TO HER FOR REAL. I TOLD HER I **LOVE HER...**
Ah!
HANG ON...!
NOW THAT I THINK ABOUT IT, EVEN THOUGH I MADE THAT BIG LOVE SPEECH TO HER...
DIDN'T SHE CALL IT A "SIGN OF MY LOYALTY," OR SOMETHING?

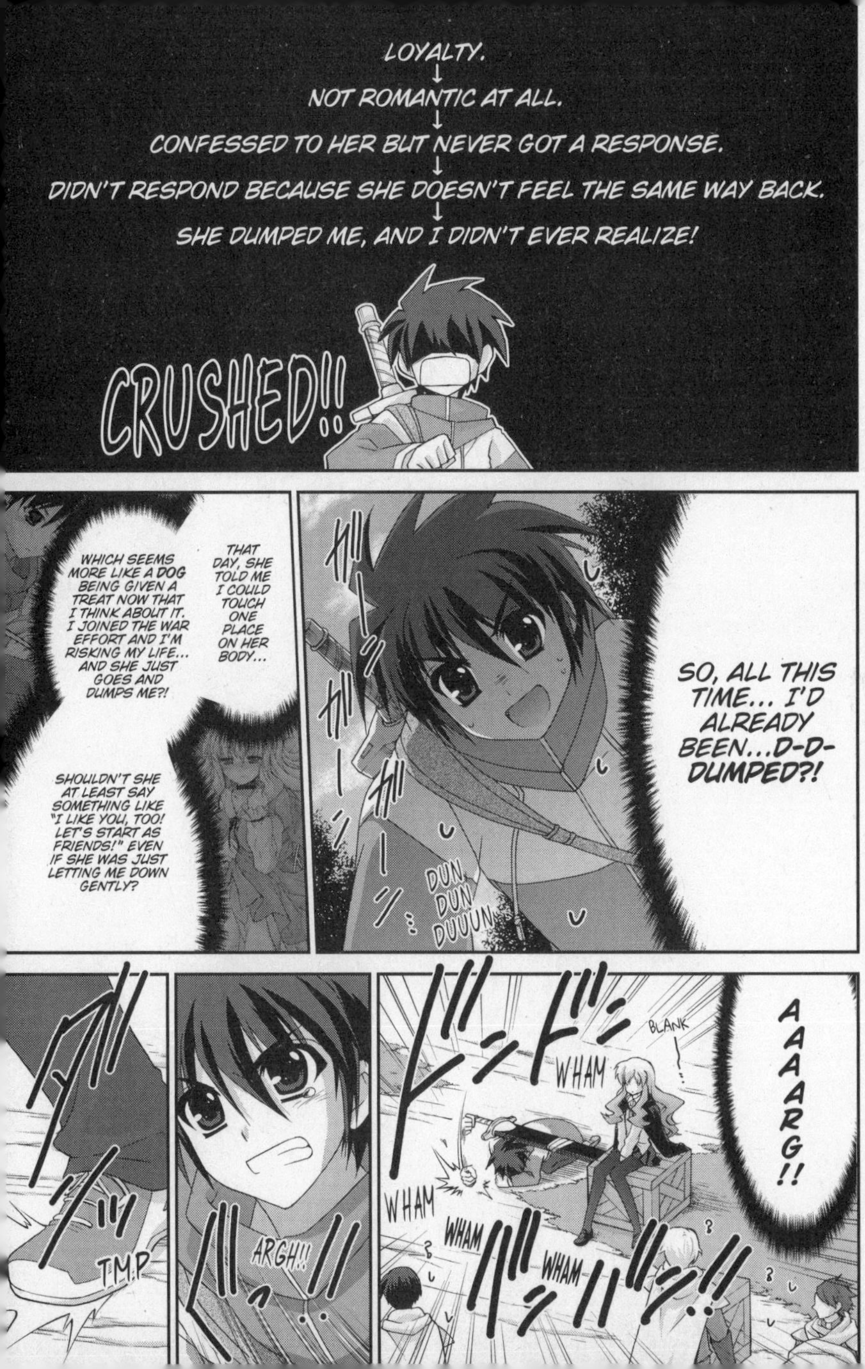
LOYALTY.
↓
NOT ROMANTIC AT ALL.
↓
CONFESSED TO HER BUT NEVER GOT A RESPONSE.
↓
DIDN'T RESPOND BECAUSE SHE DOESN'T FEEL THE SAME WAY BACK.
↓
SHE DUMPED ME, AND I DIDN'T EVER REALIZE!
CRUSHED!!
SO, ALL THIS TIME... I'D ALREADY BEEN...D-D-DUMPED?!
DUN DUN DUUUN
THAT DAY, SHE TOLD ME I COULD TOUCH ONE PLACE ON HER BODY...
WHICH SEEMS MORE LIKE A DOG BEING GIVEN A TREAT NOW THAT I THINK ABOUT IT. I JOINED THE WAR EFFORT AND I'M RISKING MY LIFE... AND SHE JUST GOES AND DUMPS ME?!
SHOULDN'T SHE AT LEAST SAY SOMETHING LIKE "I LIKE YOU, TOO! LET'S START AS FRIENDS!" EVEN IF SHE WAS JUST LETTING ME DOWN GENTLY?
AAAAARG!!
BLANK
WHAM
WHAM
WHAM
WHAM
ARGH!!
TMP

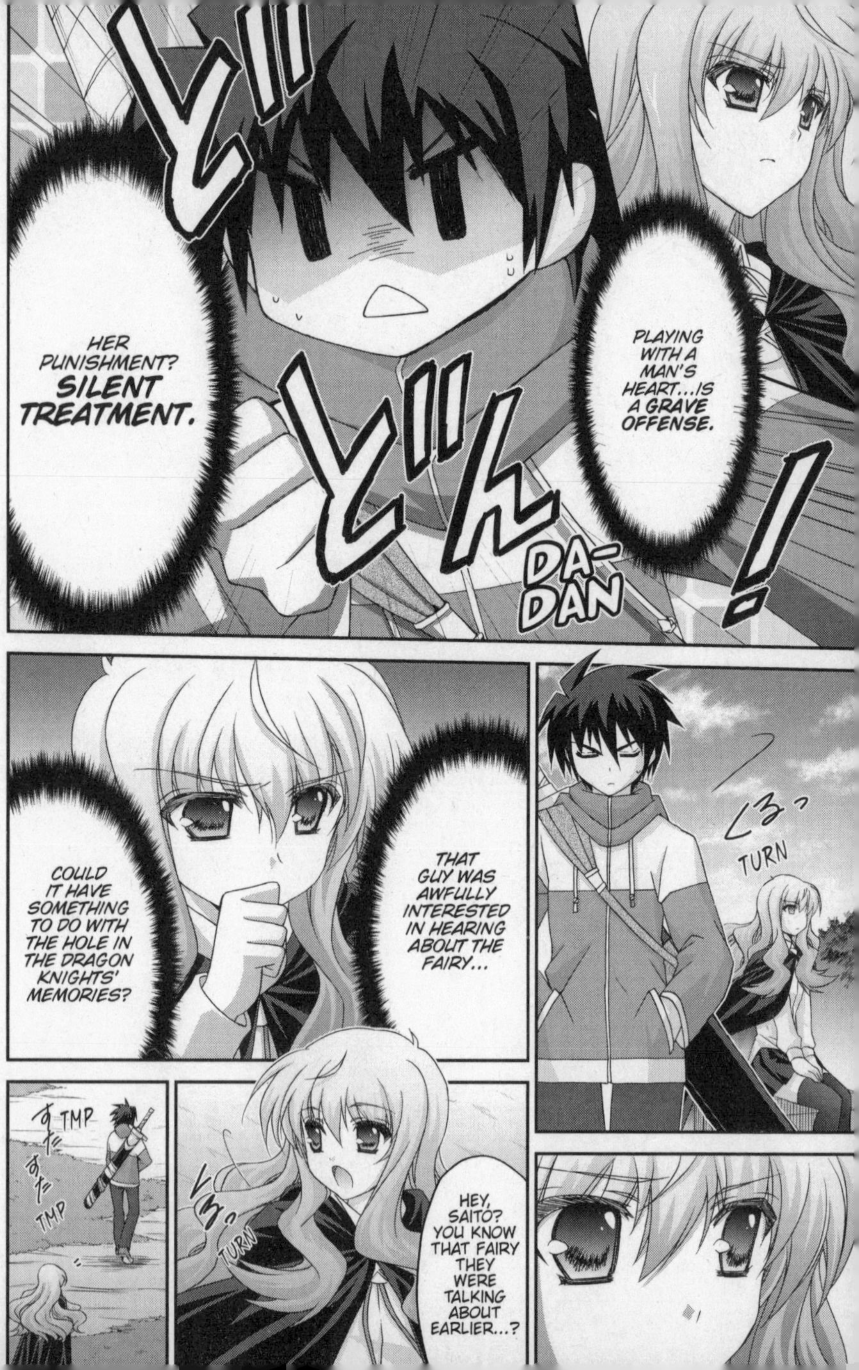
PLAYING WITH A MAN'S HEART...IS A GRAVE OFFENSE.
どどん
DA-DAN
HER PUNISHMENT? SILENT TREATMENT.
くるっ
TURN
THAT GUY WAS AWFULLY INTERESTED IN HEARING ABOUT THE FAIRY...
COULD IT HAVE SOMETHING TO DO WITH THE HOLE IN THE DRAGON KNIGHTS' MEMORIES?
HEY, SAITO? YOU KNOW THAT FAIRY THEY WERE TALKING ABOUT EARLIER...?
くるっ
TURN
TMP
TMP

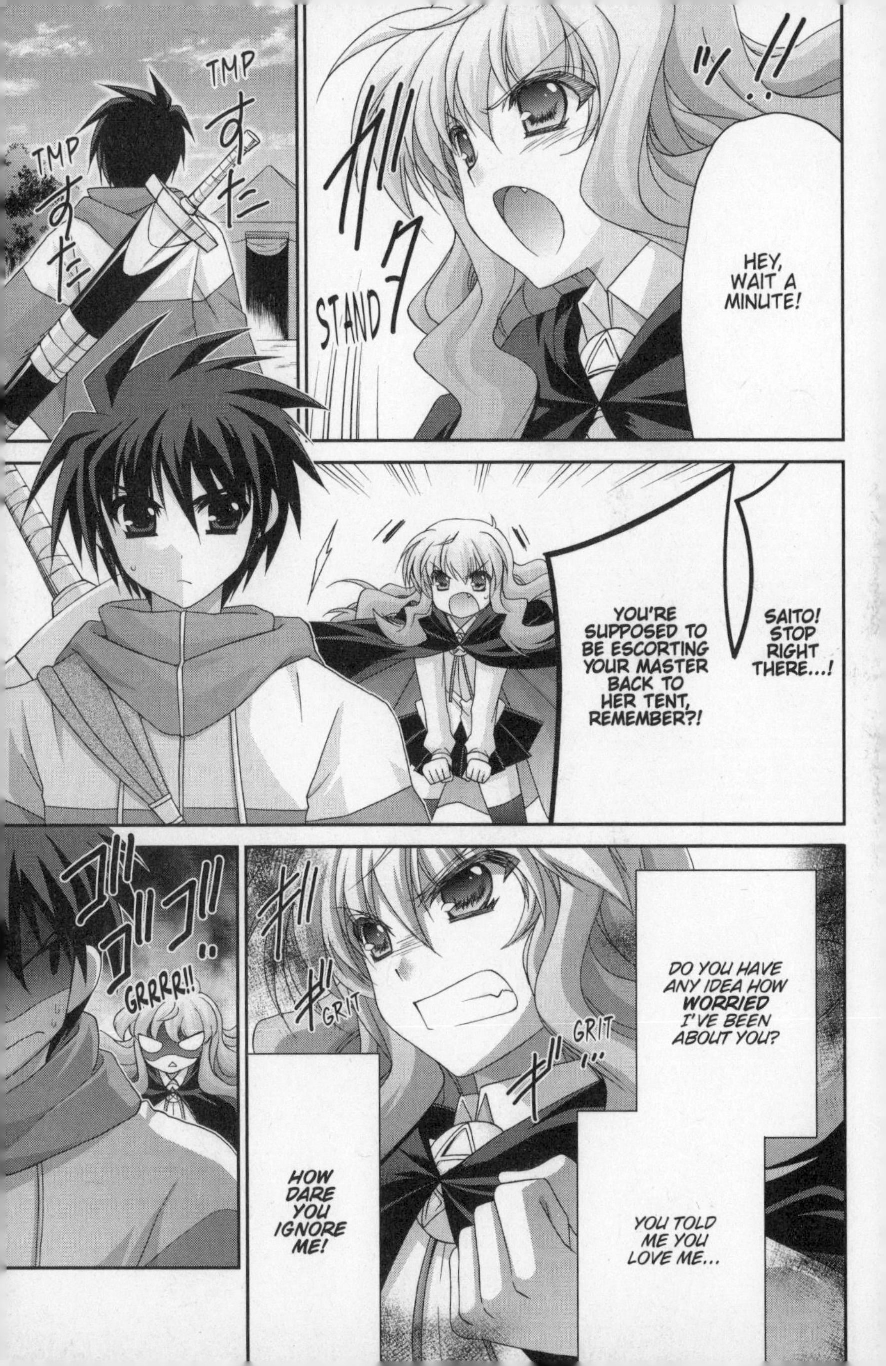
STAND
HEY, WAIT A MINUTE!
TMP
すた
TMP
すた
SAITO! STOP RIGHT THERE...!
YOU'RE SUPPOSED TO BE ESCORTING YOUR MASTER BACK TO HER TENT, REMEMBER?!
DO YOU HAVE ANY IDEA HOW WORRIED I'VE BEEN ABOUT YOU?
GRIT
GRIT
YOU TOLD ME YOU LOVE ME...
HOW DARE YOU IGNORE ME!
GRRRR!!

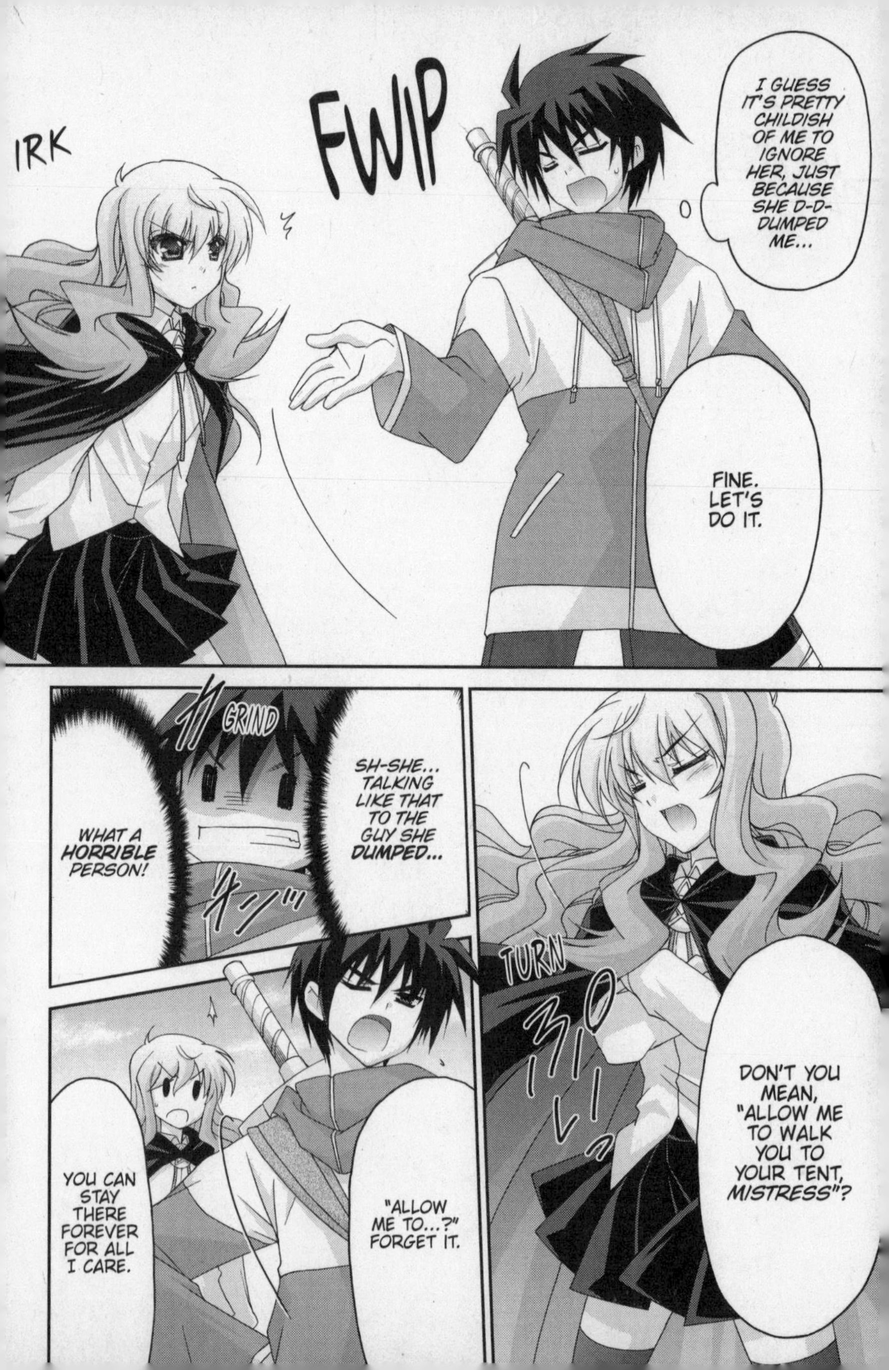

I GUESS IT'S PRETTY CHILDISH OF ME TO IGNORE HER, JUST BECAUSE SHE D-D-DUMPED ME...
FWIP
FINE. LET'S DO IT.
IRK
TURN
DON'T YOU MEAN, "ALLOW ME TO WALK YOU TO YOUR TENT, MISTRESS"?
GRIND
SH-SHE... TALKING LIKE THAT TO THE GUY SHE DUMPED...
WHAT A HORRIBLE PERSON!
"ALLOW ME TO...?" FORGET IT.
YOU CAN STAY THERE FOREVER FOR ALL I CARE.

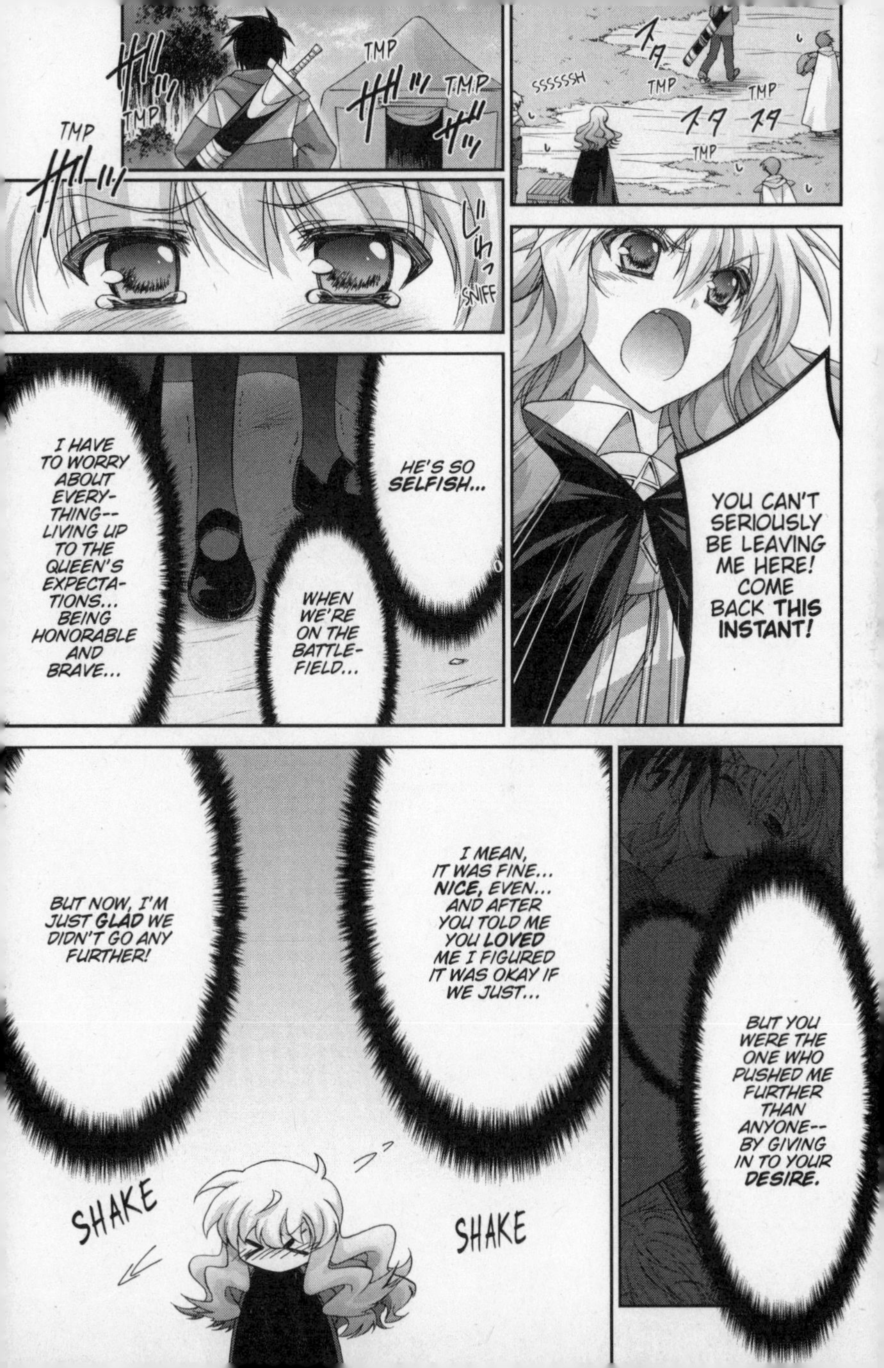
SSSSSSH
TMP
TMP
スタ スタ
TMP
TMP
TMP
TMP
TMP
YOU CAN'T SERIOUSLY BE LEAVING ME HERE! COME BACK **THIS INSTANT!**
SNIFF
HE'S SO **SELFISH...**
WHEN WE'RE ON THE BATTLEFIELD...
I HAVE TO WORRY ABOUT EVERYTHING-- LIVING UP TO THE QUEEN'S EXPECTATIONS... BEING HONORABLE AND BRAVE...
BUT YOU WERE THE ONE WHO PUSHED ME FURTHER THAN ANYONE-- BY GIVING IN TO YOUR **DESIRE.**
I MEAN, IT WAS FINE... **NICE,** EVEN... AND AFTER YOU TOLD ME YOU **LOVED** ME I FIGURED IT WAS OKAY IF WE JUST...
BUT NOW, I'M JUST **GLAD** WE DIDN'T GO ANY FURTHER!
SHAKE
SHAKE

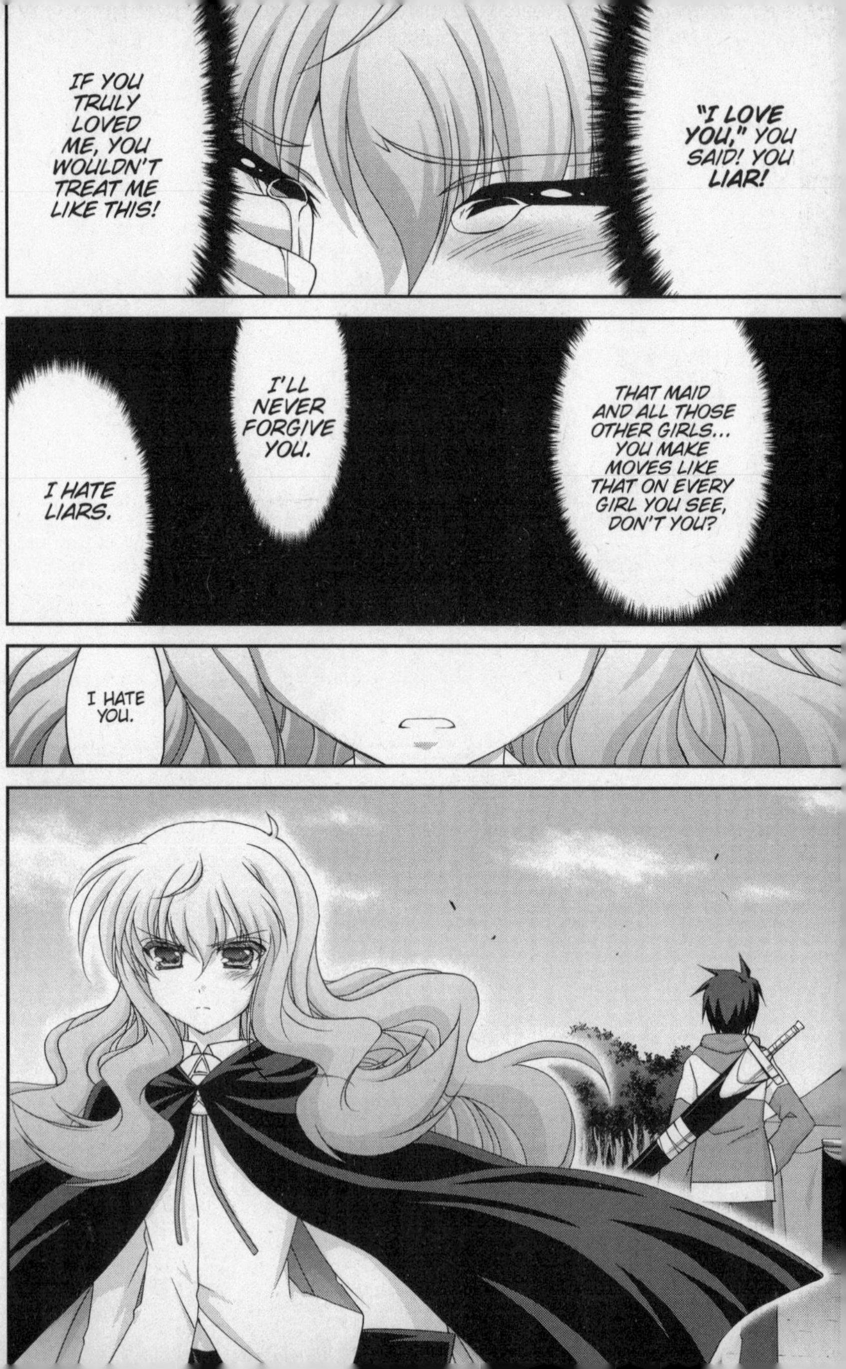
"I LOVE YOU," YOU SAID! YOU LIAR!
IF YOU TRULY LOVED ME, YOU WOULDN'T TREAT ME LIKE THIS!
THAT MAID AND ALL THOSE OTHER GIRLS... YOU MAKE MOVES LIKE THAT ON EVERY GIRL YOU SEE, DON'T YOU?
I'LL NEVER FORGIVE YOU.
I HATE LIARS.
I HATE YOU.

Chapter 18: The Priest of Romalia

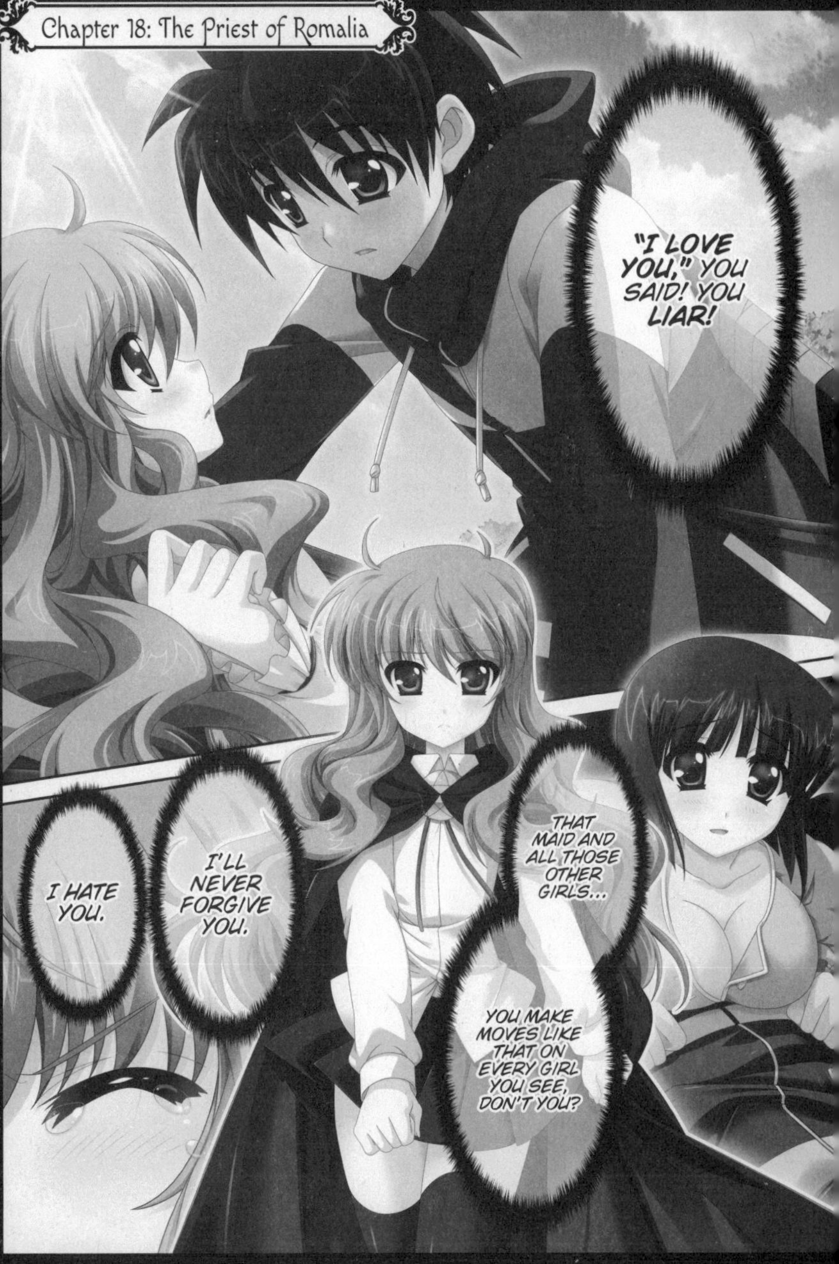
"I LOVE YOU," YOU SAID! YOU LIAR!
THAT MAID AND ALL THOSE OTHER GIRLS...
YOU MAKE MOVES LIKE THAT ON EVERY GIRL YOU SEE, DON'T YOU?
I'LL NEVER FORGIVE YOU.
I HATE YOU.

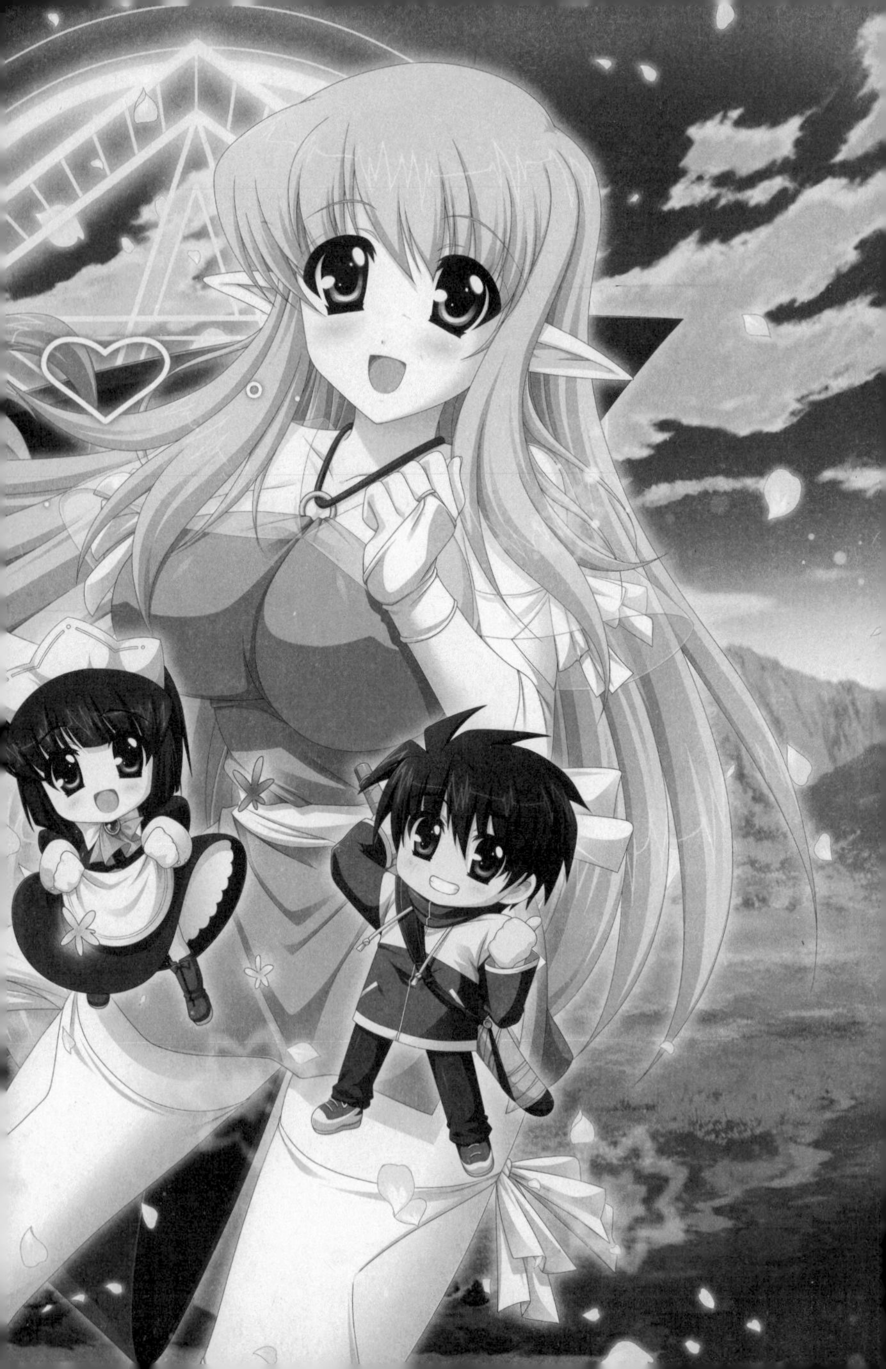

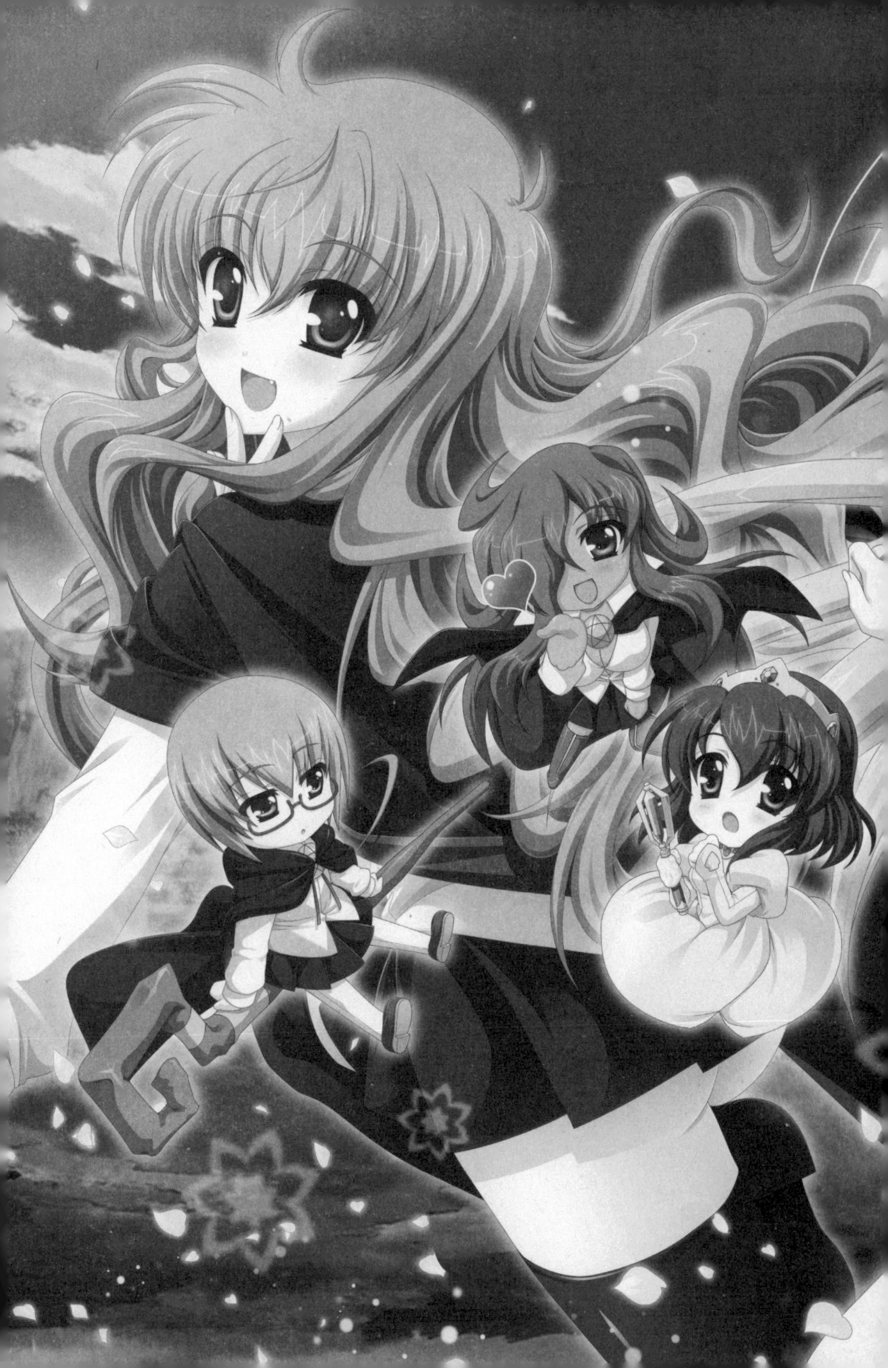

Le Familier de Zero Chevalier

ZERO'S
FAMILIAR
Chevalier

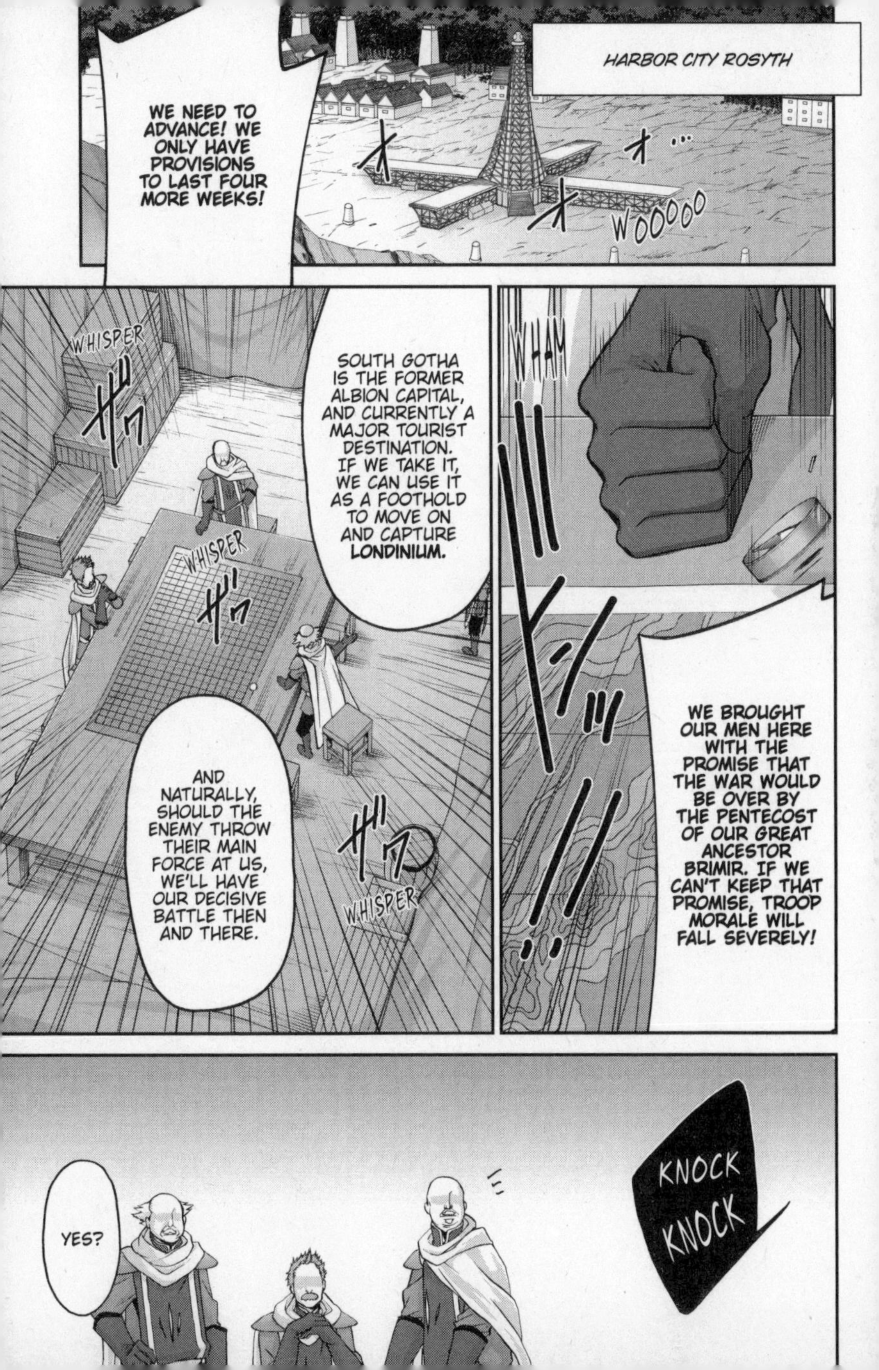
HARBOR CITY ROSYTH
WOOOOO
WE NEED TO ADVANCE! WE ONLY HAVE PROVISIONS TO LAST FOUR MORE WEEKS!
WHAM
WE BROUGHT OUR MEN HERE WITH THE PROMISE THAT THE WAR WOULD BE OVER BY THE PENTECOST OF OUR GREAT ANCESTOR BRIMIR. IF WE CAN'T KEEP THAT PROMISE, TROOP MORALE WILL FALL SEVERELY!
SOUTH GOTHA IS THE FORMER ALBION CAPITAL, AND CURRENTLY A MAJOR TOURIST DESTINATION. IF WE TAKE IT, WE CAN USE IT AS A FOOTHOLD TO MOVE ON AND CAPTURE **LONDINIUM.**
WHISPER
WHISPER
AND NATURALLY, SHOULD THE ENEMY THROW THEIR MAIN FORCE AT US, WE'LL HAVE OUR DECISIVE BATTLE THEN AND THERE.
WHISPER
KNOCK KNOCK
YES?

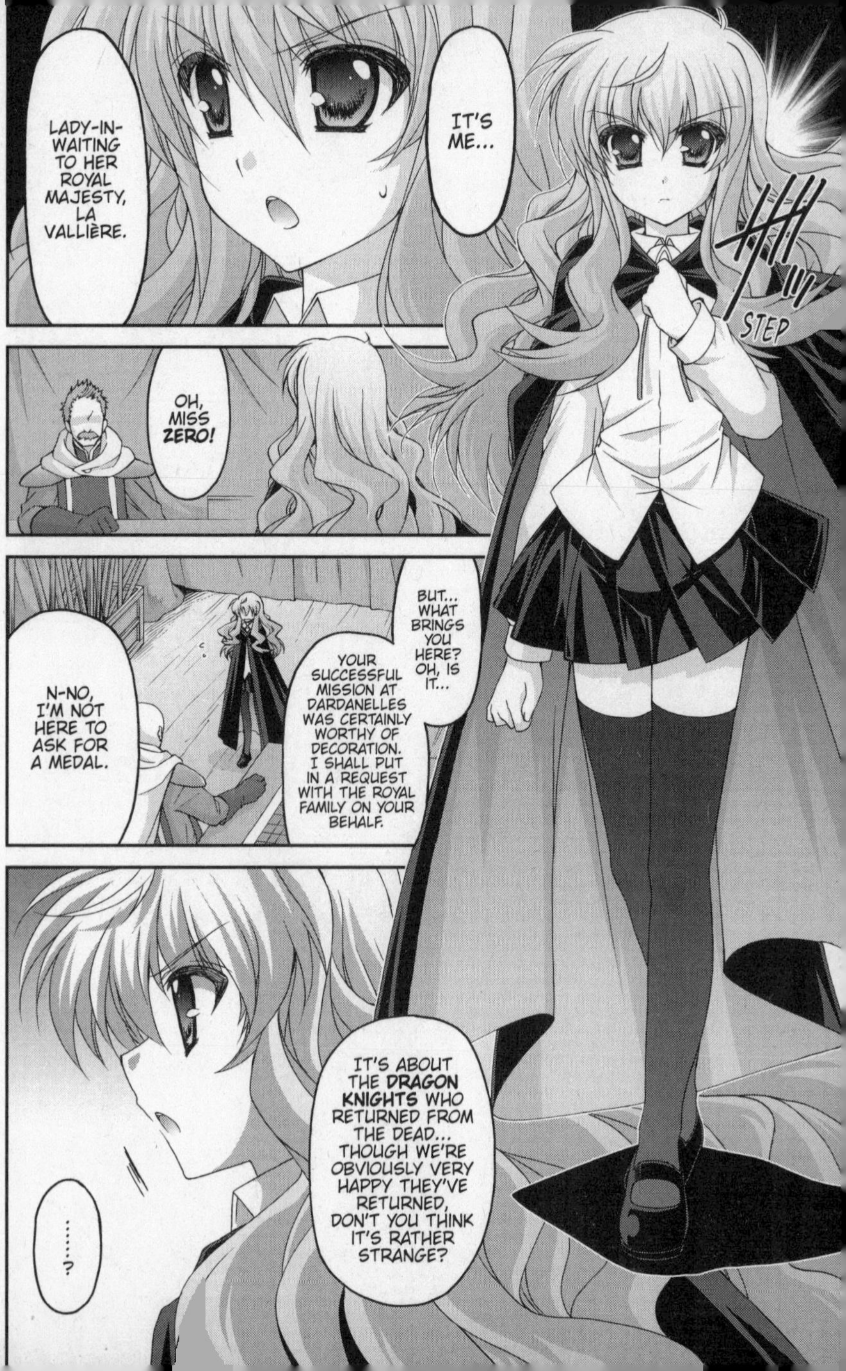
STEP
IT'S ME...
LADY-IN-WAITING TO HER ROYAL MAJESTY, LA VALLIÈRE.
OH, MISS **ZERO!**
BUT... WHAT BRINGS YOU HERE? OH, IS IT...
YOUR SUCCESSFUL MISSION AT DARDANELLES WAS CERTAINLY WORTHY OF DECORATION. I SHALL PUT IN A REQUEST WITH THE ROYAL FAMILY ON YOUR BEHALF.
N-NO, I'M NOT HERE TO ASK FOR A MEDAL.
IT'S ABOUT THE **DRAGON KNIGHTS** WHO RETURNED FROM THE DEAD... THOUGH WE'RE OBVIOUSLY VERY HAPPY THEY'VE RETURNED, DON'T YOU THINK IT'S RATHER STRANGE?
......?

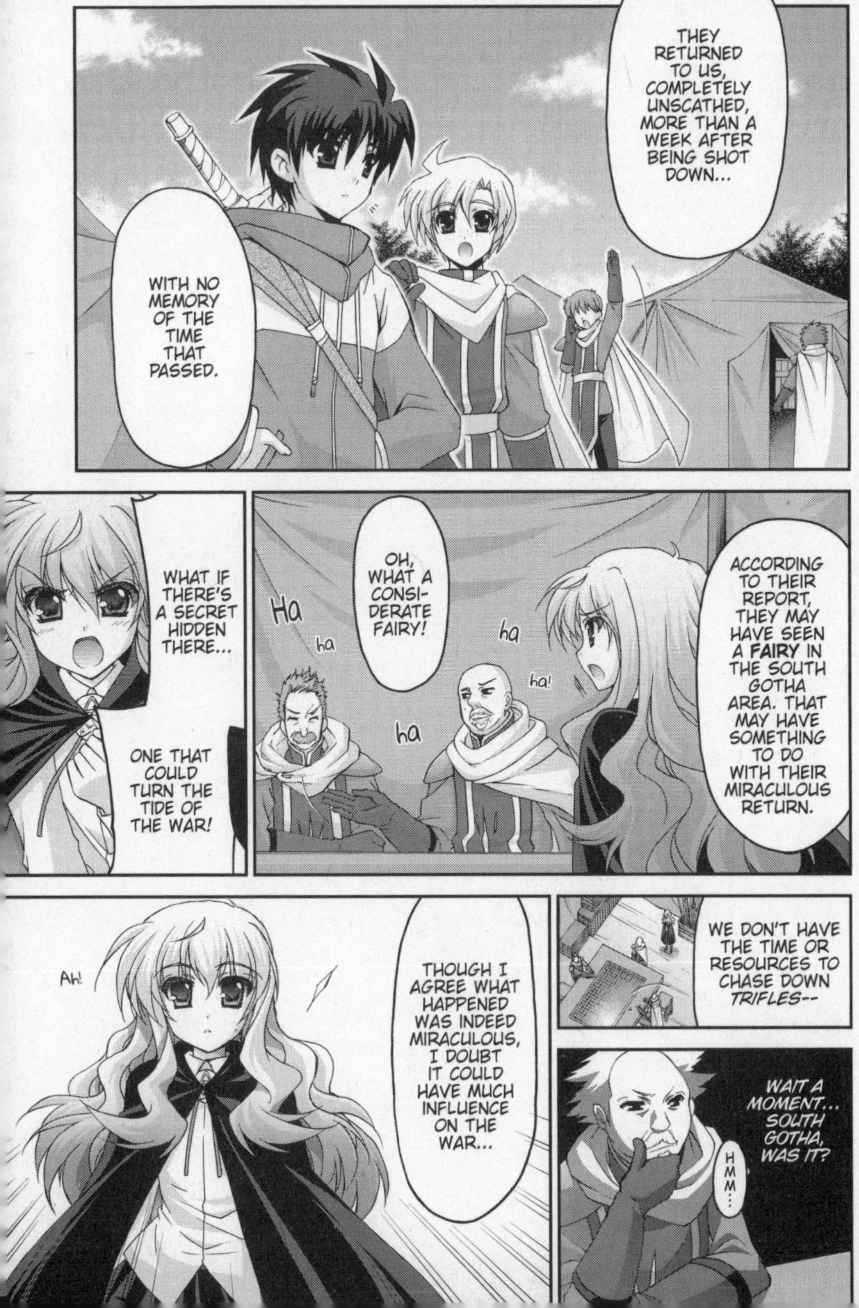
THEY RETURNED TO US, COMPLETELY UNSCATHED, MORE THAN A WEEK AFTER BEING SHOT DOWN...
WITH NO MEMORY OF THE TIME THAT PASSED.
ACCORDING TO THEIR REPORT, THEY MAY HAVE SEEN A **FAIRY** IN THE SOUTH GOTHA AREA. THAT MAY HAVE SOMETHING TO DO WITH THEIR MIRACULOUS RETURN.
ha
ha!
OH, WHAT A CONSI-DERATE FAIRY!
Ha
ha
ha
WHAT IF THERE'S A SECRET HIDDEN THERE...
ONE THAT COULD TURN THE TIDE OF THE WAR!
WE DON'T HAVE THE TIME OR RESOURCES TO CHASE DOWN *TRIFLES*--
WAIT A MOMENT... SOUTH GOTHA, WAS IT?
HMM...
THOUGH I AGREE WHAT HAPPENED WAS INDEED MIRACULOUS, I DOUBT IT COULD HAVE MUCH INFLUENCE ON THE WAR...
Ah!

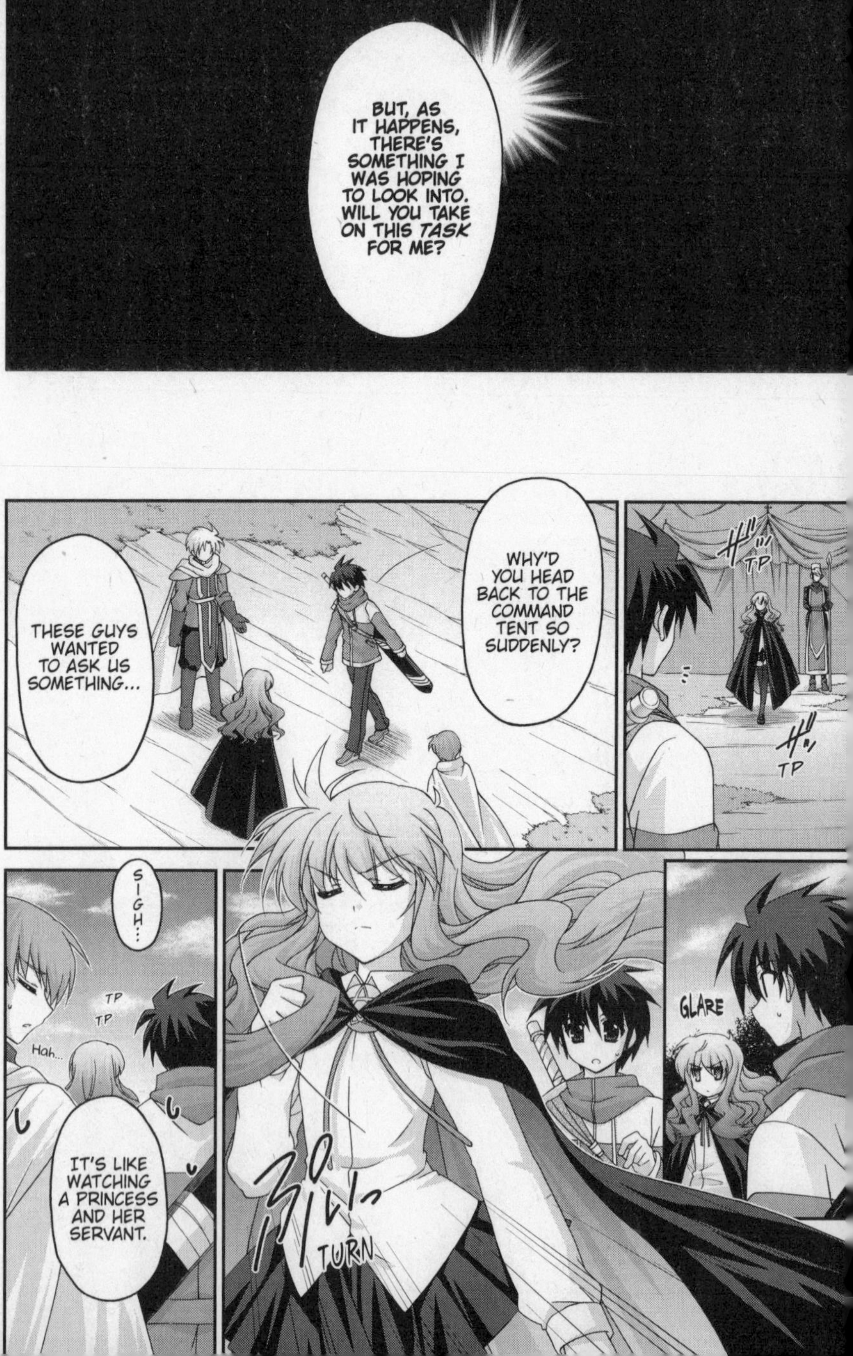
BUT, AS IT HAPPENS, THERE'S SOMETHING I WAS HOPING TO LOOK INTO. WILL YOU TAKE ON THIS *TASK* FOR ME?
TP
TP
WHY'D YOU HEAD BACK TO THE COMMAND TENT SO SUDDENLY?
THESE GUYS WANTED TO ASK US SOMETHING...
GLARE
TURN
SIGH...
TP
TP
Hah...
IT'S LIKE WATCHING A PRINCESS AND HER SERVANT.

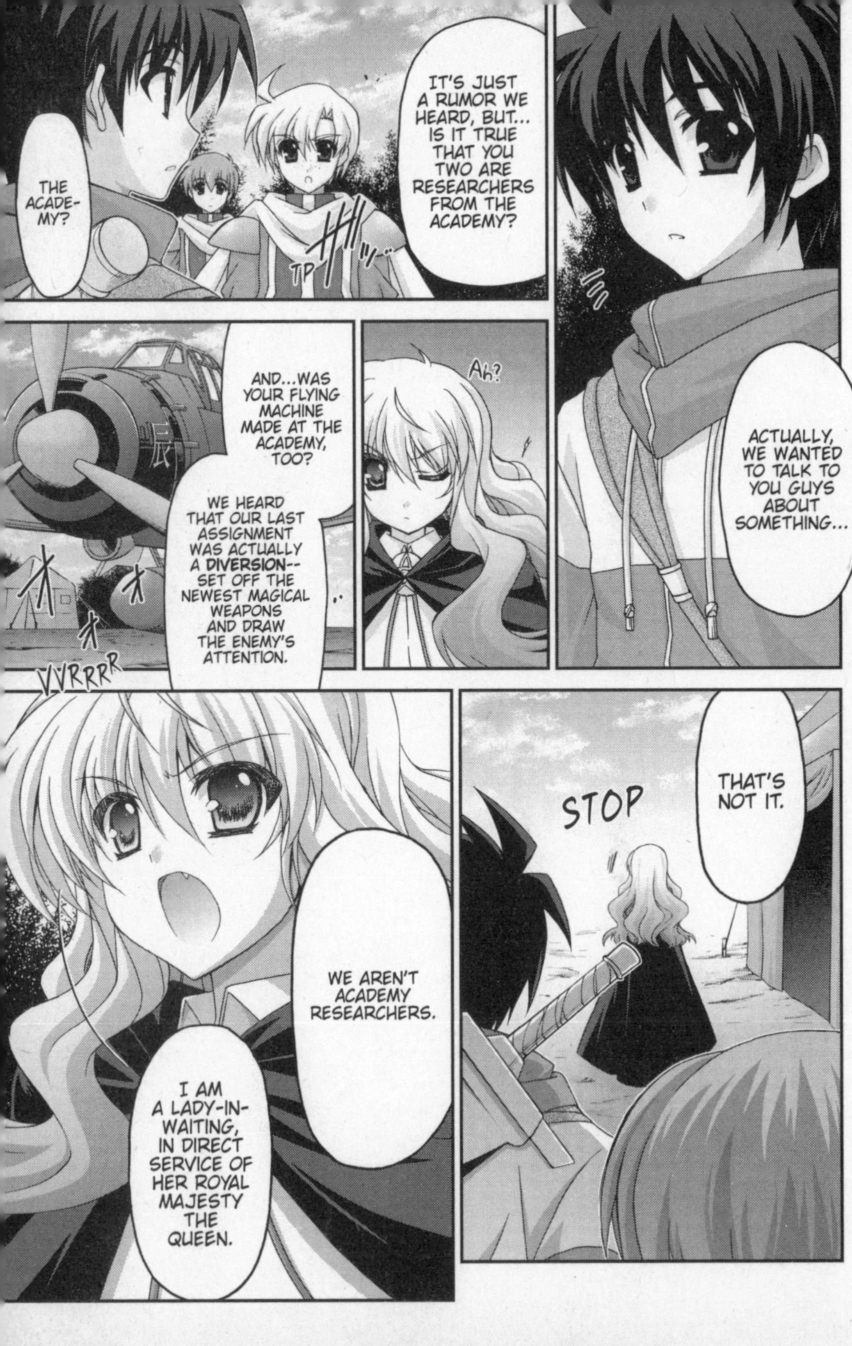
ACTUALLY, WE WANTED TO TALK TO YOU GUYS ABOUT SOMETHING...
IT'S JUST A RUMOR WE HEARD, BUT... IS IT TRUE THAT YOU TWO ARE RESEARCHERS FROM THE ACADEMY?
TP
THE ACADE-MY?
Ah?
AND...WAS YOUR FLYING MACHINE MADE AT THE ACADEMY, TOO?
WE HEARD THAT OUR LAST ASSIGNMENT WAS ACTUALLY A **DIVERSION**-- SET OFF THE NEWEST MAGICAL WEAPONS AND DRAW THE ENEMY'S ATTENTION.
VVRRRR
THAT'S NOT IT.
STOP
WE AREN'T ACADEMY RESEARCHERS.
I AM A LADY-IN-WAITING, IN DIRECT SERVICE OF HER ROYAL MAJESTY THE QUEEN.

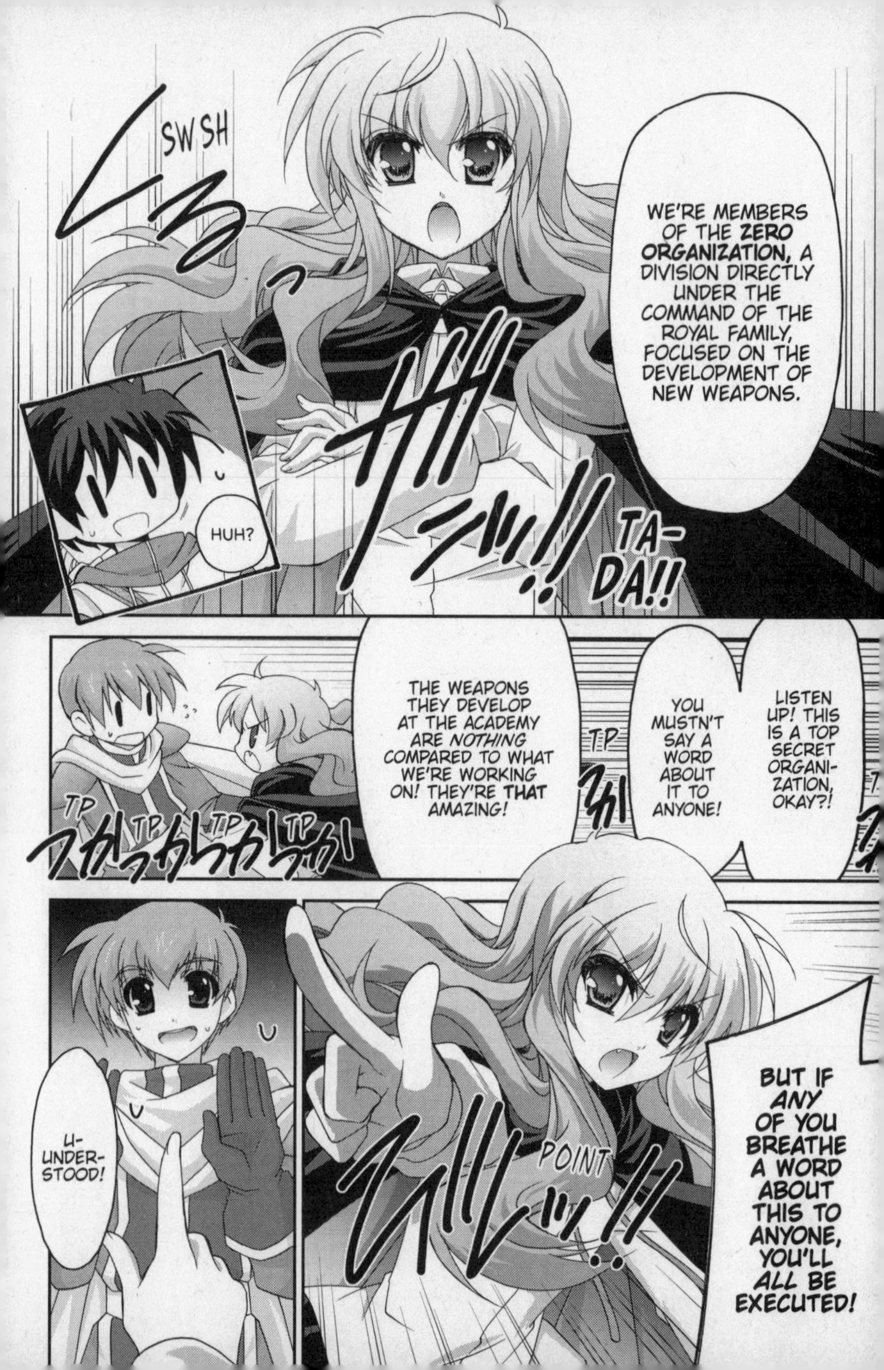
SWSH
WE'RE MEMBERS OF THE **ZERO ORGANIZATION,** A DIVISION DIRECTLY UNDER THE COMMAND OF THE ROYAL FAMILY, FOCUSED ON THE DEVELOPMENT OF NEW WEAPONS.
TA-DA!!
HUH?
LISTEN UP! THIS IS A TOP SECRET ORGANI-ZATION, OKAY?!
YOU MUSTN'T SAY A WORD ABOUT IT TO ANYONE!
TP
THE WEAPONS THEY DEVELOP AT THE ACADEMY ARE *NOTHING* COMPARED TO WHAT WE'RE WORKING ON! THEY'RE **THAT** AMAZING!
TP TP TP TP
BUT IF *ANY* OF YOU BREATHE A WORD ABOUT THIS TO ANYONE, YOU'LL *ALL* BE EXECUTED!
POINT
U-UNDER-STOOD!

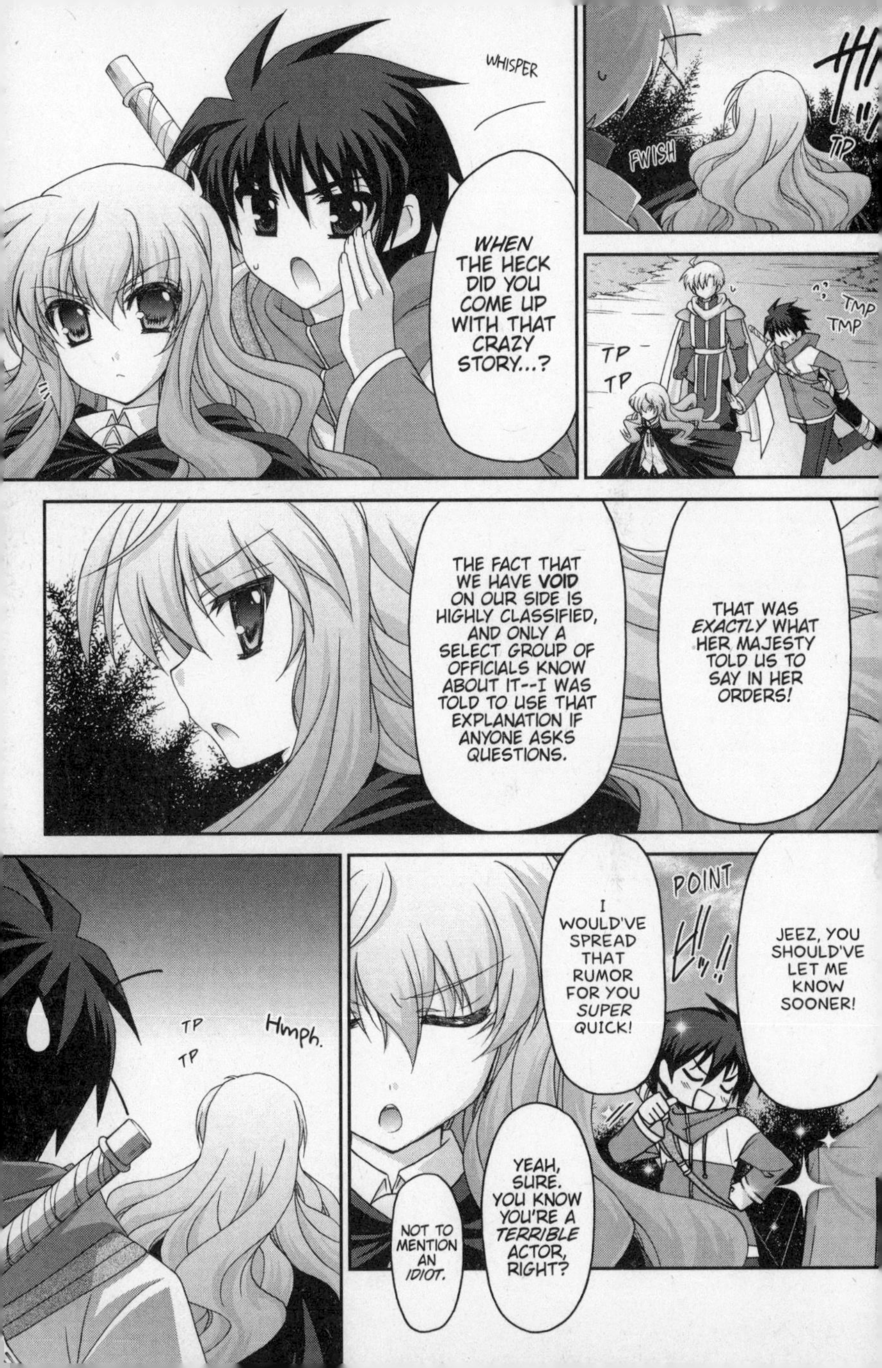
FWISH
TP
TMP
TMP
TP
TP
WHISPER
WHEN THE HECK DID YOU COME UP WITH THAT CRAZY STORY...?
THAT WAS *EXACTLY* WHAT HER MAJESTY TOLD US TO SAY IN HER ORDERS!
THE FACT THAT WE HAVE **VOID** ON OUR SIDE IS HIGHLY CLASSIFIED, AND ONLY A SELECT GROUP OF OFFICIALS KNOW ABOUT IT--I WAS TOLD TO USE THAT EXPLANATION IF ANYONE ASKS QUESTIONS.
JEEZ, YOU SHOULD'VE LET ME KNOW SOONER!
POINT
I WOULD'VE SPREAD THAT RUMOR FOR YOU *SUPER* QUICK!
YEAH, SURE. YOU KNOW YOU'RE A *TERRIBLE* ACTOR, RIGHT?
NOT TO MENTION AN *IDIOT*.
TP
TP
Hmph.

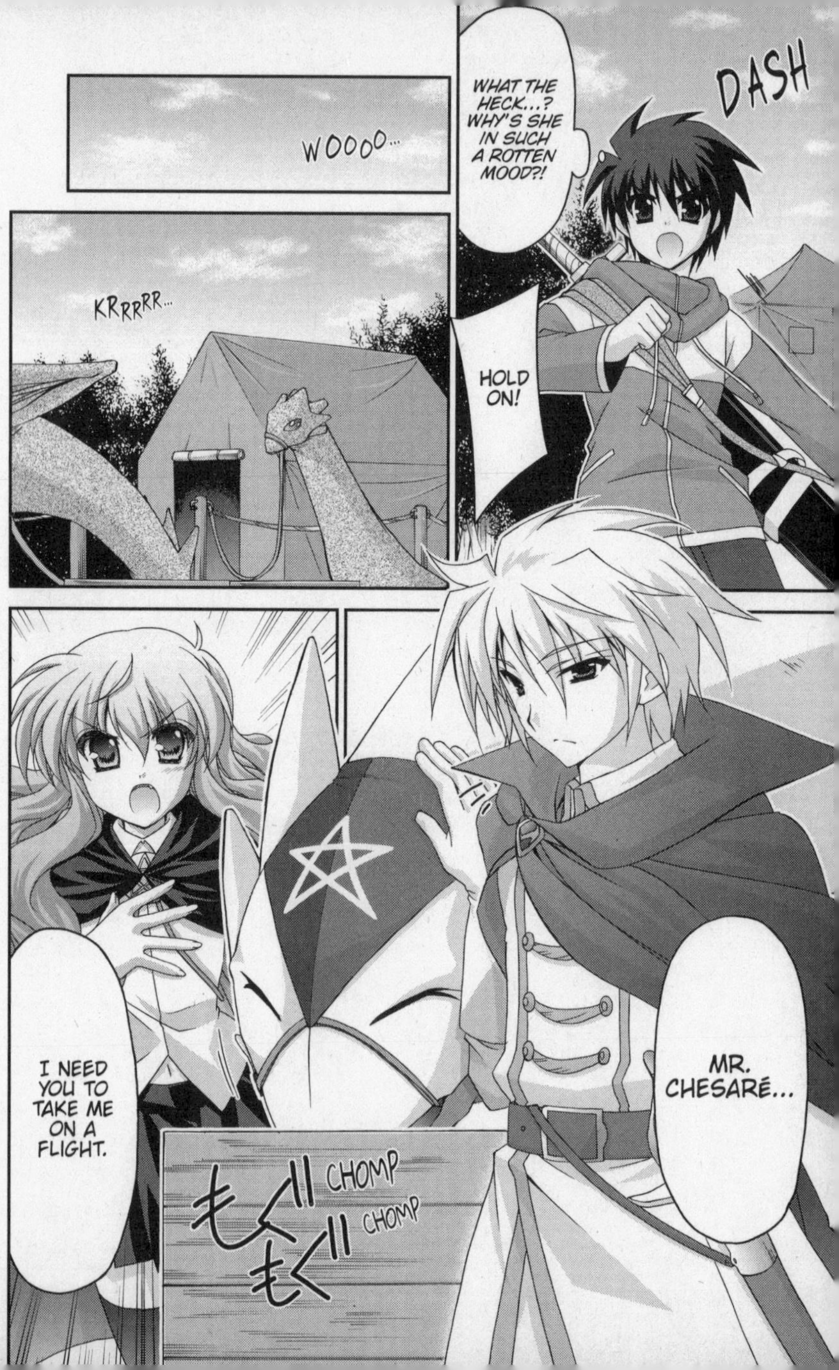
DASH
WHAT THE HECK...? WHY'S SHE IN SUCH A ROTTEN MOOD?!
HOLD ON!
WOOOO...
KRRRRR...
MR. CHESARÉ...
もぐもぐ CHOMP CHOMP
I NEED YOU TO TAKE ME ON A FLIGHT.

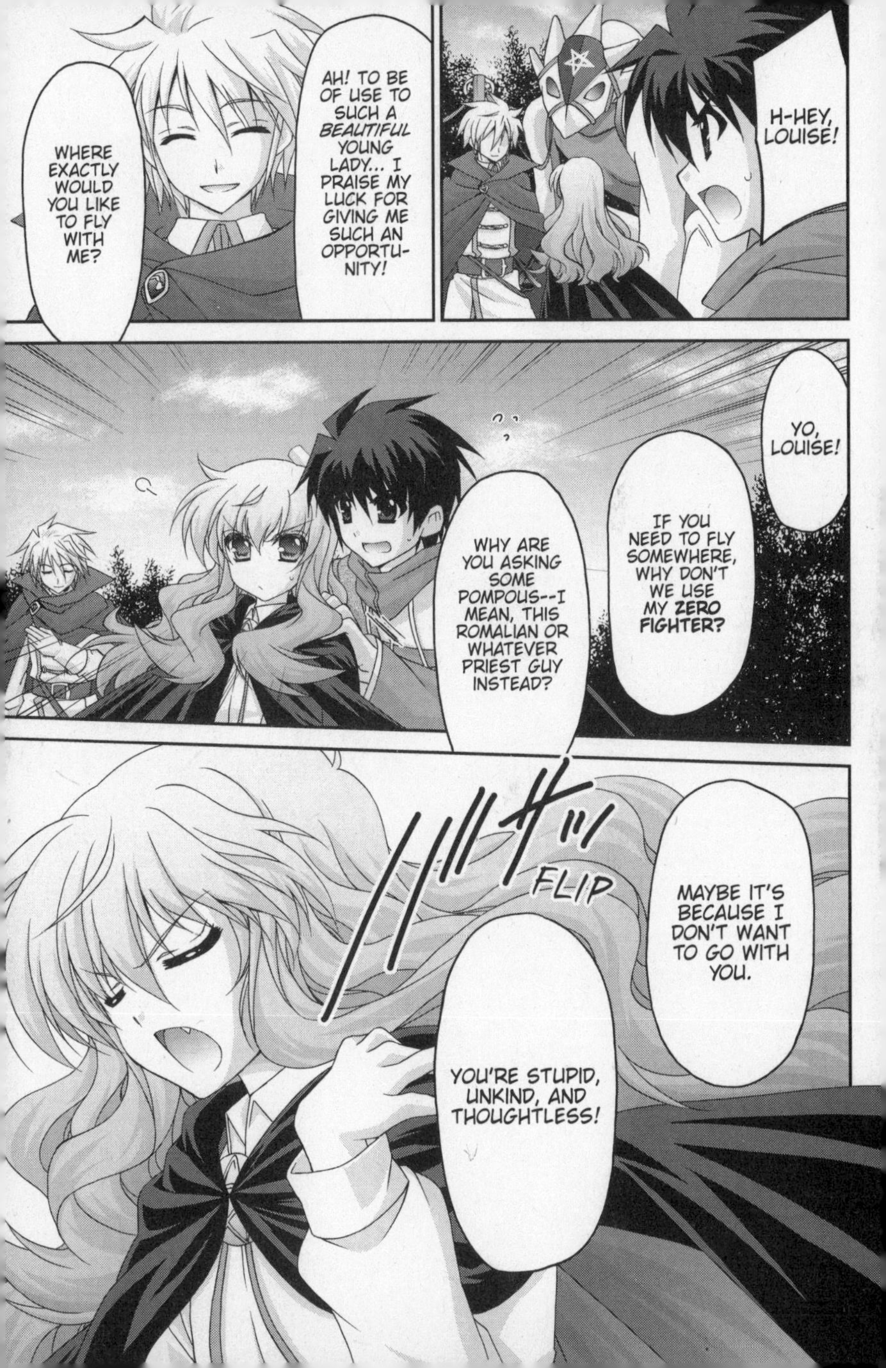
H-HEY, LOUISE!
AH! TO BE OF USE TO SUCH A *BEAUTIFUL* YOUNG LADY... I PRAISE MY LUCK FOR GIVING ME SUCH AN OPPORTU-NITY!
WHERE EXACTLY WOULD YOU LIKE TO FLY WITH ME?
YO, LOUISE!
IF YOU NEED TO FLY SOMEWHERE, WHY DON'T WE USE MY **ZERO FIGHTER**?
WHY ARE YOU ASKING SOME POMPOUS--I MEAN, THIS ROMALIAN OR WHATEVER PRIEST GUY INSTEAD?
FLIP
MAYBE IT'S BECAUSE I DON'T WANT TO GO WITH YOU.
YOU'RE STUPID, UNKIND, AND THOUGHTLESS!

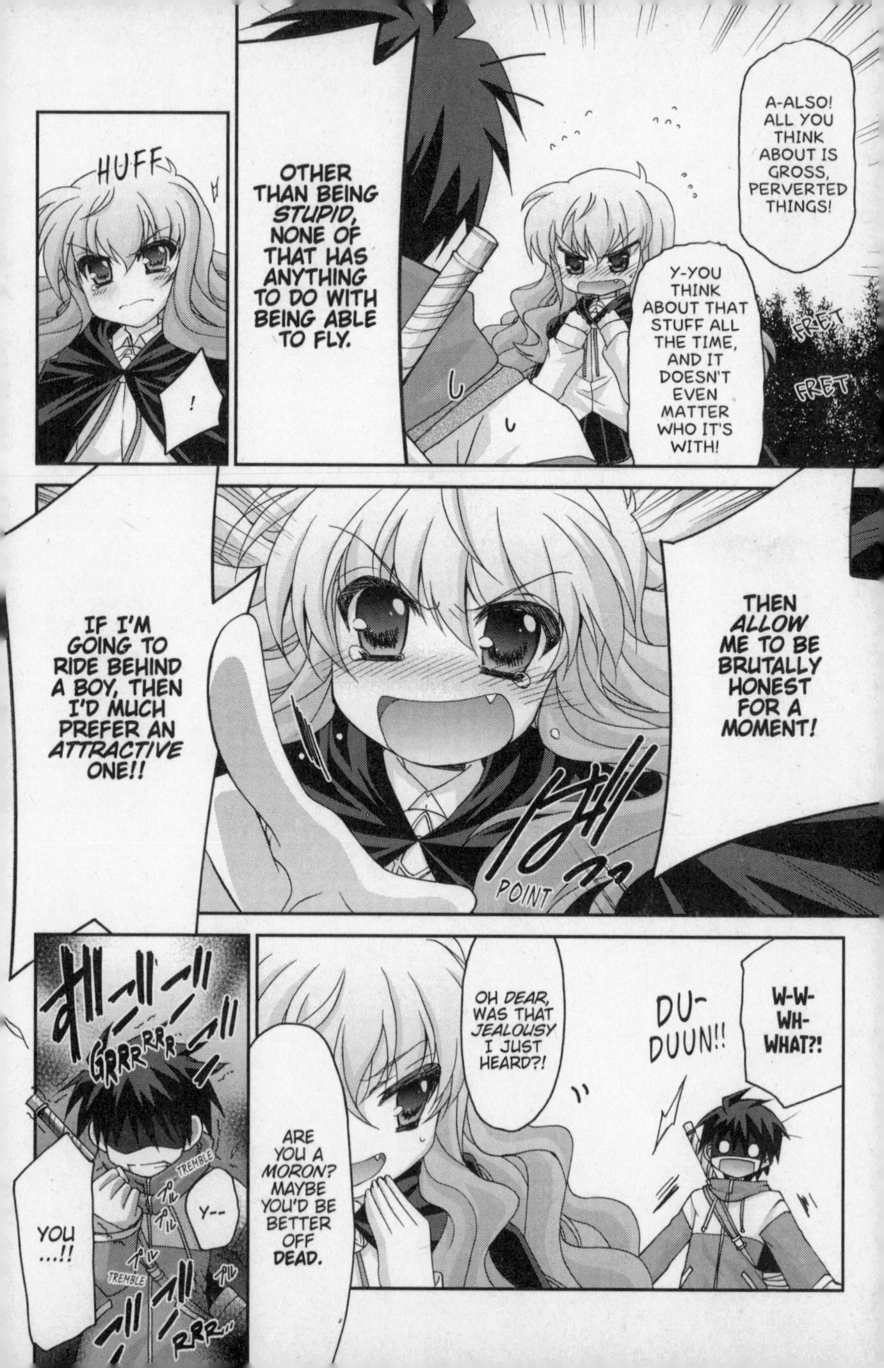
A-ALSO! ALL YOU THINK ABOUT IS GROSS, PERVERTED THINGS!
Y-YOU THINK ABOUT THAT STUFF ALL THE TIME, AND IT DOESN'T EVEN MATTER WHO IT'S WITH!
FRET
FRET
OTHER THAN BEING *STUPID*, NONE OF THAT HAS ANYTHING TO DO WITH BEING ABLE TO FLY.
HUFF
!
THEN *ALLOW* ME TO BE BRUTALLY HONEST FOR A MOMENT!
IF I'M GOING TO RIDE BEHIND A BOY, THEN I'D MUCH PREFER AN *ATTRACTIVE* ONE!!
POINT
W-W-WH-WHAT?!
DU-DUUN!!
OH DEAR, WAS THAT *JEALOUSY* I JUST HEARD?!
ARE YOU A *MORON*? MAYBE YOU'D BE BETTER OFF DEAD.
GRRRRRR
TREMBLE
Y--
YOU ...!!
TREMBLE
RRR...

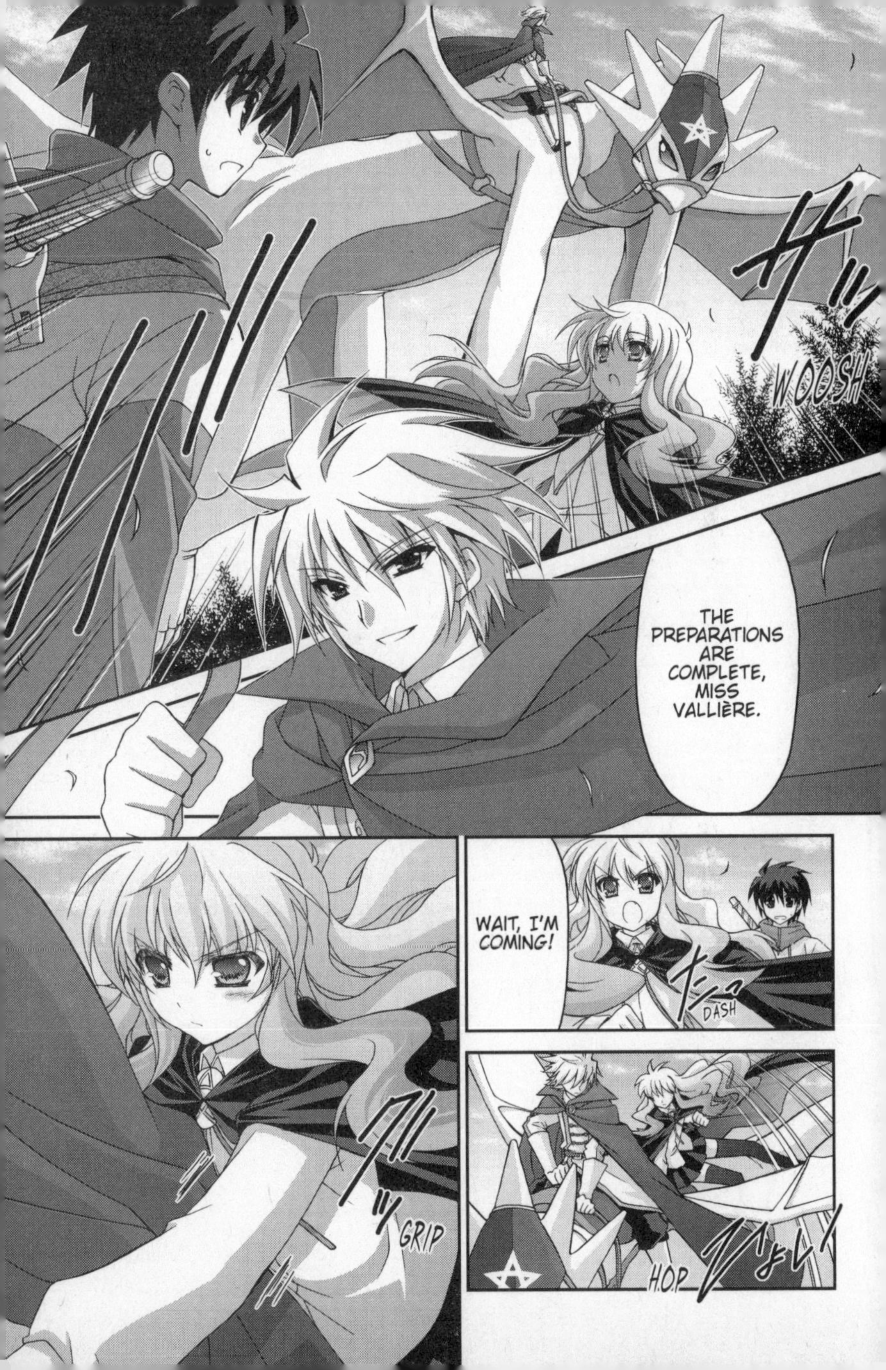
WOOSH
THE PREPARATIONS ARE COMPLETE, MISS VALLIÈRE.
WAIT, I'M COMING!
DASH
H.O.P
GRIP

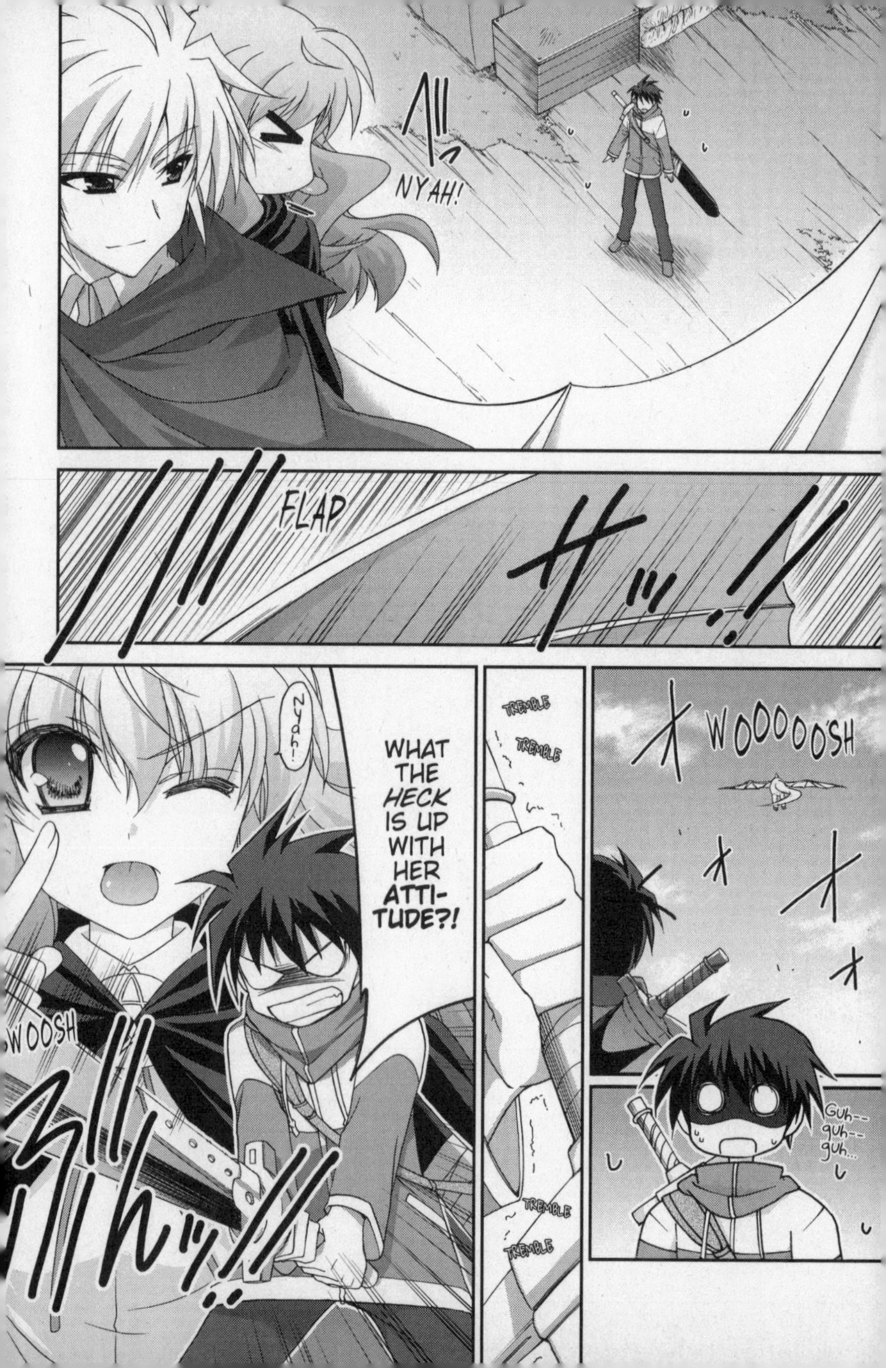
NYAH!
FLAP
サッ!!
WOOOOOSH
Guh--guh--guh...
TREMBLE
TREMBLE
TREMBLE
TREMBLE
WHAT THE HECK IS UP WITH HER ATTI-TUDE?!
Nyah!
WOOSH

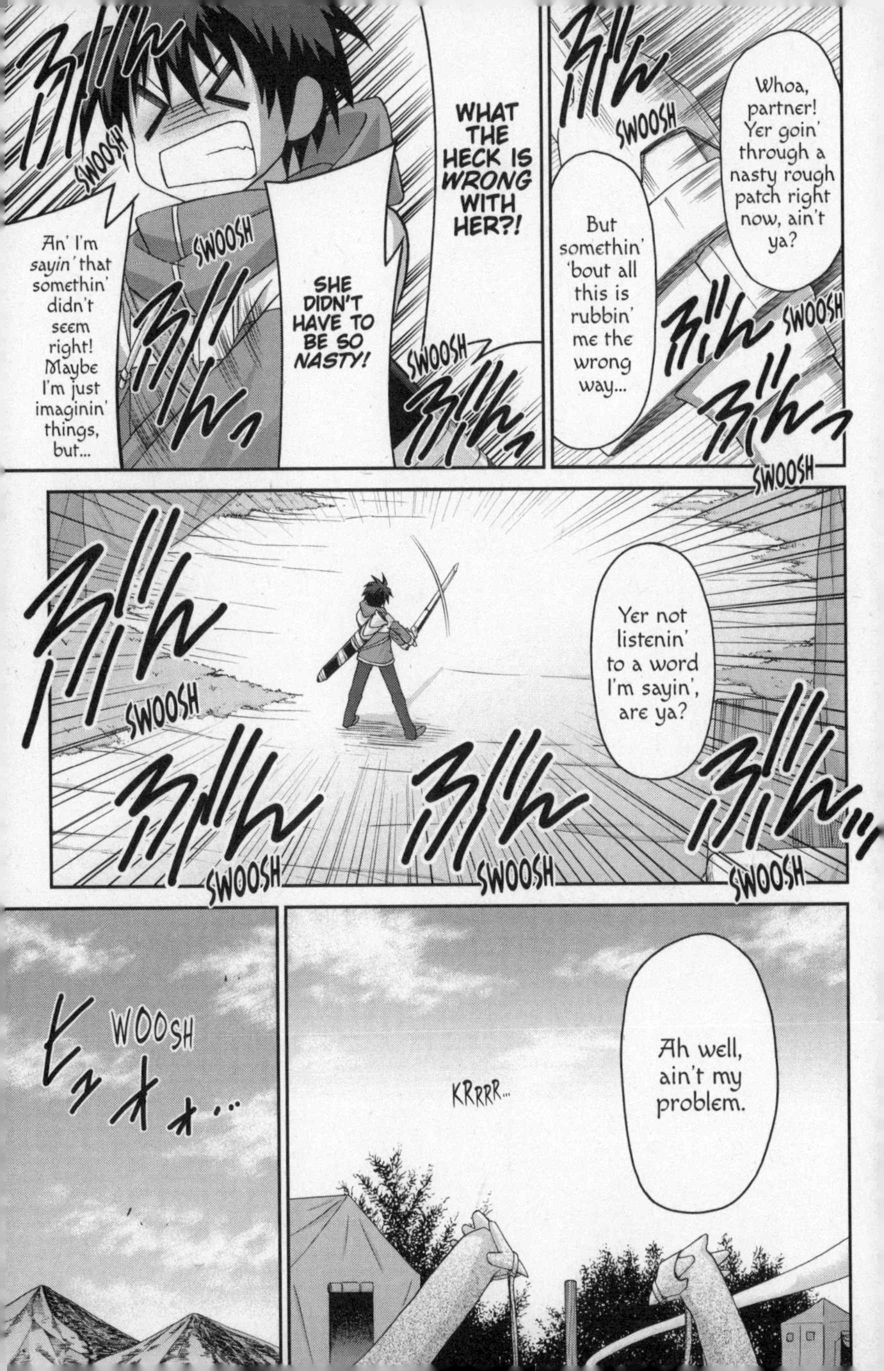

SWOOSH
Whoa, partner! Yer goin' through a nasty rough patch right now, ain't ya?
But somethin' 'bout all this is rubbin' me the wrong way...
SWOOSH
SWOOSH
WHAT THE HECK IS WRONG WITH HER?!
SHE DIDN'T HAVE TO BE SO NASTY!
SWOOSH
SWOOSH
SWOOSH
An' I'm sayin' that somethin' didn't seem right! Maybe I'm just imaginin' things, but...
Yer not listenin' to a word I'm sayin', are ya?
SWOOSH
SWOOSH
SWOOSH
SWOOSH
Ah well, ain't my problem.
KRRRR...
WOOSH
ヒュオォ…

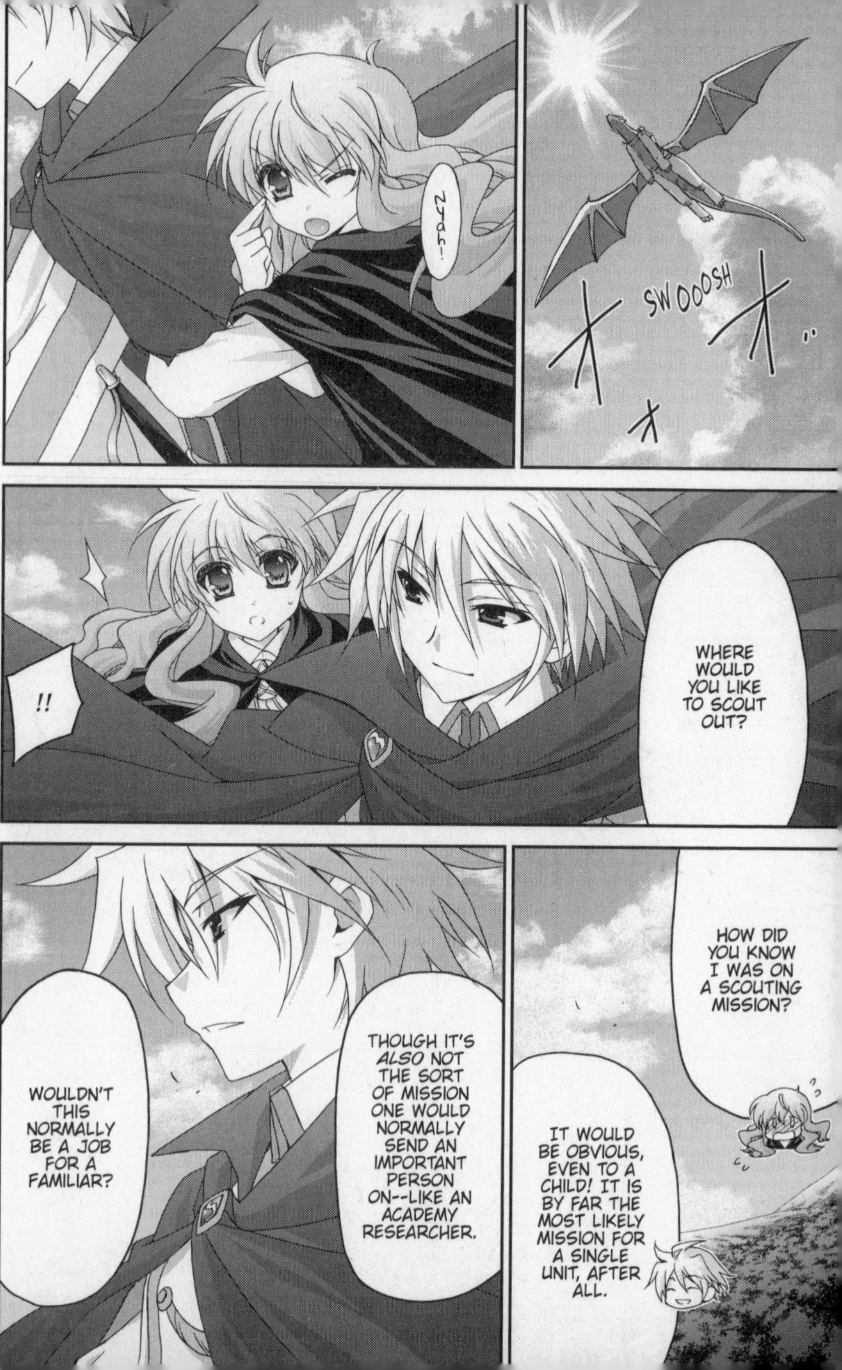
SWOOOSH
Nyah!
WHERE WOULD YOU LIKE TO SCOUT OUT?
!!
HOW DID YOU KNOW I WAS ON A SCOUTING MISSION?
IT WOULD BE OBVIOUS, EVEN TO A CHILD! IT IS BY FAR THE MOST LIKELY MISSION FOR A SINGLE UNIT, AFTER ALL.
THOUGH IT'S *ALSO* NOT THE SORT OF MISSION ONE WOULD NORMALLY SEND AN IMPORTANT PERSON ON--LIKE AN ACADEMY RESEARCHER.
WOULDN'T THIS NORMALLY BE A JOB FOR A FAMILIAR?

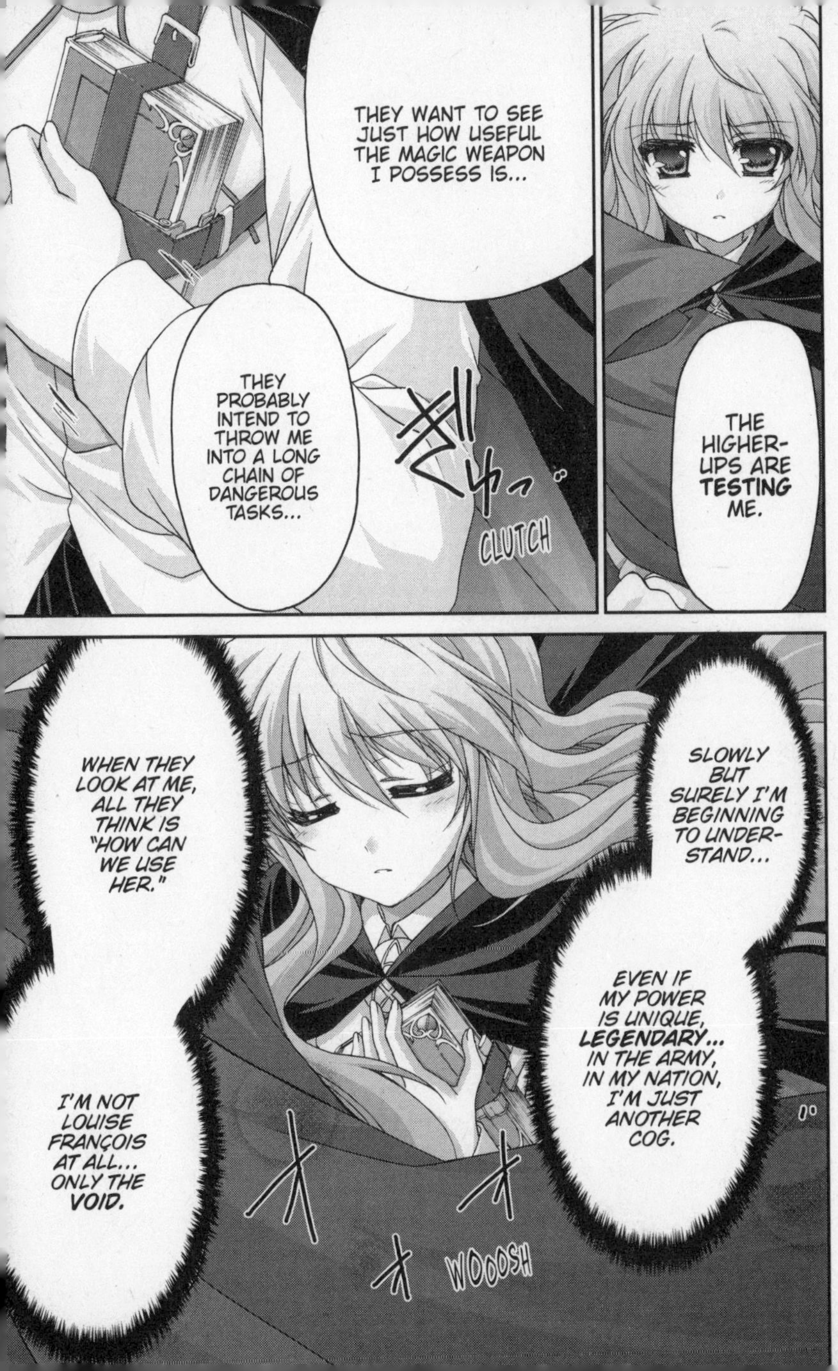
THE HIGHER-UPS ARE TESTING ME.
THEY WANT TO SEE JUST HOW USEFUL THE MAGIC WEAPON I POSSESS IS...
THEY PROBABLY INTEND TO THROW ME INTO A LONG CHAIN OF DANGEROUS TASKS...
CLUTCH
SLOWLY BUT SURELY I'M BEGINNING TO UNDER-STAND...
WHEN THEY LOOK AT ME, ALL THEY THINK IS "HOW CAN WE USE HER."
EVEN IF MY POWER IS UNIQUE, LEGENDARY... IN THE ARMY, IN MY NATION, I'M JUST ANOTHER COG.
I'M NOT LOUISE FRANÇOIS AT ALL... ONLY THE VOID.
WOOOSH

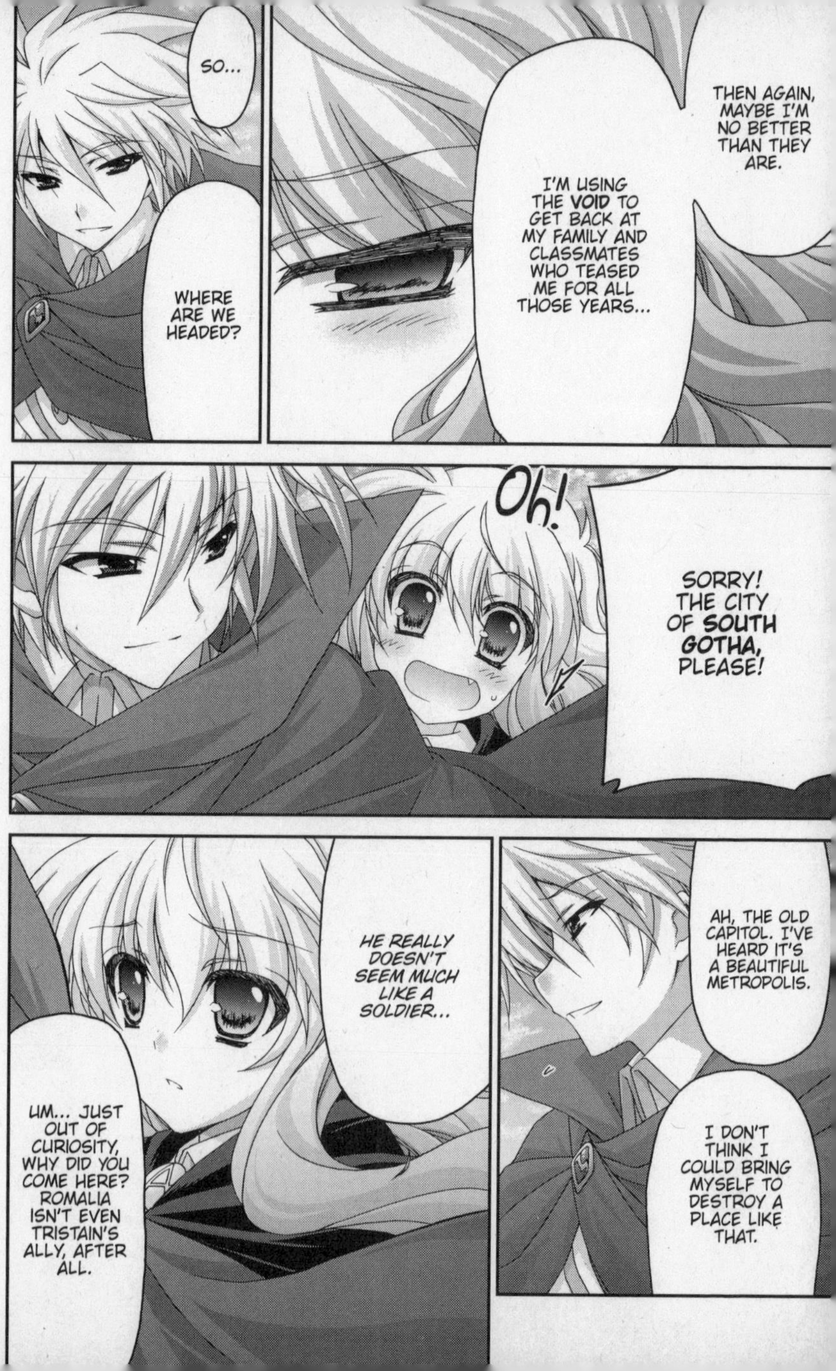
THEN AGAIN, MAYBE I'M NO BETTER THAN THEY ARE.
I'M USING THE **VOID** TO GET BACK AT MY FAMILY AND CLASSMATES WHO TEASED ME FOR ALL THOSE YEARS...
SO...
WHERE ARE WE HEADED?
Oh!
SORRY! THE CITY OF **SOUTH GOTHA,** PLEASE!
AH, THE OLD CAPITOL. I'VE HEARD IT'S A BEAUTIFUL METROPOLIS.
I DON'T THINK I COULD BRING MYSELF TO DESTROY A PLACE LIKE THAT.
HE REALLY DOESN'T SEEM MUCH LIKE A SOLDIER...
UM... JUST OUT OF CURIOSITY, WHY DID YOU COME HERE? ROMALIA ISN'T EVEN TRISTAIN'S ALLY, AFTER ALL.

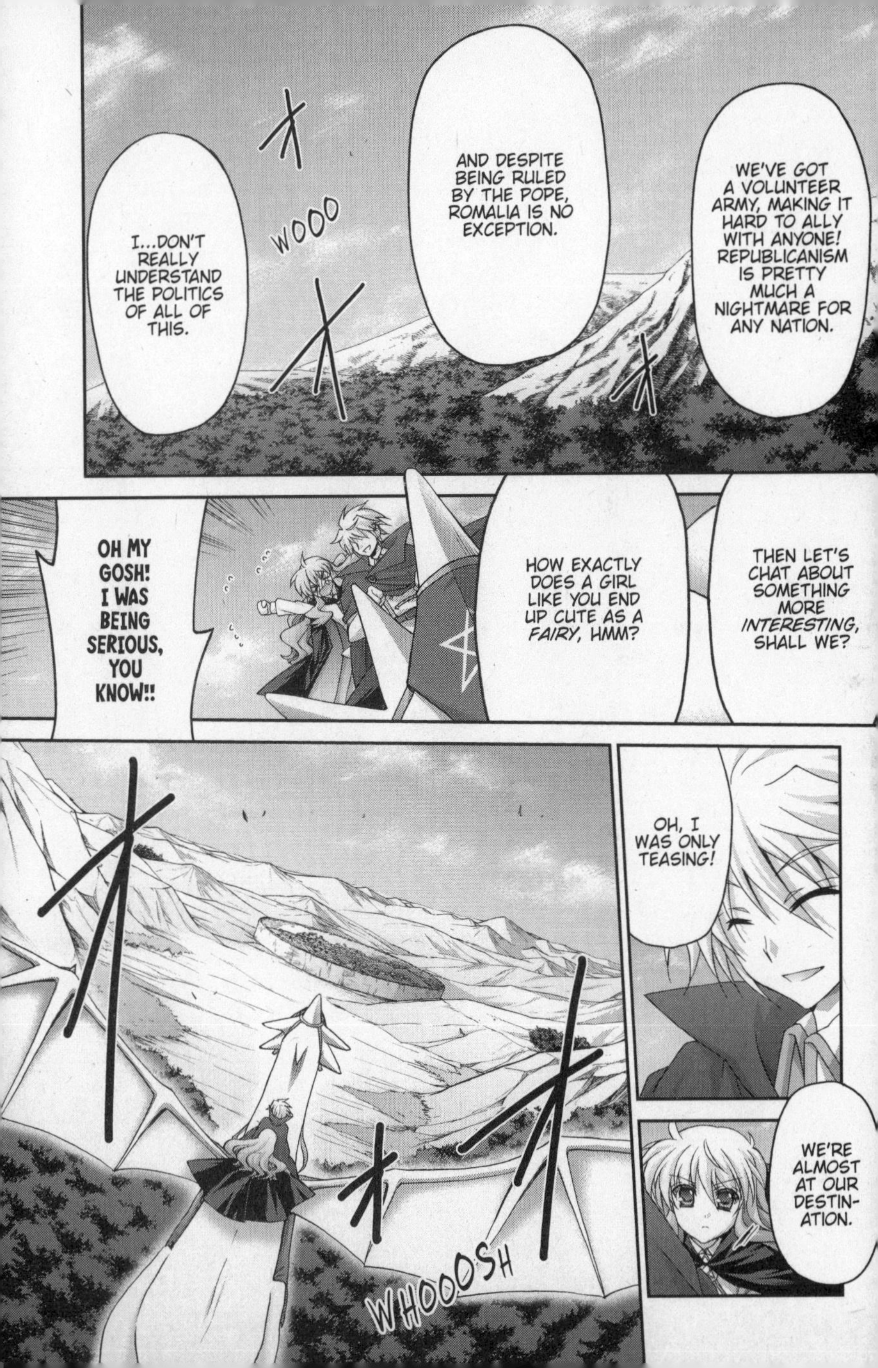
WE'VE GOT A VOLUNTEER ARMY, MAKING IT HARD TO ALLY WITH ANYONE! REPUBLICANISM IS PRETTY MUCH A NIGHTMARE FOR ANY NATION.
AND DESPITE BEING RULED BY THE POPE, ROMALIA IS NO EXCEPTION.
WOOO
I...DON'T REALLY UNDERSTAND THE POLITICS OF ALL OF THIS.
THEN LET'S CHAT ABOUT SOMETHING MORE *INTERESTING*, SHALL WE?
HOW EXACTLY DOES A GIRL LIKE YOU END UP CUTE AS A *FAIRY*, HMM?
OH MY GOSH! I WAS BEING SERIOUS, YOU KNOW!!
OH, I WAS ONLY TEASING!
WE'RE ALMOST AT OUR DESTIN-ATION.
WHOOOSH

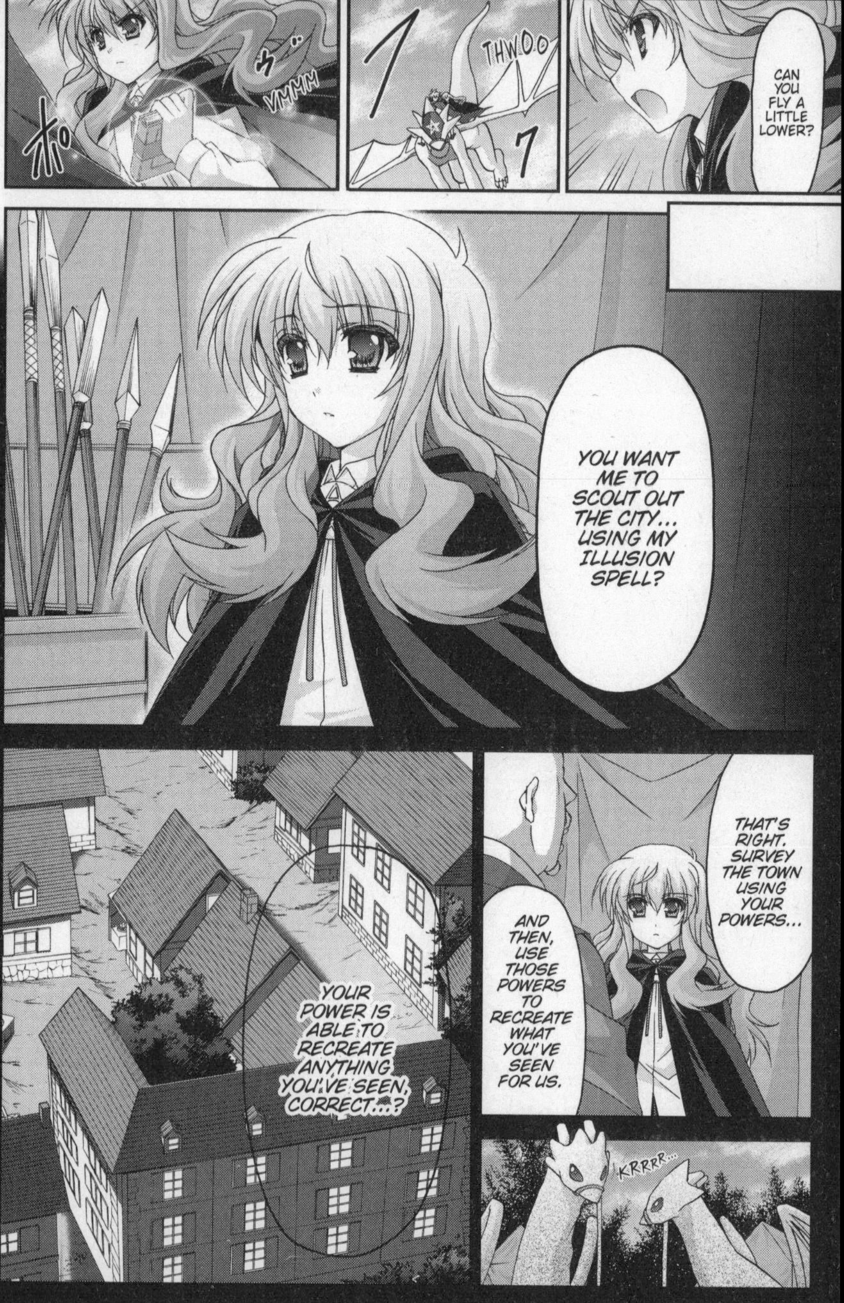
CAN YOU FLY A LITTLE LOWER?
THWOOO
VMMM
YOU WANT ME TO SCOUT OUT THE CITY... USING MY ILLUSION SPELL?
THAT'S RIGHT. SURVEY THE TOWN USING YOUR POWERS...
AND THEN, USE THOSE POWERS TO RECREATE WHAT YOU'VE SEEN FOR US.
KRRRR...
YOUR POWER IS ABLE TO RECREATE ANYTHING YOU'VE SEEN, CORRECT...?

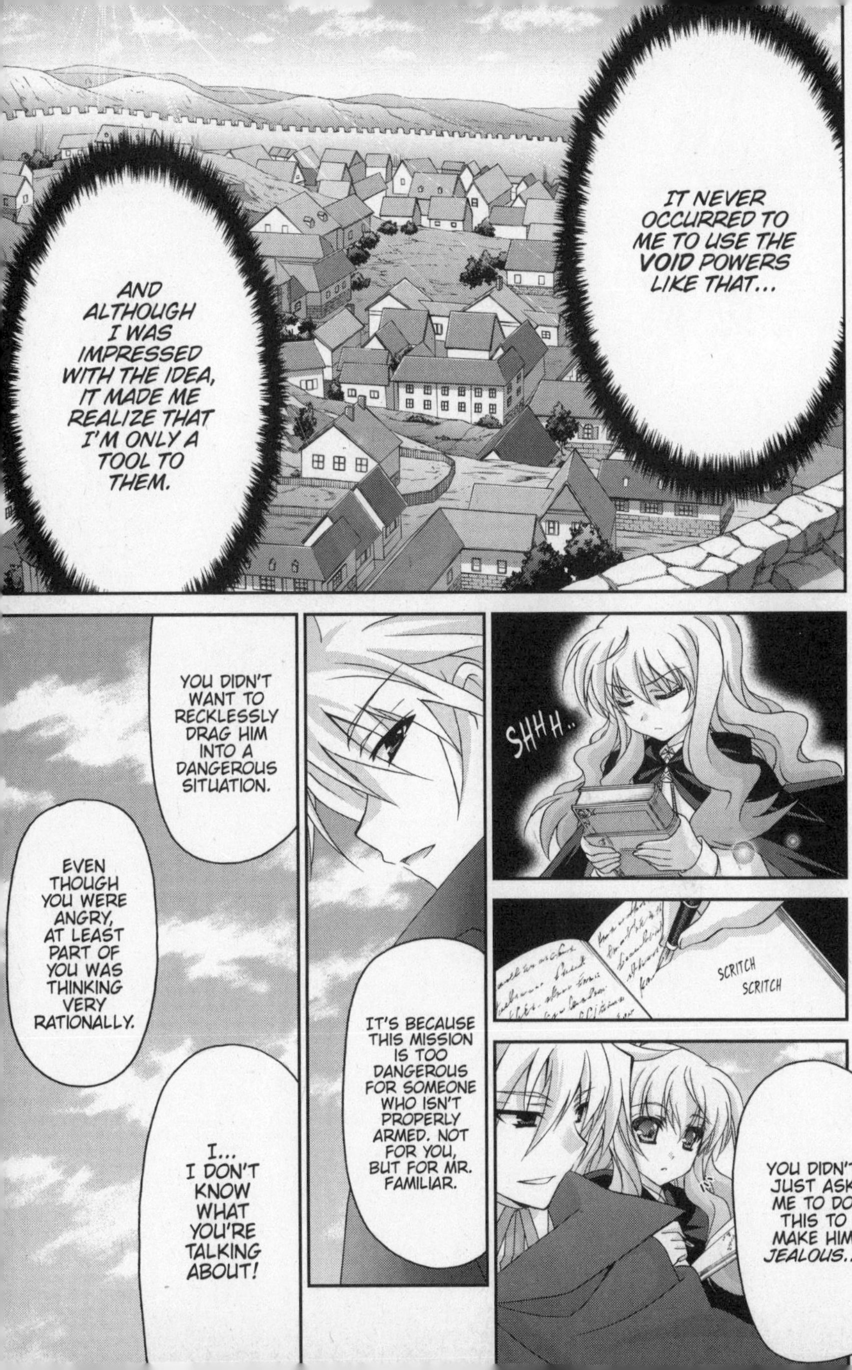
IT NEVER OCCURRED TO ME TO USE THE VOID POWERS LIKE THAT...
AND ALTHOUGH I WAS IMPRESSED WITH THE IDEA, IT MADE ME REALIZE THAT I'M ONLY A TOOL TO THEM.
SHHH..
SCRITCH SCRITCH
YOU DIDN'T JUST ASK ME TO DO THIS TO MAKE HIM JEALOUS...
IT'S BECAUSE THIS MISSION IS TOO DANGEROUS FOR SOMEONE WHO ISN'T PROPERLY ARMED. NOT FOR YOU, BUT FOR MR. FAMILIAR.
YOU DIDN'T WANT TO RECKLESSLY DRAG HIM INTO A DANGEROUS SITUATION.
EVEN THOUGH YOU WERE ANGRY, AT LEAST PART OF YOU WAS THINKING VERY RATIONALLY.
I... I DON'T KNOW WHAT YOU'RE TALKING ABOUT!

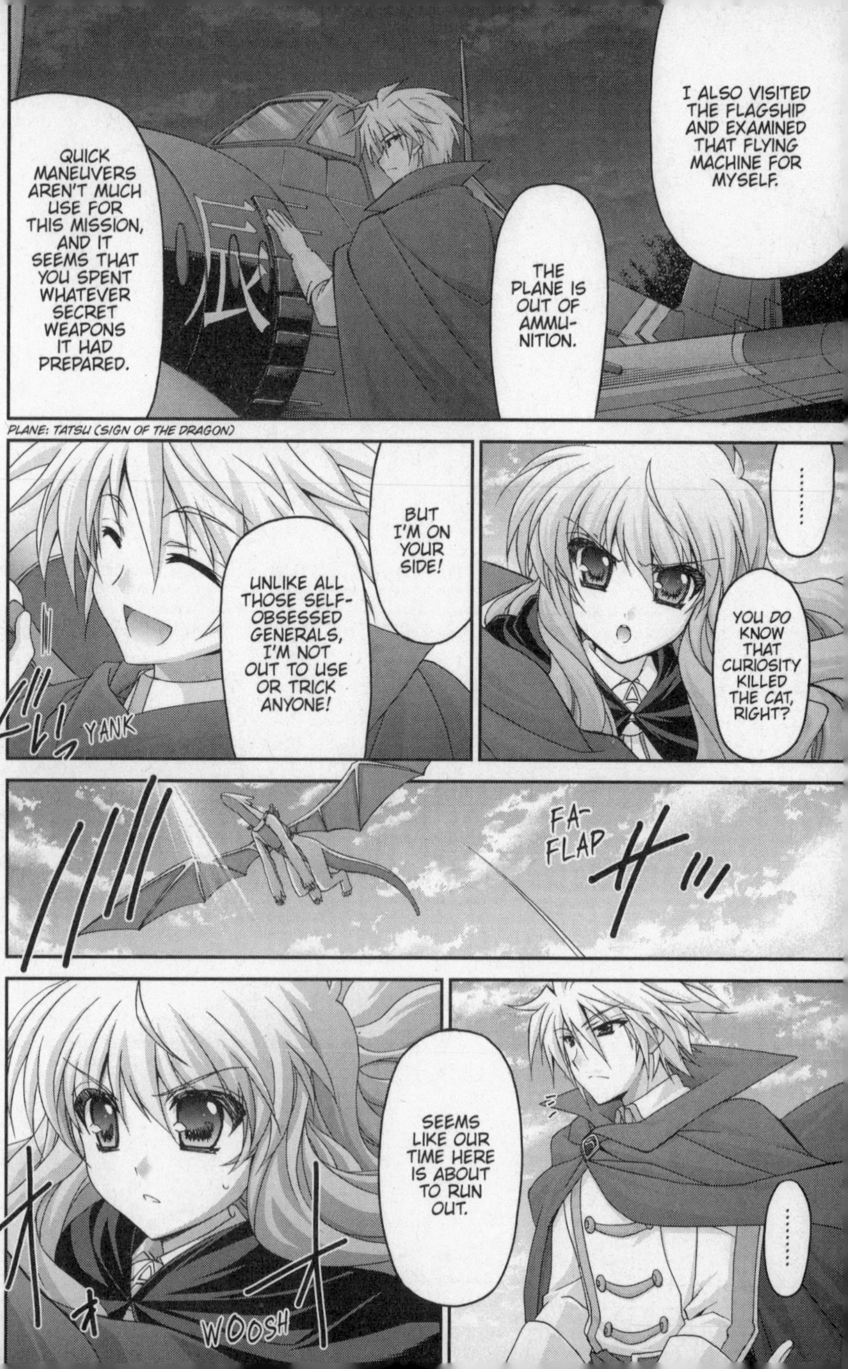
I ALSO VISITED THE FLAGSHIP AND EXAMINED THAT FLYING MACHINE FOR MYSELF.
THE PLANE IS OUT OF AMMUNITION.
QUICK MANEUVERS AREN'T MUCH USE FOR THIS MISSION, AND IT SEEMS THAT YOU SPENT WHATEVER SECRET WEAPONS IT HAD PREPARED.
PLANE: TATSU (SIGN OF THE DRAGON)
......
YOU *DO* KNOW THAT CURIOSITY KILLED THE CAT, RIGHT?
BUT I'M ON YOUR SIDE!
UNLIKE ALL THOSE SELF-OBSESSED GENERALS, I'M NOT OUT TO USE OR TRICK ANYONE!
YANK
FA-FLAP
......
SEEMS LIKE OUR TIME HERE IS ABOUT TO RUN OUT.
WOOSH

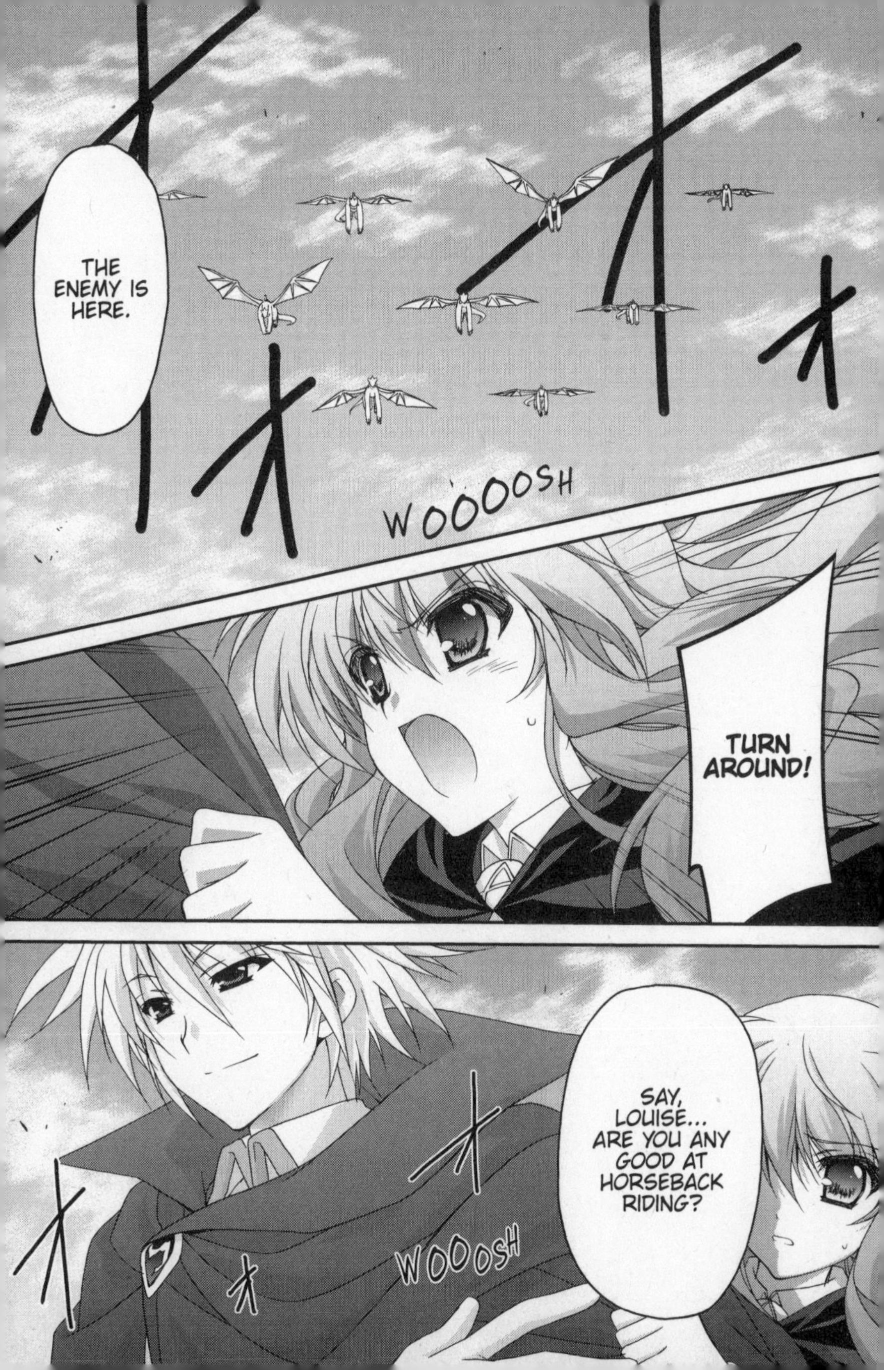
THE ENEMY IS HERE.
WOOOOSH
TURN AROUND!
SAY, LOUISE... ARE YOU ANY GOOD AT HORSEBACK RIDING?
WOOOSH

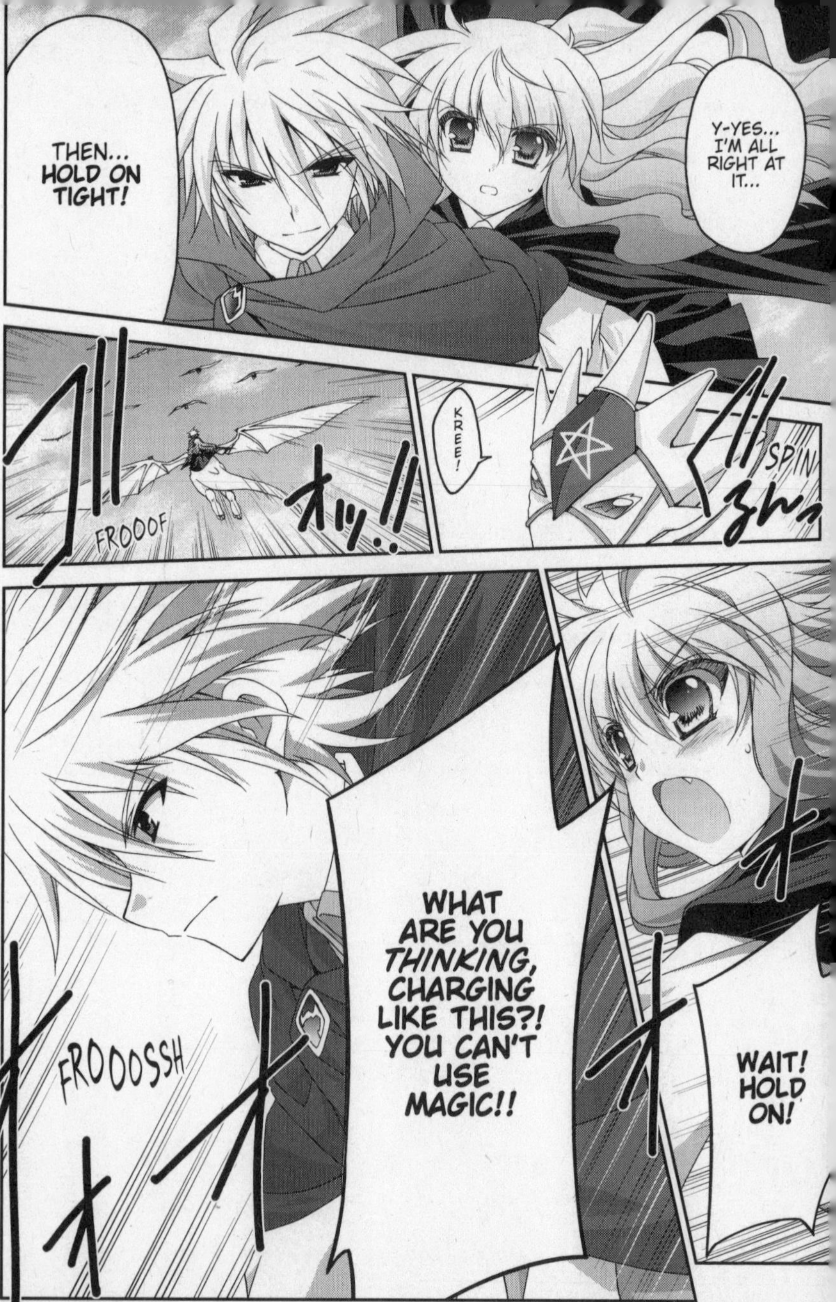
Y-YES... I'M ALL RIGHT AT IT...
THEN... HOLD ON TIGHT!
SPIN
KREE!
オッ!!
FROOOF
WAIT! HOLD ON!
WHAT ARE YOU *THINKING*, CHARGING LIKE THIS?! YOU CAN'T USE MAGIC!!
FROOOSSH

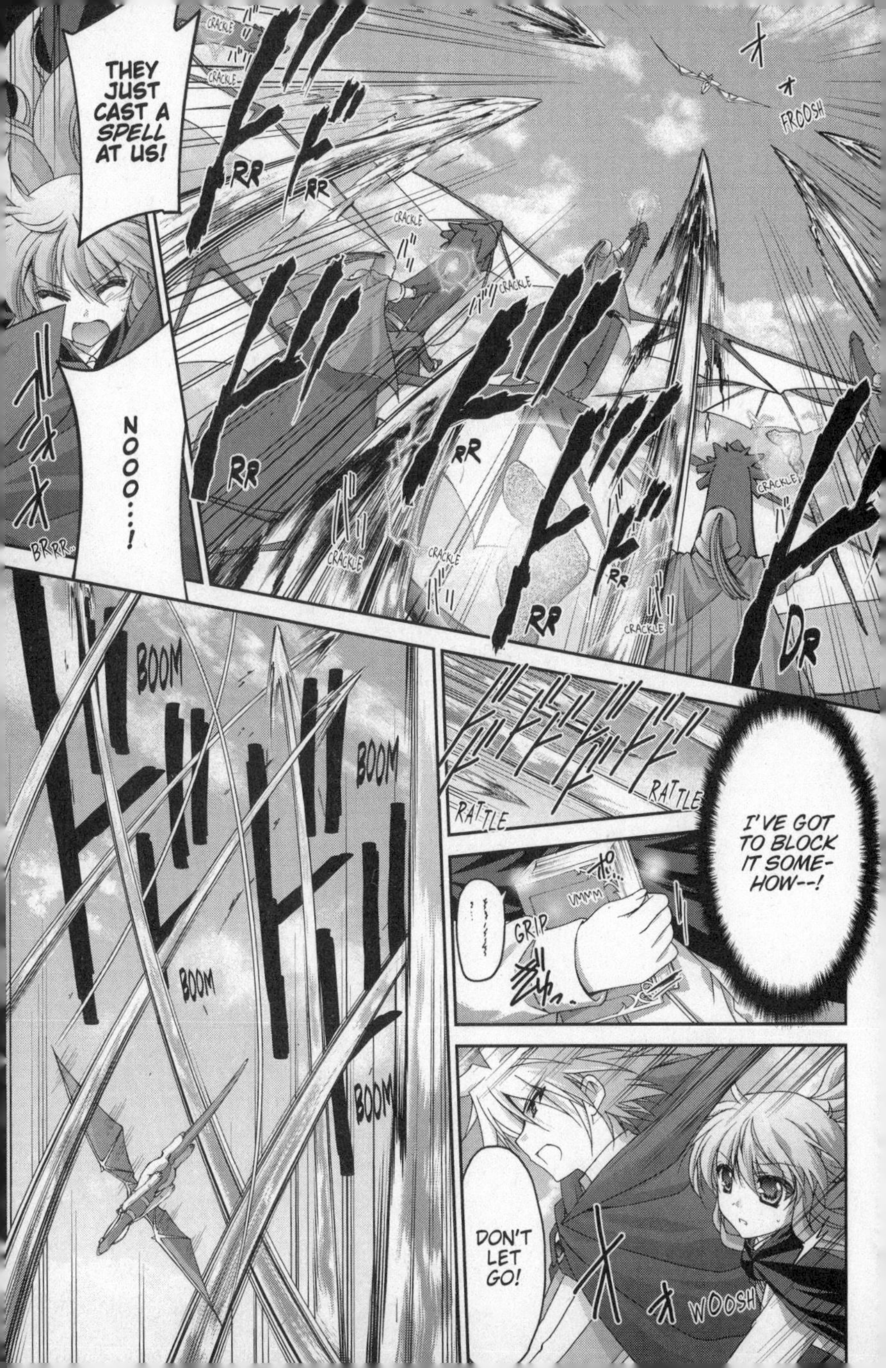
FROOSH
CRACKLE
CRACKLE
RR
RR
CRACKLE
CRACKLE
CRACKLE
DR
RR
RR
CRACKLE
CRACKLE
RR
RR
THEY JUST CAST A SPELL AT US!
NOOO...!
BRRR..
RATTLE
RATTLE
I'VE GOT TO BLOCK IT SOMEHOW--!
VMMM
GRIP
DON'T LET GO!
WOOSH
BOOM
BOOM
BOOM
BOOM

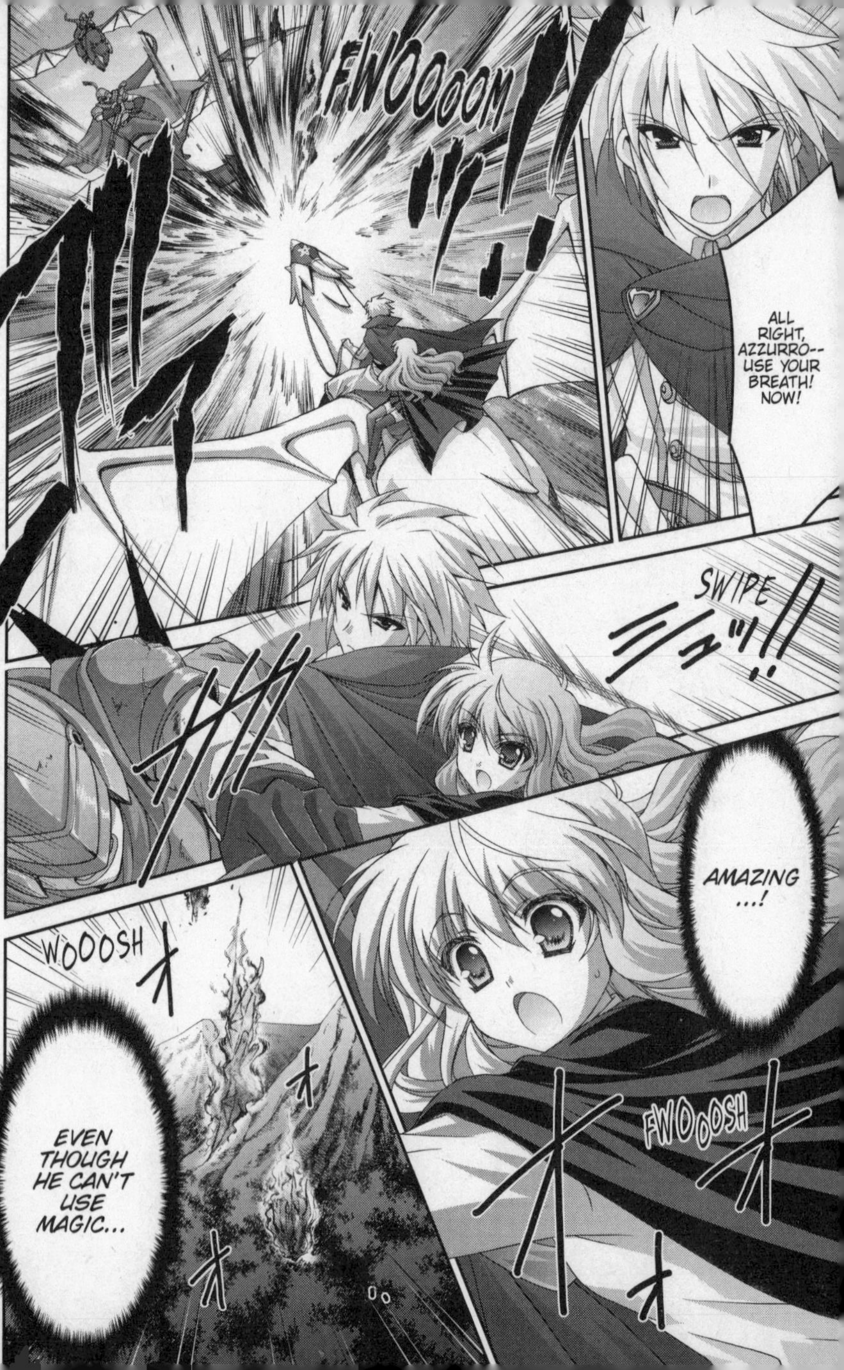
ALL RIGHT, AZZURRO-- USE YOUR BREATH! NOW!
FWOOOOM
SWIPE
AMAZING ...!
FWOOOSH
WOOOSH
EVEN THOUGH HE CAN'T USE MAGIC...

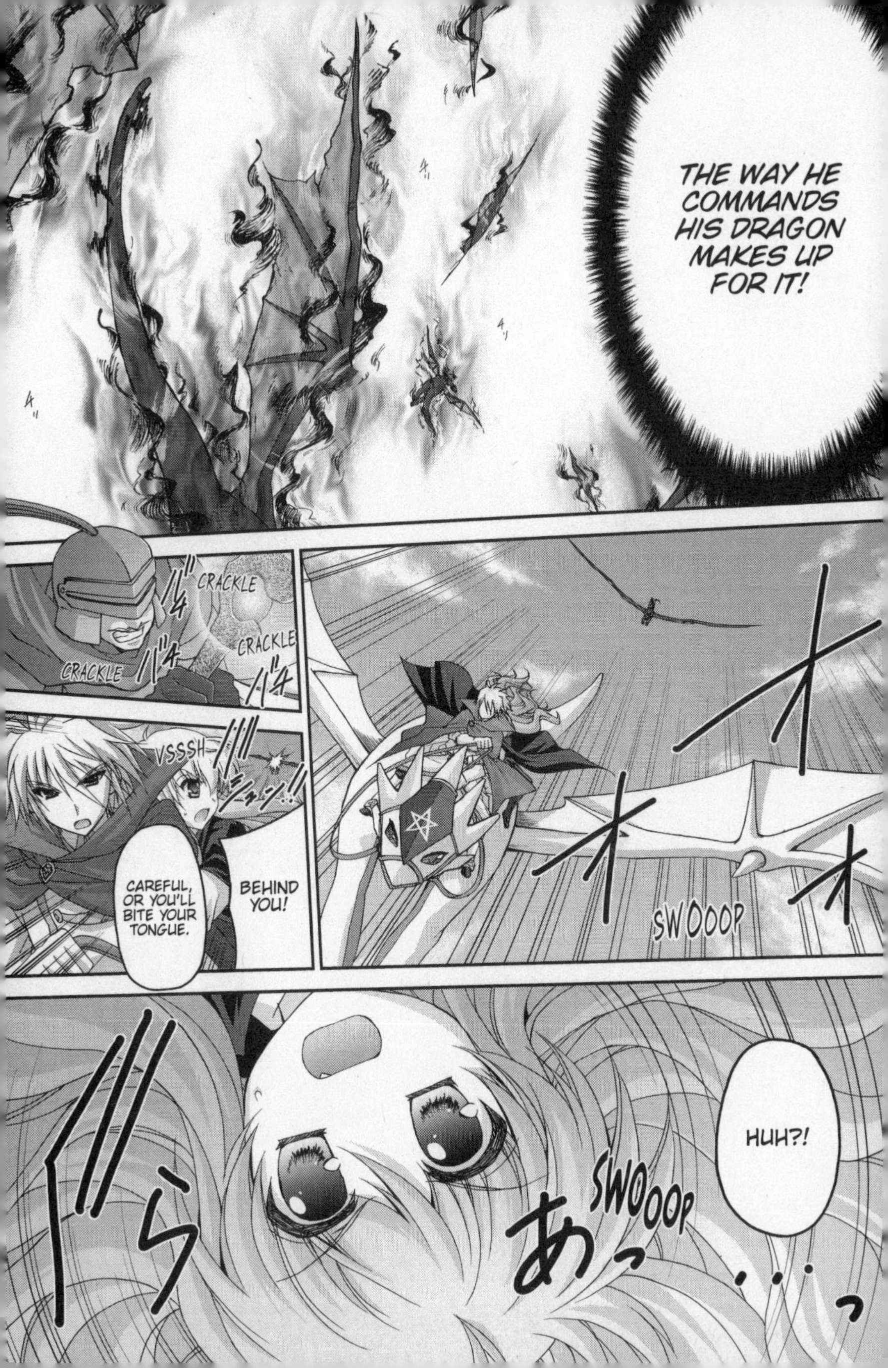
THE WAY HE COMMANDS HIS DRAGON MAKES UP FOR IT!
SWOOOP
CRACKLE
CRACKLE
CRACKLE
VSSSH
BEHIND YOU!
CAREFUL, OR YOU'LL BITE YOUR TONGUE.
HUH?!
SWOOOP

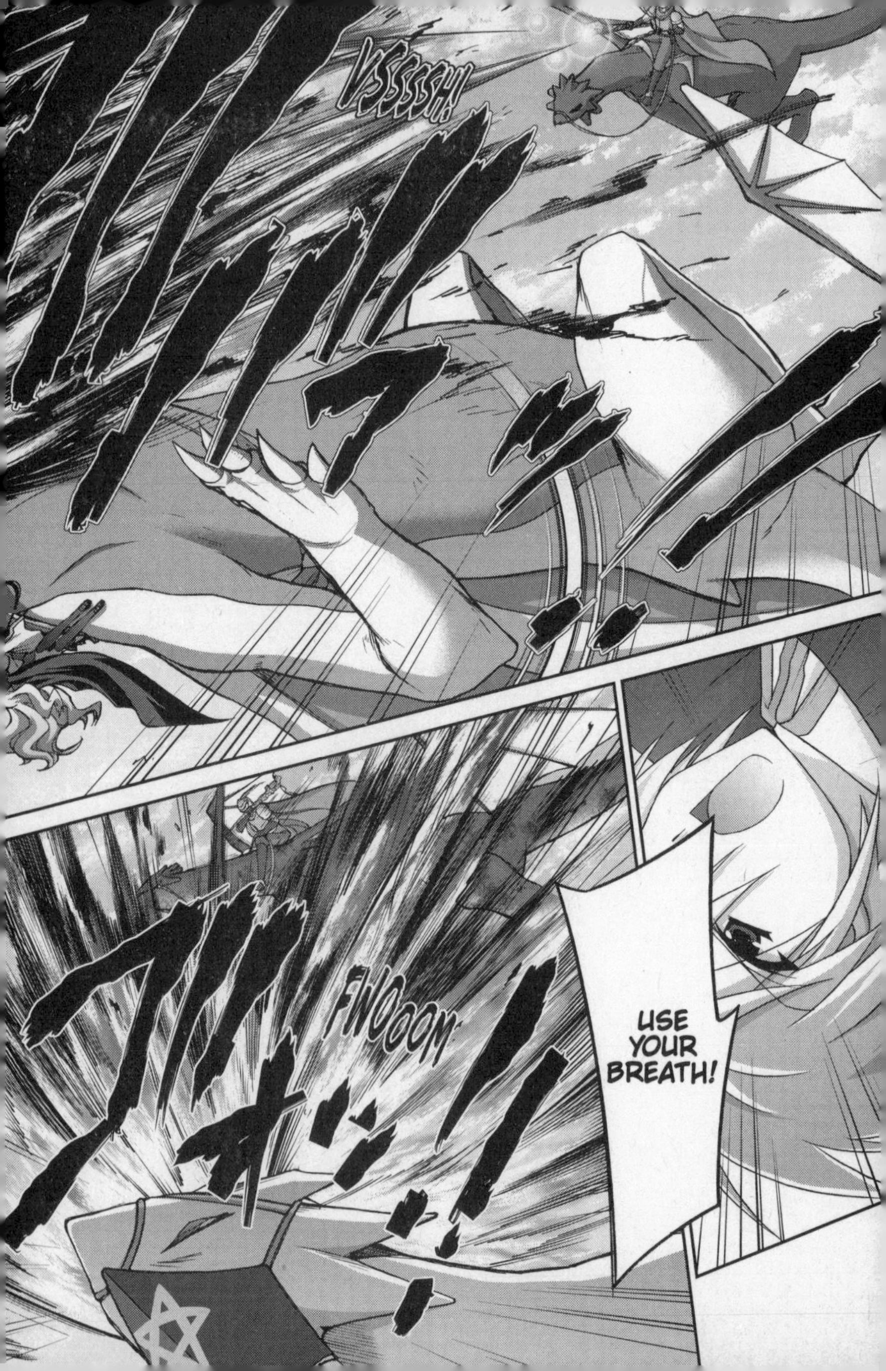
VSSSSSH!
USE YOUR BREATH!
FWOOOM

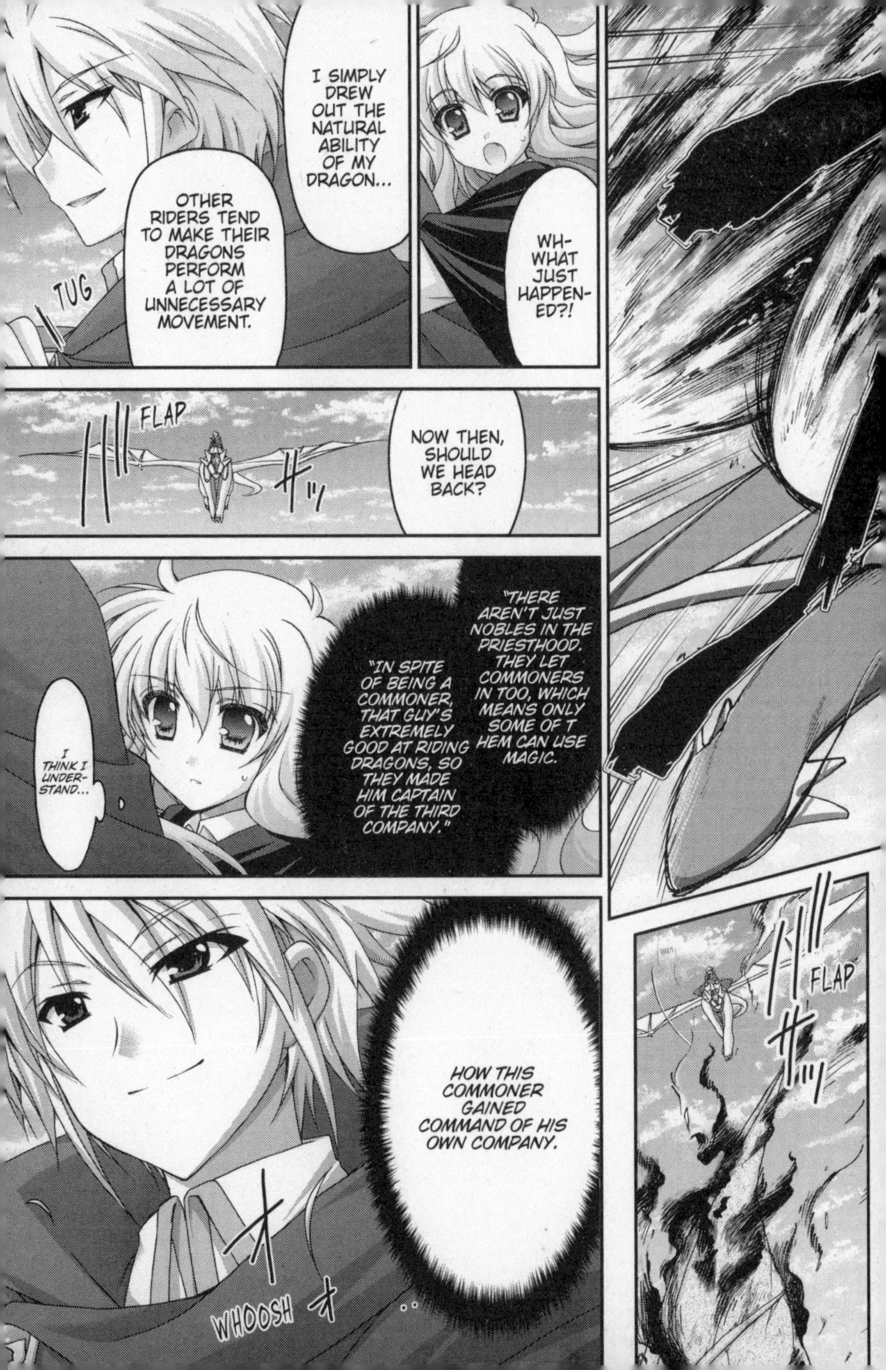
WH-WHAT JUST HAPPEN-ED?!
I SIMPLY DREW OUT THE NATURAL ABILITY OF MY DRAGON...
OTHER RIDERS TEND TO MAKE THEIR DRAGONS PERFORM A LOT OF UNNECESSARY MOVEMENT.
TUG
NOW THEN, SHOULD WE HEAD BACK?
FLAP
"THERE AREN'T JUST NOBLES IN THE PRIESTHOOD. THEY LET COMMONERS IN TOO, WHICH MEANS ONLY SOME OF T HEM CAN USE MAGIC.
"IN SPITE OF BEING A COMMONER, THAT GUY'S EXTREMELY GOOD AT RIDING DRAGONS, SO THEY MADE HIM CAPTAIN OF THE THIRD COMPANY."
I THINK I UNDER-STAND...
FLAP
HOW THIS COMMONER GAINED COMMAND OF HIS OWN COMPANY.
WHOOSH

Le Familier de Zero Chevalier

ZERO'S
FAMILIAR
Chevalier

Chapter 19: The Secretary and the Emperor

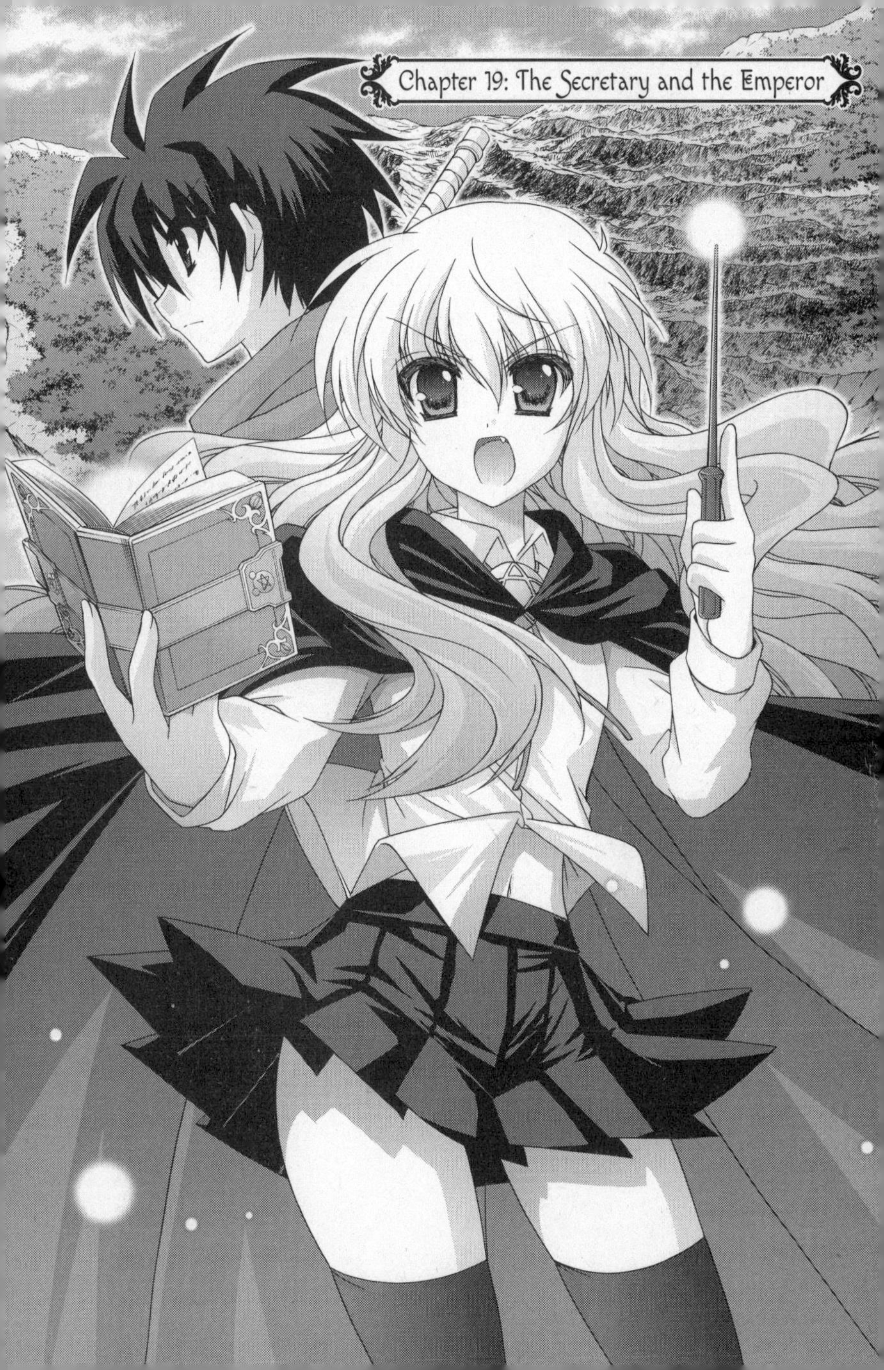

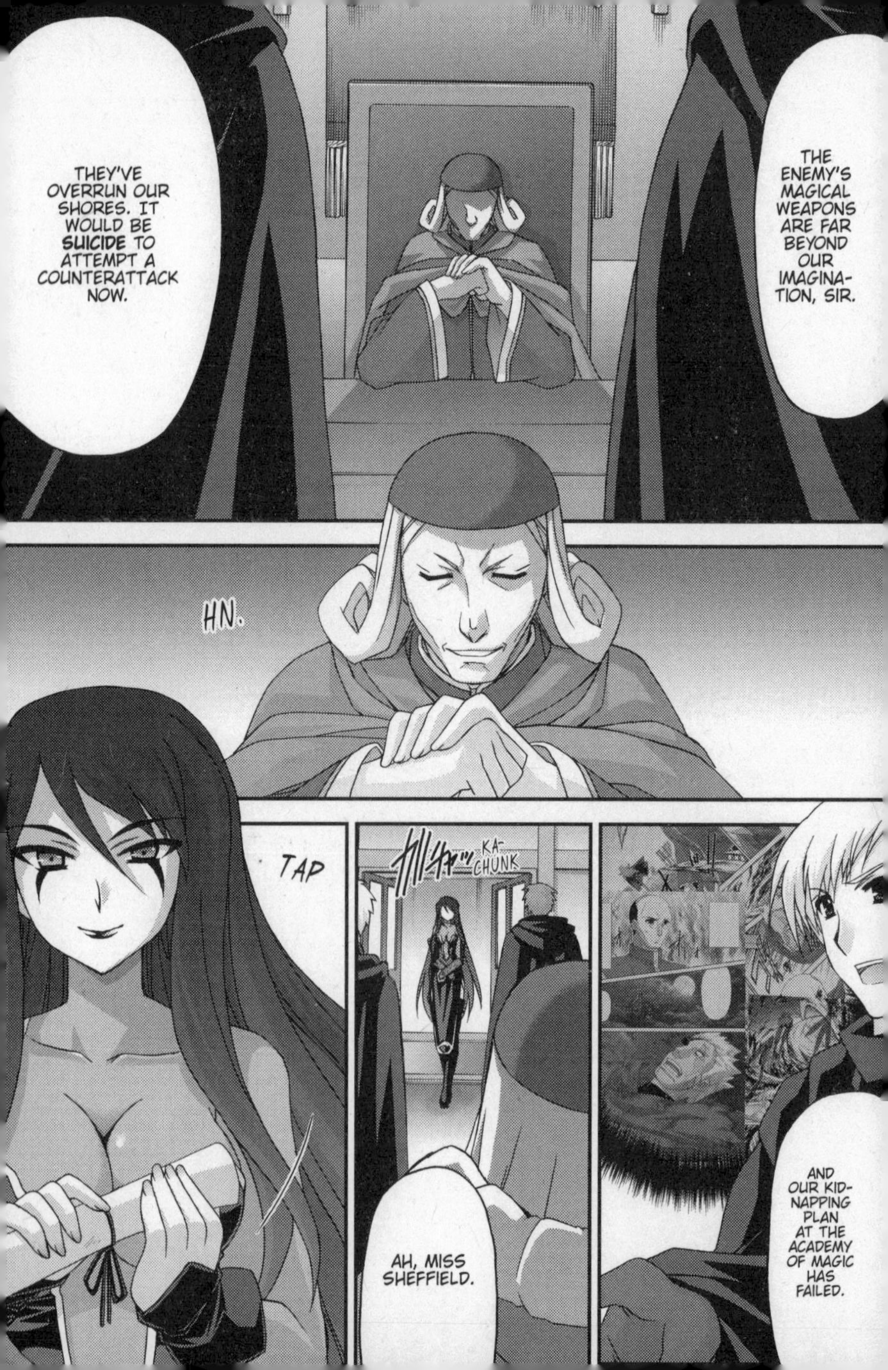
THE ENEMY'S MAGICAL WEAPONS ARE FAR BEYOND OUR IMAGINATION, SIR.
THEY'VE OVERRUN OUR SHORES. IT WOULD BE **SUICIDE** TO ATTEMPT A COUNTERATTACK NOW.
HN.
AND OUR KID-NAPPING PLAN AT THE ACADEMY OF MAGIC HAS FAILED.
KA-CHUNK
AH, MISS SHEFFIELD.
TAP

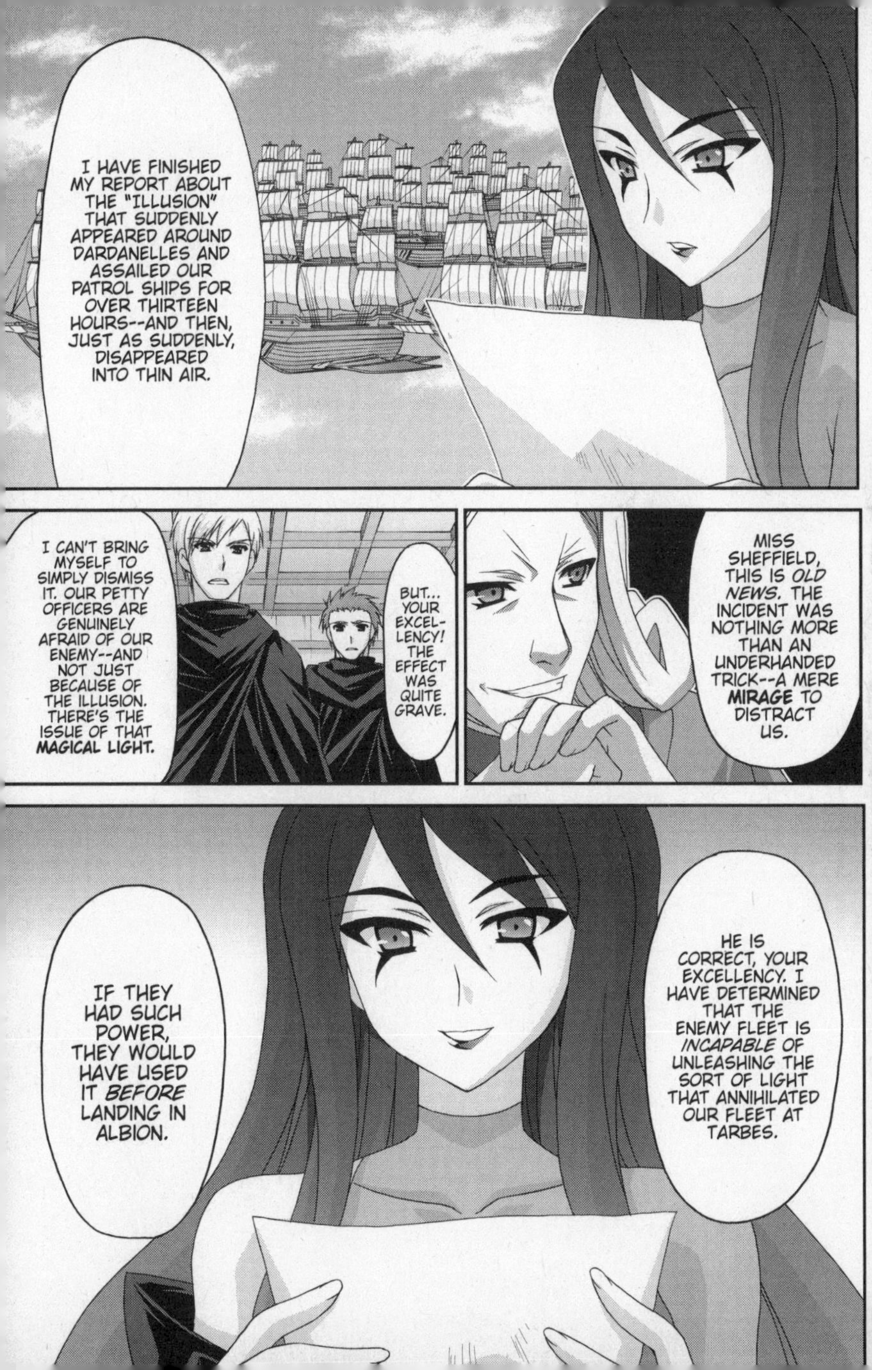
I HAVE FINISHED MY REPORT ABOUT THE "ILLUSION" THAT SUDDENLY APPEARED AROUND DARDANELLES AND ASSAILED OUR PATROL SHIPS FOR OVER THIRTEEN HOURS--AND THEN, JUST AS SUDDENLY, DISAPPEARED INTO THIN AIR.
MISS SHEFFIELD, THIS IS *OLD NEWS*. THE INCIDENT WAS NOTHING MORE THAN AN UNDERHANDED TRICK--A MERE **MIRAGE** TO DISTRACT US.
BUT... YOUR EXCEL-LENCY! THE EFFECT WAS QUITE GRAVE.
I CAN'T BRING MYSELF TO SIMPLY DISMISS IT. OUR PETTY OFFICERS ARE GENUINELY AFRAID OF OUR ENEMY--AND NOT JUST BECAUSE OF THE ILLUSION. THERE'S THE ISSUE OF THAT **MAGICAL LIGHT.**
HE IS CORRECT, YOUR EXCELLENCY. I HAVE DETERMINED THAT THE ENEMY FLEET IS *INCAPABLE* OF UNLEASHING THE SORT OF LIGHT THAT ANNIHILATED OUR FLEET AT TARBES.
IF THEY HAD SUCH POWER, THEY WOULD HAVE USED IT *BEFORE* LANDING IN ALBION.

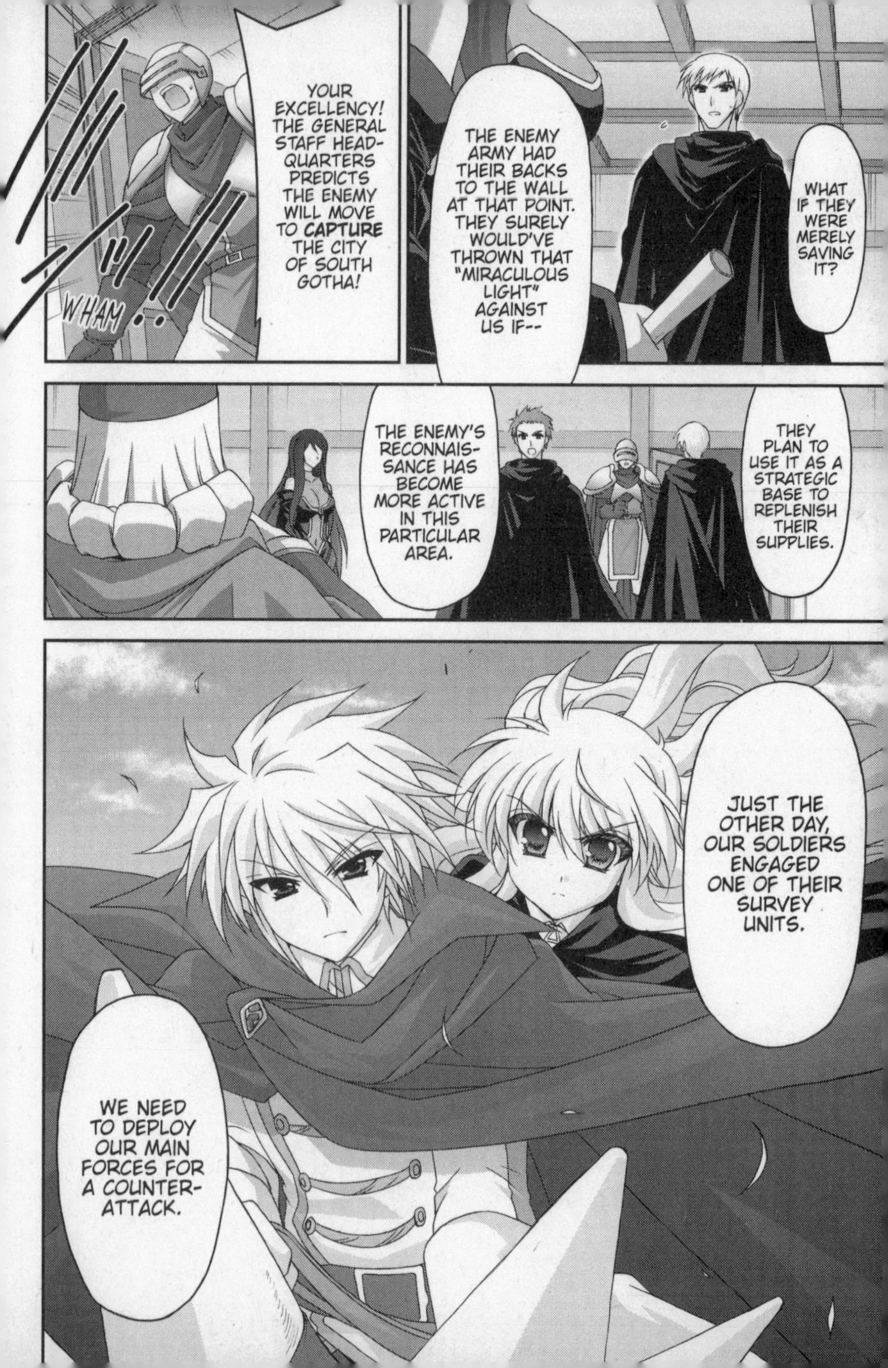
THE ENEMY ARMY HAD THEIR BACKS TO THE WALL AT THAT POINT. THEY SURELY WOULD'VE THROWN THAT "MIRACULOUS LIGHT" AGAINST US IF--
WHAT IF THEY WERE MERELY SAVING IT?
YOUR EXCELLENCY! THE GENERAL STAFF HEAD-QUARTERS PREDICTS THE ENEMY WILL MOVE TO **CAPTURE** THE CITY OF SOUTH GOTHA!
WHAM
THEY PLAN TO USE IT AS A STRATEGIC BASE TO REPLENISH THEIR SUPPLIES.
THE ENEMY'S RECONNAIS-SANCE HAS BECOME MORE ACTIVE IN THIS PARTICULAR AREA.
JUST THE OTHER DAY, OUR SOLDIERS ENGAGED ONE OF THEIR SURVEY UNITS.
WE NEED TO DEPLOY OUR MAIN FORCES FOR A COUNTER-ATTACK.

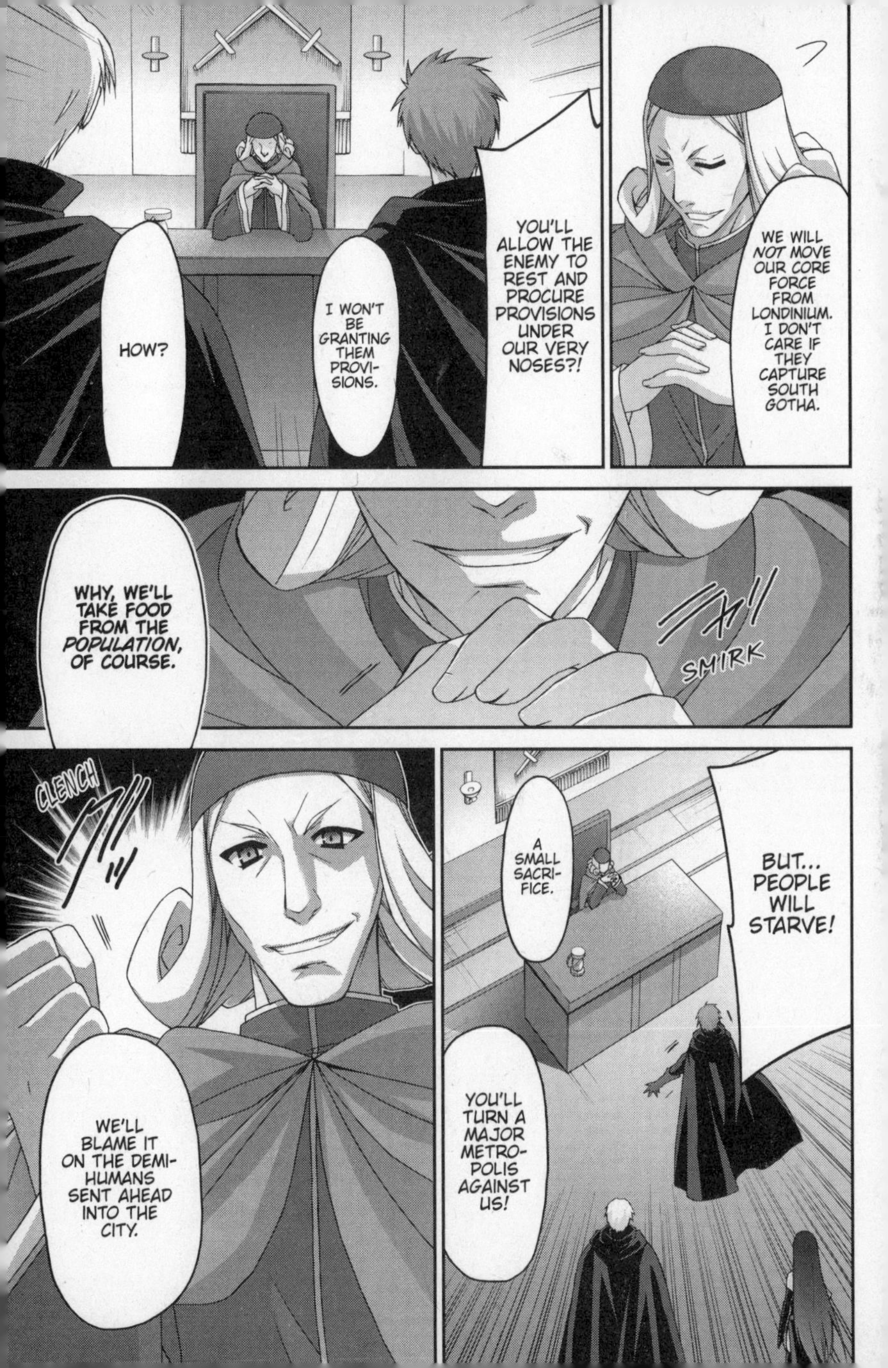
WE WILL *NOT* MOVE OUR CORE FORCE FROM LONDINIUM. I DON'T CARE IF THEY CAPTURE SOUTH GOTHA.
YOU'LL ALLOW THE ENEMY TO REST AND PROCURE PROVISIONS UNDER OUR VERY NOSES?!
I WON'T BE GRANTING THEM PROVI-SIONS.
HOW?
SMIRK
WHY, WE'LL TAKE FOOD FROM THE *POPULATION*, OF COURSE.
BUT... PEOPLE WILL STARVE!
A SMALL SACRI-FICE.
YOU'LL TURN A MAJOR METRO-POLIS AGAINST US!
CLENCH
WE'LL BLAME IT ON THE DEMI-HUMANS SENT AHEAD INTO THE CITY.

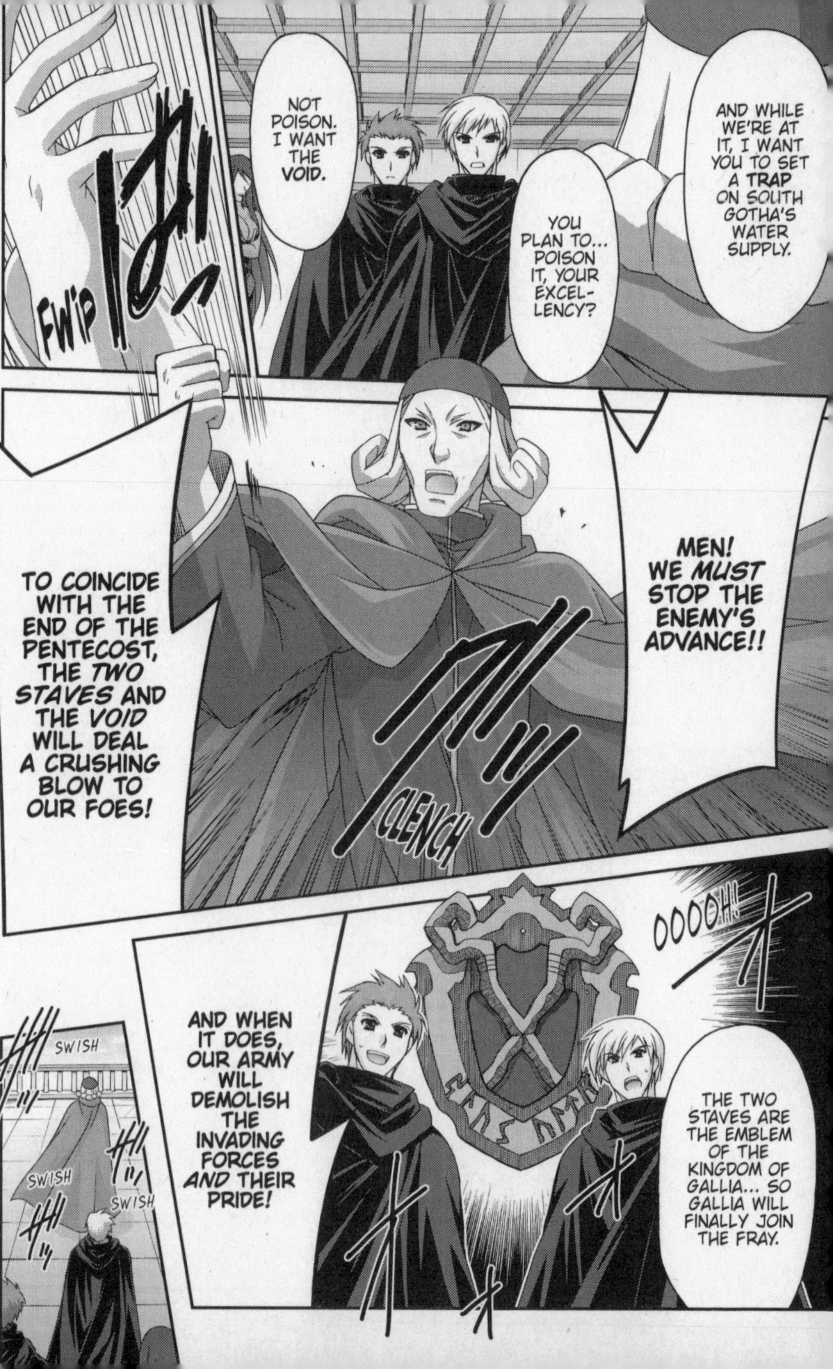
AND WHILE WE'RE AT IT, I WANT YOU TO SET A TRAP ON SOUTH GOTHA'S WATER SUPPLY.
YOU PLAN TO... POISON IT, YOUR EXCEL-LENCY?
NOT POISON. I WANT THE VOID.
FWIP
MEN! WE MUST STOP THE ENEMY'S ADVANCE!!
TO COINCIDE WITH THE END OF THE PENTECOST, THE TWO STAVES AND THE VOID WILL DEAL A CRUSHING BLOW TO OUR FOES!
CLENCH
OOOOH!!
THE TWO STAVES ARE THE EMBLEM OF THE KINGDOM OF GALLIA... SO GALLIA WILL FINALLY JOIN THE FRAY.
AND WHEN IT DOES, OUR ARMY WILL DEMOLISH THE INVADING FORCES AND THEIR PRIDE!
SWISH
SWISH
SWISH

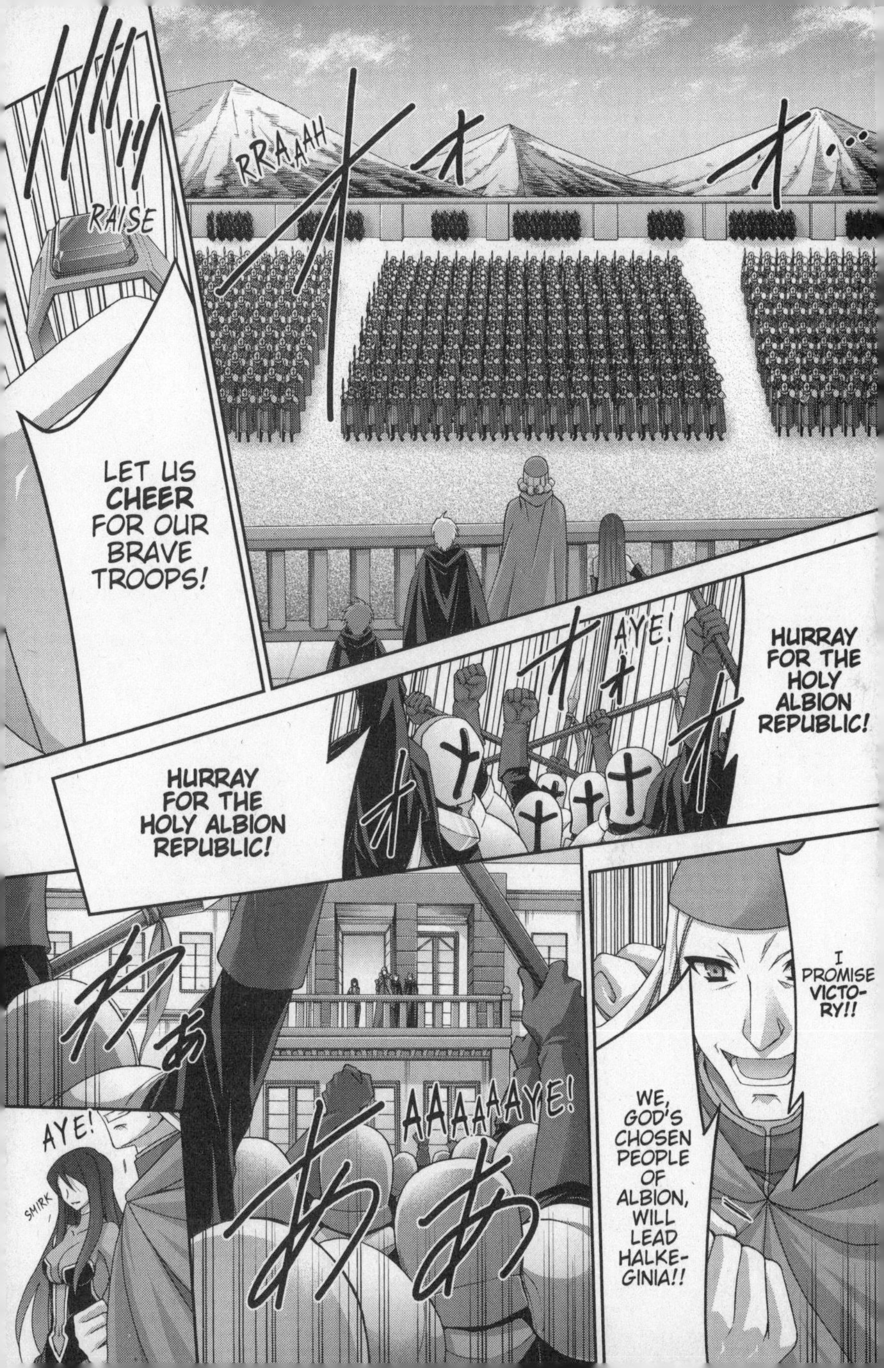
RRAAAH
RAISE
LET US CHEER FOR OUR BRAVE TROOPS!
HURRAY FOR THE HOLY ALBION REPUBLIC!
AYE!
HURRAY FOR THE HOLY ALBION REPUBLIC!
I PROMISE VICTO-RY!!
WE, GOD'S CHOSEN PEOPLE OF ALBION, WILL LEAD HALKE-GINIA!!
AAAAAAYE!
AYE!
SMIRK

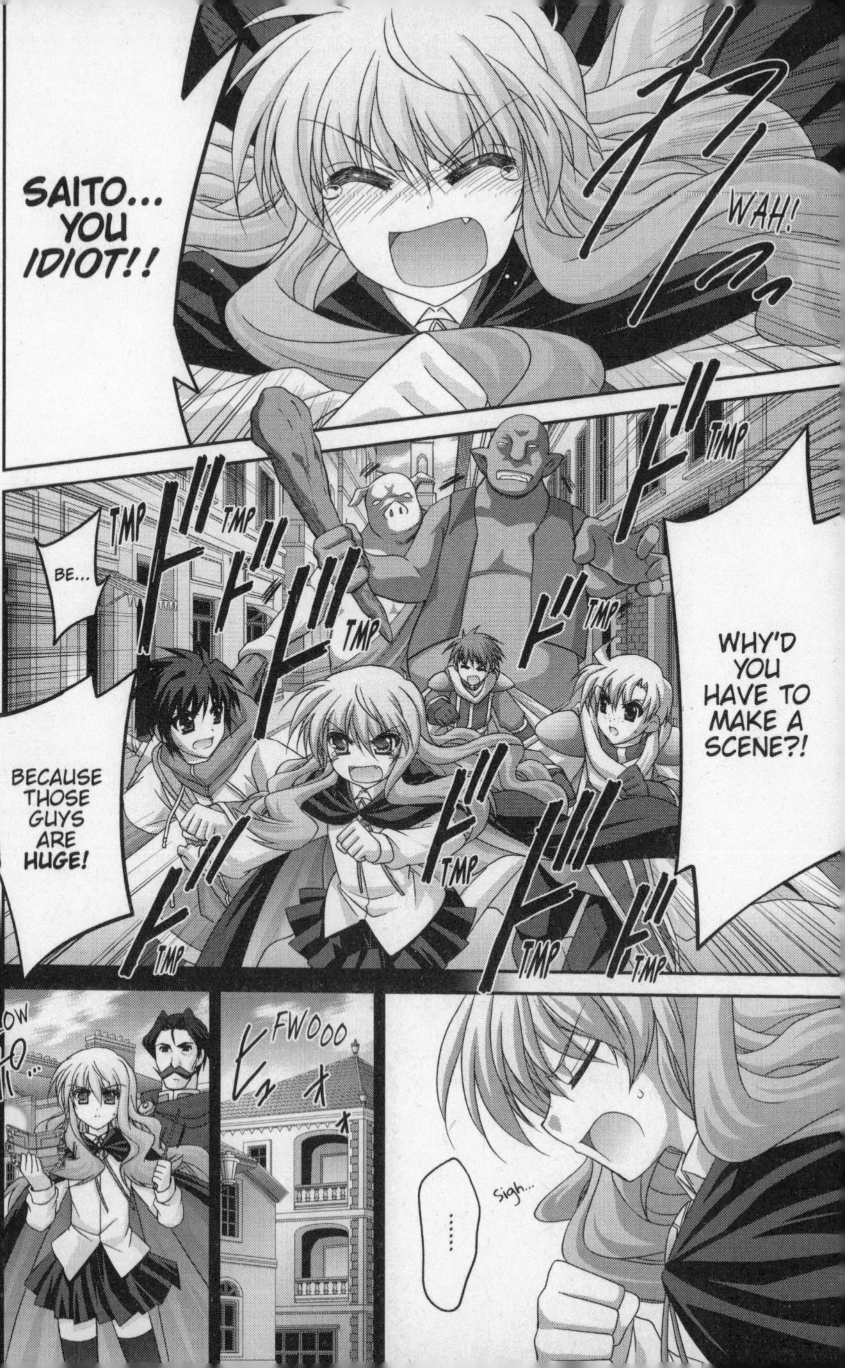
WAH!
SAITO... YOU IDIOT!!
TMP
TMP
WHY'D YOU HAVE TO MAKE A SCENE?!
TMP
TMP
TMP
TMP
BE...
BECAUSE THOSE GUYS ARE HUGE!
TMP
TMP
TMP
Sigh...
......
FWOOO
GLOW

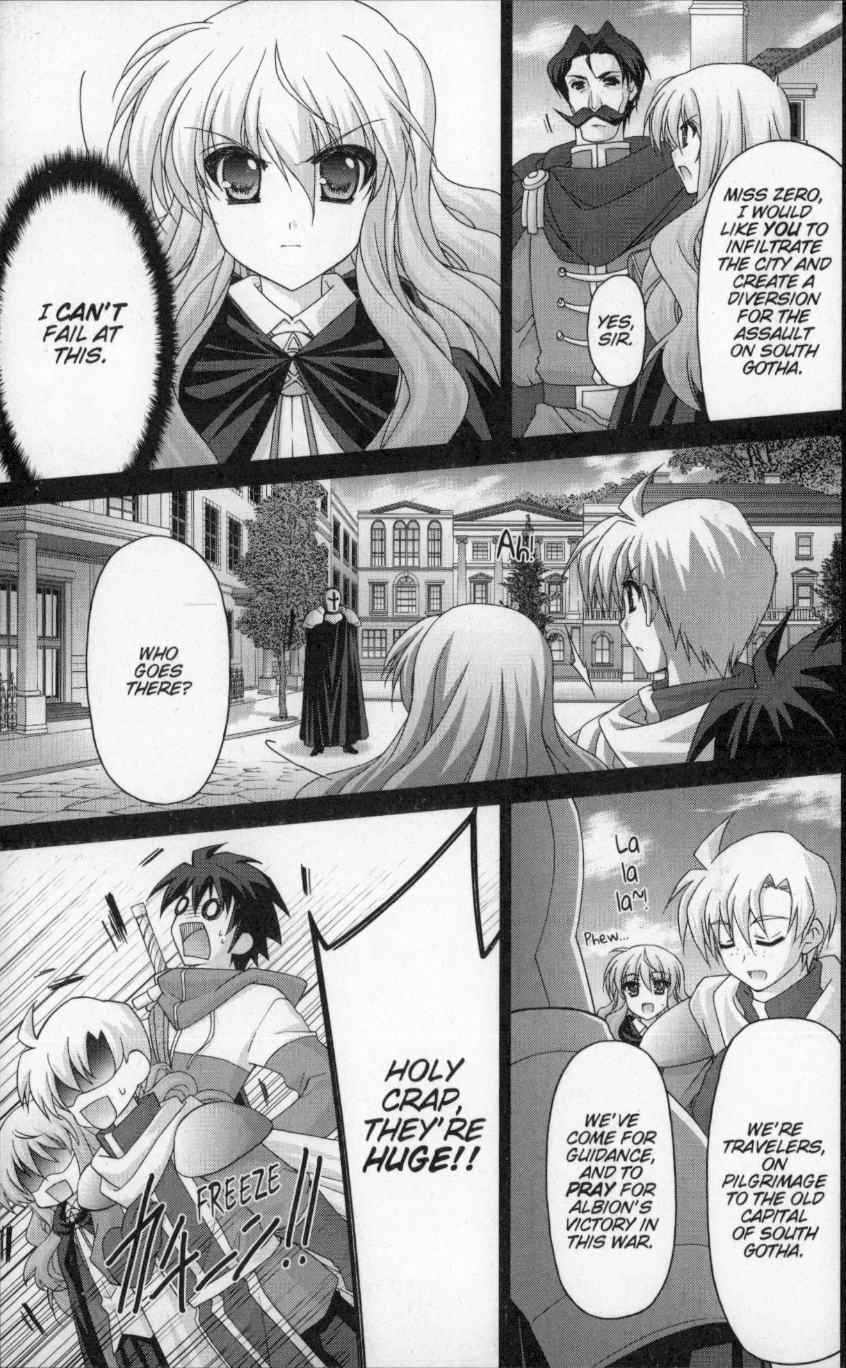

MISS ZERO, I WOULD LIKE **YOU** TO INFILTRATE THE CITY AND CREATE A DIVERSION FOR THE ASSAULT ON SOUTH GOTHA.
YES, SIR.
I **CAN'T** FAIL AT THIS.
Ah!
WHO GOES THERE?
La la la~!
Phew...
WE'RE TRAVELERS, ON PILGRIMAGE TO THE OLD CAPITAL OF SOUTH GOTHA.
WE'VE COME FOR GUIDANCE, AND TO **PRAY** FOR ALBION'S VICTORY IN THIS WAR.
HOLY CRAP, THEY'RE **HUGE!!**
FREEZE
カチーン!!

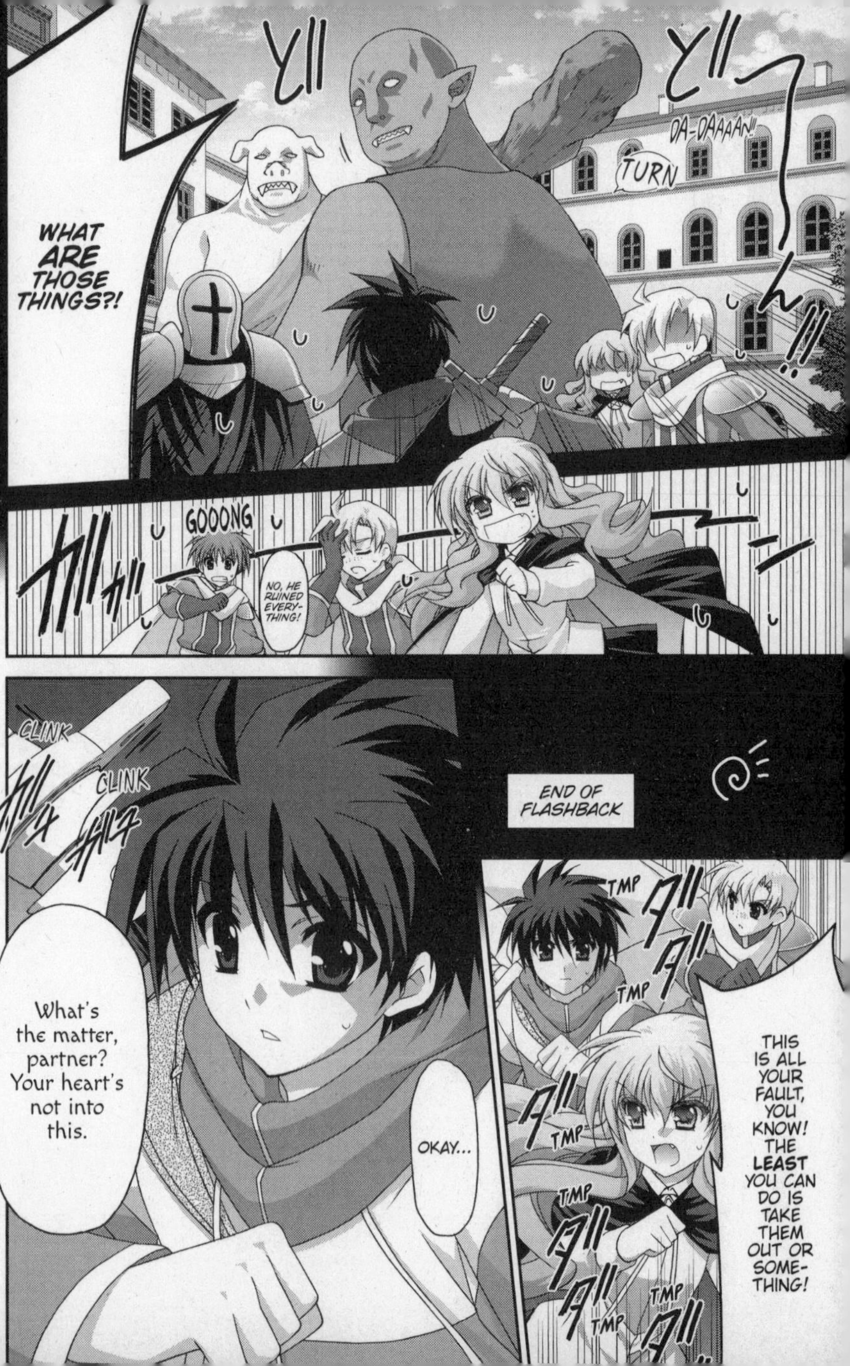
DA-DAAAAN!!
TURN
WHAT ARE THOSE THINGS?!
GOOONG
NO, HE RUINED EVERYTHING!
END OF FLASHBACK
TMP
TMP
THIS IS ALL YOUR FAULT, YOU KNOW! THE LEAST YOU CAN DO IS TAKE THEM OUT OR SOME-THING!
TMP
TMP
TMP
TMP
CLINK
CLINK
What's the matter, partner? Your heart's not into this.
OKAY...

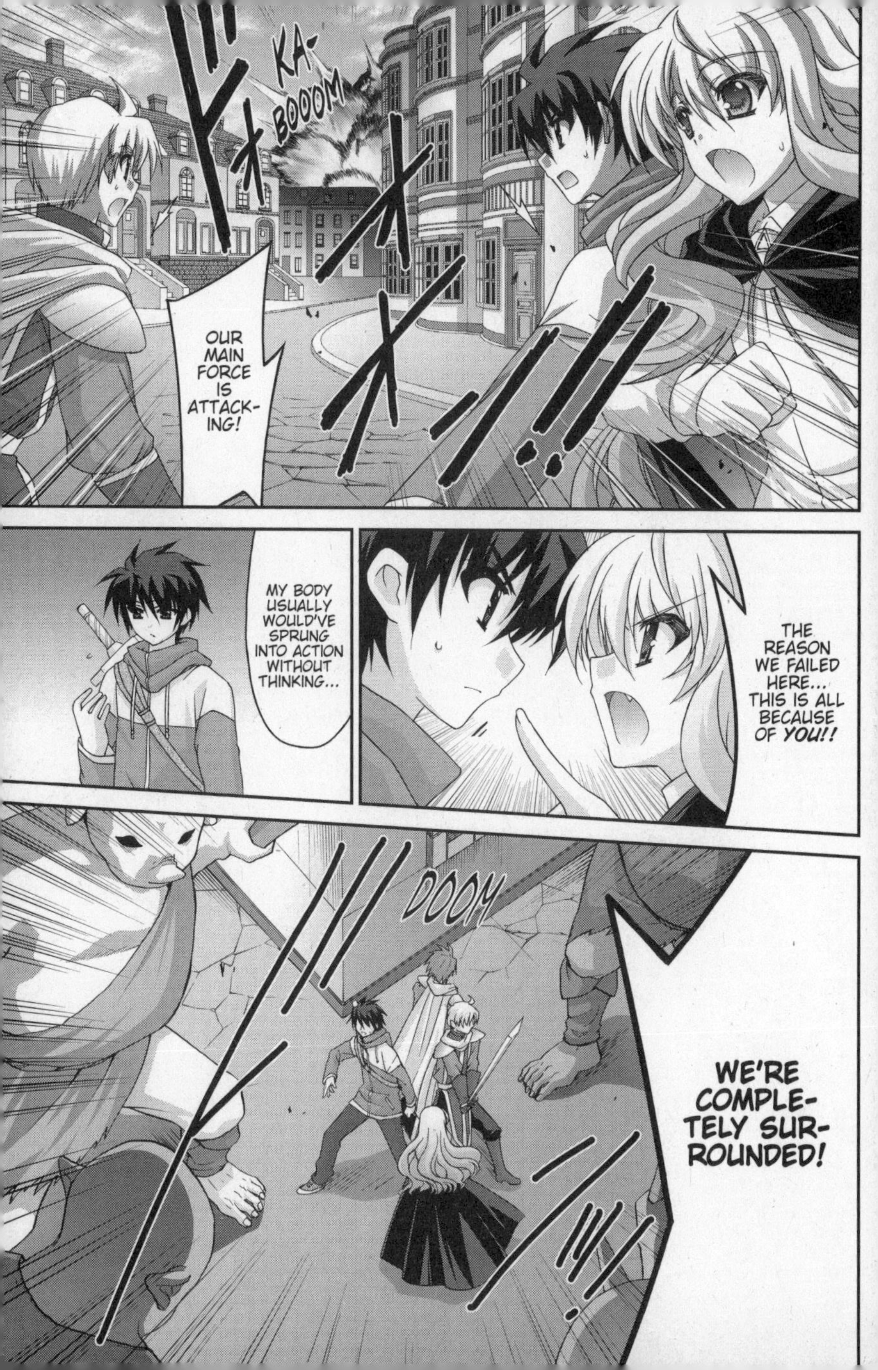
KA-BOOOM
OUR MAIN FORCE IS ATTACKING!
THE REASON WE FAILED HERE... THIS IS ALL BECAUSE OF ***YOU!!***
MY BODY USUALLY WOULD'VE SPRUNG INTO ACTION WITHOUT THINKING...
DOOM
WE'RE COMPLETELY SURROUNDED!

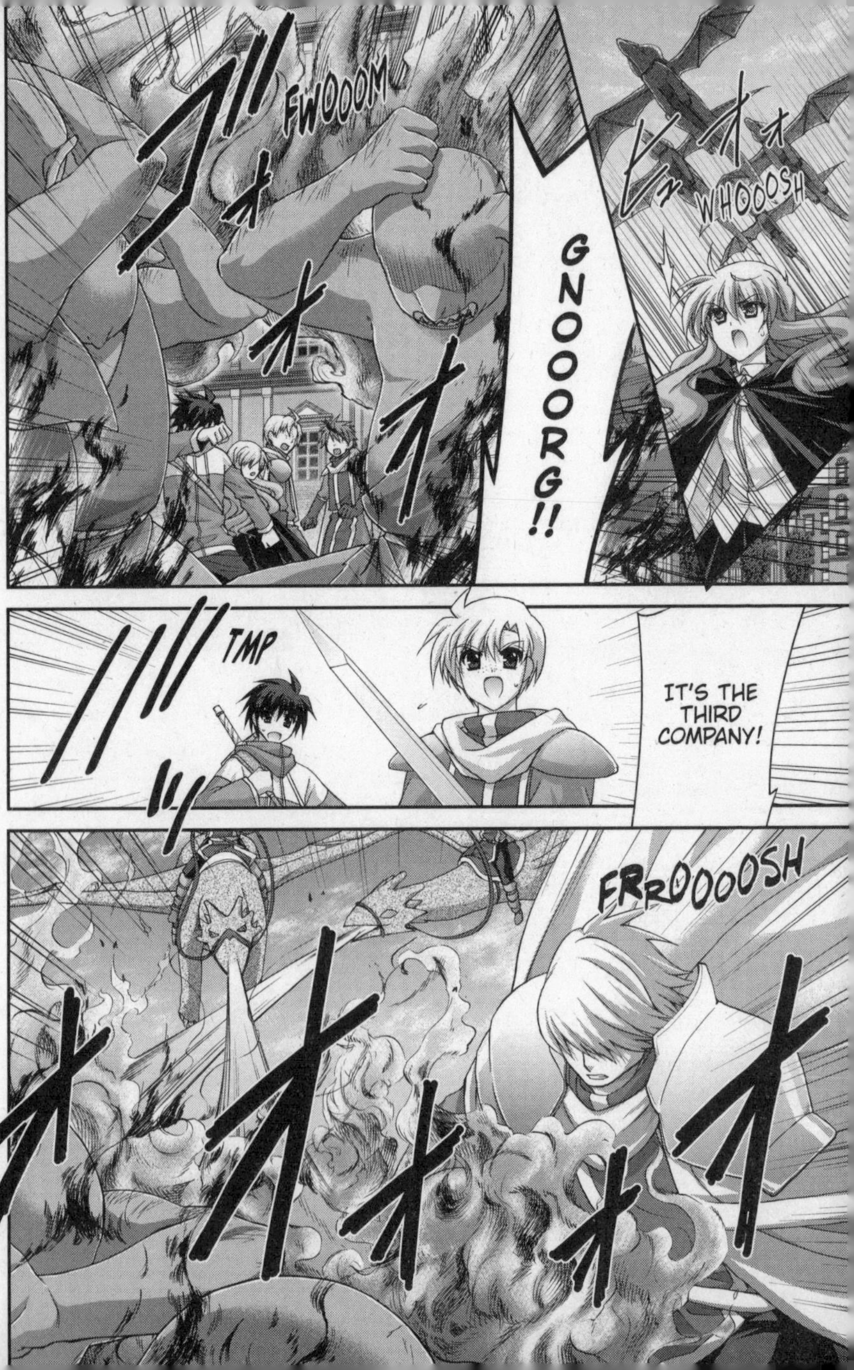
WHOOOSH
GNOOOORG!!
FWOOOM
IT'S THE THIRD COMPANY!
TMP
FRROOOOSH

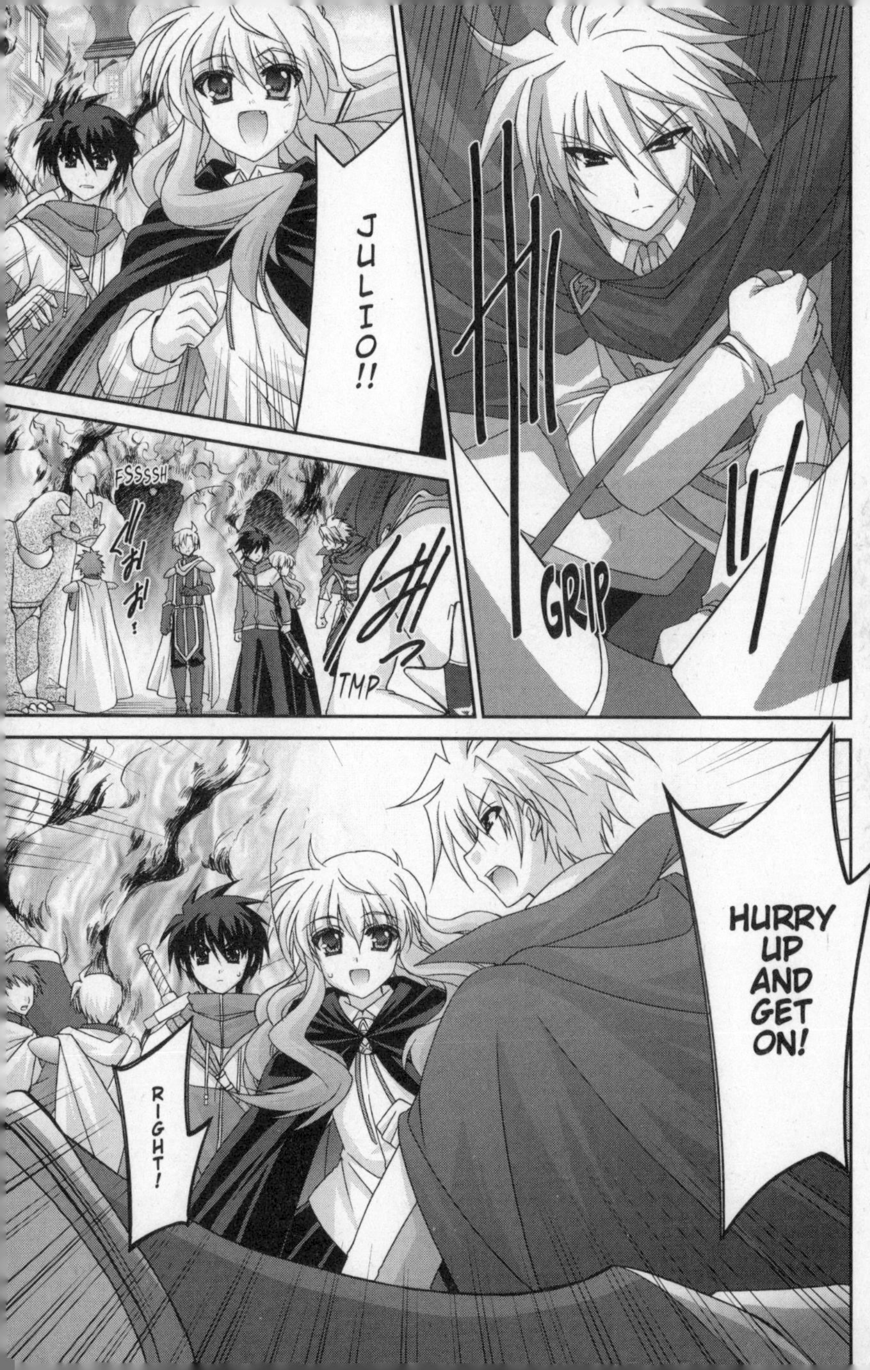
GRIP
JULIO!!
FSSSSH
TMP
HURRY UP AND GET ON!
RIGHT!

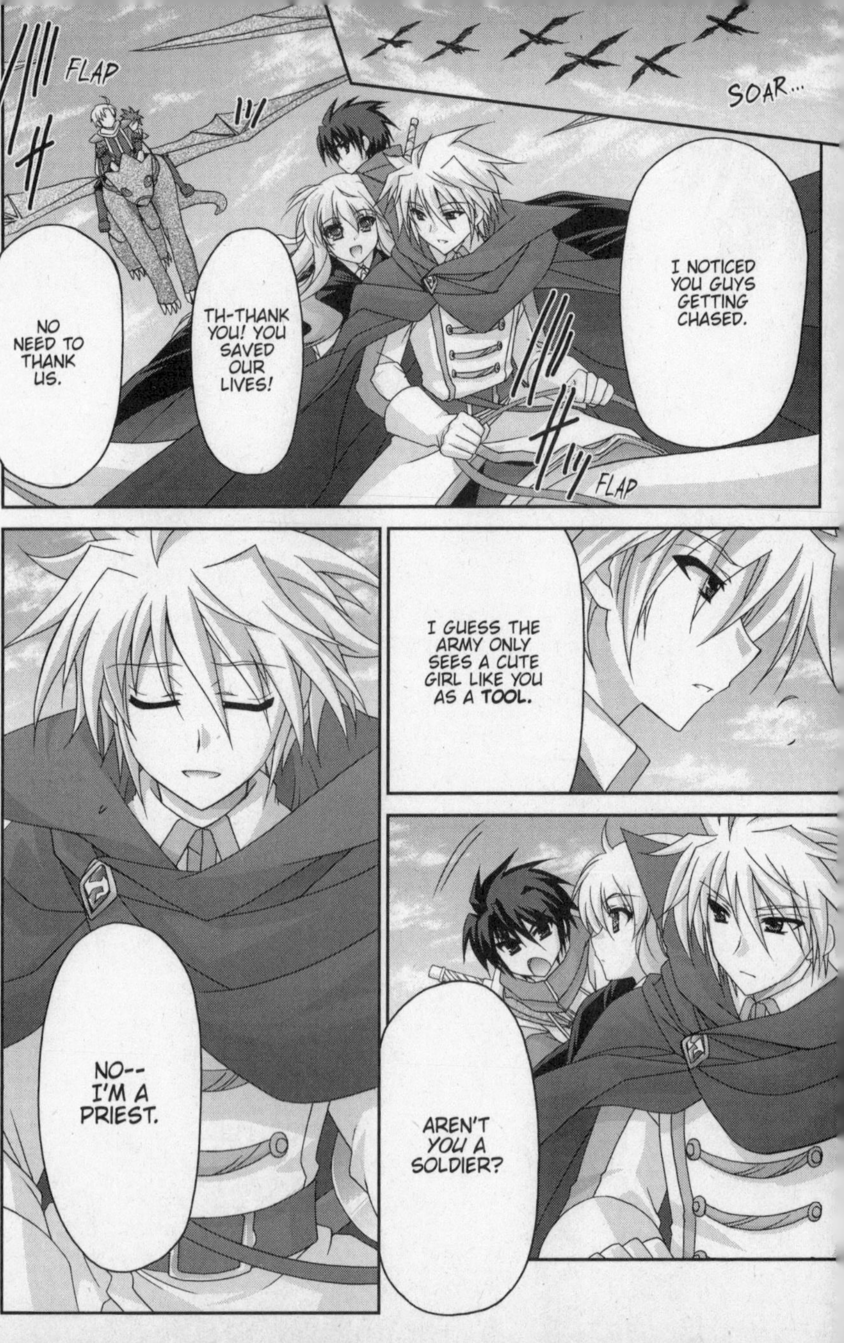
SOAR...
I NOTICED YOU GUYS GETTING CHASED.
FLAP
TH-THANK YOU! YOU SAVED OUR LIVES!
NO NEED TO THANK US.
FLAP
I GUESS THE ARMY ONLY SEES A CUTE GIRL LIKE YOU AS A **TOOL.**
AREN'T *YOU* A SOLDIER?
NO-- I'M A PRIEST.

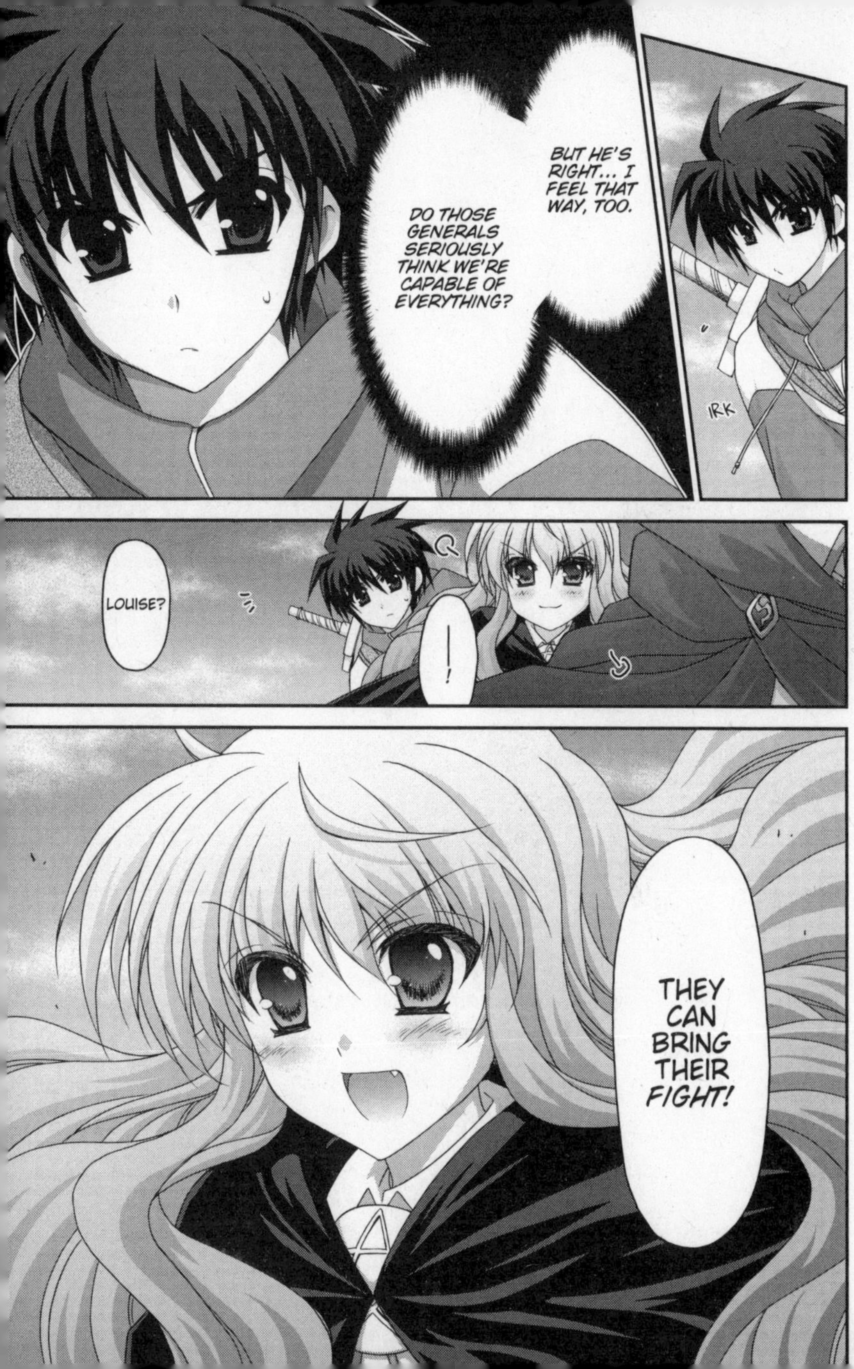
IRK
BUT HE'S RIGHT... I FEEL THAT WAY, TOO.
DO THOSE GENERALS SERIOUSLY THINK WE'RE CAPABLE OF EVERYTHING?
!
LOUISE?
THEY CAN BRING THEIR *FIGHT!*

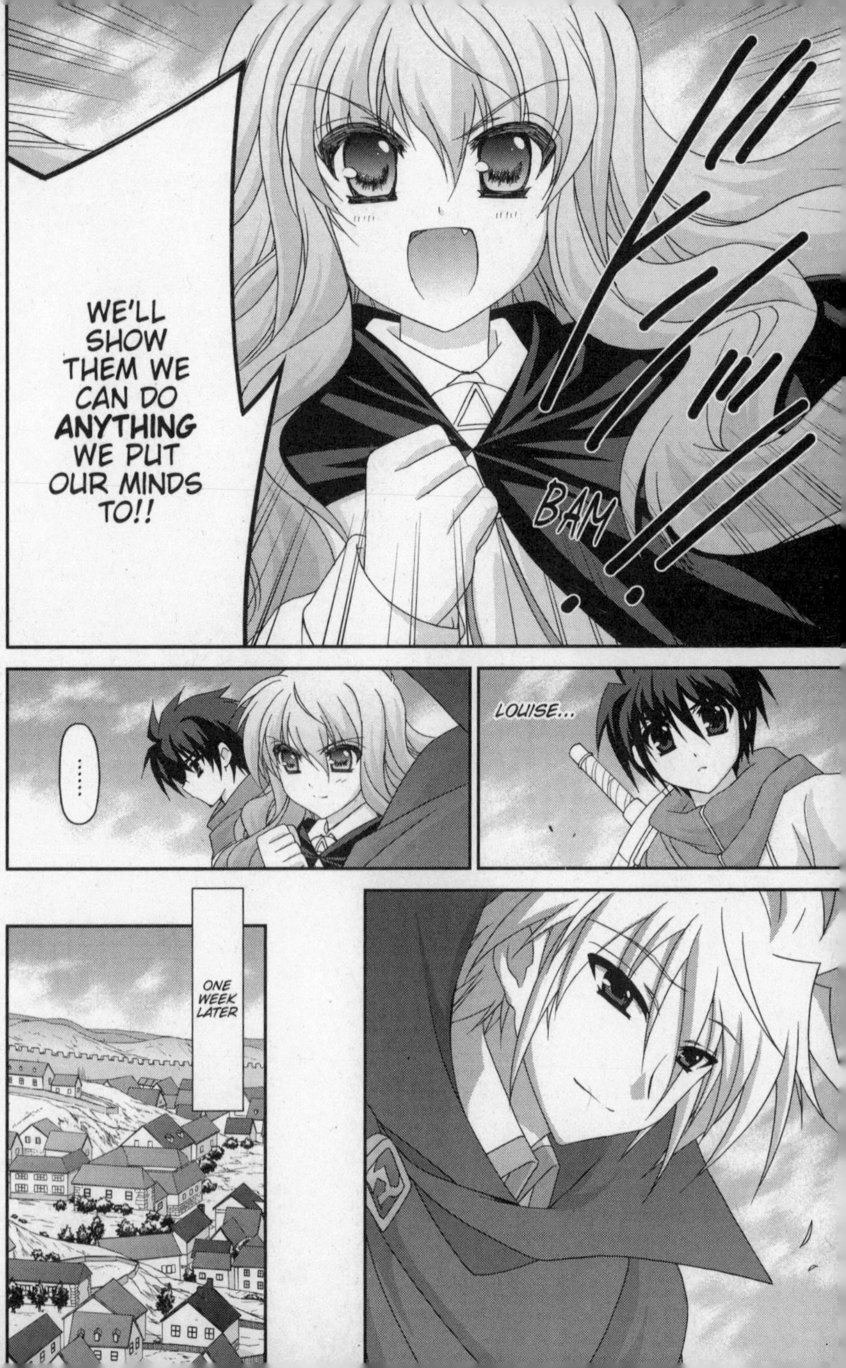
WE'LL SHOW THEM WE CAN DO ANYTHING WE PUT OUR MINDS TO!!
BAM
LOUISE...
......
ONE WEEK LATER

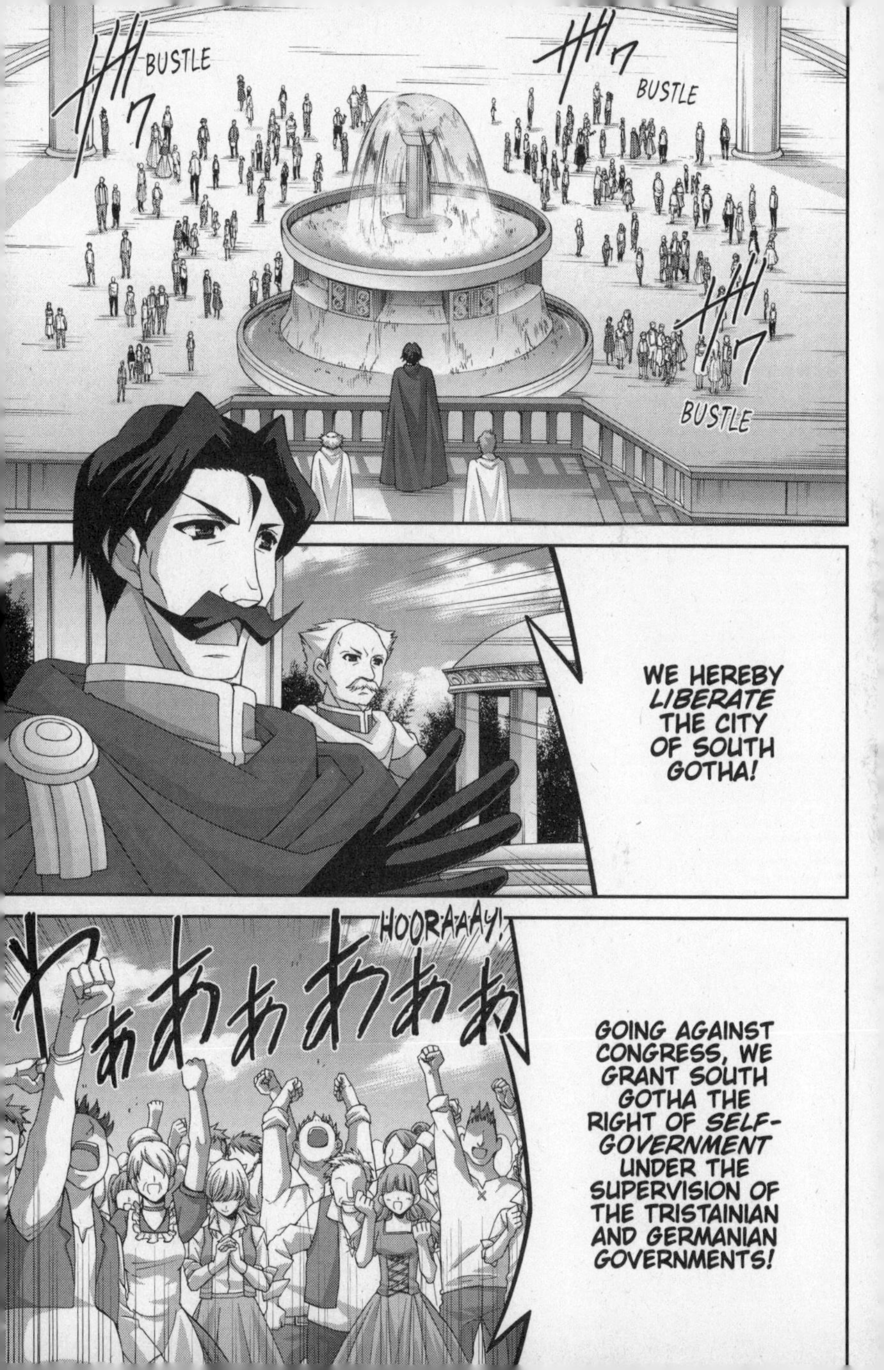
ザワ BUSTLE
ザワ BUSTLE
ザワ BUSTLE
WE HEREBY LIBERATE THE CITY OF SOUTH GOTHA!
GOING AGAINST CONGRESS, WE GRANT SOUTH GOTHA THE RIGHT OF SELF-GOVERNMENT UNDER THE SUPERVISION OF THE TRISTAINIAN AND GERMANIAN GOVERNMENTS!
わぁあぁあぁあぁあ HOORAAAY!

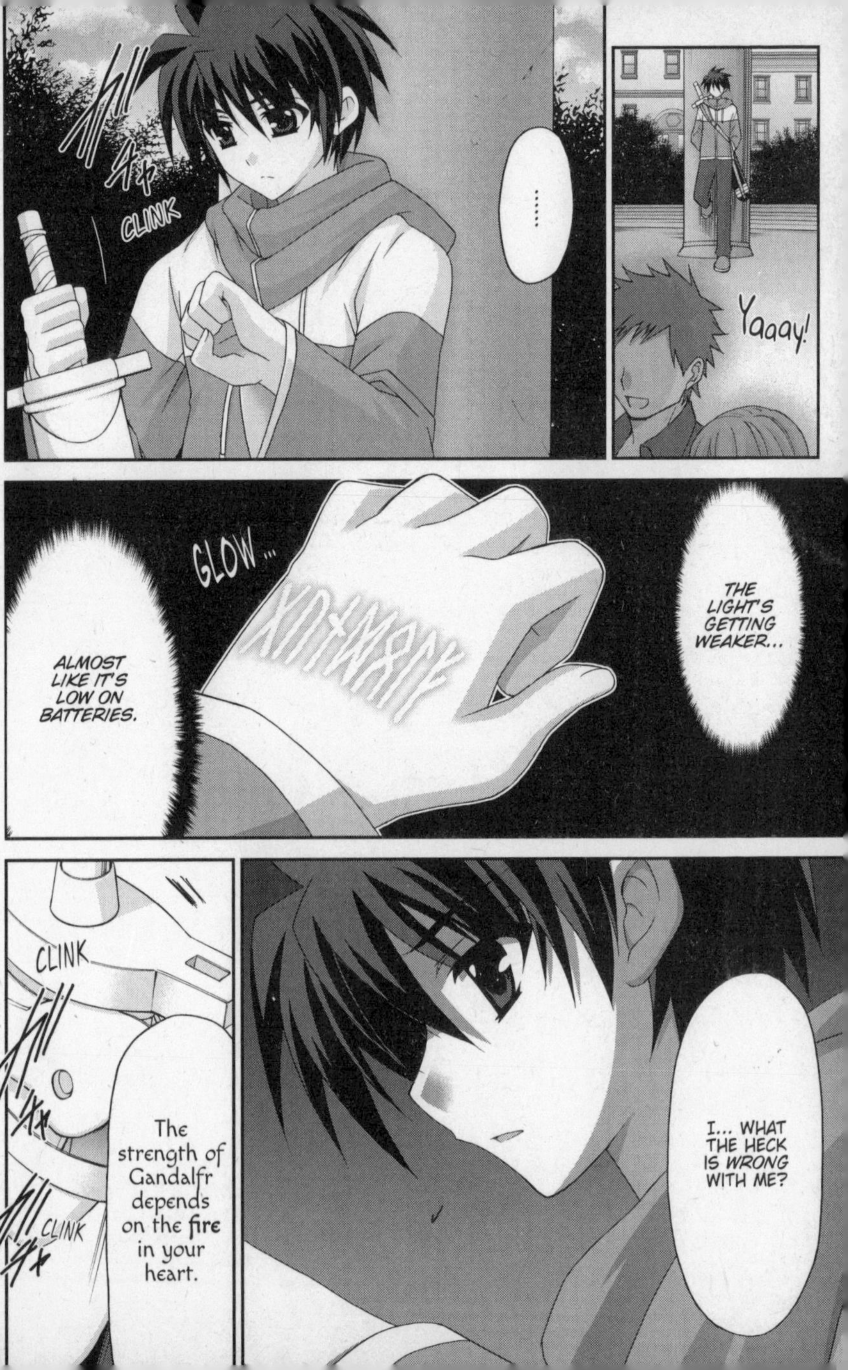
Yaaay!
CLINK
......
THE LIGHT'S GETTING WEAKER...
GLOW...
ALMOST LIKE IT'S LOW ON BATTERIES.
I... WHAT THE HECK IS WRONG WITH ME?
The strength of Gandalfr depends on the fire in your heart.
CLINK
CLINK

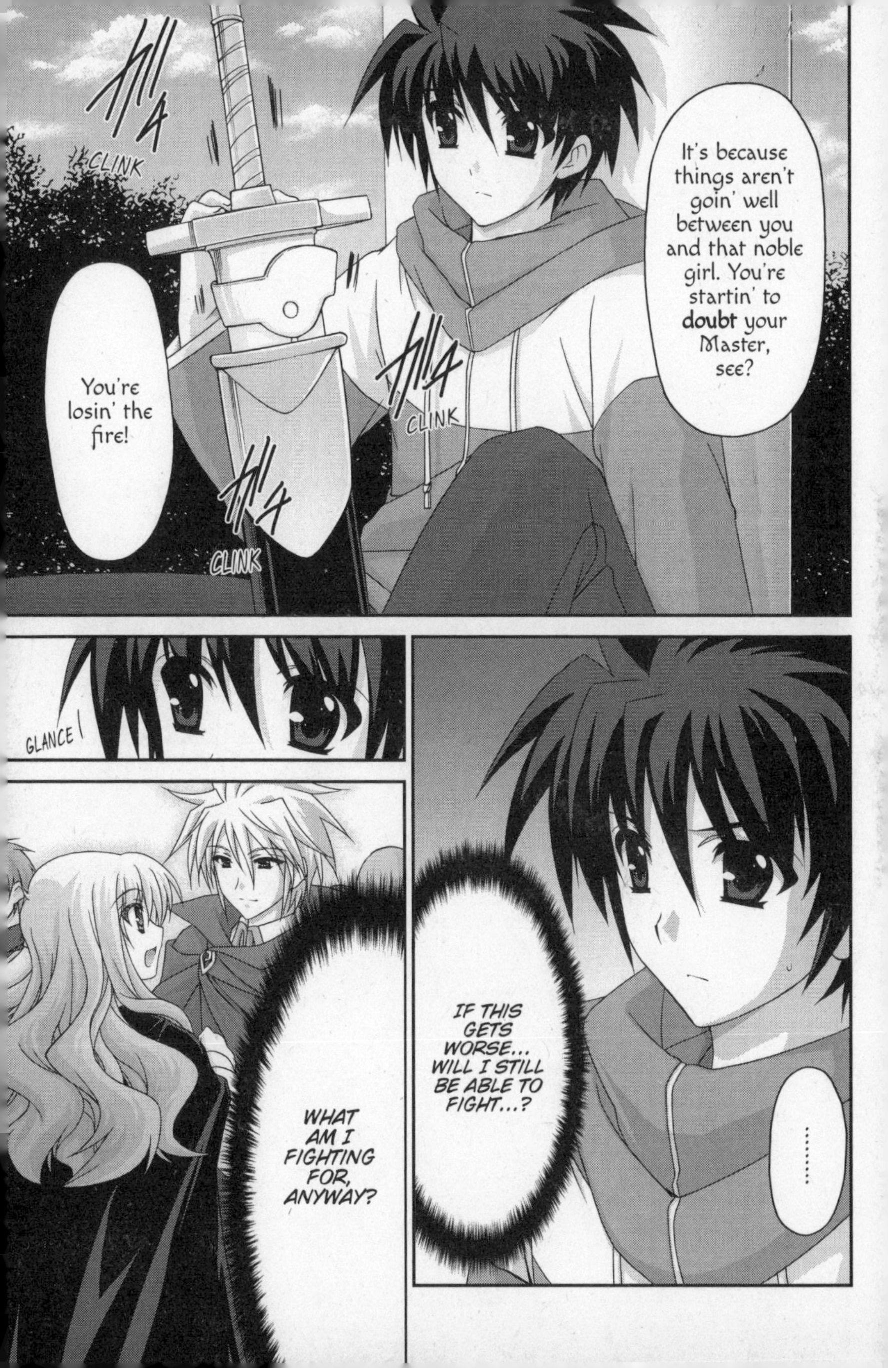
It's because things aren't goin' well between you and that noble girl. You're startin' to **doubt** your Master, see?
CLINK
CLINK
CLINK
You're losin' the fire!
......
IF THIS GETS WORSE... WILL I STILL BE ABLE TO FIGHT...?
WHAT AM I FIGHTING FOR, ANYWAY?
GLANCE

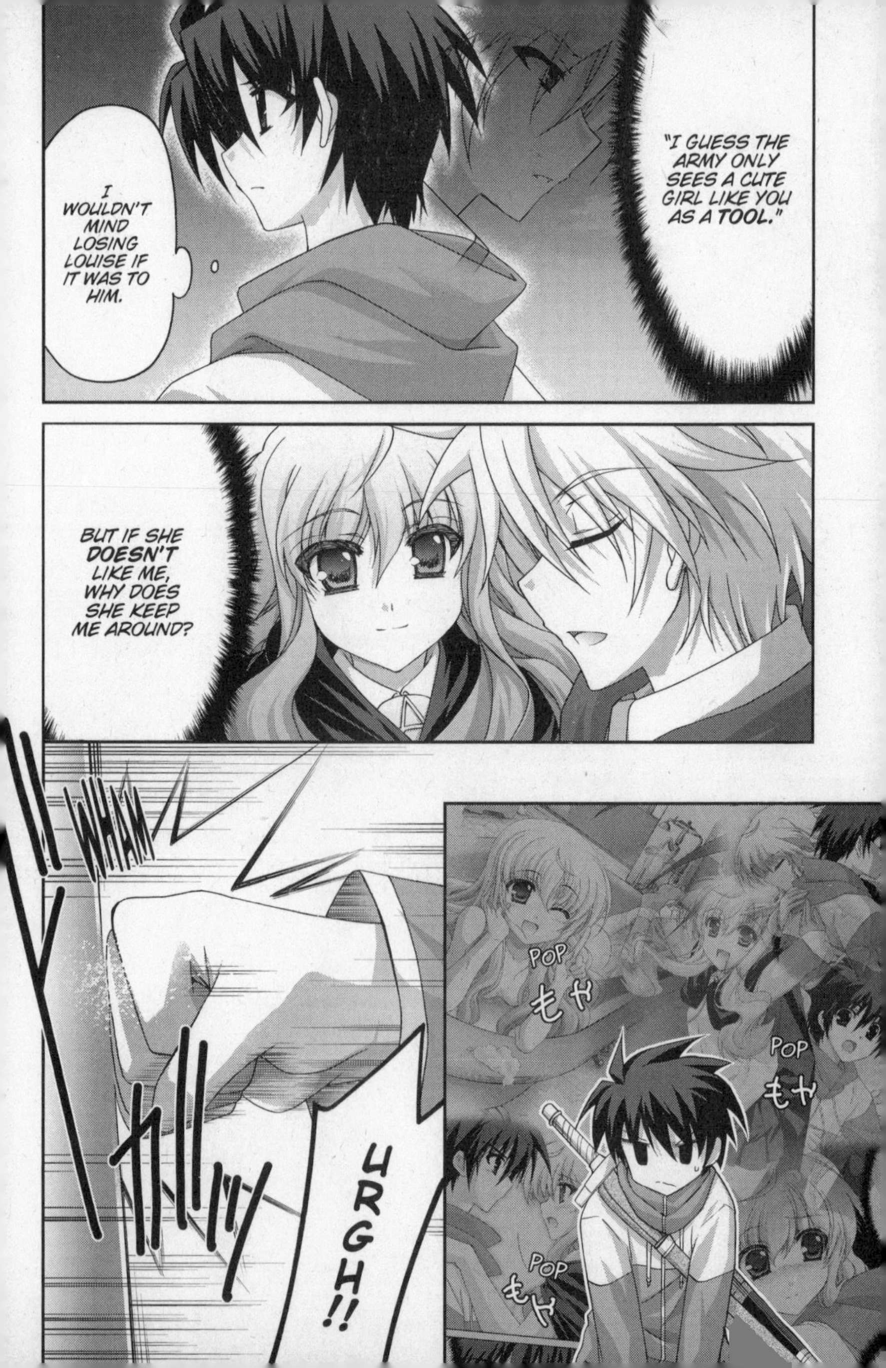
"I GUESS THE ARMY ONLY SEES A CUTE GIRL LIKE YOU AS A TOOL."
I WOULDN'T MIND LOSING LOUISE IF IT WAS TO HIM.
BUT IF SHE DOESN'T LIKE ME, WHY DOES SHE KEEP ME AROUND?
POP
もや
POP
もや
POP
もや
WHAM
URGH!!

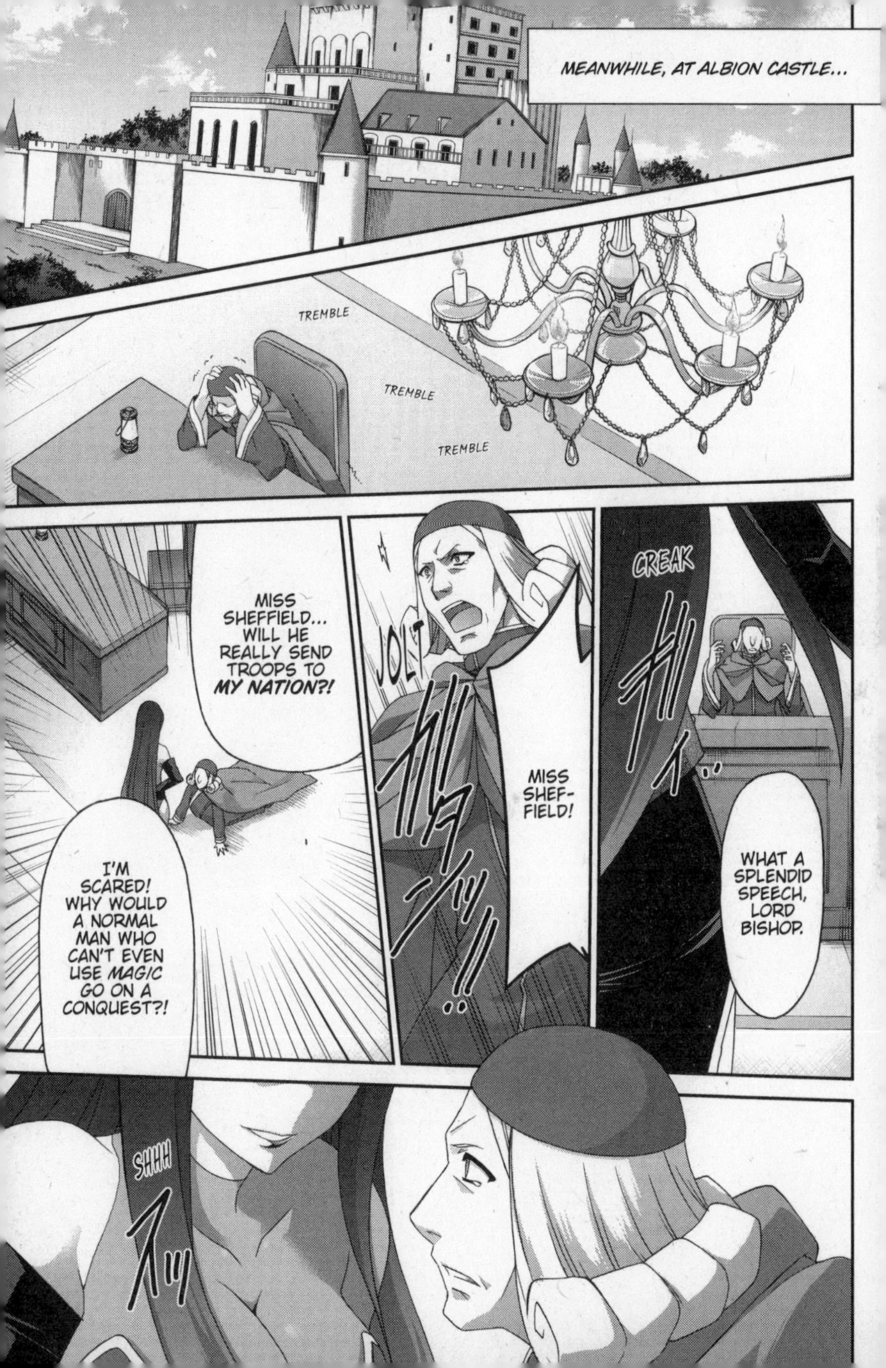

MEANWHILE, AT ALBION CASTLE...
TREMBLE
TREMBLE
TREMBLE
CREAK
WHAT A SPLENDID SPEECH, LORD BISHOP.
JOLT
MISS SHEFFIELD!
MISS SHEFFIELD... WILL HE REALLY SEND TROOPS TO MY NATION?!
I'M SCARED! WHY WOULD A NORMAL MAN WHO CAN'T EVEN USE MAGIC GO ON A CONQUEST?!
SHHH

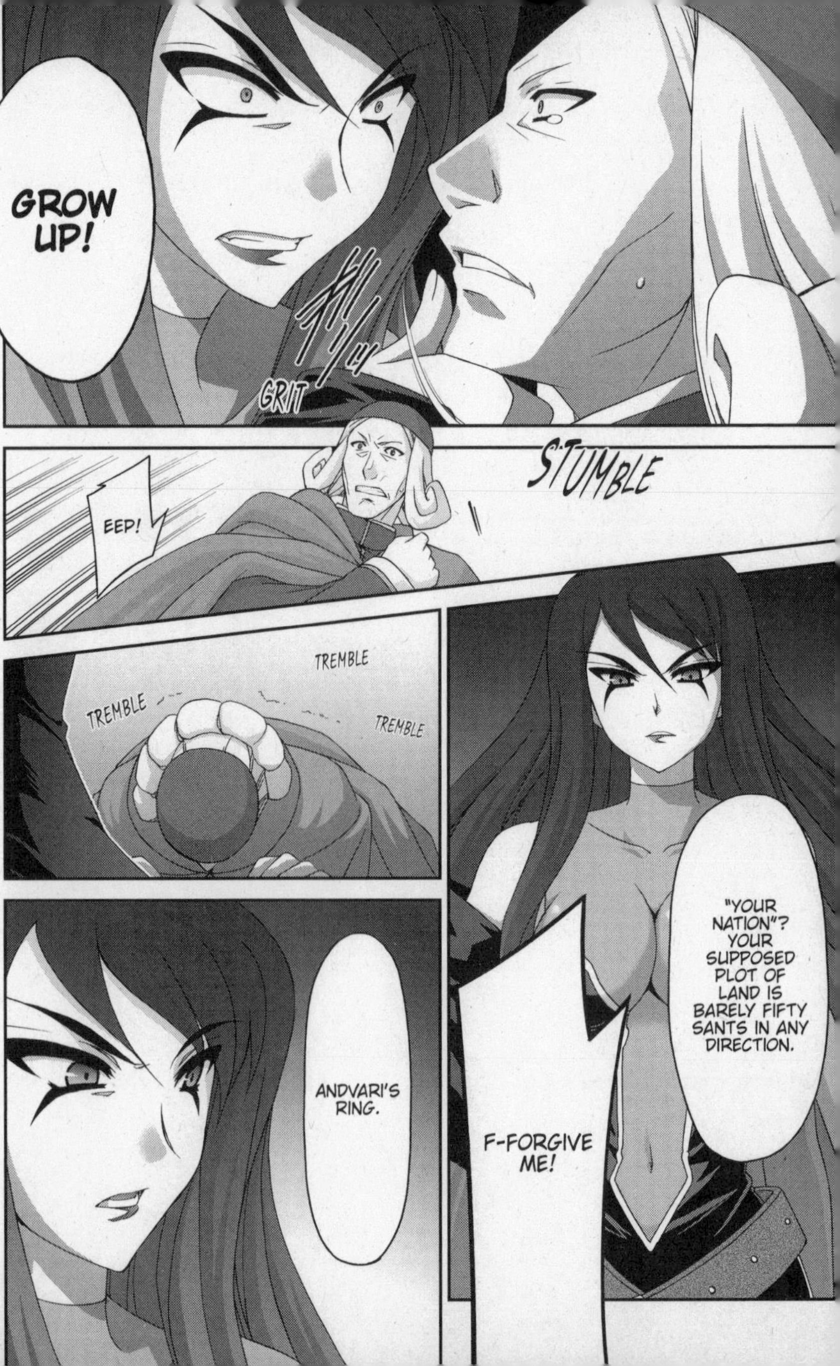
GROW UP!
GRIT
STUMBLE
EEP!
"YOUR NATION"? YOUR SUPPOSED PLOT OF LAND IS BARELY FIFTY SANTS IN ANY DIRECTION.
F-FORGIVE ME!
TREMBLE
TREMBLE
TREMBLE
ANDVARI'S RING.

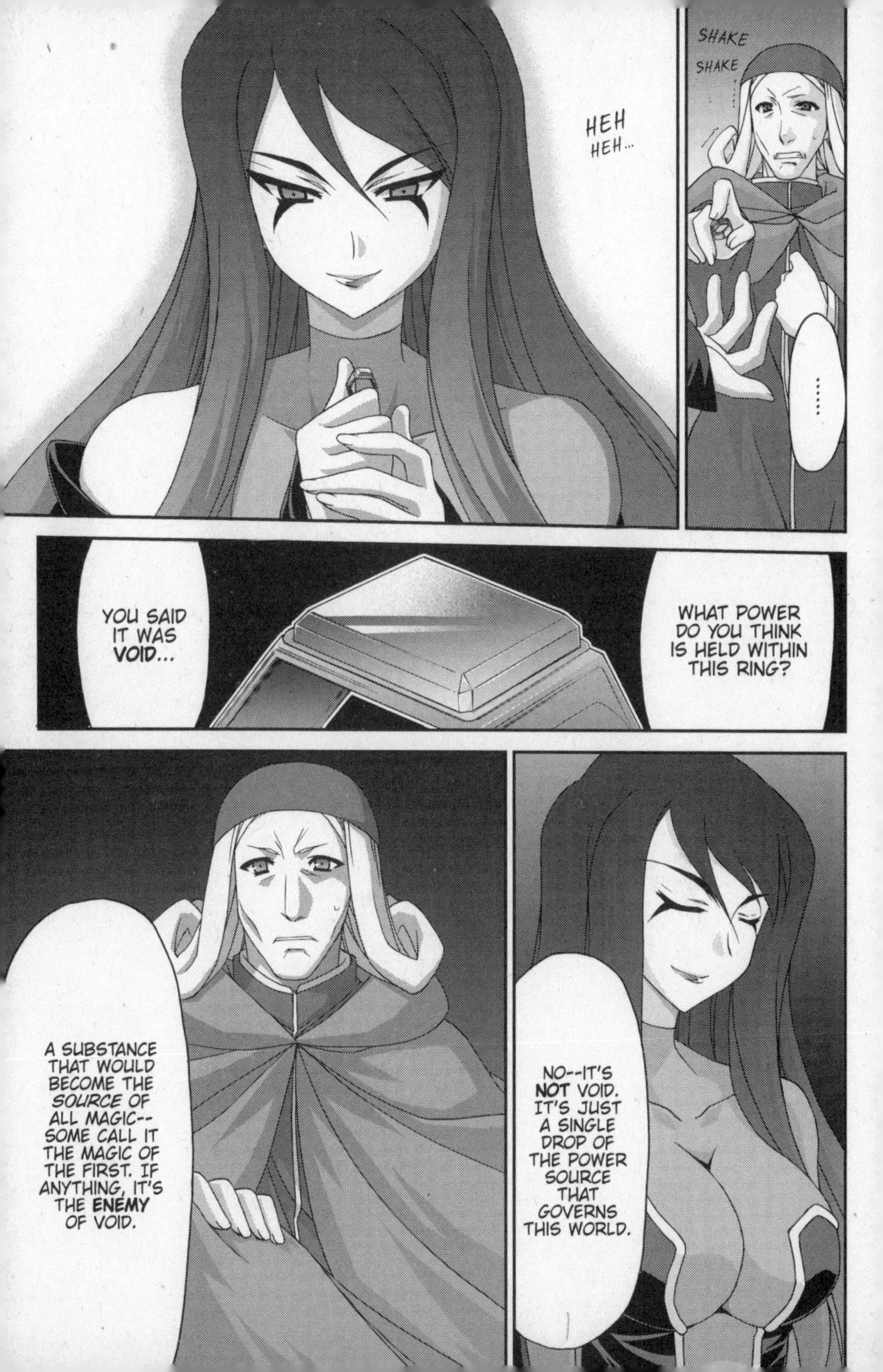
SHAKE
SHAKE
......
HEH HEH...
WHAT POWER DO YOU THINK IS HELD WITHIN THIS RING?
YOU SAID IT WAS **VOID**...
NO--IT'S **NOT** VOID. IT'S JUST A SINGLE DROP OF THE POWER SOURCE THAT GOVERNS THIS WORLD.
A SUBSTANCE THAT WOULD BECOME THE *SOURCE* OF ALL MAGIC--SOME CALL IT THE MAGIC OF THE FIRST. IF ANYTHING, IT'S THE **ENEMY** OF VOID.

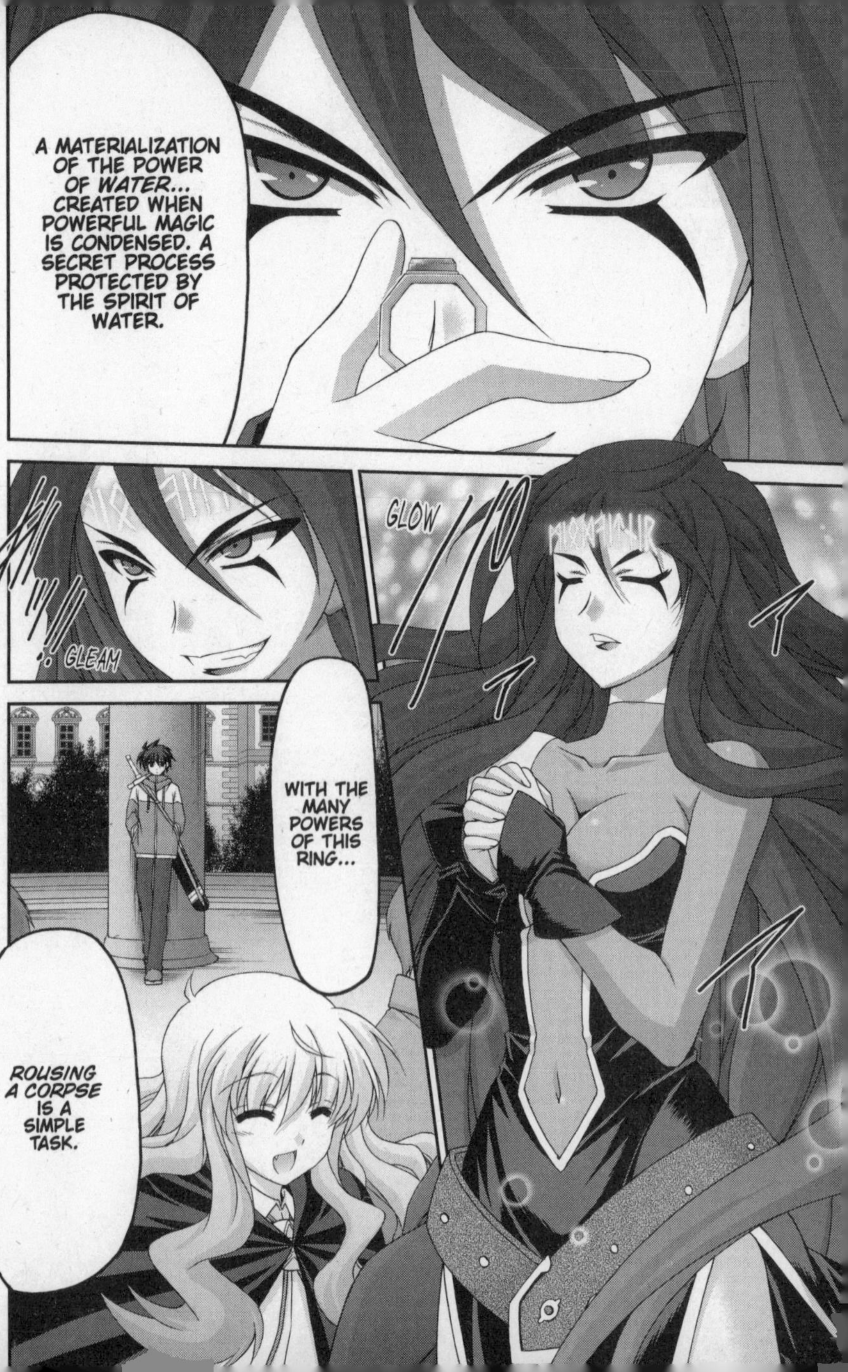
A MATERIALIZATION OF THE POWER OF *WATER*... CREATED WHEN POWERFUL MAGIC IS CONDENSED. A SECRET PROCESS PROTECTED BY THE SPIRIT OF WATER.
GLOW
GLEAM
WITH THE MANY POWERS OF THIS RING...
ROUSING A CORPSE IS A SIMPLE TASK.

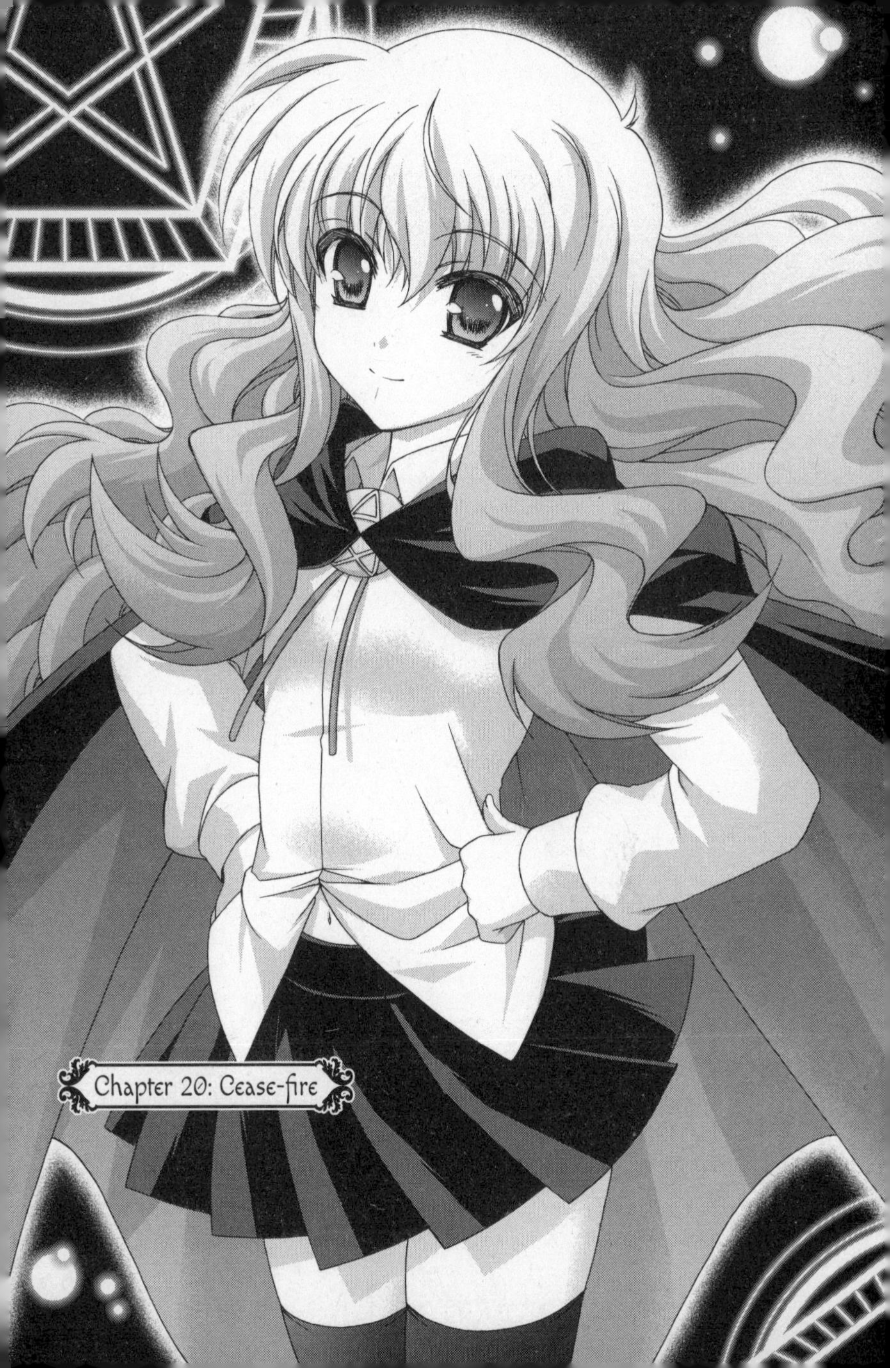
Chapter 20: Cease-fire

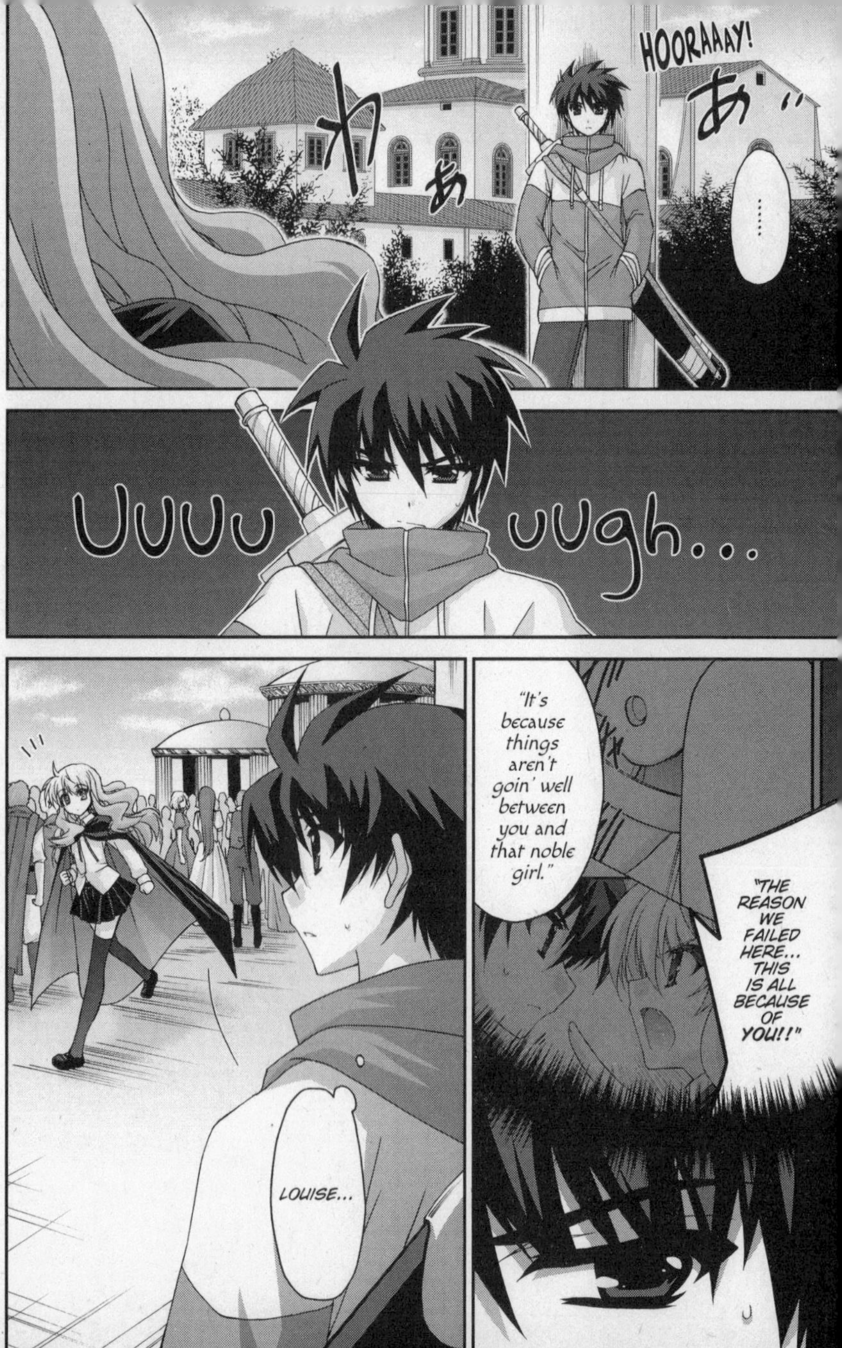
HOORAAAY!
あぃ
……
わぁ
Uuuu uugh...
"It's because things aren't goin' well between you and that noble girl."
"THE REASON WE FAILED HERE... THIS IS ALL BECAUSE OF YOU!!"
LOUISE...

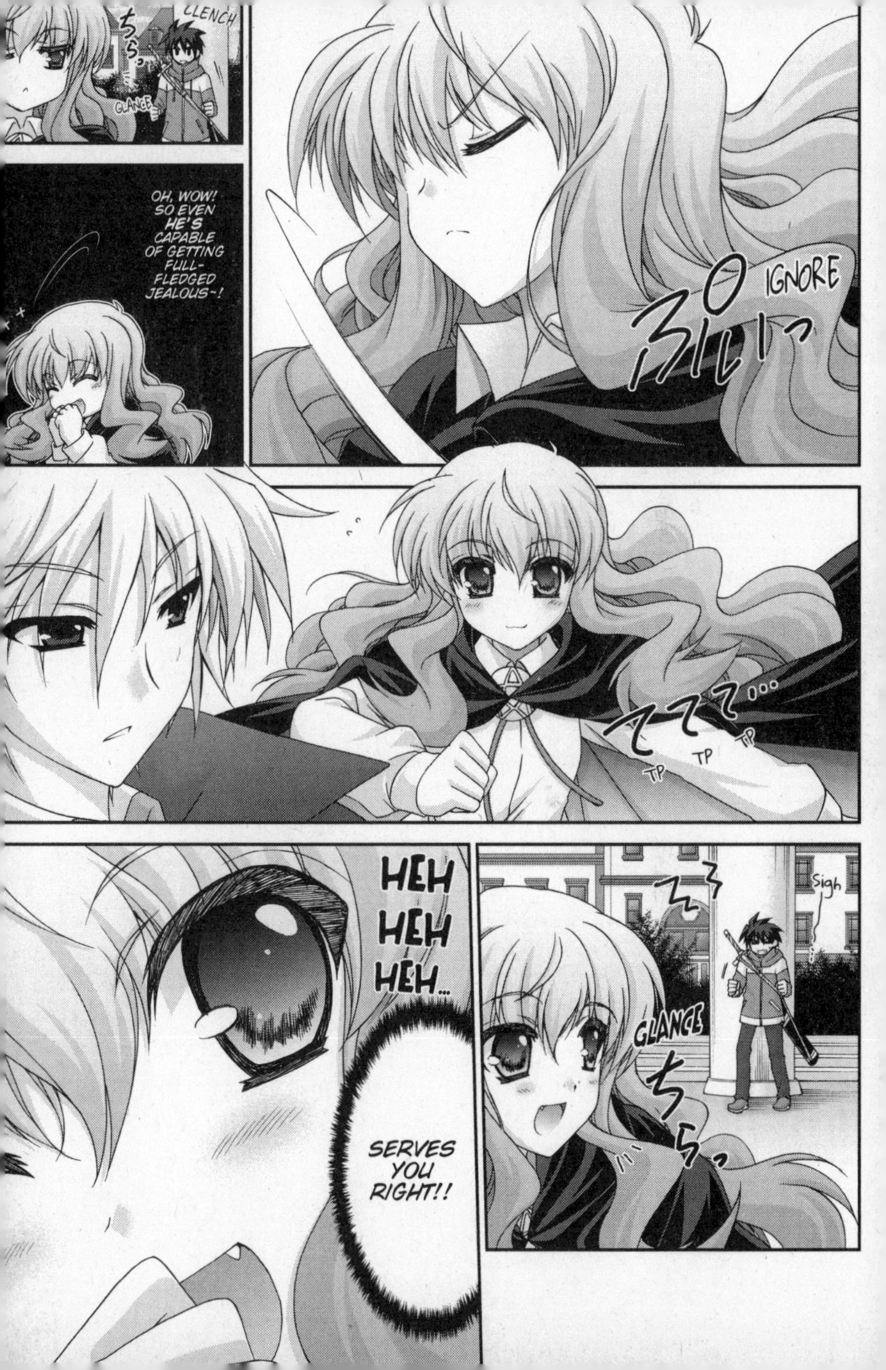

ふいっ
IGNORE
CLENCH
ちらっ
GLANCE
OH, WOW! SO EVEN HE'S CAPABLE OF GETTING FULL-FLEDGED JEALOUS-!
てててっ...
TP
TP
TP
Sigh
GLANCE
ちらっ
HEH HEH HEH...
SERVES YOU RIGHT!!

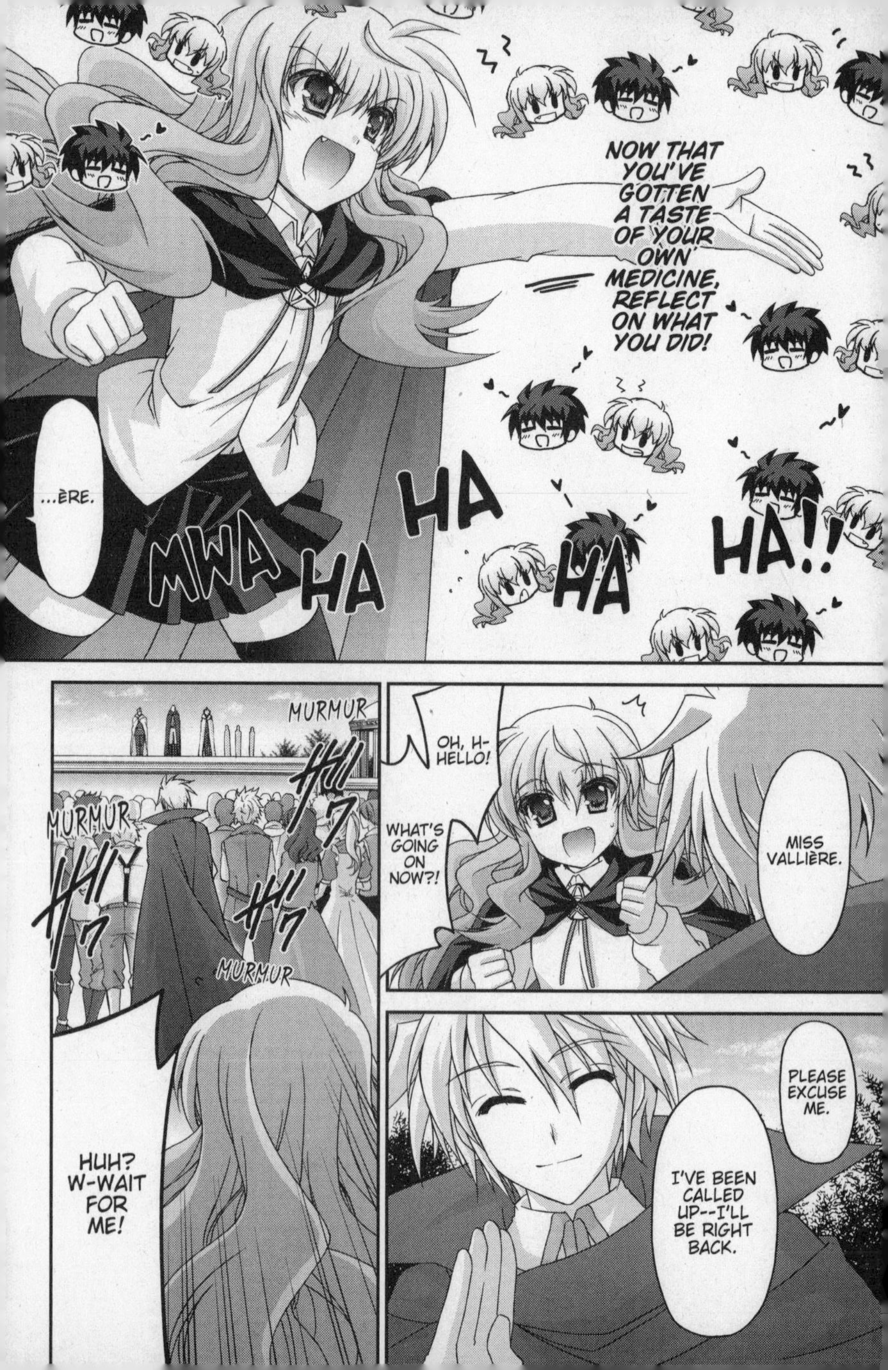
NOW THAT YOU'VE GOTTEN A TASTE OF YOUR OWN MEDICINE, REFLECT ON WHAT YOU DID!
MWA HA HA HA HA!!
...ÈRE.
MISS VALLIÈRE.
OH, H-HELLO!
WHAT'S GOING ON NOW?!
PLEASE EXCUSE ME.
I'VE BEEN CALLED UP--I'LL BE RIGHT BACK.
MURMUR
MURMUR
MURMUR
HUH? W-WAIT FOR ME!

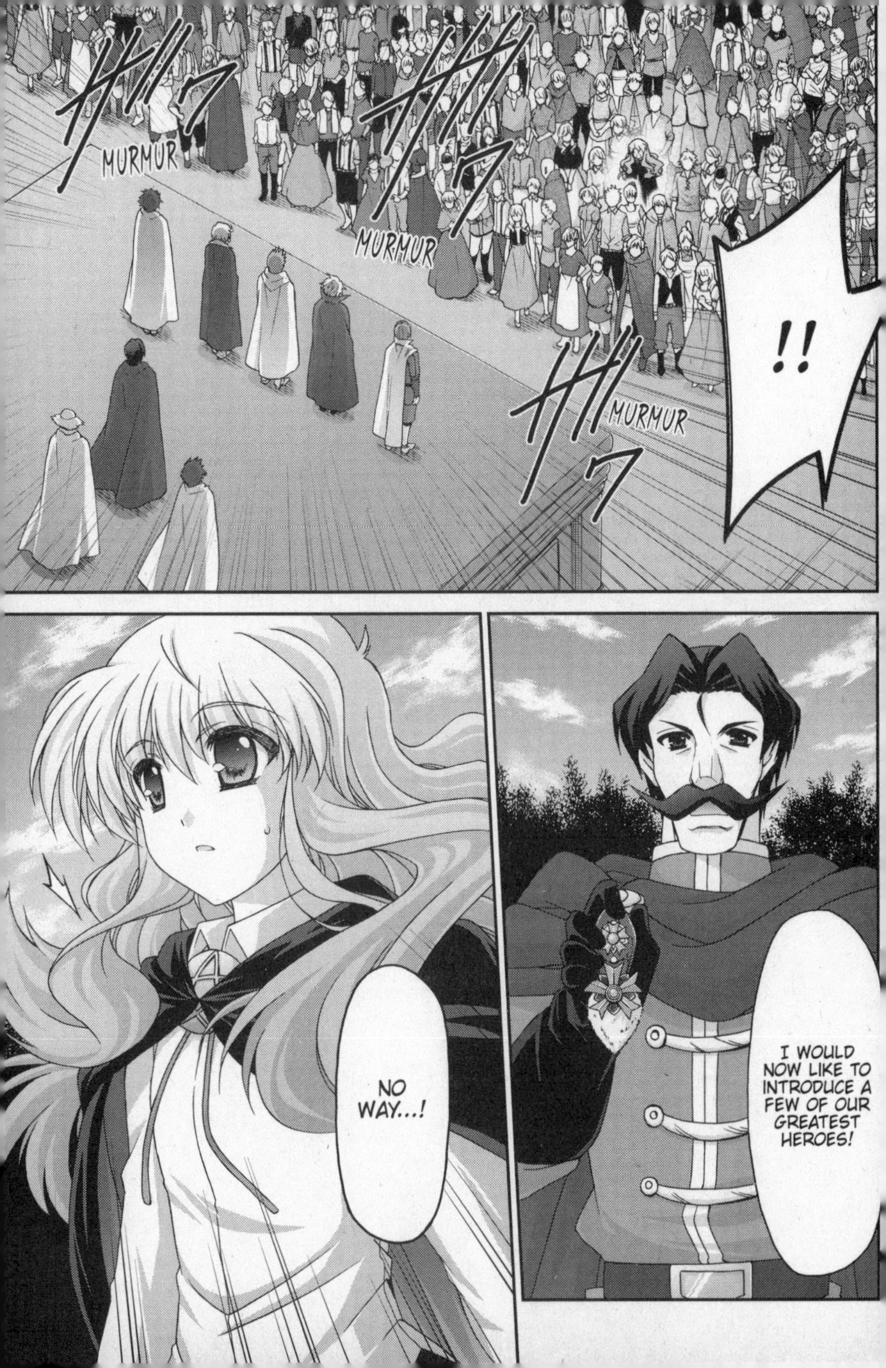
!!
MURMUR
MURMUR
MURMUR
MURMUR
I WOULD NOW LIKE TO INTRODUCE A FEW OF OUR GREATEST HEROES!
NO WAY...!

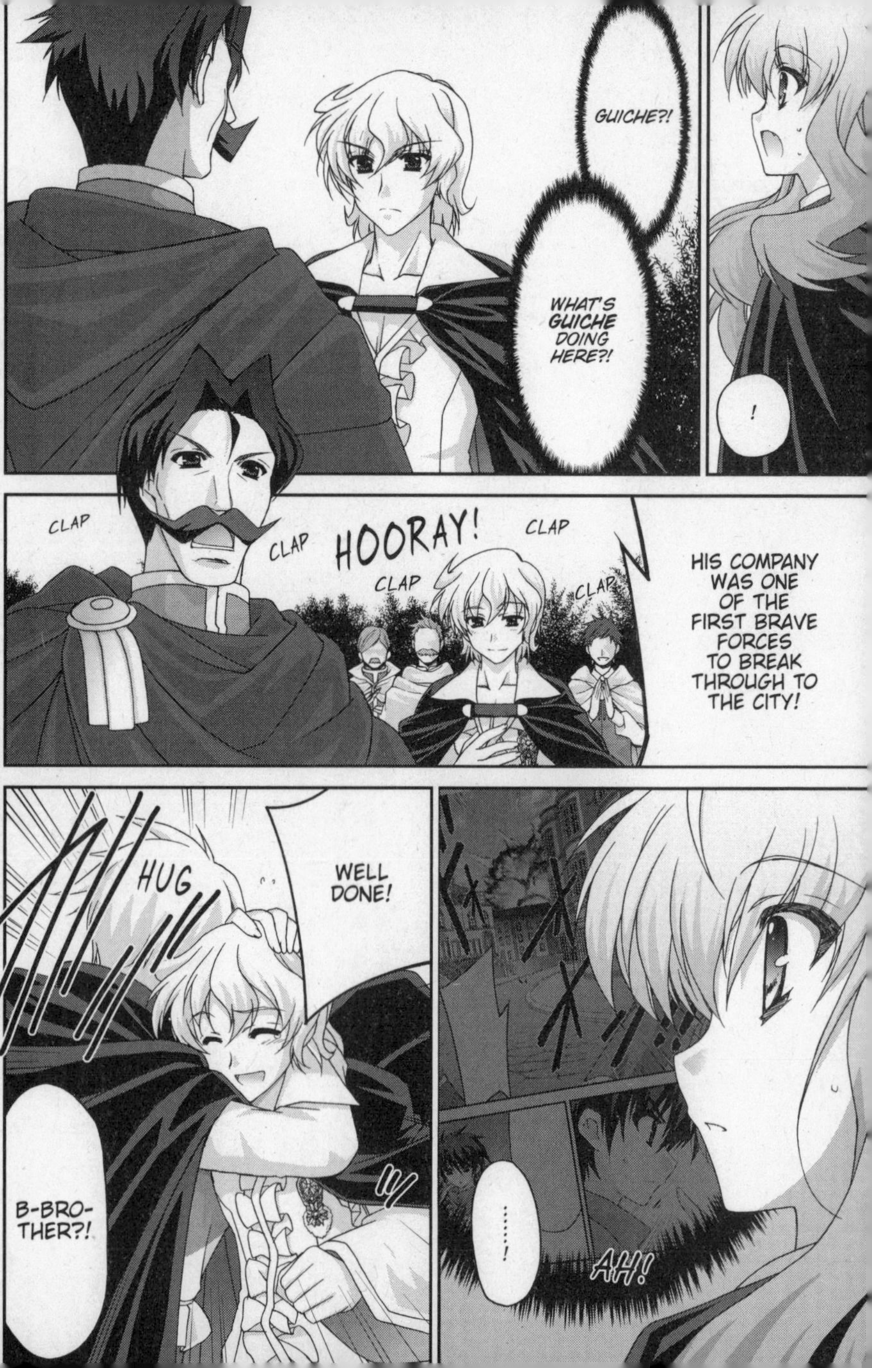
!
GUICHE?!
WHAT'S GUICHE DOING HERE?!
HIS COMPANY WAS ONE OF THE FIRST BRAVE FORCES TO BREAK THROUGH TO THE CITY!
CLAP
CLAP
HOORAY!
CLAP
CLAP
CLAP
......!
AH!
WELL DONE!
HUG
B-BROTHER?!

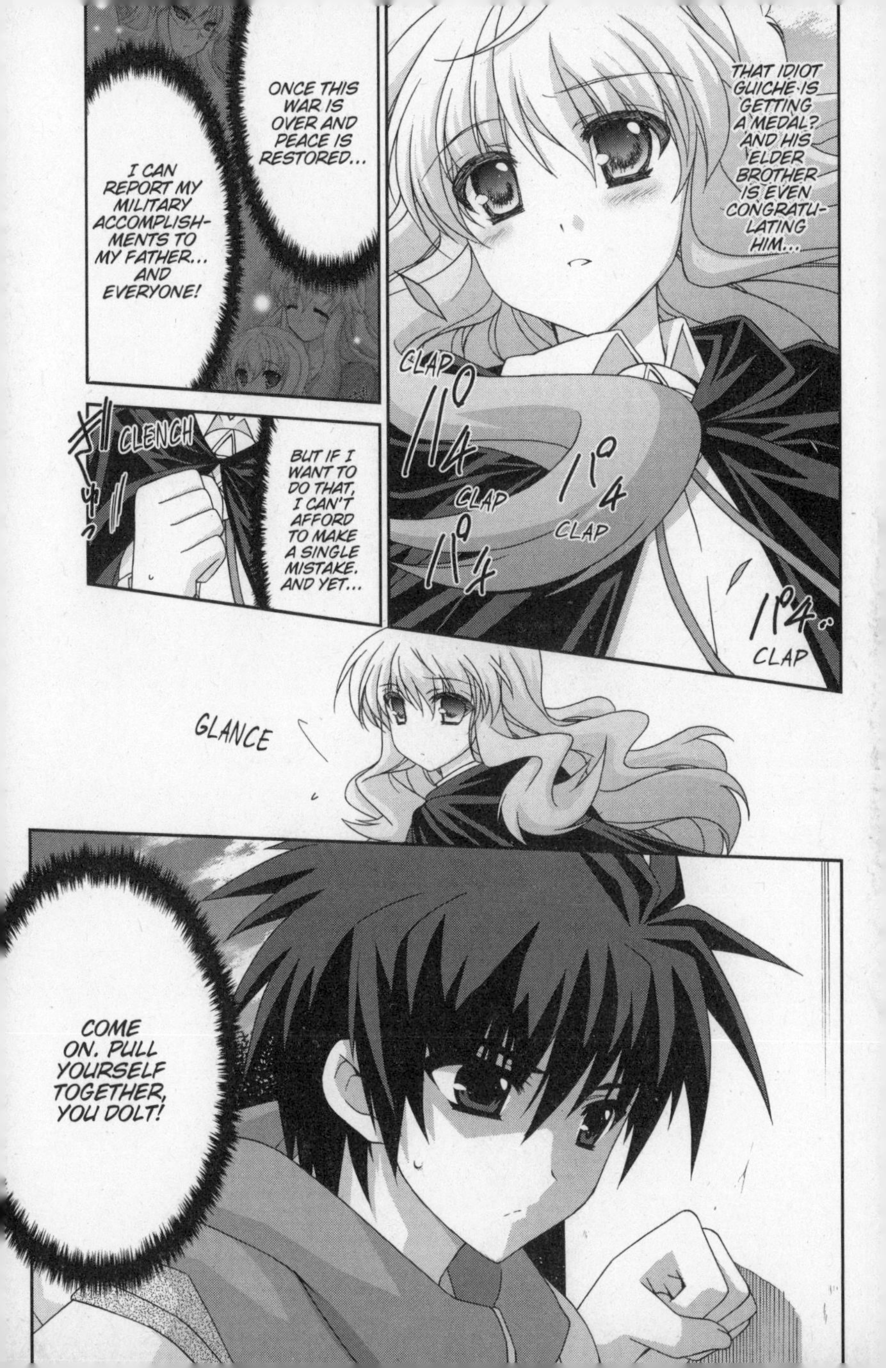
THAT IDIOT GUICHE IS GETTING A MEDAL? AND HIS ELDER BROTHER IS EVEN CONGRATULATING HIM...
CLAP
CLAP
CLAP
CLAP
ONCE THIS WAR IS OVER AND PEACE IS RESTORED...
I CAN REPORT MY MILITARY ACCOMPLISHMENTS TO MY FATHER... AND EVERYONE!
CLENCH
BUT IF I WANT TO DO THAT, I CAN'T AFFORD TO MAKE A SINGLE MISTAKE. AND YET...
GLANCE
COME ON. PULL YOURSELF TOGETHER, YOU DOLT!

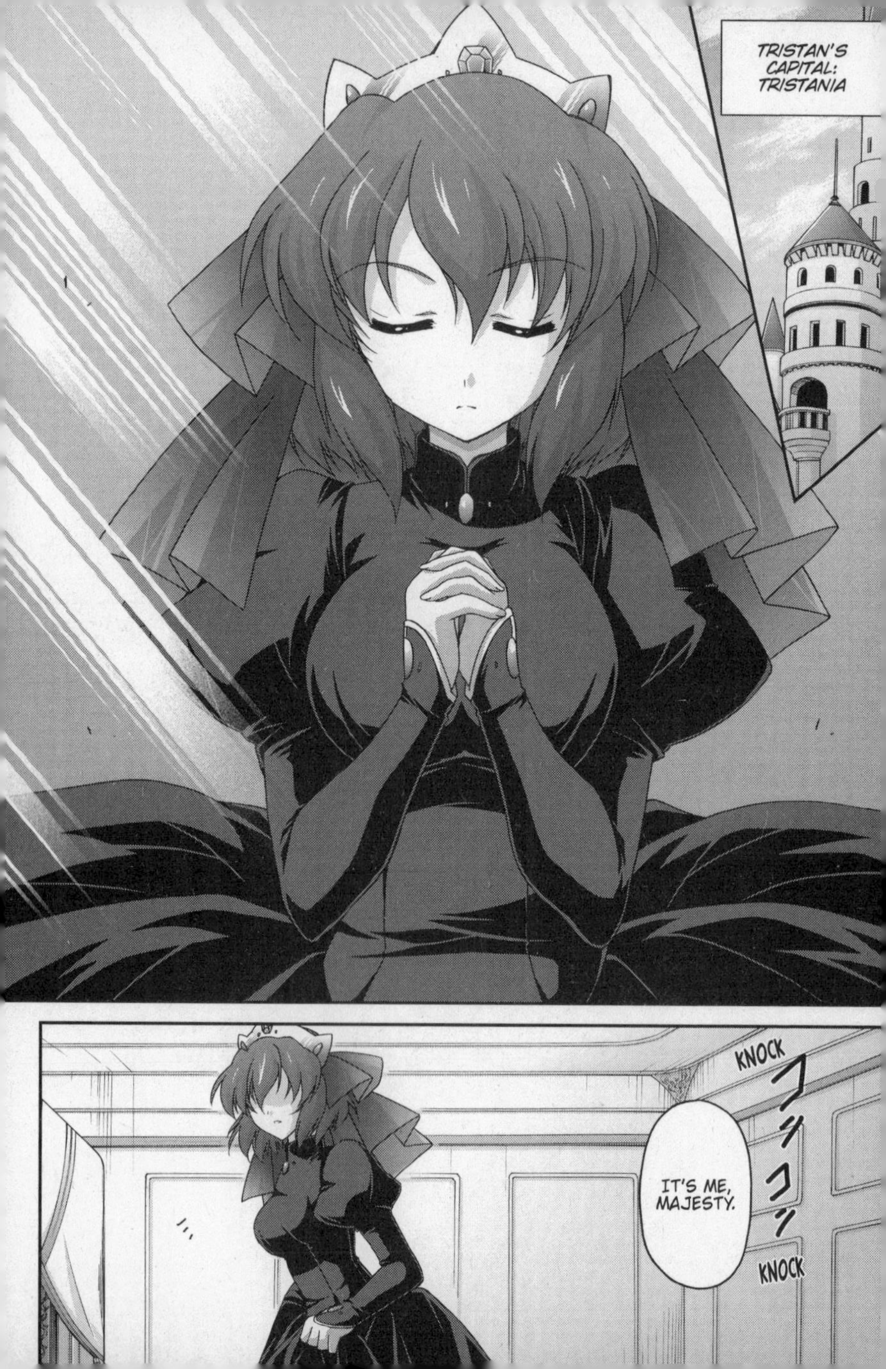
TRISTAN'S CAPITAL: TRISTANIA
KNOCK
KNOCK
IT'S ME, MAJESTY.

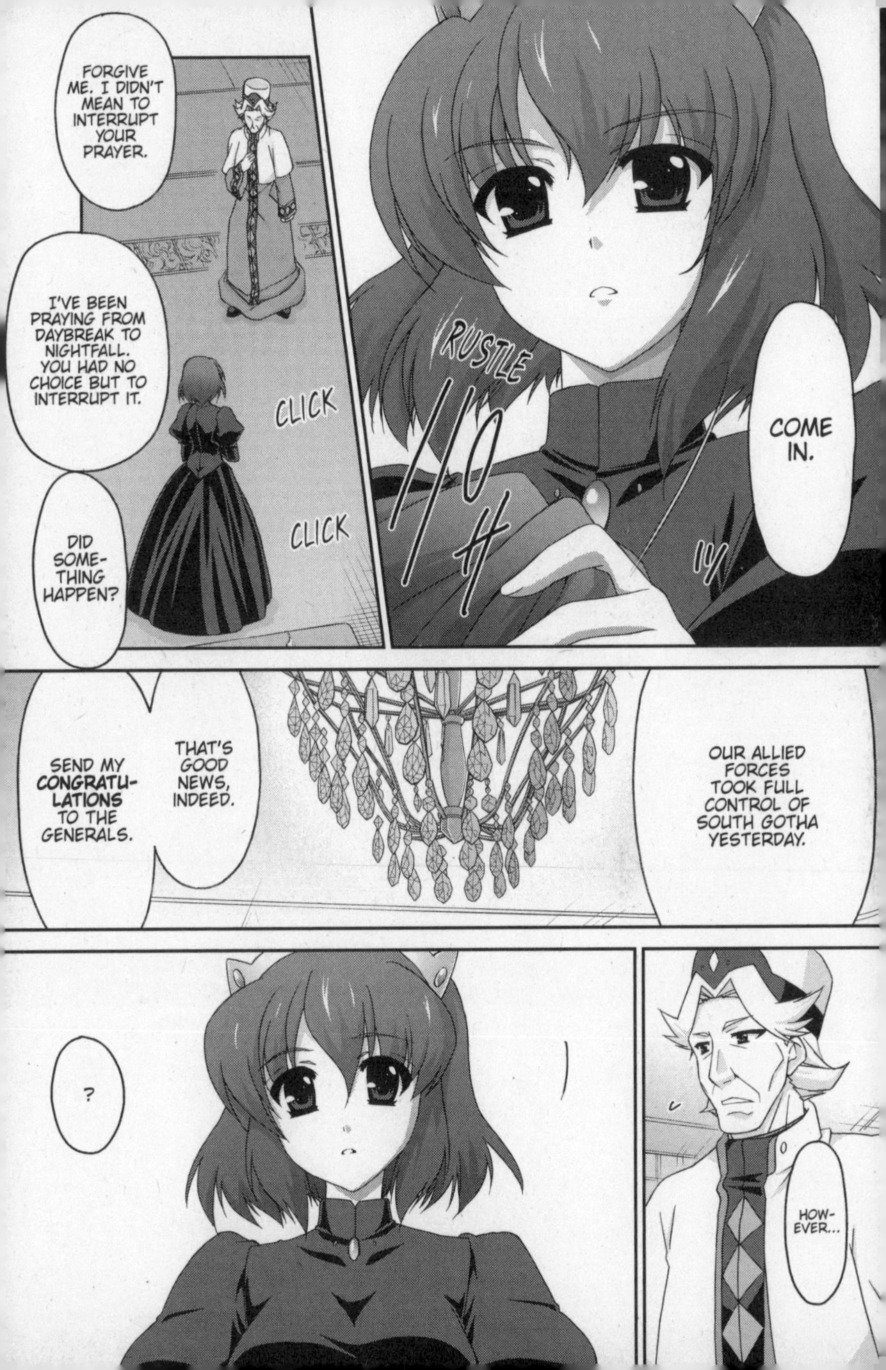
RUSTLE
COME IN.
FORGIVE ME. I DIDN'T MEAN TO INTERRUPT YOUR PRAYER.
I'VE BEEN PRAYING FROM DAYBREAK TO NIGHTFALL. YOU HAD NO CHOICE BUT TO INTERRUPT IT.
CLICK
CLICK
DID SOMETHING HAPPEN?
OUR ALLIED FORCES TOOK FULL CONTROL OF SOUTH GOTHA YESTERDAY.
THAT'S GOOD NEWS, INDEED.
SEND MY **CONGRATULATIONS** TO THE GENERALS.
HOWEVER...
?

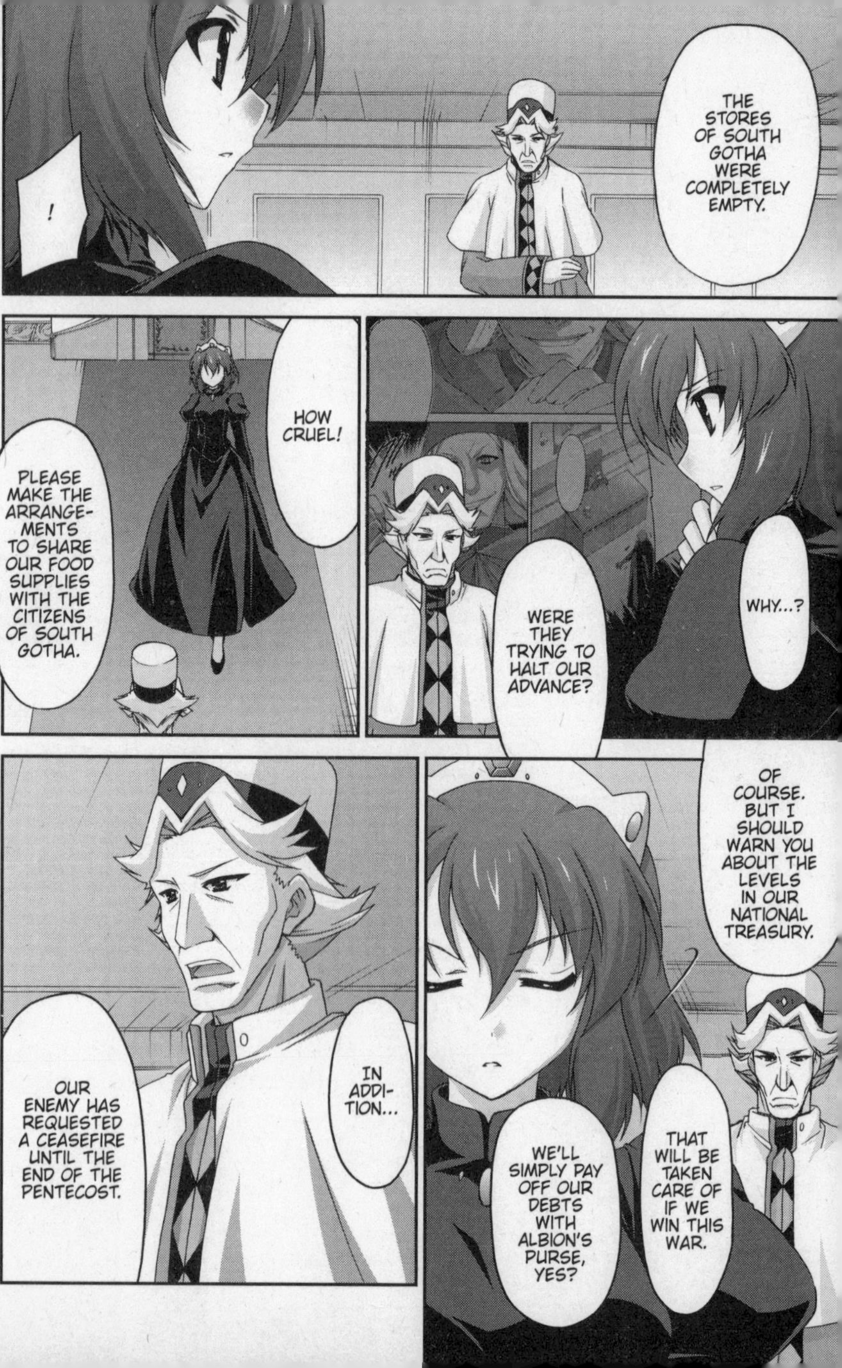
THE STORES OF SOUTH GOTHA WERE COMPLETELY EMPTY.
!
WHY...?
WERE THEY TRYING TO HALT OUR ADVANCE?
HOW CRUEL!
PLEASE MAKE THE ARRANGE-MENTS TO SHARE OUR FOOD SUPPLIES WITH THE CITIZENS OF SOUTH GOTHA.
OF COURSE. BUT I SHOULD WARN YOU ABOUT THE LEVELS IN OUR NATIONAL TREASURY.
THAT WILL BE TAKEN CARE OF IF WE WIN THIS WAR.
WE'LL SIMPLY PAY OFF OUR DEBTS WITH ALBION'S PURSE, YES?
IN ADDI-TION...
OUR ENEMY HAS REQUESTED A CEASEFIRE UNTIL THE END OF THE PENTECOST.

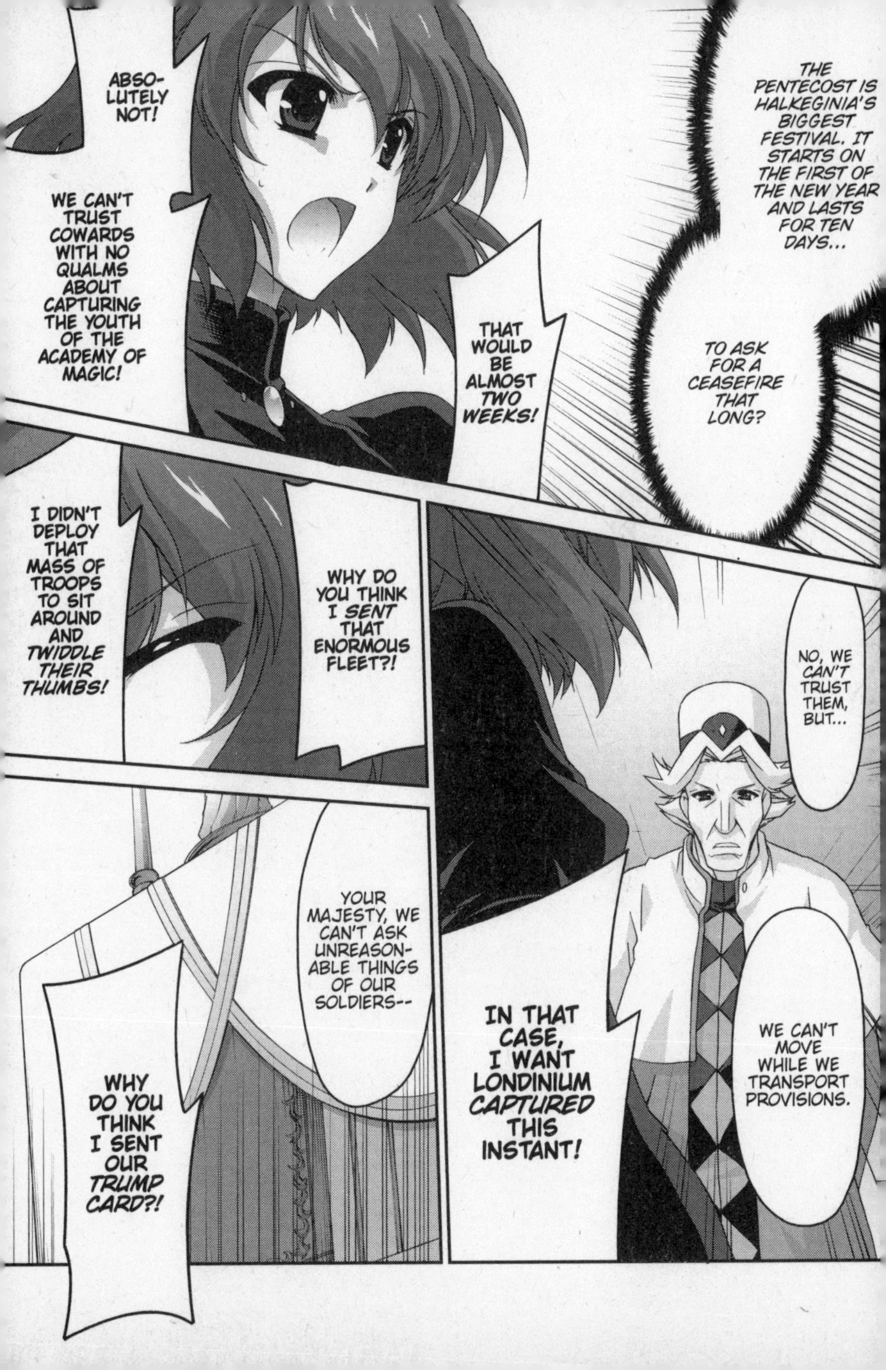

THE PENTECOST IS HALKEGINIA'S BIGGEST FESTIVAL. IT STARTS ON THE FIRST OF THE NEW YEAR AND LASTS FOR TEN DAYS...
TO ASK FOR A CEASEFIRE THAT LONG?
THAT WOULD BE ALMOST *TWO WEEKS!*
ABSO-LUTELY NOT!
WE CAN'T TRUST COWARDS WITH NO QUALMS ABOUT CAPTURING THE YOUTH OF THE ACADEMY OF MAGIC!
NO, WE *CAN'T* TRUST THEM, BUT...
WE CAN'T MOVE WHILE WE TRANSPORT PROVISIONS.
IN THAT CASE, I WANT LONDINIUM *CAPTURED* THIS INSTANT!
WHY DO YOU THINK I *SENT* THAT ENORMOUS FLEET?!
I DIDN'T DEPLOY THAT MASS OF TROOPS TO SIT AROUND AND *TWIDDLE THEIR THUMBS!*
YOUR MAJESTY, WE CAN'T ASK UNREASON-ABLE THINGS OF OUR SOLDIERS--
WHY DO YOU THINK I SENT OUR *TRUMP CARD?!*

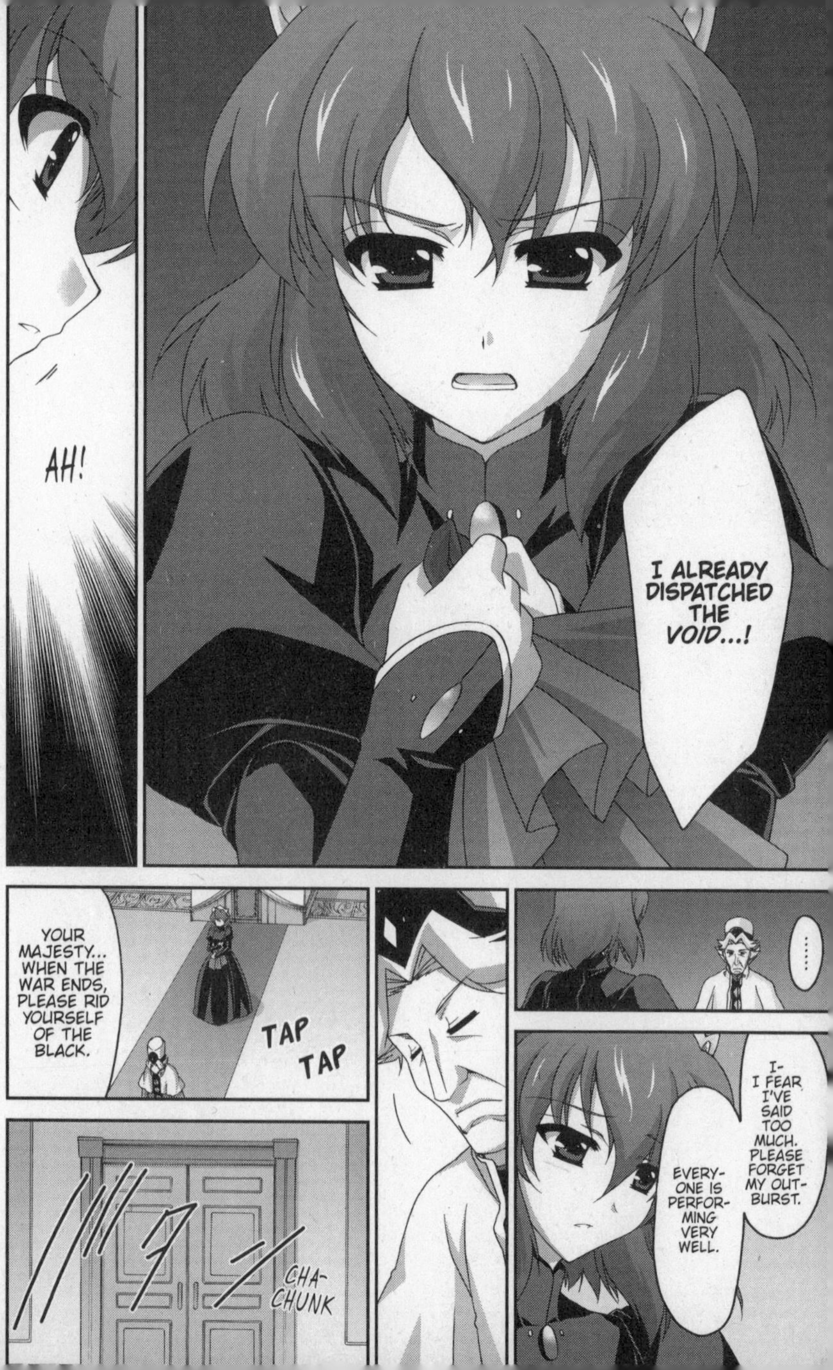
I ALREADY DISPATCHED THE VOID...!
AH!
......
I- I FEAR I'VE SAID TOO MUCH. PLEASE FORGET MY OUTBURST.
EVERYONE IS PERFORMING VERY WELL.
YOUR MAJESTY... WHEN THE WAR ENDS, PLEASE RID YOURSELF OF THE BLACK.
TAP TAP
CHA-CHUNK

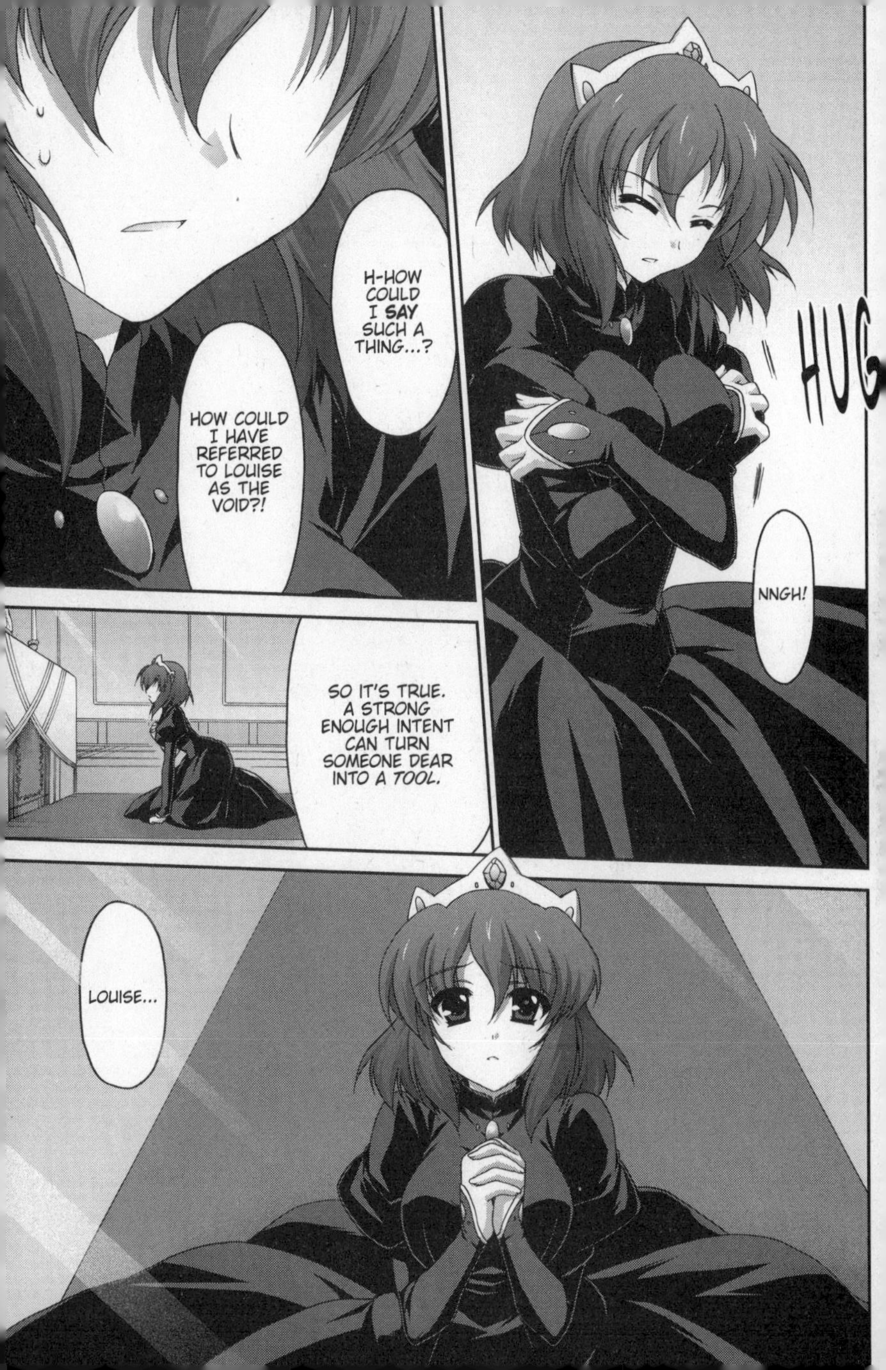
HUG
NNGH!
H-HOW COULD I **SAY** SUCH A THING...?
HOW COULD I HAVE REFERRED TO LOUISE AS THE VOID?!
SO IT'S TRUE. A STRONG ENOUGH INTENT CAN TURN SOMEONE DEAR INTO A *TOOL.*
LOUISE...

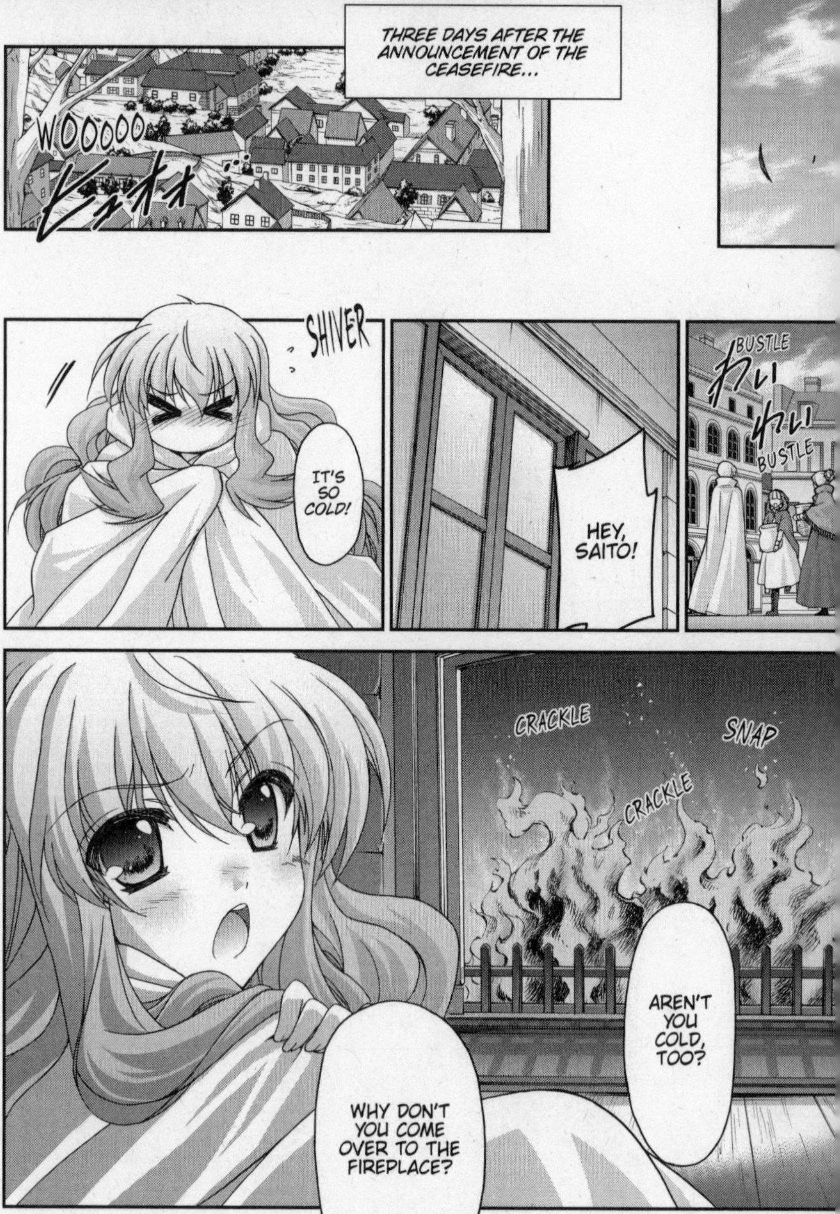
THREE DAYS AFTER THE ANNOUNCEMENT OF THE CEASEFIRE...
WOOOOO
ヒュオォ
BUSTLE
わいわい
BUSTLE
HEY, SAITO!
SHIVER
IT'S SO COLD!
SNAP
CRACKLE
CRACKLE
AREN'T YOU COLD, TOO?
WHY DON'T YOU COME OVER TO THE FIREPLACE?

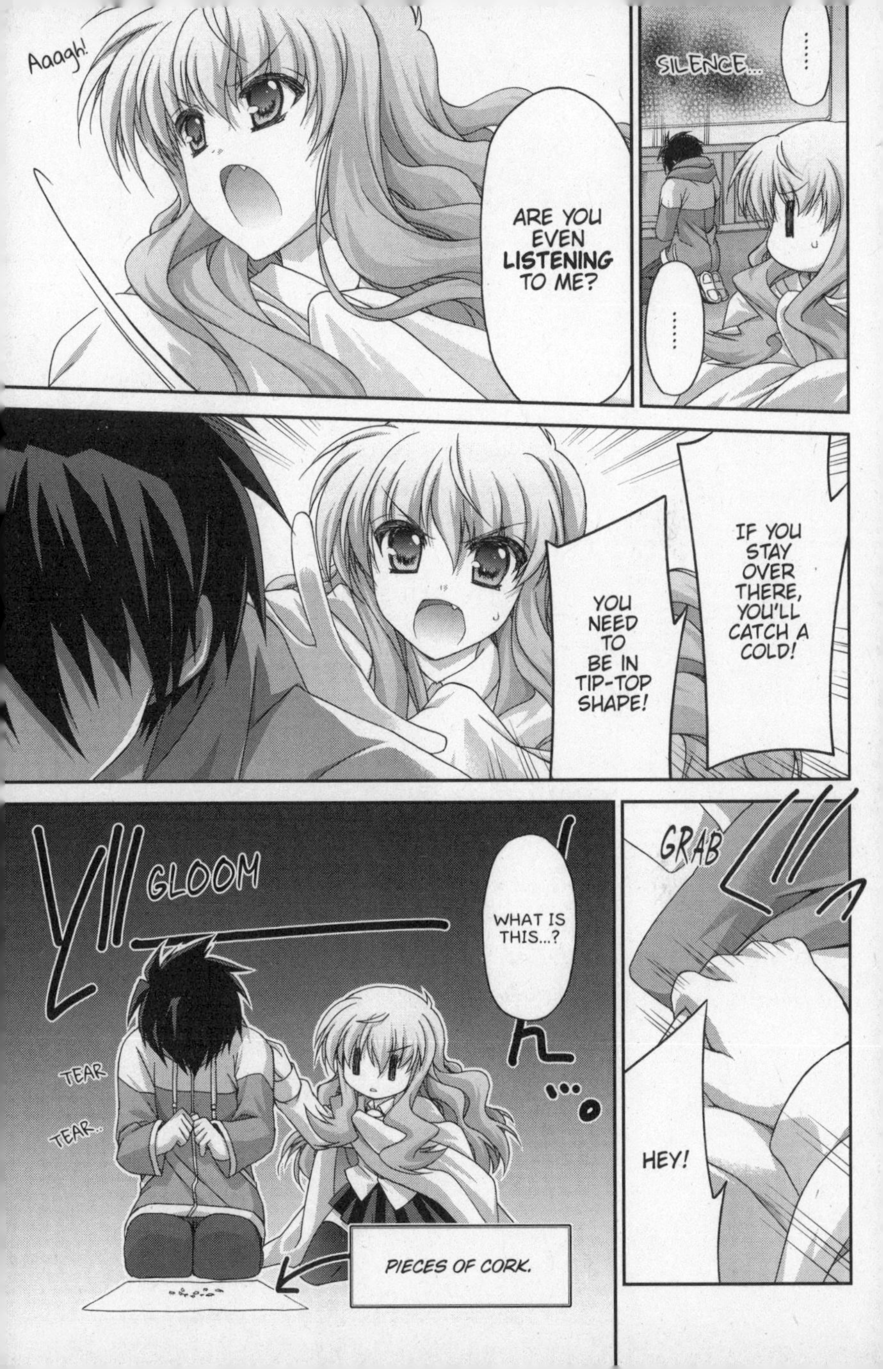
......
SILENCE...
......
ARE YOU EVEN LISTENING TO ME?
Aaaagh!
IF YOU STAY OVER THERE, YOU'LL CATCH A COLD!
YOU NEED TO BE IN TIP-TOP SHAPE!
GRAB
HEY!
WHAT IS THIS...?
GLOOM
TEAR
TEAR..
PIECES OF CORK.

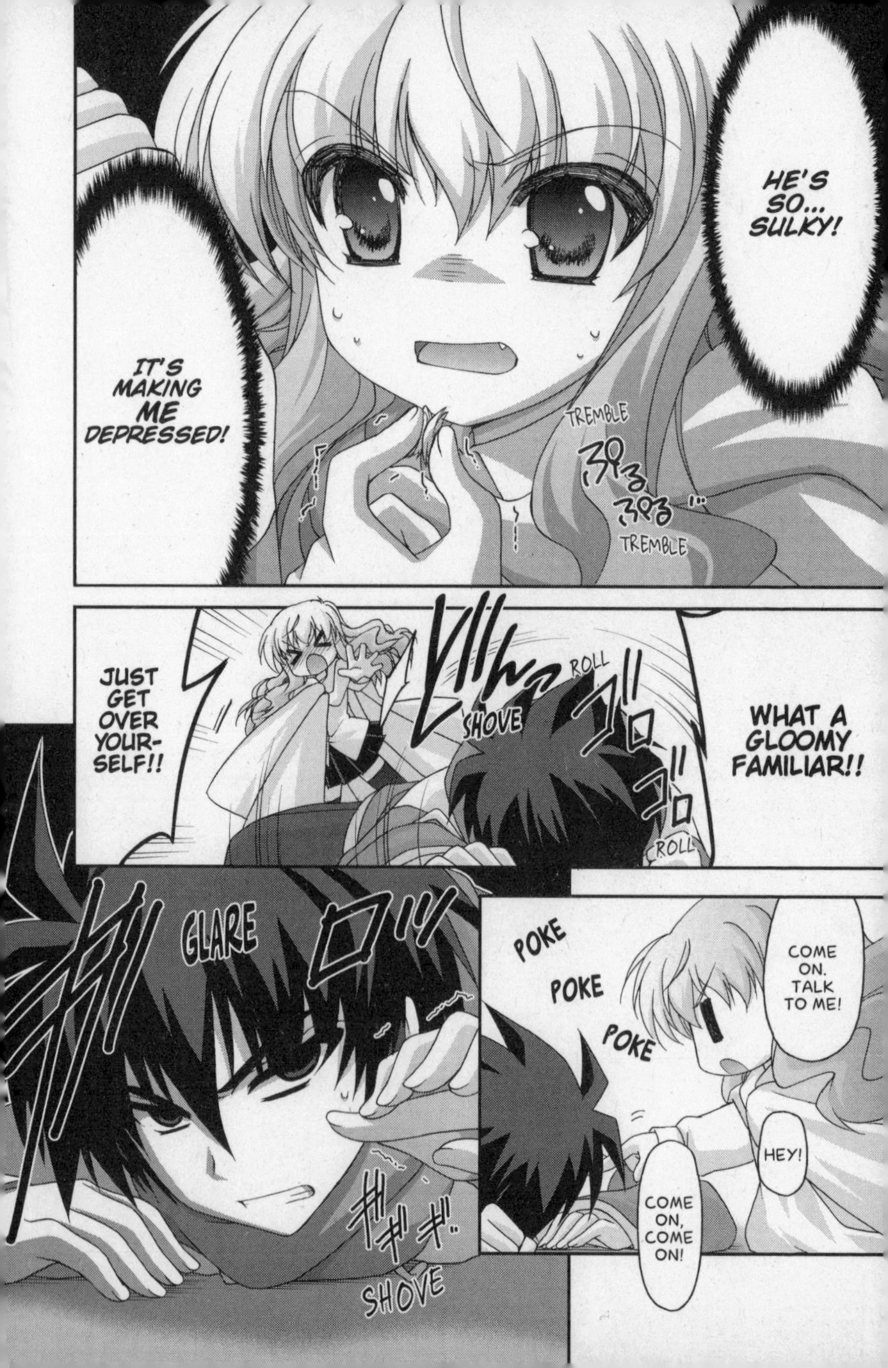
HE'S SO... SULKY!
IT'S MAKING ME DEPRESSED!
TREMBLE
TREMBLE
WHAT A GLOOMY FAMILIAR!!
ROLL
SHOVE
ROLL
JUST GET OVER YOURSELF!!
COME ON. TALK TO ME!
POKE
POKE
POKE
HEY!
COME ON, COME ON!
GLARE
SHOVE

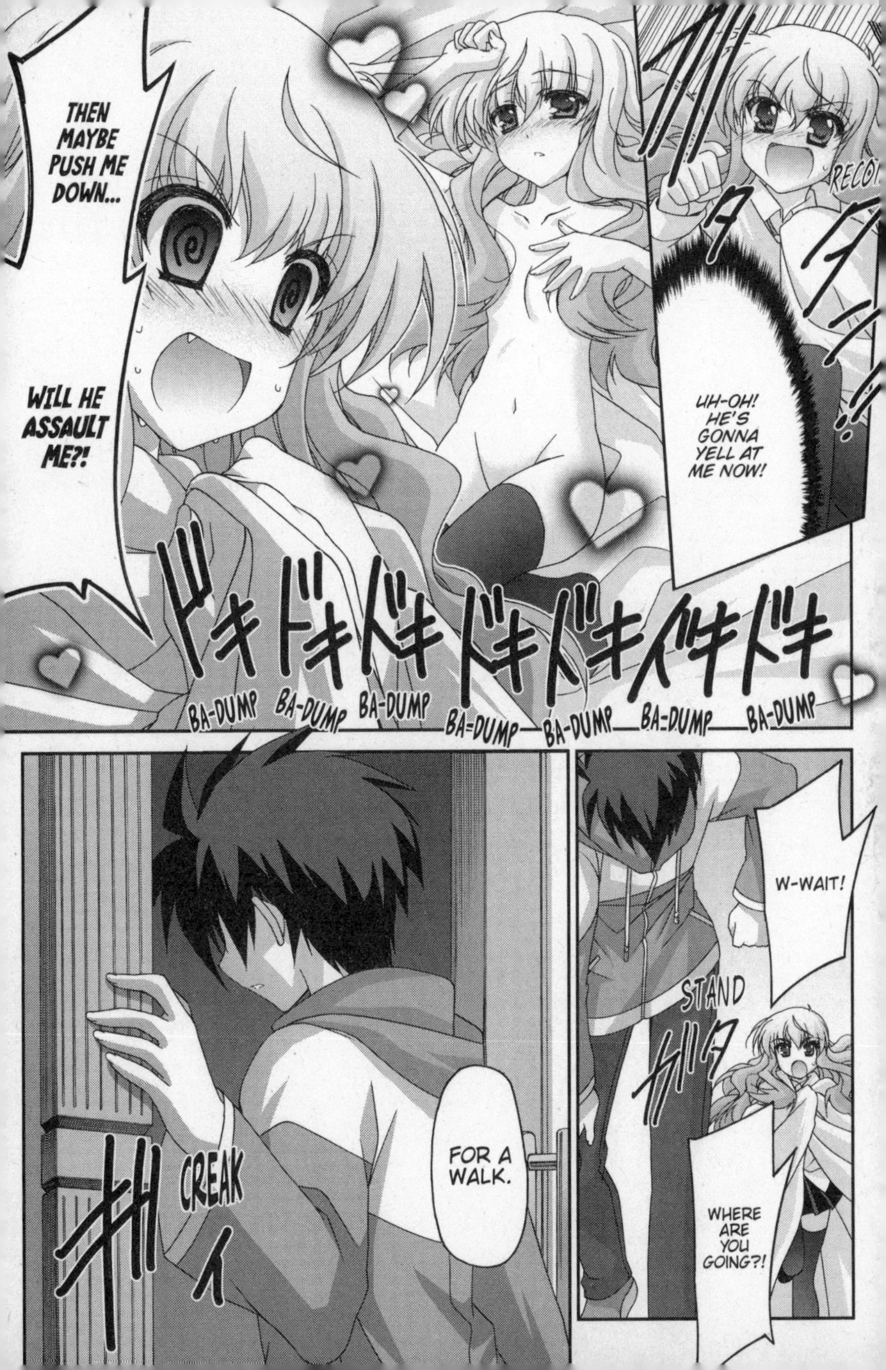
RECOI
UH-OH! HE'S GONNA YELL AT ME NOW!
THEN MAYBE PUSH ME DOWN...
WILL HE ASSAULT ME?!
BA-DUMP BA-DUMP BA-DUMP BA-DUMP BA-DUMP BA-DUMP BA-DUMP
W-WAIT!
STAND
WHERE ARE YOU GOING?!
FOR A WALK.
CREAK

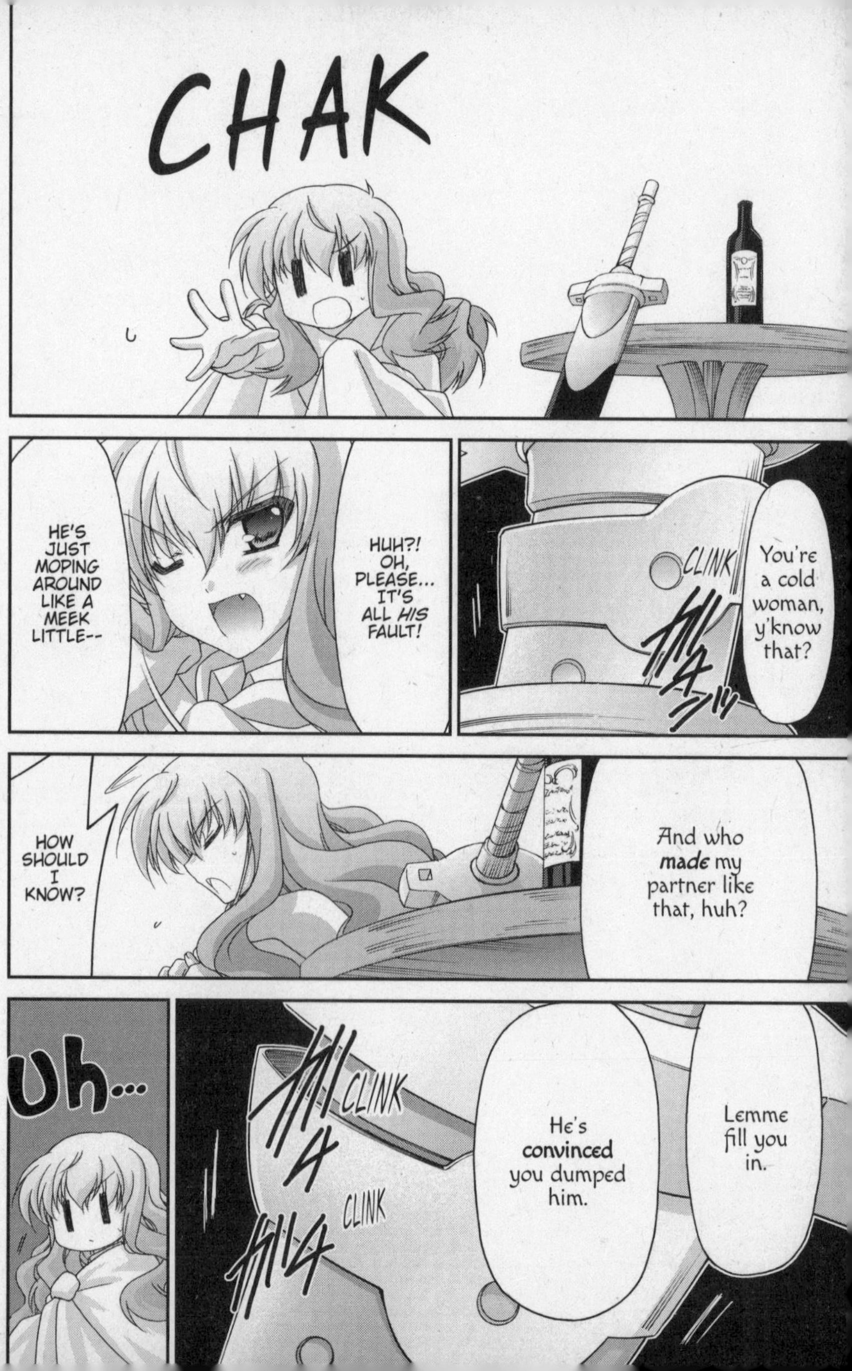
CHAK
You're a cold woman, y'know that?
CLINK
HUH?! OH, PLEASE... IT'S ALL *HIS* FAULT!
HE'S JUST MOPING AROUND LIKE A MEEK LITTLE--
And who **made** my partner like that, huh?
HOW SHOULD I KNOW?
Lemme fill you in.
He's **convinced** you dumped him.
CLINK
CLINK
Uh...

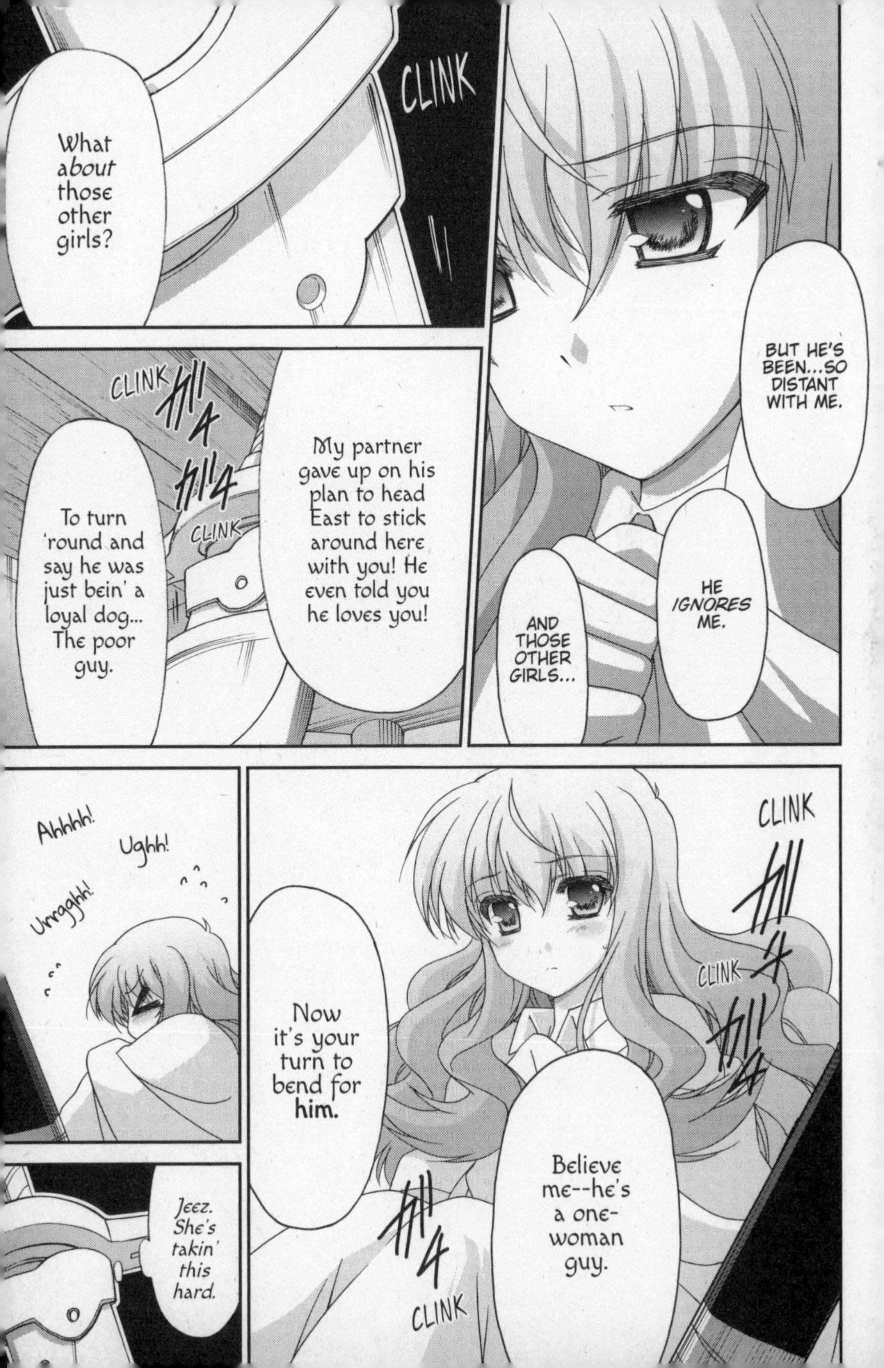

BUT HE'S BEEN...SO DISTANT WITH ME.
HE IGNORES ME.
AND THOSE OTHER GIRLS...
CLINK
What about those other girls?
CLINK
My partner gave up on his plan to head East to stick around here with you! He even told you he loves you!
CLINK
To turn 'round and say he was just bein' a loyal dog... The poor guy.
CLINK
CLINK
Now it's your turn to bend for him.
Believe me--he's a one-woman guy.
CLINK
Ahhhh!
Ughh!
Urrgghh!
Jeez. She's takin' this hard.

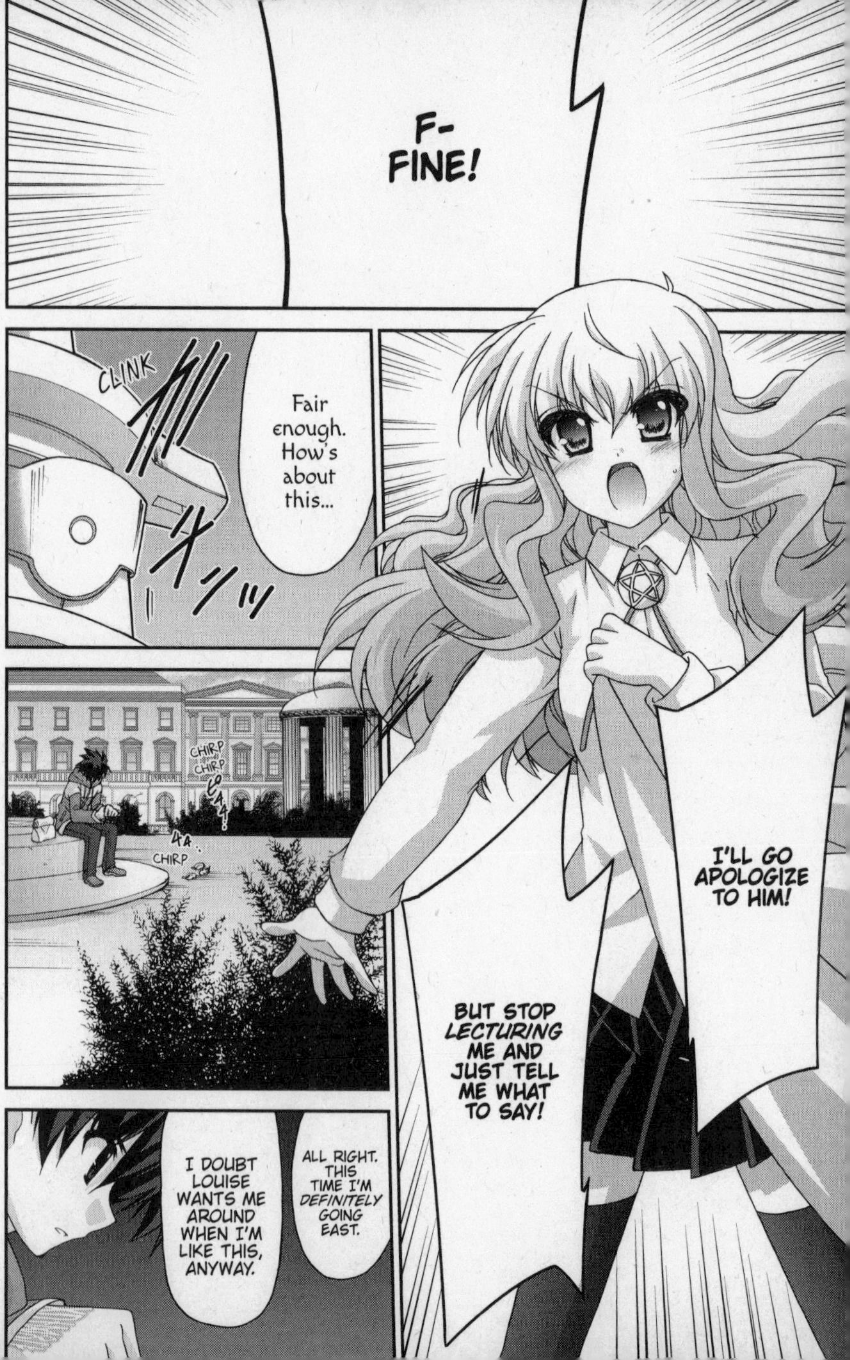
F-
FINE!
I'LL GO APOLOGIZE TO HIM!
BUT STOP *LECTURING* ME AND JUST TELL ME WHAT TO SAY!
CLINK
Fair enough. How's about this...
CHIRP
CHIRP
CHIRP
ALL RIGHT. THIS TIME I'M *DEFINITELY* GOING EAST.
I DOUBT LOUISE WANTS ME AROUND WHEN I'M LIKE THIS, ANYWAY.

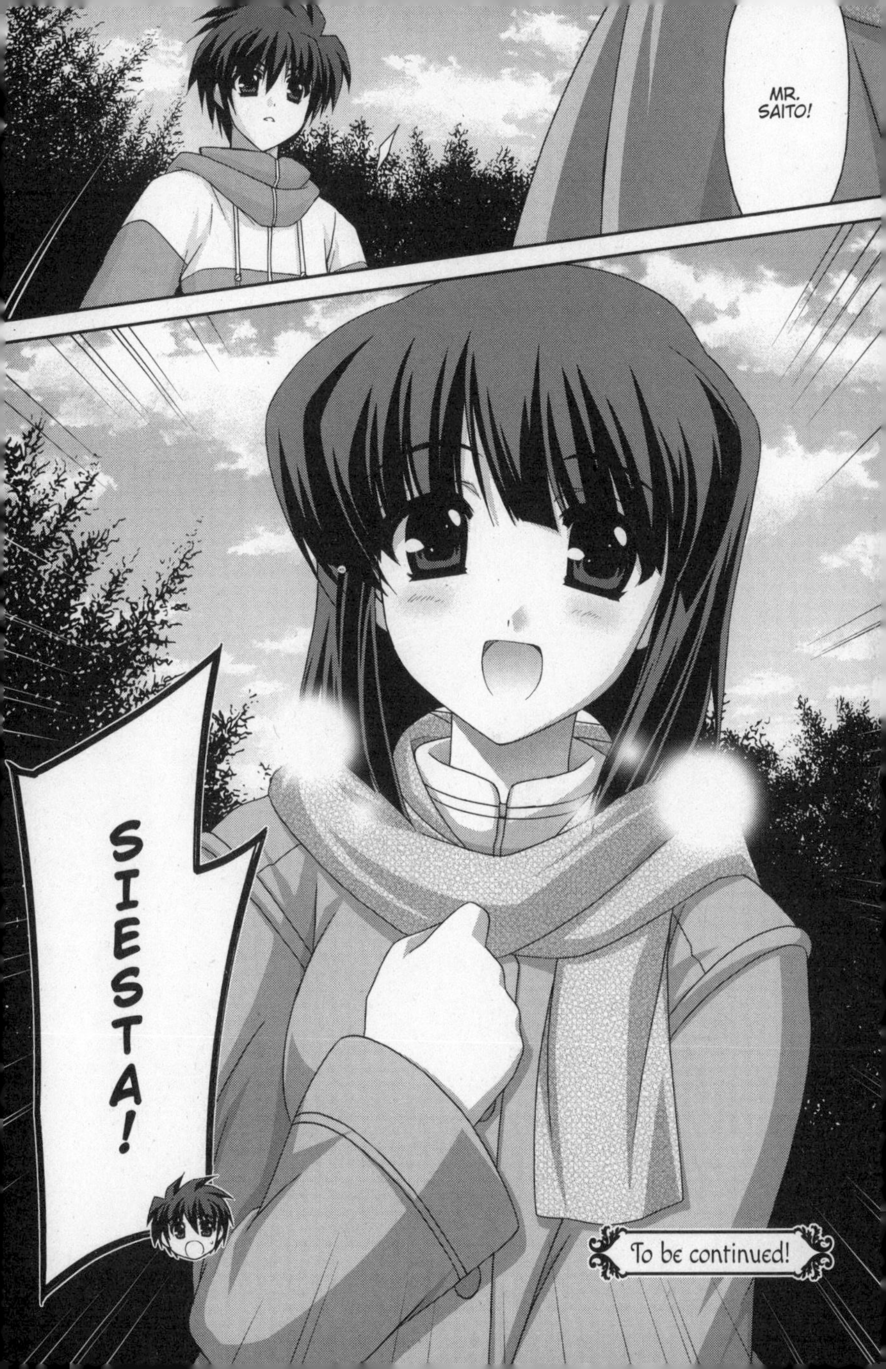
MR. SAITO!
SIESTA!
To be continued!

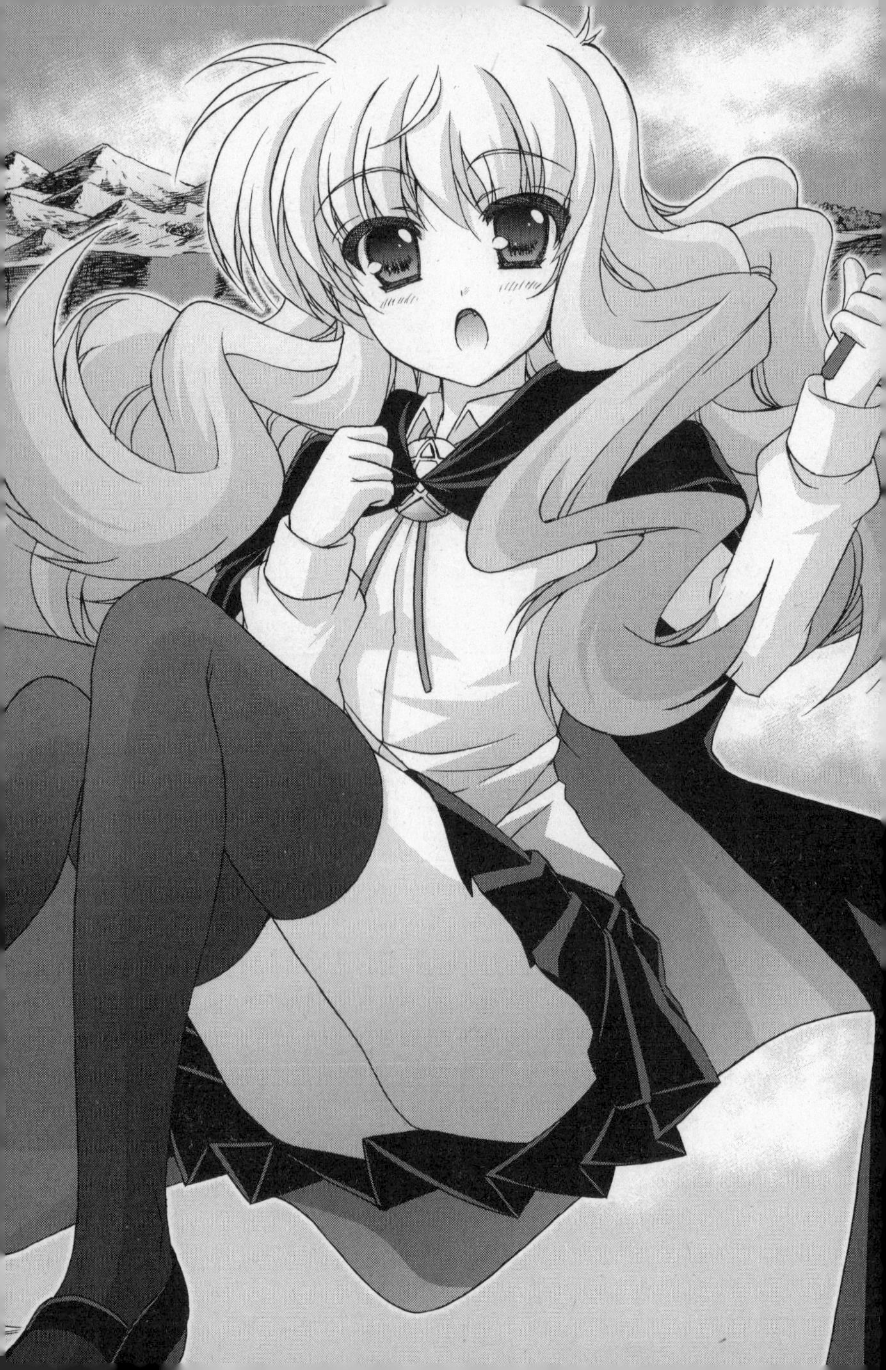

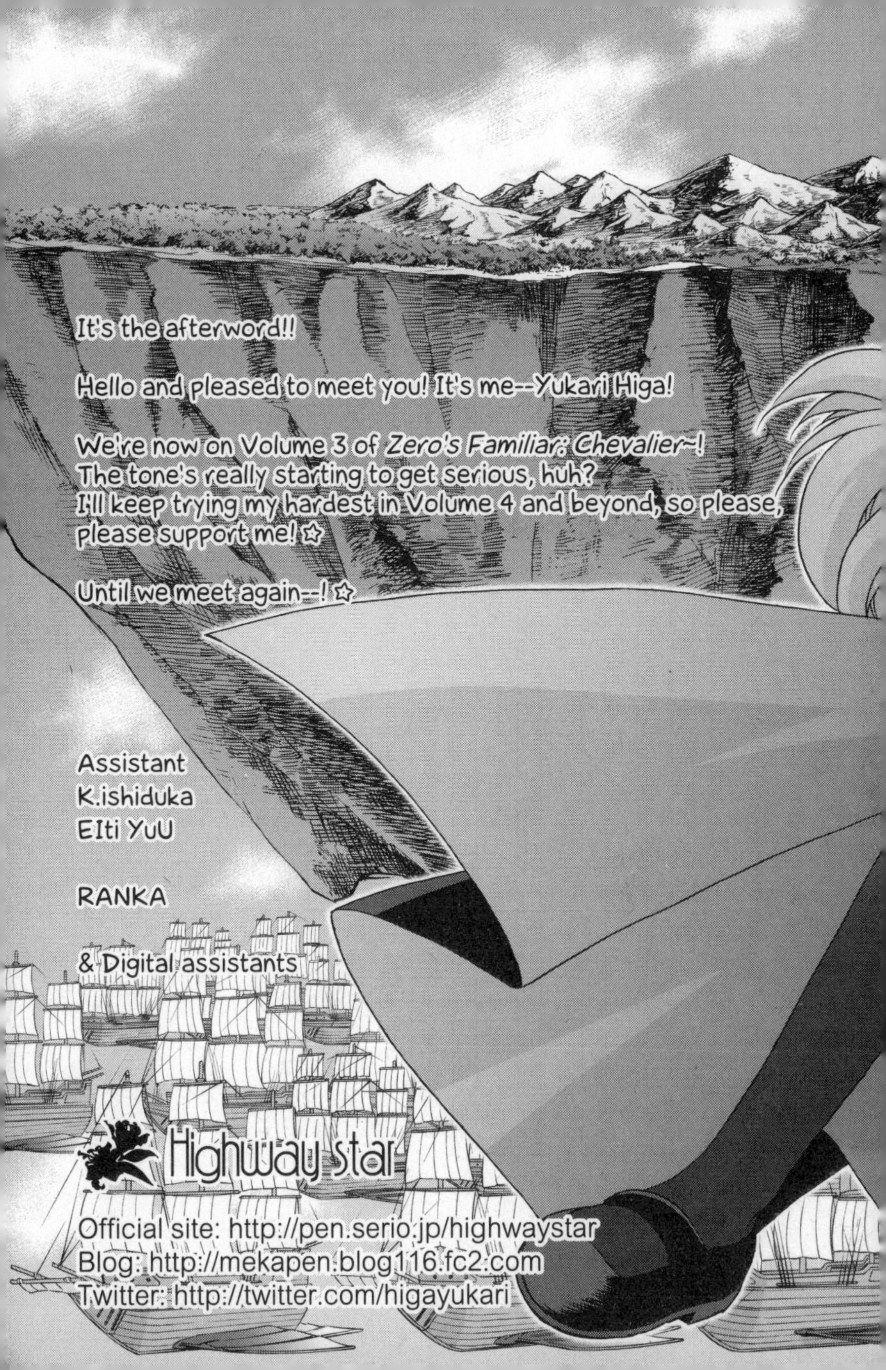

It's the afterword!!

Hello and pleased to meet you! It's me--Yukari Higa!

We're now on Volume 3 of *Zero's Familiar: Chevalier*~!
The tone's really starting to get serious, huh?
I'll keep trying my hardest in Volume 4 and beyond, so please, please support me! ☆

Until we meet again--! ☆

Assistant
K.ishiduka
EIti YuU

RANKA

& Digital assistants

Highway star

Official site: http://pen.serio.jp/highwaystar
Blog: http://mekapen.blog116.fc2.com
Twitter: http://twitter.com/higayukari

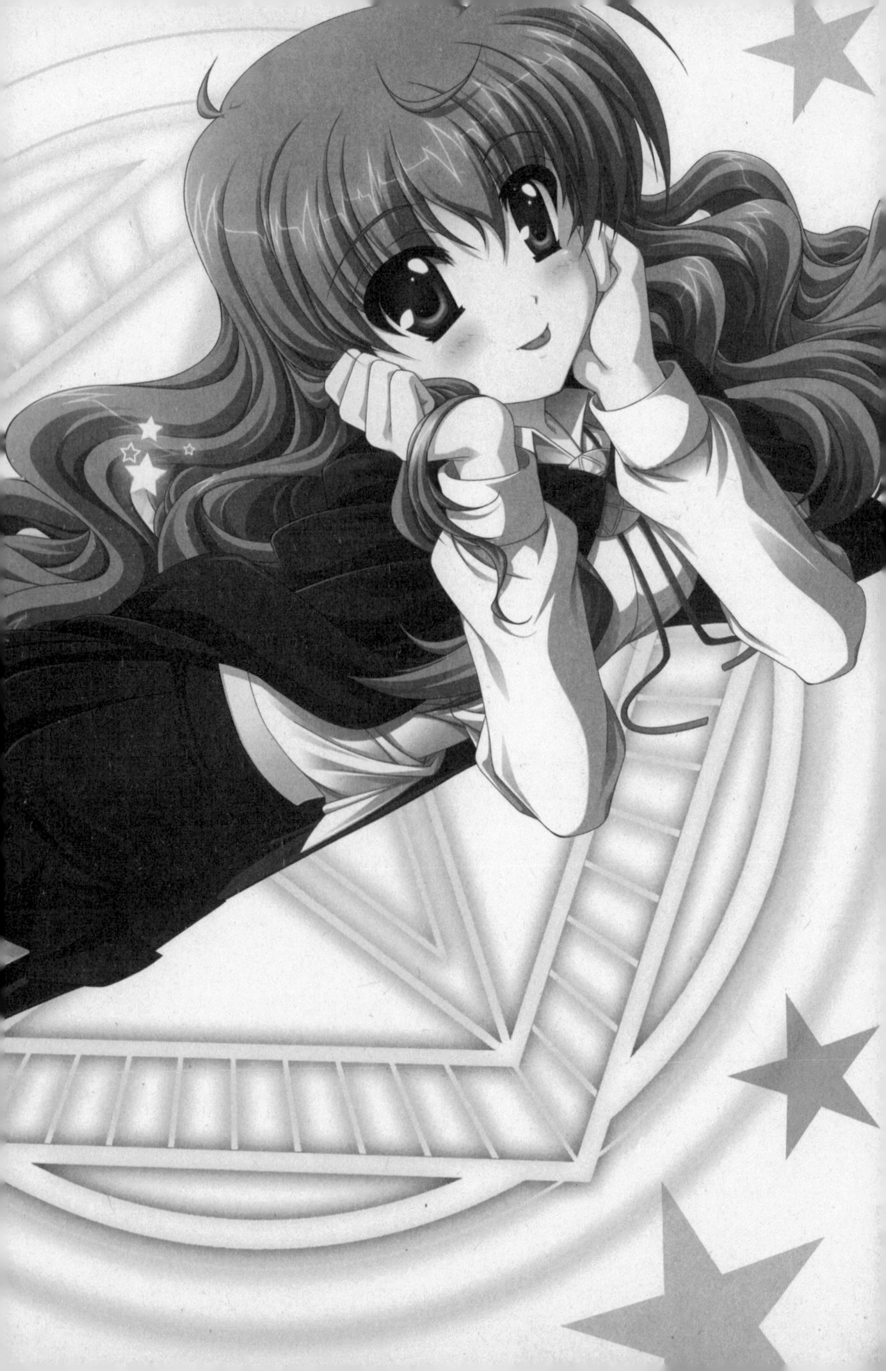

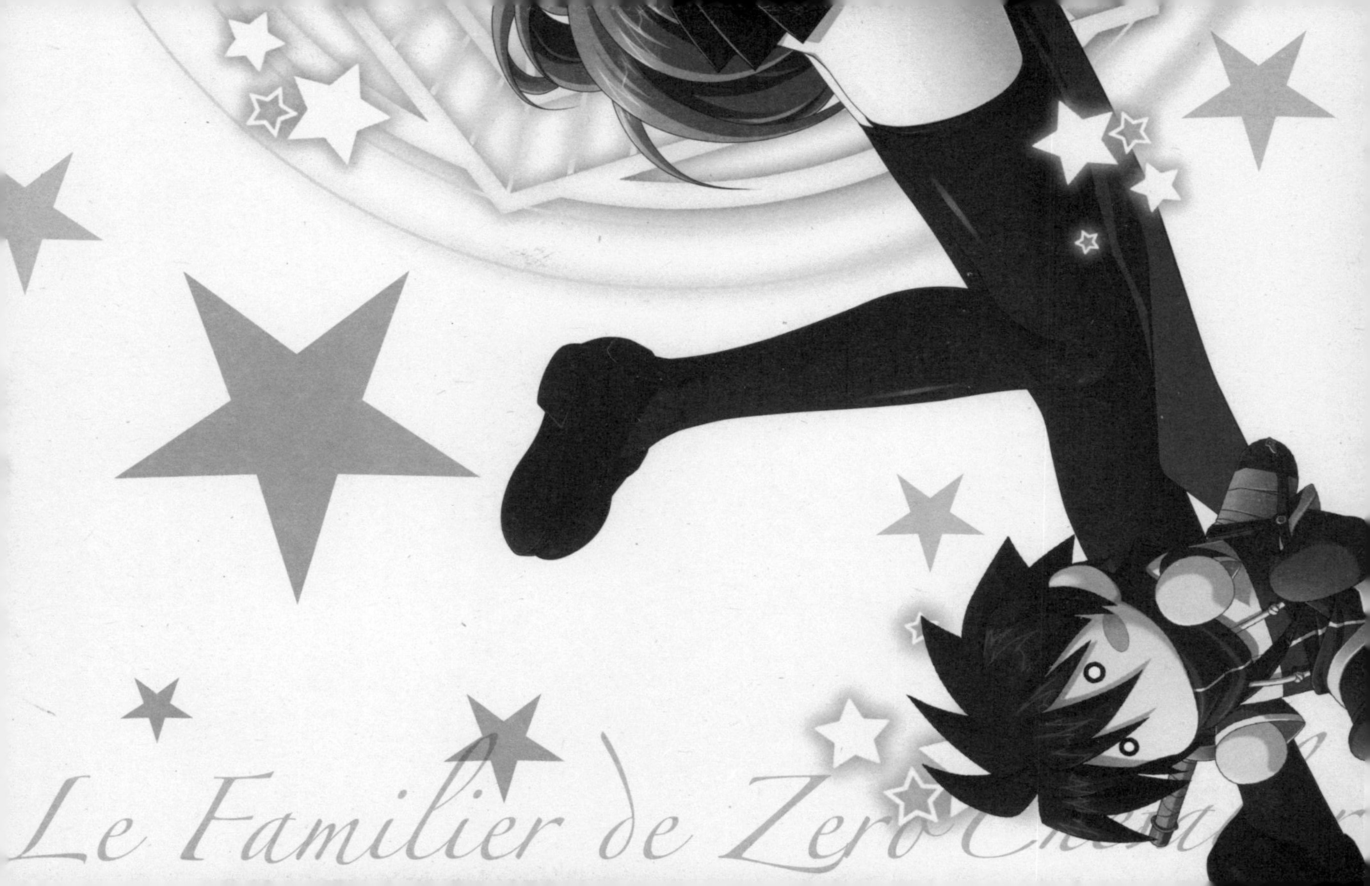
Le Familier de Zero

Le Familier de Zero Chevalier

ZERO'S FAMILIAR Chevalier

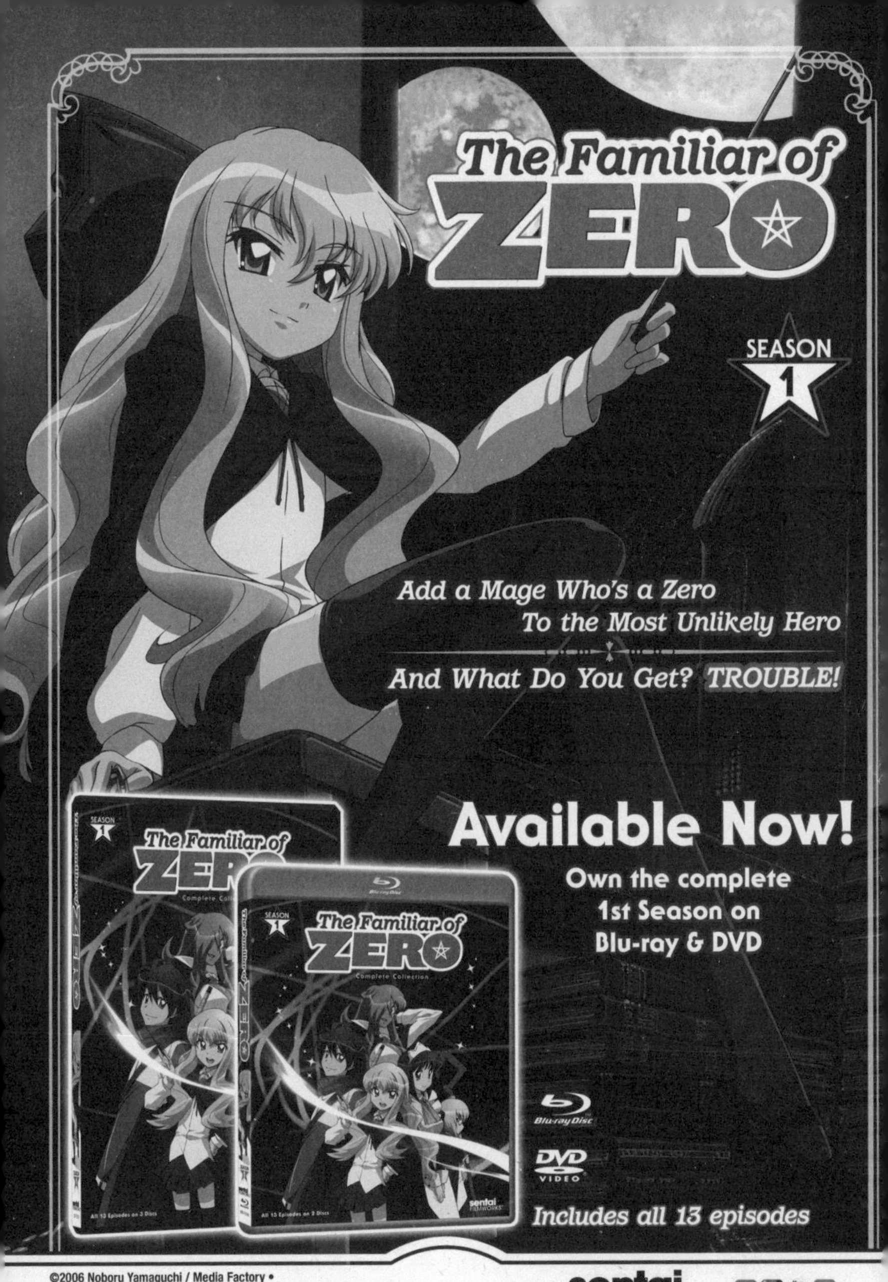
The Familiar of ZERO
SEASON 1
Add a Mage Who's a Zero
To the Most Unlikely Hero
And What Do You Get? TROUBLE!
Available Now!
Own the complete
1st Season on
Blu-ray & DVD
Blu-ray Disc
DVD VIDEO
Includes all 13 episodes

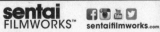

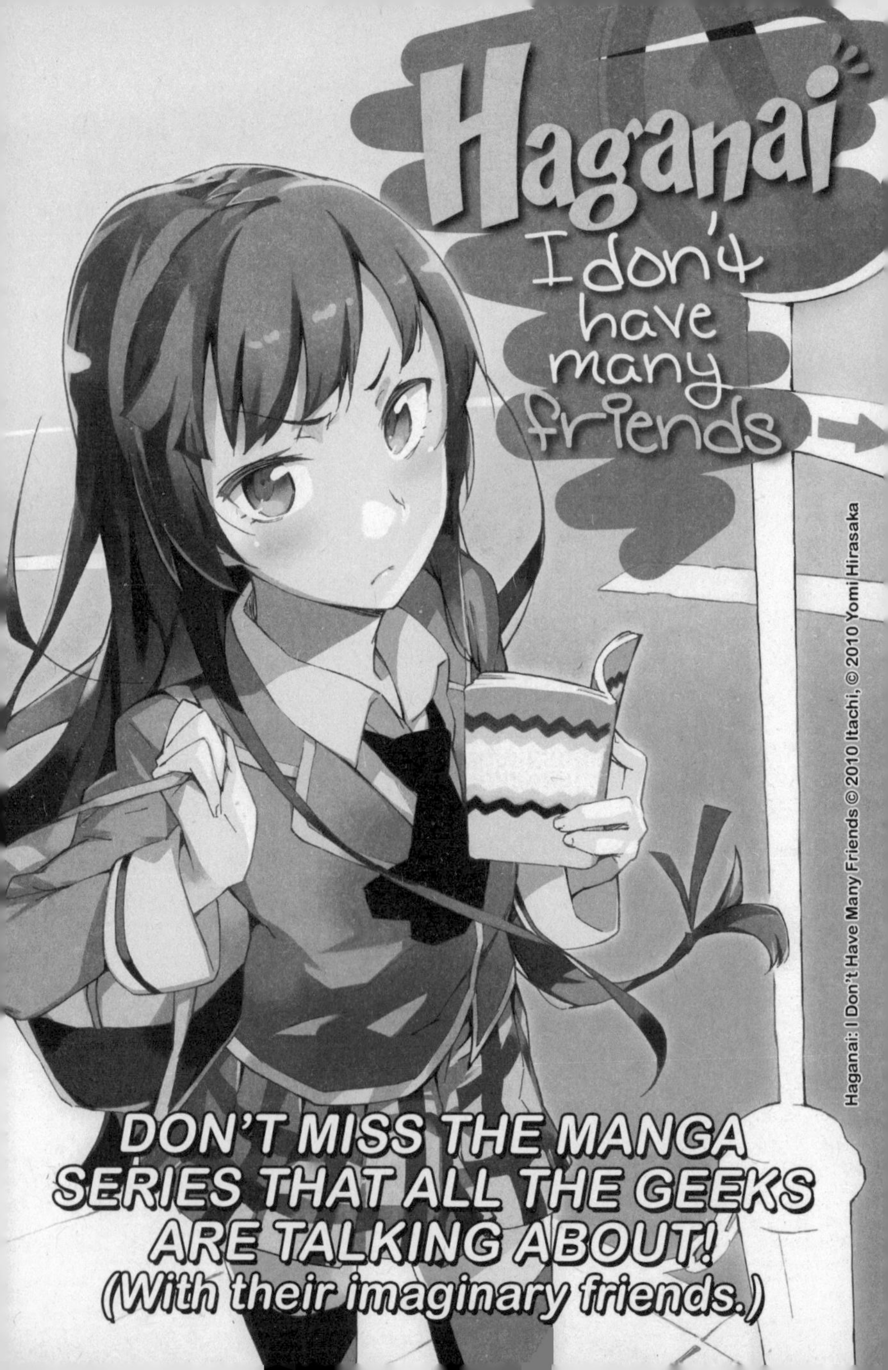
Haganai
I don't have many friends
DON'T MISS THE MANGA SERIES THAT ALL THE GEEKS ARE TALKING ABOUT!
(With their imaginary friends.)
Haganai: I Don't Have Many Friends © 2010 Itachi, © 2010 Yomi Hirasaka

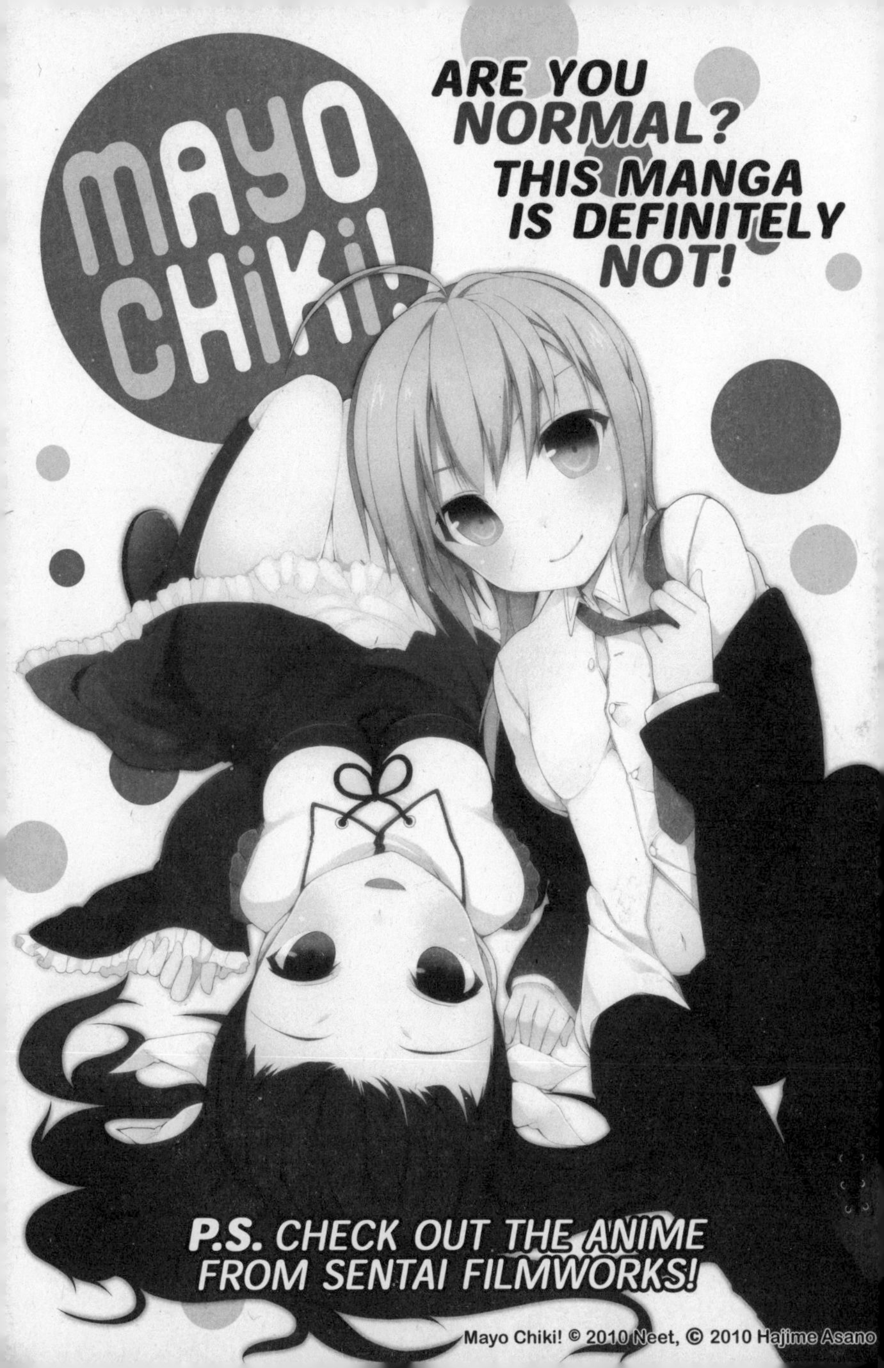

MAYO CHIKI!
ARE YOU NORMAL? THIS MANGA IS DEFINITELY NOT!
P.S. CHECK OUT THE ANIME FROM SENTAI FILMWORKS!
Mayo Chiki! © 2010 Neet, © 2010 Hajime Asano

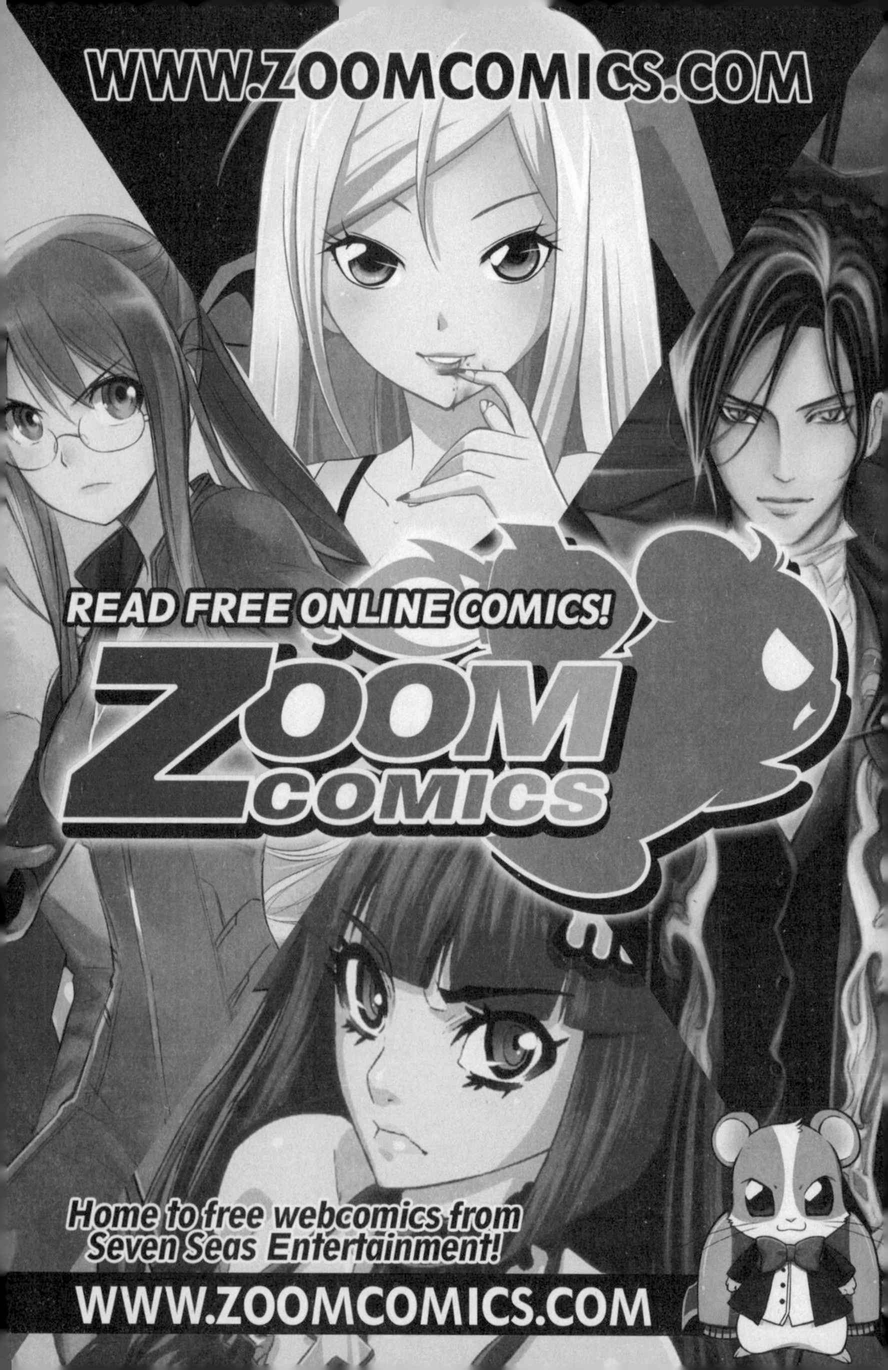
WWW.ZOOMCOMICS.COM
READ FREE ONLINE COMICS!
ZOOM COMICS
Home to free webcomics from Seven Seas Entertainment!
WWW.ZOOMCOMICS.COM

SEVEN SEAS ENTERTAINMENT PRESENTS

ZERO'S FAMILIAR Chevalier

art by **YUKARI HIGA** / story by **NOBORU YAMAGUCHI**   VOLUME **3**

Original Character Designs by **EIJI USATSUKA**

TRANSLATION
Nan Rymer

ADAPTATION
Rebecca Scoble

LETTERING AND LAYOUT
Alice Baker

COVER DESIGN
Nicky Lim

PROOFREADER
Katherine Bell
Conner Crooks

MANAGING EDITOR
Adam Arnold

PUBLISHER
Jason DeAngelis

FOLLOW US ONLINE: *www.gomanga.com*

READING DIRECTIONS

This book reads from *right to left*, Japanese style.
If this is your first time reading manga, you start
reading from the top right panel on each page and
take it from there. If you get lost, just follow the
numbered diagram here. It may seem backwards at
first, but you'll get the hang of it! Have fun!!